Writing

INSIDE

LANGUAGE · LITERACY · CONTENT

PROGRAM AUTHOR

Gretchen Bernabei

Acknowledgments

Grateful acknowledgment is given to the authors, artists, photographers, museums, publishers, and agents for permission to reprint copyrighted material. Every effort has been made to secure the appropriate permission. If any omissions have been made or if corrections are required, please contact the Publisher.

Photographic Credits

Cover: Submerged Alligator, Andrew Masur. Photograph © Andrew Masur/Flikr/Getty Images.

Acknowledgments continue on page 540W.

For product information and technology assistance, contact us at **Cengage Learning Customer & Sales Support, 888-915-3276**

For permission to use material from this text or product, submit all requests online at **www.cengage.com/permissions** Further permissions questions can be emailed to **permissionrequest@cengage.com**

National Geographic Learning | Cengage Learning
1 Lower Ragsdale Drive
Building 1, Suite 200
Monterey, CA 93940

Cengage Learning is a leading provider of customized learning solutions with office locations around the globe, including Singapore, the United Kingdom, Australia, Mexico, Brazil, and Japan. Locate your local office at **www.cengage.com/global**.

Visit National Geographic Learning online at **ngl.cengage.com**
Visit our corporate website at **www.cengage.com**

Printer: Quad/Graphics, Versailles, KY

ISBN: 978-12854-37156

Printed in the United States of America
18 19 20 21 22
10 9 8 7 6 5 4

Contents

THE Building Blocks OF WRITING

Project 1 Paragraph Structure:
Ways to Organize · INFORMATIVE/EXPLANATORY

THE Writing Process

Project 2 **Use the Writing Process** ▪ ARGUMENT

At Each Stage of the Writing Process—

THE Many Writers YOU ARE

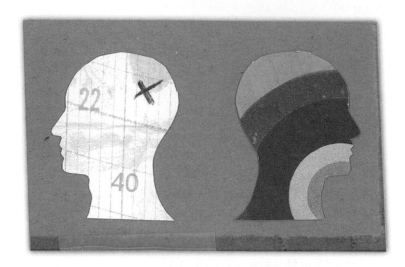

Project 3 Write as an Eyewitness · NARRATIVE

Chapter 3, continued

Chapter 3, continued

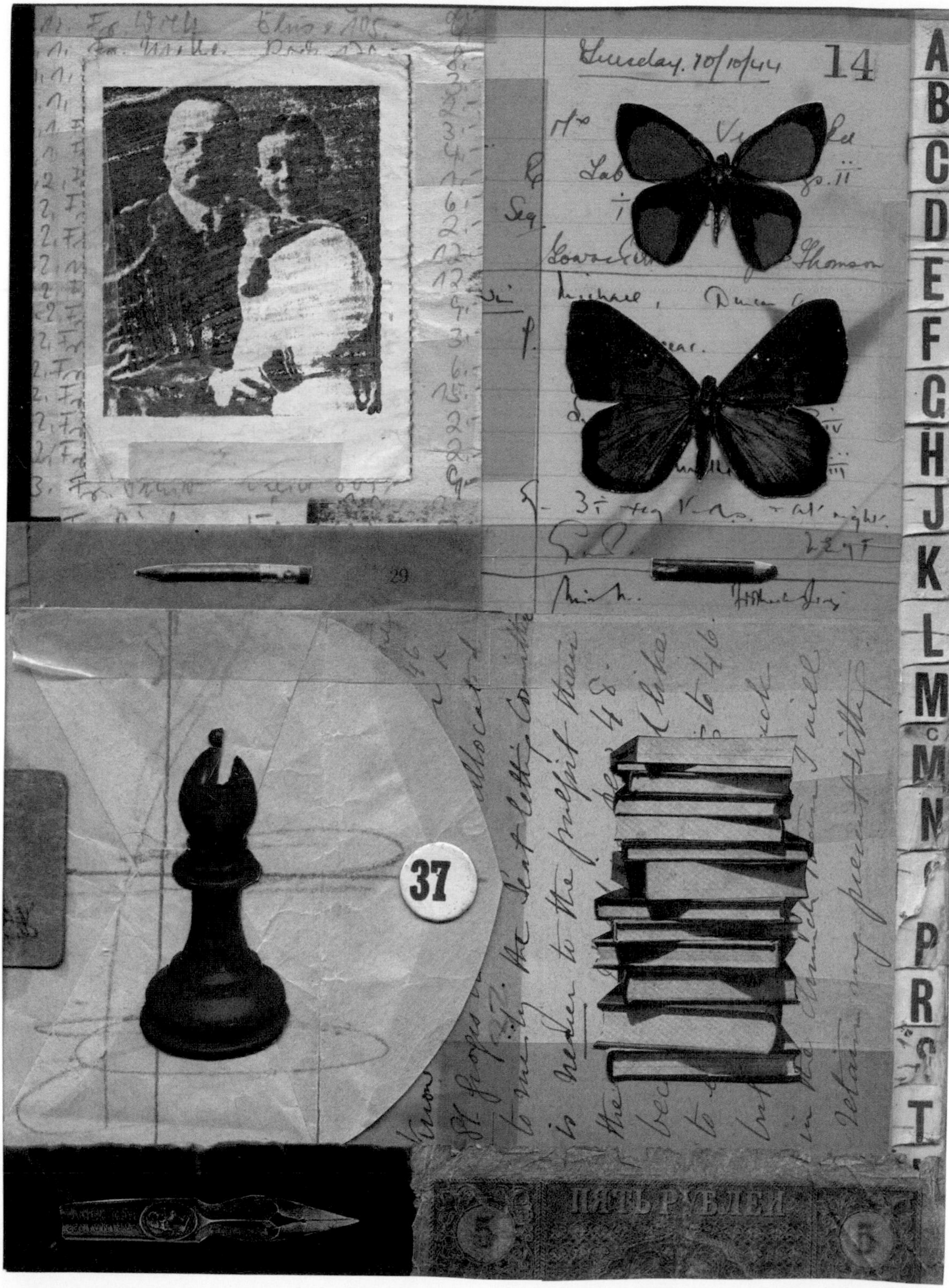
14
29
37
ПЯТЬ РУБЛЕЙ
A B C D E F G H J K L M M N P R S T

THE Building Blocks
OF WRITING

Paragraph Structure:
Ways to Organize

"I had a great dream. And I wrote a great paragraph in my dream journal this morning."

—Alma

Model Study

Sentences and Paragraphs

One great way to express your ideas is through writing. When you write, your reader can understand your ideas more easily if they are presented clearly and in an organized way.

Start with Sentences

You start with writing a group of words that tell a complete thought. There are four types of sentences:

Type of Sentence	Example
A **statement** tells something.	Greg created many versions of Crittercam.
A **question** asks something.	What do turtles do underwater?
An **exclamation** shows strong emotion.	Crittercam is the best invention ever!
A **command** tells you to do something.	Look at these underwater pictures. Learn more about penguins!

Build to Paragraphs

When you write, you put sentences together in an organized way to create **paragraphs.** Make sure that each paragraph has a clear **main idea** stated in a **topic sentence.** The other details in the paragraph should support the main idea with **details** and **examples.**

The **topic sentence** tells the main idea of the paragraph.

Greg Marshall invented the Crittercam to study ocean life. How does it work? The Crittercam is a machine made with a metal tube and a camera. He attaches the Crittercam to animals and lets the animals back into the ocean. Scientists are able to watch through the Crittercam to see just what the animals see as they swim in the ocean. Life in the ocean is still mysterious. But with the Crittercam, scientists are making many new discoveries that would have been impossible before Marshall came along.

This is a **detail** that supports the main idea.

Professional Model

PARAGRAPH

A good paragraph

☑ has a topic sentence that states the main idea

☑ contains details that tell more about the main idea.

Feature Checklist

Strapping the Crittercam to an animal's back allows scientists to study how it lives. ▶

Organize Your Paragraphs

What's It Like ?

Look at this tropical aquarium! You may not know about every sea creature that lives in a tropical reef. But when you hear the words "tropical aquarium," you have a good sense of what to expect. A topic sentence works that way, too. It doesn't give away all of the details, but it tells the reader what to expect.

Getting to a Topic Sentence

First, you need to decide what to write about. That will be your topic. Then think about what you want to say in general about your topic—that will be your main idea. Next, follow these steps to get to a topic sentence:

- Write as many details as you can that support your main idea.

- Look to see how the details are related to each other and to the main idea.

- Write a full statement that expresses your main idea as it relates to the details you plan to cover in your paragraph.

Here's how one student got to her topic sentence.

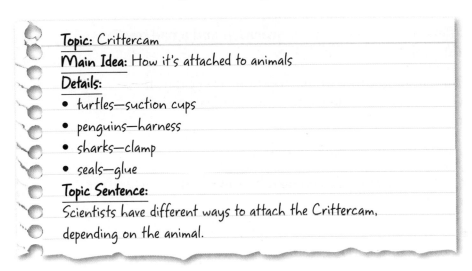

Topic: Crittercam
Main Idea: How it's attached to animals
Details:
- turtles—suction cups
- penguins—harness
- sharks—clamp
- seals—glue

Topic Sentence:
Scientists have different ways to attach the Crittercam, depending on the animal.

Topic Sentence

Your topic sentence and supporting details will determine how your paragraph is organized. Below are four common types of paragraph organization. We'll go through each type in more detail on pages 6W–13W.

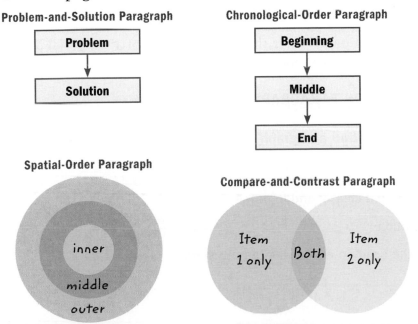

Problem-and-Solution Paragraph

Problem → Solution

Chronological-Order Paragraph

Beginning → Middle → End

Spatial-Order Paragraph

inner
middle
outer

Compare-and-Contrast Paragraph

Item 1 only — Both — Item 2 only

Problem-and-Solution Paragraph

What is the difference between a good invention and a bad one? A good invention solves a problem.

People face problems and think about solutions every day. If you want to write about a problem and a solution, you need to organize your ideas clearly:

- Begin by describing the problem in detail.

- Explain how you think the problem can be solved, or describe how it was solved.

Before you start writing, you can use a problem-and-solution chart to help organize your thoughts.

Problem-and-Solution Chart

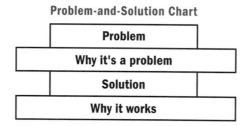

Read the student model on page 7W. It shows the features of a good problem-and-solution paragraph.

PROBLEM-AND-SOLUTION PARAGRAPH

A good problem-and-solution paragraph

☑ presents a problem

☑ explains the problem clearly and in detail

☑ presents a solution

☑ explains how the solution addresses the problem.

Feature Checklist

Perfecting the Crittercam
by Carly Rogers

At first, Greg Marshall's Crittercam was too bulky and heavy to work effectively. Marshall first tried out the Crittercam on a captive nurse shark. The shark was not able to swim as quickly as usual. The weight of the camera was causing drag, which slowed the shark down. Marshall redesigned the Crittercam. He made it smaller and lighter. These changes improved its usefulness, because the shark could swim more normally.

The topic sentence states the **problem**.

Then, the writer shows the **solution**.

Student Model

Problem
Crittercam was too bulky, heavy.

Why it's a problem
Shark couldn't swim well.

Solution
Redesign camera to make it smaller and lighter.

Why it works
Shark will be able to swim more normally.

The Crittercam's improved design helped scientists learn more about sharks.

Chronological-Order Paragraph

You often tell about things that happen to you. When you describe events, you usually tell them in the order they happened. If you mix present and past events, your listener will have a hard time following what you are saying.

When you want to write about a series of events, retell the events in the sequence in which they occurred. This sequence is called **chronological order.** Start with what happened first, and lead the reader to the final event. When you write events in chronological order, use words such as *first, then, after,* and *finally.*

Read the professional model on page 9W. It shows the features of a good chronological-order paragraph.

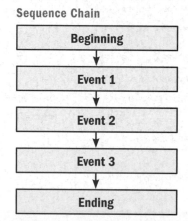

Sequence Chain

Beginning
Event 1
Event 2
Event 3
Ending

CHRONOLOGICAL-ORDER PARAGRAPH

A good chronological-order paragraph

☑ tells events in the order they happened

☑ uses signal words like *first, next, then, after,* and *finally* to show the sequence of events.

Feature Checklist

from **Hitching a Ride**
by Rebecca L. Johnson

These two events are in **chronological order**.

The team learned how penguins dive. First the penguins dive down and then turn to look up at the ice overhead. Against the bright white of the ice, they can easily spot their favorite fish. They go up to grab a meal. Next, they go down again for another look at the ice. The penguins make a few of these food-finding trips. Then the penguins pop out of the water with stomachs bulging full of fish.

Signal words help the reader understand when something happened.

Professional Model

Beginning
The penguins dive down.

↓

Event 1
They look up and spot their favorite fish.

↓

Event 2
They go up to grab a meal.

↓

Event 3
They go down to take another look at the ice.

↓

Ending
They pop out of the water with stomachs full of fish.

◀ Penguins dive under ice to catch fish.

Spatial-Order Paragraph

How would you describe the way someone was dressed on a special occasion? You might start by describing the person's hairstyle or hat. Then you'd move down, describing each item of clothing until you got to the person's shoes. To do this a different way, you could start with the shoes and then move up.

When you write to describe something you see, choose a starting point and then move in a clear direction. Use **spatial order** to describe something so your reader can picture what it's like. Proceed from inside to outside, left to right, or top to bottom.

You might want to begin by drawing and labeling a picture. This will help you organize the details of your description.

Read the student model on page 11W. It shows the features of a good spatial-order paragraph.

SPATIAL-ORDER PARAGRAPH

A good spatial-order paragraph

☑ proceeds from a visual starting point to an ending point

☑ takes the reader logically from one place to the other

☑ uses signal words like *above* and *underneath* to show spatial order.

Feature Checklist

The Blue Whale
by Emma Triches

The writer describes the whale from front to back.

The blue whale has a long, cone-shaped head. On the top of its head, the blue whale has two blowholes. On its sides, there are the flippers. On its back and close to the tail, the blue whale has a small triangular fin. The blue whale has a huge back fin with broad flukes.

Student Model

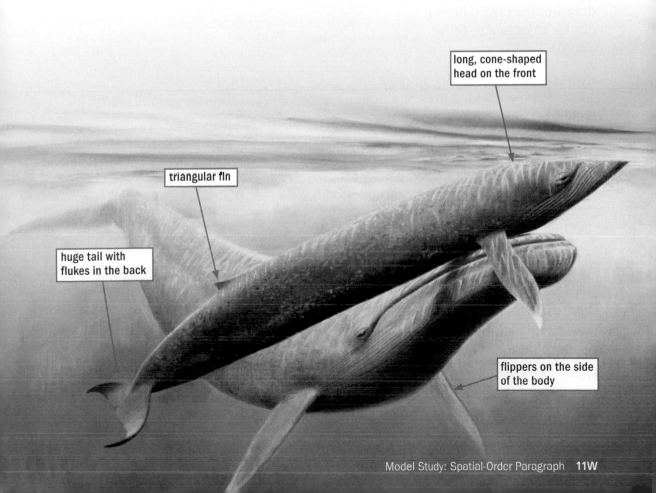

long, cone-shaped head on the front

triangular fin

huge tail with flukes in the back

flippers on the side of the body

Compare-and-Contrast Paragraph

When you want to bring attention to the similarities or differences between two things, you write a paragraph that compares and contrasts.

When you **compare,** you write about how two things are similar. When you **contrast,** you write to show how two things are different.

You can use a **Venn diagram** to show the similarities and differences between two things. A Venn diagram uses overlapping circles to organize these details.

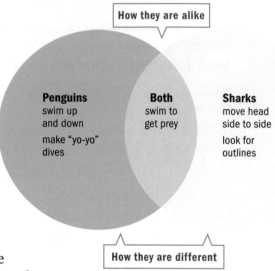

How they are alike

Penguins
swim up and down

make "yo-yo" dives

Both
swim to get prey

Sharks
move head side to side

look for outlines

How they are different

Read the student model on page 13W. It shows the features of a good compare-and-contrast paragraph.

COMPARE-AND-CONTRAST PARAGRAPH

A good compare-and-contrast paragraph

☑ names the items being compared

☑ describes ways the items are similar

☑ describes ways the items are different

☑ includes signal words like *both, same, different,* and *however* to show similarities and differences.

Feature Checklist

Grizzly Bears and Great White Sharks
by Mamoun Rahman

The writer **names the animals** being compared.

The writer tells how grizzly bears and sharks are different.

The writer tells what the animals have in common.

Grizzly bears and great white sharks are both scary predators that can sometimes terrorize people. Grizzly bears are mammals and live on land, while great white sharks are fish and live in the ocean. Grizzly bears protect themselves from the cold with their fur. Great white sharks, on the other hand, are covered in special scales that protect them. Both animals have been observed through the Crittercam. Apparently, both grizzly bears and great white sharks are a little more friendly than you might think. One way in which they are alike is that they often share their space with other animals of their own species.

These **signal words** cue the contrasts.

These **signal words** cue the similarities.

▲ Student Model

▲ A grizzly bear's fur protects it from cold temperatures.

Great white sharks are common ▲ off the coast of California.

Write a Paragraph

WRITING PROMPT There are more things to write about than there are fish in the ocean! Now that you have learned about different ways of organizing paragraphs, pick your favorite critter and write a paragraph. You can choose any of the four structures you have learned about.

Be sure you include

* a topic sentence
* a clear organization
* interesting details that support your topic sentence.

Plan and Write

Here are some ideas for how you can plan and then get started on your writing.

1 Choose a Topic

Decide what to write about. You can't tell everything about your favorite animal in one paragraph, so what is it that you want readers to understand? This will be your main idea.

> The Great White Shark
> —in aquariums
> —adapted for hunting
> —many different species

2 Get Some Details Down on Paper

After you choose your topic and decide what you want to say about it, list some details and examples that support your main idea.

> —large, saw-edged teeth
> —can weigh more than 7000 lbs.
> —mottled skin
> —has small, hidden ears to help hear prey

3 Choose an Organization and Write a Topic Sentence

Think about how your details relate to one another and to the main idea. Your main idea and details will usually suggest a specific organization. Write a topic sentence that expresses your main idea fully and reflects your organization.

> **Topic Sentence for a Spatial-Order Paragraph**
> From nose to tail fin, the great white shark is an efficient, deadly hunting machine.

4 Turn Your Details into Supporting Sentences

Turn each detail on your list into a supporting sentence to flesh out your paragraph. Each sentence should explain the main idea or give an example of it. A graphic organizer might help you arrange the sentences effectively.

> From nose to tail fin, the great white shark is an efficient, deadly hunting machine. Its mouth, on the underside of its head, is filled with rows of sharp, saw-edged teeth.

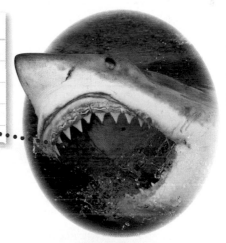

Reflect

- Is your main idea clear in your topic sentence?

- Are all of your details connected?

THE Writing Process

Writing Strategy

The Writing Process

Writing is like playing basketball or the piano. If you want to be good at it, you have to work on it. And there's a process involved. Some things you do first; some things you do later.

What Are the Steps of the Writing Process?

Writers follow a process to make their writing the best it can be. The writing process usually involves five stages—**prewriting, drafting, revising, editing and proofreading,** and **publishing.**

1 **Prewrite—Get Ready to Write**

Prewriting is what you do before you write. You choose a topic, think about what to say, and develop a plan. What is the plan that works best for you? You can write notes, make an outline, or even sketch drawings.

2 **Draft—Get It Down on Paper**

Drafting is the next step. Writing down that first draft is sometimes the hardest part. But it can also be the most exciting. Remember, your first draft doesn't have to be perfect. You can go back and make changes later, so relax and enjoy the work.

❸ Revise—Get It to Sing

After you finish your draft, put it aside for a while. Then you can come back to it with fresh eyes. You might end up making major changes! You might move sentences around or add new ideas. You can show your work to someone else, too, and ask for comments.

❹ Edit and Proofread—Get It Right

Once you've made the big changes, work on getting the details right. This is when you correct your sentences and fix any mistakes in grammar, spelling, or punctuation.

❺ Publish, Share, and Reflect—Get It Out There

Do you want other people to read your work? Then publish it! Writers share their work in newspapers, magazines, and books. Sharing your writing with your family, friends, and classmates is another form of publishing. Don't forget to reflect on your writing yourself—think about what you have worked so hard to create!

Your Job as a Writer

Good writers have many trade secrets. One of them is using the writing process. Try it on this project.

Write Problem-and-Solution Paragraphs

WRITING PROMPT Inventions are created for a reason: to solve problems. What are some inventions that make your life easier? What do you think life was like before they were invented? Think about an invention that you think really makes life easier. Then write two paragraphs about it. Your paragraphs should:

- present a problem
- explain the problem clearly and in detail
- make a claim about the solution
- give reasons and evidence that support the claim as a good solution for the problem.

Prewrite: Collect Ideas

Where can you get ideas for your writing? Start by looking around. Reading news stories and books can also help you get an idea. Sometimes ideas come from your past experiences. Once you start looking, you can find ideas everywhere!

Ways to Come Up with Ideas

Get your idea wheel spinning. Think about:

- items you use every day that help you with difficult tasks

- famous inventions of the past

- news articles you've read about recent inventions

- projects you saw at the science fair

- how life in the past was different from life today

- what your life would be without modern technology

- your top ten favorite inventions.

Top Ten Inventions
1. Video games
2. The umbrella
3. Headphones
4. Sunglasses

Where to Keep Your Ideas

Start an idea file to keep your ideas together in one place. Any container will do. For example, you could:

- keep a journal of your thoughts and ideas

- put articles, stories, and photos you like in a file folder

- keep a few pages of your Writer's Notebook just for your ideas

- write your ideas on strips of paper and put them in a cereal box or in a basket.

On-the-Go Inspiration

When you don't have your idea file with you, ask yourself questions like these:

- What objects that I use are good inventions?

- What inventions could change my life at school?

- Who are my favorite inventors?

- What have people invented in recent years?

- If I were an inventor, what would I try to create?

- What big problems did famous inventions solve?

TechTIP

You can record your ideas on an electronic device when you're on the go. Look for a microphone, find out how it works, and speak your ideas! You can even talk to a voicemail system.

Prewrite: Collect Ideas, continued

Some things, like science or spelling, you know in your head. Other things, about people or the world, you know in your heart. That's your truth. When you write about one thing you believe in your heart, your writing will not wander.

Speak Your Truth

What do you believe is true about people or the world? You may already have an idea in your head, but sometimes looking at a photograph can help you discover your truth. What truth would you add to this list?

Truths
1. Everyone needs help to learn new things.
2. Families spend time together.
3. Not everyone can get things right without some help.
4. People change as they get older.
5. There are many ways to define a family.

Something that is true for one person is not necessarily true for others. When you look at these photographs, does a different truth come to mind?

Working together is so much better than working alone.

Communication mistakes can cause serious problems.

Sometimes you have to look from a distance to see something clearly.

Shopping is like searching for treasure; you never know what you're going to bring home.

Prewrite: Choose Your Topic

You can use your idea collection to come up with a topic to write about. You want to make sure your topic is not too general, or broad, for the kind of writing you'll do.

A specific, or smaller, topic is easier to write about. It is also much more interesting for your readers. Take a look at how one writer narrowed the topic of "Inventors" for a problem-and-solution essay.

Inventors

This topic would take pages and pages to cover. Why?

Broad

Inventions used in my town

This is better, but still too broad. How many inventions can you write about?

The trash-sorting machine that cleaned my town's landfill

This topic is interesting because it is specific. How could you write a problem-and-solution essay about this?

Narrow

Your Topic is Too Broad When . . .

- you type key words into a search engine and get thousands of hits

- you search the library database and find hundreds of books

- there are so many ideas, you don't know where to start

Prewrite: Choose Your Audience

After choosing a good topic, think about your **audience**. These are the people who will read your writing. When you know your audience, you can choose the right tone for your writing.

Audience	Tone	Language
your best friend or someone your age	very informal	Hey Lindsey- Have you ever heard of Linus Yale? He invented the lock.
an older relative	somewhat informal	Hello, Uncle Jim, I'm doing a report about locks. Could you tell me about locks you put in doors when you build them? Thanks.
your teacher	somewhat formal	Dear Mrs. Smith, I would like to invite my Uncle Jim to class to talk about locks. He is a carpenter. When would be a good time to talk more about this?
someone you do not know	very formal	Dear Prof. Goodis, I am doing a report on the invention of locks for school. Would you answer the three questions I've included in this e-mail? I would really appreciate it. Thank you.

Who is the audience for each of these e-mails?

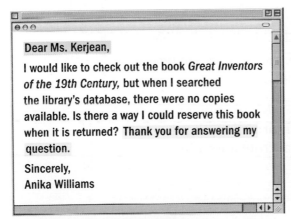

Dear Ms. Kerjean,

I would like to check out the book *Great Inventors of the 19th Century,* but when I searched the library's database, there were no copies available. Is there a way I could reserve this book when it is returned? Thank you for answering my question.

Sincerely,
Anika Williams

The writer uses a **formal greeting** and words that give her message a **polite, formal tone.**

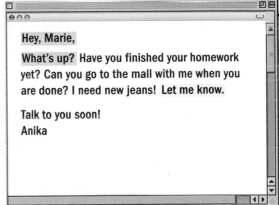

Hey, Marie,

What's up? Have you finished your homework yet? Can you go to the mall with me when you are done? I need new jeans! Let me know.

Talk to you soon!
Anika

The writer uses an **informal greeting** and words that give her message a **friendly, casual tone.**

Prewrite: Choose Your Purpose

What do you want your audience to know or do? That'll be your **purpose,** or reason, for writing. When you write, choose a tone that fits your purpose.

What is the writer's purpose in the e-mail below? What is the writer's purpose in the journal entry?

E-mail

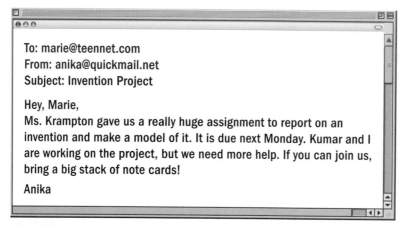

To: marie@teennet.com
From: anika@quickmail.net
Subject: Invention Project

Hey, Marie,
Ms. Krampton gave us a really huge assignment to report on an invention and make a model of it. It is due next Monday. Kumar and I are working on the project, but we need more help. If you can join us, bring a big stack of note cards!

Anika

Journal Entry

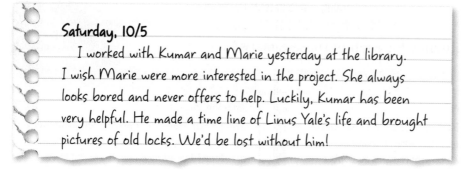

Saturday, 10/5
    I worked with Kumar and Marie yesterday at the library.
I wish Marie were more interested in the project. She always looks bored and never offers to help. Luckily, Kumar has been very helpful. He made a time line of Linus Yale's life and brought pictures of old locks. We'd be lost without him!

Anika wrote the e-mail to give Marie information about the project. In the journal entry, Anika wrote about her private feelings.

What was her purpose for writing this letter to her friend Bernie?

Letter

> Dear Bernie,
>   Thank you so much for all the information that you sent me about Linus Yale's invention. However, I think we should do more research about his life growing up in New York. Adding these details will make our report more convincing and interesting to read! Call me if you want to talk more about this. I can explain more why I really think this is the way to go.

Are Your Audience and Purpose Connected?

Yes. Your audience and purpose are related to one another. One way to get clear about your purpose is to consider how you want your audience to react to what you have to say.

If You Want Your Audience to	Your Purpose Is	For Quick Topic Ideas, List . . .
• learn something new • understand something better	to inform or explain	• ten things people can learn from you • ten things you can do really well
• laugh • feel deep emotion • enjoy reading your work • enjoy reading about a real experience or event	to narrate	• ten situations that made you laugh • funny or strange situations you experienced
• believe something • take action on an important issue • know what you think	to argue	• five things you would like to change, how you would change them, and why • your ideas about what you like or dislike, and why

Prewrite: Choose Your Purpose, continued

Does Your Form Connect to Your Purpose?

You can change how and what you write to fit your purpose.
Look at the examples on these pages.

To Inform or Explain

You might want to explain how to do something.

How to Start a Research Project

1. Go to the library and read all you can about your subject.
2. Take notes and write where the information comes from.
3. Make copies of interesting material.

Instructions

Or, you could give your audience important information.

When you start a research project, you need to find material. The best place to start is the library. Once you're there, look for books about your subject. As you skim through the pages, take notes. You can also make copies of interesting material.

Paragraph

You might want to describe something.

The tablet is one of the most practical inventions of the past few years. Measuring about 7 x 10 inches and weighing about a pound and a half, this powerful computer can do almost everything a laptop can do but in a smaller, lighter package.

Description

You might want to give information about the life of a real person.

The next time you use tape to wrap a package, thank Richard Drew. Drew was an engineer in the 1920s and 1930s. He invented masking tape—a tan paper strip with adhesive—to help painters paint a straight line.

Biography

In an editorial, you make a claim and support it with reasons and evidence.

Recycle Tech Devices

Every year, we get excited about some new electronic device. Every year, millions of old electronic devices get thrown away. The Environmental Protection Agency says that discarding these devices in landfills is dangerous because electronics contain many harmful metals and chemicals. In landfills, these metals and chemicals can seep into groundwater and poison whole water systems. This is why people need better ways to dispose of old electronics. Recycling them can be part of the solution.

Editorial for School Newspaper

In an advertisement, you can use reasons and evidence to argue why someone should buy something.

Bike Locks
ON SALE NOW!

Bike thefts are at an all-time high in our town. You need the sturdiest lock to protect your bike. Police tests rate U-Locks as the best choice for keeping bikes safe. Choose from the largest selection of U-Locks in town at Locks in Stock. Hurry while supplies last!

LOCKS IN STOCK
14 Oak Street • (555) 555-3421

Ad

You could write a funny essay about a real experience that has a logical sequence of events.

Laura's Invention

Laura unveiled her invention. It was a spoon with a straw attached to it. "It is for drinking the last drops of soup in the bowl," she explained.

Then she demonstrated her invention. She poured a little bit of orange juice into a bowl. She spooned out as much as she could. Then she used the straw. She made a horrible gurgling sound. Everyone laughed. "Science doesn't care about manners!" Laura exclaimed.

Essay

You could write a story about an imagined experience and use lots of descriptive details.

The Robot

Josh and Sam stared at their creation. The robot creaked and blinked its little shiny eyes. Then it started talking. Instead of repeating the script Josh and Sam had written, the robot started talking in a strange language. At first, Josh and Sam could not understand what the robot was saying. Then, they began to hear their names, repeated over and over. The robot seemed to mock them. What was happening?

Short Story

Prewrite: Organize Your Ideas

You know your topic, your purpose, and the form. You know who your audience will be. Sum them up in an FATP chart.

FATP Chart

Form: _problem-and-solution paragraphs_

Audience: _classmates_

Topic: _how my town solved the landfill problem_

Purpose: _to explain a problem and its solution_

First Paragraph

For a problem-and-solution essay, your first paragraph should present the problem.

1. Maybe you want to describe the problem and give details about it. You could use **logical order**, like this:

Save Sunnydale!

Our landfill has gotten so big, it is blocking the sun from shining on Sunnydale. It is a big, ugly, smelly problem. The pile of trash is so high that many people are worried it might collapse.

The **topic sentence** introduces the **claim**.

The **reasons** support the claim.

2. Maybe you want to describe how the problem started and then got worse, step by step. Then you would use **chronological order.**

Save Sunnydale!

Last year, my town decided to put all of the trash we collected in a landfill. At first, the pile was small, but then as people kept throwing things away, it got bigger and bigger. By the end of the year, the pile was so big, it blocked out the sun.

Time words and phrases help to show chronological order.

3. Maybe you want to describe the scene, so that readers can picture it in their minds. Then you would use **spatial order.**

Save Sunnydale!

The landfill towers over the town. The base is covered with old trash that smells terrible. The sides are covered by small objects that have fallen from the top. At the top, you can see the seagulls searching for food.

The writer describes the landfill from **bottom to top**.

Check out pages 444W–453W for some tools you can use to organize ideas.

Second Paragraph

Once you have described the problem, you need to move on to the solution. This second paragraph tells the audience how the problem was solved.

At the town meeting, we found the perfect solution: buying a trash-sorting machine. The machine is able to sort glass from paper, wood from metal. Although some people pointed out that the machine is very expensive, in the long run, it is worth the expense. Sorting trash will help our town recycle more easily, reducing the amount of trash. According to expert estimates, recycling will reduce the amount of trash that ends up in our giant landfill by 42%. And reducing the size of the landfill is our goal.

The writer states the **claim** and provides **reasons** and **evidence** to support it. The writer offers a different, or an **alternative claim** and refutes it to strengthen the claim.

Reflect

- What do you want your audience to understand about the problem?

- How can you explain the solution clearly?

Draft

What's It Like?

The first model an inventor creates almost never looks like the final invention. An inventor starts with an idea, sees how the model works, and then keeps toying around with it until the invention does exactly what it is supposed to do. Drafting is like that. You have a plan and good ideas, and you go for it! The whole point is to get your ideas down on paper so that you can see how they work out.

How Do You Face a Blank Page?

Now that you have a plan, it's time to start the first draft of your problem-and-solution paper. Sometimes, the hardest part of writing a paper is getting started! As you will see, there is no one right way to write a first draft.

All drafts start with a blank piece of paper—or a blank computer screen. Here are some ideas to help you get started:

- Gather all the tools you need. Get pencils and paper. Collect the notes and graphic organizers that you made during prewriting. If you are using a computer, create a folder for your files.

- Find a good place to write. It doesn't have to be a desk, but make sure there are no distractions.

- Start writing! Remember, a draft does not have to be perfect. Just get your ideas down on paper!

Look at Jaime's draft on page 33W. What makes it a good start? How much does it matter if there are spelling mistakes in the first draft?

An Easier Time for Wheelchair Users

by Jaime Rivera

Thanks to 12-year-old Chandler Macocha, wheelchair users now have an easier time getting things out of backpacks. Chandler invented a swing-out backpack holder for wheelchairs.

The seed for this invention began with Chandler's young next-door neighbor who used a wheelchair. His neighbor always had problems with reaching around the back of her wheelchair for her backpack. Sometimes she had to ask others for help. Chandler figured that a lot of people had this same problem.

Chandler had an idea for a solution, so he developed a working model. Then his neighbor tried out the model. By pulling a lever, she could make the backpack swivel forward.

Chandler's neighbor wasn't the only one who thought the swing-out backpack holder was a good idea. for this invention, Chandler receive a Da Vinci Award, which is given for innovations that help people overcome physical limitations. In addition, the U.S. Patent Office gave Chandler a patent on the invention. Now, with Chandler's swing-out backpack holder, Chandler's neighbor and other wheelchair user no longer have to struggle to get their backpacks.

Jaime wrote without worrying about little mistakes. Now he has a draft to work with.

DRAFTING CHECKLIST

In a good draft:

☑ the title and first sentence identify the claim

☑ the writing includes logical reasons and relevant evidence

☑ the concluding sentence supports the claim

☑ writers set down ideas quickly, without worrying about spelling or grammar mistakes.

Draft, continued

Writing is like playing sports. You don't have to be perfect. You just need to do your best. On the next few pages are some ideas about writing a first draft. Which ideas sound familiar? Which ideas seem like they would work for you?

Getting Started

Q: What do I need to get started?

A: Find a quiet place where you can work. Make sure you have enough pencils and paper, or a computer. You should also have your notes and your graphic organizers. These materials will help you when you are unsure about how to organize your writing.

Q: What's the right way to start a draft?

A: Writers are like snowflakes. No two are exactly alike. While there's no "right" way to start, here are some ideas:

- Draw pictures to get yourself thinking. You can also write whatever comes into your head to get your ideas flowing. It's like doodling with words.

- Write your ideas down quickly. Don't worry about finding exactly the right word.

- Spend some time working on the first paragraph. This will help you find a direction for the body of the paper.

- Work out of order if you need to. Write the parts you feel more comfortable with. Then move to the other paragraphs.

How Do You Start Writing a Draft?

" I spend five or ten minutes writing down anything I can think of about my topic, even if it sounds silly. Freewriting really helps me get my ideas out. "

—Karen

" I draw pictures of something that has to do with my topic. If I need to describe something, my picture helps me organize my thoughts. "

—Matthew

" I talk to my friends about my story first. It helps me figure out what I'm going to write about. Sometimes we instant-message each other to talk about our ideas. "

—Gilberto

" I create lists or webs of ideas that relate to the topic of my essay. Graphic organizers give me a lot of ideas to start with. "

—Sylvia

Draft, continued

Staying on Track

Q: Sometimes when I'm writing, my mind wanders and I get away from the point. How can I stay on track?

A: Keep your notes and graphic organizer around you to keep you focused. They will remind you of your plan for your essay.

You can also try to work with a partner. You can ask your partner to read your paper. You can also read your paper out loud and ask your friend what he or she thinks.

Another way to stay on track is by writing a "kernel essay" before you write your paper. A kernel essay shows just the main points of your story. It doesn't have any details. See how this writer used a kernel essay in his final paper.

Matt's Kernel Essay

The Invention of Earmuffs

Inventions solve a problem.	Chester Greenwood's earmuffs were brilliant.	They solved the problem of cold ears.	The earmuffs covered his ears.	With earmuffs on, his ears stayed warm in cold weather.

From Matt's Essay

Chester Greenwood's invention was a brilliant solution to a problem. Winters were really harsh where Chester lived. One thing that bothered him was that his ears would get cold when he was outside during the winter.

How Do You Stay on Track?

" I need silence when I write. I turn off my phone and the radio so that I won't be distracted. Quiet helps me focus on my writing. "

—Fatima

" I write for five or ten minutes and then reread what I've written. If I like it, I write for ten more minutes. If not, I take a short break and then come back with fresh eyes. Then I decide how I want to fix it. "

—Mark

" Sometimes it helps to take a short break when I am having a hard time writing. If I keep struggling with a tough paragraph, sometimes I get frustrated and I need to walk away from it for a while. Taking a break helps me go back to my writing with fresh ideas. "

—Melanie

" After every couple of paragraphs, I like to share my writing with a friend. It has to be someone I trust and feel comfortable with. It is helpful to hear my essay out loud and ask my friend for questions and comments. "

—Dean

Draft, continued

Knowing When You're Done

Q: How do I know when I'm done with the draft and I can move on to the next step?

A: You know you are finished when your ideas are all down on paper (or on your computer). Reread your essay and ask yourself some questions:

- Is my opening paragraph interesting? Is my argument clear? Will it make a reader want to know the reasons for my claim?

- Are my reasons clear and logical? Is my evidence relevant? Does it come from accurate and credible sources?

- Does the ending flow smoothly? Does it seem tacked on? Does it follow from and support the argument I presented?

The Truth About Drafting

FICTION: You should write your entire draft at once.
FACT: Sometimes you can write a draft all at once. But most drafts will take more time. Take a break if you need to!

FICTION: You should use a pencil and lined notebook paper to write a draft.
FACT: Use whatever works best for you. Some writers take notes on lots of scraps of paper. Others write on plain paper with colored pens. Some people use a computer to write. The important thing is to keep writing.

FICTION: You should never, ever write a draft without doing prewriting first.
FACT: Prewriting is a good way to organize your ideas. But sometimes the best way to figure out what you want to say is to just start writing! That way, you have some ideas down on paper. You can always go back and reorganize your ideas later.

FICTION: You should always stick to your plan when you're writing.
FACT: It's a good idea to stick to your writing plan. But that doesn't mean you can't change your mind. As you write, you might come up with new and better ideas. Don't be afraid to be flexible and change your plan if you need to.

What's One Truth You Want to Share About Drafting?

" Don't feel like you have to fill up the page. The only thing you have to do is share your thoughts as clearly as you can, so your readers can understand. "

—Greg

" You can get ideas anywhere. You can be singing in the shower or eating ice cream when you think of a great idea for your essay. Inspiration is exciting! "

—Monica

" Remember, you can change your plan while you're drafting. I, for example, change my mind all the time while I'm drafting. Be flexible. "

—Sam

" Don't feel like you have to use regular notebook paper for drafting. Some writers draft in brown journals or on flower-scented paper. Others type on their laptops. It doesn't matter how or where you write, just that you do! "

—Angela

Reflect

- What helps you get started with writing?

- Which ideas from other writers will be most helpful to you?

Write Effective Sentences

Combine Sentences

Good writing has a rhythm to it. The sentences are varied and interesting to read. If your writing sounds choppy, try to combine some sentences.

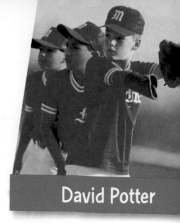

David Potter

Short, Choppy Sentences

The Prosthetic Catch-and-Throw Device is such a worthwhile invention. It was invented to help one young amputee throw a baseball. The device could also help other kids. The kids are amputees.

One Way to Combine the Sentences

The Prosthetic Catch-and-Throw Device is such a worthwhile invention. It was invented to help one young amputee throw a baseball. The device could also help other kids. The kids are amputees.

because

who

This writer combined sentences 1 and 2 and sentences 3 and 4.

Another Way to Combine the Sentences

The Prosthetic Catch-and-Throw Device is such a worthwhile invention. It was invented to help one young amputee throw a baseball. The device could also help other kids. The kids are amputees.

but

who

This writer combined sentences 2–4.

Inventor: Josh Parsons

Hometown: Houston, Texas

Vary Your Sentences

Your writing will be livelier if you make some sentences short and others long. That way you can create a nice rhythm and flow. Use different kinds of sentences, too.

x

Boring

The All-in-One Washer/Dryer

I think that the All-in-One Washer/Dryer is a better invention than an automatic rabbit feeder. First the washer/dryer can help more people. Two professors from San José State University studied U.S. homes. Seventy-six percent of U.S homes have a washing machine. Seventy-three percent have a dryer. There are more than 114 million households in the U.S. There are only about 5 million pet rabbits in the U.S. Compare the numbers. The washer/dryer would benefit many people.

All the sentences are statements, and most are about the same length.

Interesting

The All-in-One Washer/Dryer: A Better Invention

The All-in-One Washer/Dryer is a better invention than an automatic rabbit feeder. Why, you ask? First the washer/dryer can help more people. According to two professors from San José State University, 76 percent of U.S homes have a washing machine and 73 percent have a dryer. And the U.S. has more than 114 million households. Compare these numbers to the mere 5 million pet rabbits in the U.S. You can see that many more people would benefit from the washer/dryer.

The writer uses a question, and the sentences vary in length.

Revise: Gather Ideas

You are going to a party and you are almost ready. Before you go out the door, you take a few minutes to look at yourself in the mirror: *How does my hair look? Did I choose the best shirt? Is that a stain on my jeans?* Revising is like that. Before you share your writing, make sure that everything looks just fine.

What Is Revising?

When you revise your draft, you are making your writing better. Here are some tips for revising:

- make your claim clearer

- check that the reasons for your claim are clear and the evidence is relevant

- remove reasons and evidence that you don't really need

- add signal words to clarify the relationships among the claims, reasons, and evidence.

How do you know what's good about your draft and what needs more work? Getting feedback from other people will help you improve your writing. Ask someone you trust if there are parts of your writing that are confusing. Gather ideas about how to make your writing better.

You can choose to get help during the revising process in different ways. Here are some techniques you might want to try.

Read Your Paper Out Loud

Perhaps the most important person who can help you is . . . *you*!
Try reading your paper aloud to yourself. Do you hear anything
confusing? Is the paper easy to follow? Is the writing clumsy?
How can you make the writing better?

An Easier Time for Wheelchair Users
by Jaime Rivera

Thanks to 12-year-old Chandler Macocha, wheelchair
users now have an easier time getting things out of
backpacks. Chandler invented a swing-out backpack
holder for wheelchairs.

The seed for this invention began with Chandler's
young next-door neighbor who used a wheelchair. His
neighbor always had problems with reaching around the
back of her wheelchair for her backpack. Sometimes she
had to ask others for help. Chandler figured that a lot of
people had this same problem.

Chandler had an idea for a solution, so he developed a
working model. Then his neighbor tried out the model.
By pulling a lever, she could make the backpack swivel
forward.

Jaime thinks:
**" I think I might
need to add
more evidence
to support the
claim.
Otherwise it's
not clear."**

Revise: Gather Ideas, continued

Read Your Paper to a Friend

Ask a friend to sketch your work. If your friend can "see" your ideas, it means you're on the right track. Next, ask your partner to write three questions about your draft. This will show what you need to change and help you revise your paper.

> Chandler had an idea for a solution, so he developed a working model. Then his neighbor tried out the model. By pulling a lever, she could make the backpack swivel forward.
>
> Chandler's neighbor wasn't the only one who thought the swing-out backpack holder was a good idea. for this invention, Chandler receive a Da Vinci Award, which is given for innovations that help people overcome physical limitations. In addition, the U.S. Patent Office gave Chandler a patent on the invention. Now, with Chandler's swing-out backpack holder, Chandler's neighbor and other wheelchair user no longer have to struggle to get their backpacks.

- What happened when the neighbor tried the model? Did it work?
- Wouldn't that evidence support your claim?
- Is all the evidence relevant?

Jaime thinks:

> " I didn't clearly support my claim that the invention made things easier for wheelchair users. I need to add evidence.**"**

Read Your Paper to Different People

Share your problem-and-solution paragraphs with at least one adult and one classmate. Use some of these ideas to ask what they thought.

5 Good Ways to Ask for Feedback

1. Is my claim clearly introduced?

2. Do any of the reasons confuse you?

3. Is the evidence relevant and credible?

4. Are the relationships between my claim and evidence clear?

5. Are there parts where the paragraphs don't "flow" quite right?

Share Your Draft

Let some other people read your draft. They can tell you what they think about it.

- Have your friends and family read your draft. What did they like most? What didn't they understand?

- Post your paper on your school's Web site or on a bulletin board. Ask for comments.

- Share your writing with your classmates. Write down what they tell you. Think about what your readers want you to change, and why.

How to Have a Peer Conference

GETTING FEEDBACK	GIVING FEEDBACK
• Don't explain your ideas before your classmates read your paper. Let it speak for itself.	• Look for the claim and supporting reasons and evidence. Does the flow of ideas make sense?
• Ask how your reader reacted to the whole paper. Was the argument effective? Did you understand it? What reasons and evidence were the most or least convincing?	• How did you feel about the whole paper? Did you understand it? What parts did you like the most or least? Why?
• Ask for ideas about what to change. What parts could be cut out or explained more fully? Do the ideas flow smoothly and make sense?	• Give specific suggestions. What reasons need more evidence? What parts could be deleted? Does the paper need to be reorganized?
	• Don't focus just on problems. Explain what the writer does well.

Revision in Action

You have seen some strategies for finding out what needs work in your writing. Keep your audience and purpose in mind as you complete these steps.

1 **Evaluate Your Work**

Choose one of the techniques you have read about to gather ideas for your revision. Answer these questions.

- **About the Form** Am I giving clear reasons and evidence to support my claim? Is all my evidence relevant?

- **About the Sentences and Paragraphs** Do I need to make my sentences clearer? Do the sentences flow together?

Revision in Action

From Jaime's Draft

Chandler had an idea for a solution, so he developed a working model. Then his neighbor tried out the model. By pulling a lever, she could make the backpack swivel forward.

Chandler's neighbor wasn't the only one who thought the swing-out backpack holder was a good idea. for this invention, Chandler receive a Da Vinci Award, which is given for innovations that help people overcome physical limitations. In addition, the U.S. Patent Office gave Chandler a patent on the invention. Now, with Chandler's swing-out backpack holder, Chandler's neighbor and other wheelchair user no longer have to struggle to get their backpacks.

Jaime thinks:

" A big piece of evidence to support my claim is that Chandler's idea worked. I need to add that information."

" I could delete a few words to simplify some sentences."

② Mark Your Changes

Add Text To fully support your claim, sometimes you need to add information. Use this mark ∧ to add:

- more evidence.
- a clearer explanation of how the evidence supports the claim.

Delete Text Sometimes you have given information that really isn't necessary. Use this mark: ⟶ℓ to take out words and sentences that you don't need. You might take out:

- evidence that doesn't relate to a claim.
- repeated words or ideas.

Reflect

- Do you present your claim, reasons, and evidence clearly?
- Do you need to add or delete information?

Revising Marks

MARK	∧	⟶ℓ
WHAT IT MEANS	Insert something.	Take out.

Revised Draft

Chandler had an idea for a solution, so he developed a working model. Then his neighbor tried out the model. By pulling a lever, she could make the backpack swivel forward. *Chandler's idea worked.* ∧

Chandler's neighbor wasn't the only one who thought the swing-out backpack holder was a good idea. for this invention, Chandler receive a Da Vinci Award, which is given for innovations that help people overcome physical limitations. In addition, the U.S. Patent Office gave Chandler a patent on the invention. Now, with Chandler's swing-out backpack holder, Chandler's neighbor and other wheelchair user no longer ~~have to~~ struggle to get their backpacks.

Jaime added evidence to support the claim better and make the reason clear.

Jaime deleted extra words that did not add meaning to a sentence.

Edit and Proofread

You played with your puppy before the party, and now you have dog hair all over your sweater. You want to look as nice as you can, so you clean it off. Editing and proofreading is like that. You take time to fix the little mistakes so they won't take attention away from your paper.

Make Your Paper Ready for Your Readers

You have revised your paper to make sure your ideas are clear. Now it's time to fix any mistakes in spelling and grammar.

- Look for errors in grammar, spelling, and mechanics. Reading your paper out loud may help you catch these errors.

- Sometimes something looks wrong, but you're not sure why. Check a dictionary, or get help from your teacher.

- Reread your paper many times, looking for different mistakes each time.

- After you fix any mistakes, be sure to make a clean copy of your paper.

Look at the edited paper on page 49W. What kind of changes is the writer making?

Edited Draft

An Easier Time for Wheelchair Users
by Jaime Rivera

Thanks to 12-year-old Chandler Macocha, wheelchair users now have an easier time getting things out of backpacks. Chandler invented a swing-out backpack holder for wheelchairs.

The seed for this invention began with Chandler's young next-door neighbor who used a wheelchair. His neighbor always had problems with reaching around the back of her wheelchair for her backpack. Sometimes she had to ask others for help. Chandler figured that a lot of people had this same problem.

Chandler had an idea for a solution, so he developed a working model. Then his neighbor tried out the model. By pulling a lever, she could make the backpack swivel forward. Chandler's idea worked.

Chandler's neighbor wasn't the only one who thought the swing-out backpack holder was a good idea. for this invention, Chandler received a Da Vinci Award, which is given for innovations that help people overcome physical limitations. In addition, the U.S. Patent Office gave Chandler a patent on the invention. Now, with Chandler's swing-out backpack holder, Chandler's neighbor and other wheelchair users no longer struggle to get their backpacks.

Editing and Proofreading Marks

MARK	WHAT IT MEANS	MARK	WHAT IT MEANS
∧	Insert something.	/	Make lowercase.
⋏	Add a comma.	ℒ	Delete, take something out.
⋏	Add a semicolon.	¶	Make new paragraph.
⊙	Add a period.	◯	Spell out.
⊙	Add a colon.	⌃	Replace with this.
⌄ ⌄	Add quotation marks.	∼	Change order of letters or words.
⌄	Add an apostrophe.	#	Insert space.
≡	Capitalize.	◠	Close up, no space here.

Edit and Proofread, continued

Tools: The Dictionary

The right tool makes any job easier. The dictionary is a tool you can use for editing and proofreading. It can help you check the spelling of a word, of course. But it can also tell you how to use words the right way.

Guide words: first and last entries on the page

Pronunciation

Part of speech

345

farrier • fastball

far·ri·er \'fär-ē-ər\ *n* : a blacksmith who shoes horses [Medieval French *ferrour*, derived from Latin *ferrum* iron]
¹**far·row** \'far-ō\ *vb* : to give birth to pigs [Middle English *farwen*, derived from Old English *fearh* "young pig"]
²**farrow** *n* : a litter of pigs
far·see·ing \'fär-'sē-ing\ *adj* : FARSIGHTED 1
Far·si \'fär-sē\ *n* : PERSIAN 2b
far·sight·ed \-'sīt-əd\ *adj* **1 a** : seeing or able to see to a great distance **b** : able to judge how something will work out in the future **2** : affected with hyperopia — **far·sight·ed·ly** *adv* — **far·sight·ed·ness** *n*
¹**far·ther** \'fär-thər\ *adv* **1** : at or to a greater distance or more advanced point **2** : more completely [Middle English *ferther*, alteration of *further*]
  usage *Farther* and *further* have been used more or less interchangeably throughout most of their history, but currently they are showing signs of going in different directions. As adverbs, they continue to be used interchangeably whenever distance in space or time is involved, or when the distance is metaphorical. But when there is no notion of distance, *further* is used 〈our techniques can be *further* refined〉. *Further* is also used as a sentence modifier 〈*further*, the new students were highly motivated〉, but *farther* is not. A difference is also appearing in their adjective use. *Farther* is taking over the meaning of distance 〈the *farther* shore〉 and *further* the meaning of addition 〈needs no *further* improvement〉.
²**farther** *adj* **1** : more distant : REMOTER **2** : ³FURTHER 2, ADDITIONAL
far·ther·most \-ˌmōst\ *adj* : most distant : FARTHEST
¹**far·thest** \'fär-thəst\ *adj* : most distant in space or time
²**farthest** *adv* **1** : to or at the greatest distance in space or time : REMOTEST **2** : to the most advanced point **3** : by the greatest degree or extent : MOST
far·thing \'fär-thing\ *n* : a former British monetary unit equal to ¼ of a penny; *also* : a coin representing this unit [Old English *fēorthung*]
far·thin·gale \'fär-thən-ˌgāl, -thing-\ *n* : a support (as of hoops) worn especially in the 16th century to swell out a skirt [Middle French *verdugale*, from Spanish *verdugado*, from *verdugo* "young shoot of a tree," from *verde* "green," from Latin *viridis*]
fas·ces \'fas-ˌēz\ *n sing or pl* : a bundle of

Word History The English words *fascism* and *fascist* are borrowings from Italian *fascismo* and *fascista*, derivatives of *fascio* (plural *fasci*), "bundle, fasces, group." *Fascista* was first used in 1914 to refer to members of a *fascio*, or political group. In 1919 *fascista* was applied to the black-shirted members of Benito Mussolini's organization, the *Fasci di combattimento* ("combat groups"), who seized power in Italy in 1922. Playing on the word *fascista*, Mussolini's party adopted the fasces, a bundle of rods with an ax among them, as a symbol of the Italian people united and obedient to the single authority of the state. The English word *fascist* was first used for members of Mussolini's *fascisti*, but it has since been generalized to those of similar beliefs.
Fa·sci·sta \fä-'shē-stä\ *n, pl* **-sti** \-stē\ : a member of the Italian Fascist movement [Italian]
¹**fash·ion** \'fash-ən\ *n* **1** : the make or form of something **2** : MANNER, WAY 〈behaving in a strange *fashion*〉 **3 a** : a prevailing custom, usage, or style **b** : the prevailing style (as in dress) during a particular time or among a particular group 〈*fashions* in women's hats〉 [Medieval French *façun, fauschoun*, "shape, manner," from Latin *factio* "act of making, faction"] —
  after a fashion : in a rough or approximate way 〈did the job *after a fashion*〉
  synonyms FASHION, STYLE, MODE, VOGUE mean the usage accepted by those who want to be up-to-date. FASHION may apply to any way of dressing, behaving, writing, or performing that is favored at any one time or place 〈the current *fashion*〉. STYLE often implies the fashion approved by the wealthy or socially prominent 〈a superstar used to traveling in *style*〉. MODE suggests the fashion among those anxious to appear elegant and sophisticated 〈muscled bodies are the *mode* at this resort〉. VOGUE applies to a temporary widespread style 〈long skirts are back in *vogue*〉.
²**fashion** *vt* **fash·ioned; fash·ion·ing** \'fash-ning, -ə-ning\ : to give shape or form to : MOLD, CONSTRUCT — **fash·ion·er** \'fash-nər, -ə-nər\ *n*
fash·ion·able \'fash-nə-bəl, -ə-nə-\ *adj* **1** : following the fashion or established style : STYLISH 〈*fashionable* clothes〉 **2** : of or relating to the world of fashion : popular among those who conform to fashion 〈*fashionable* stores〉 — **fash·ion·able·ness** *n* — **fash·ion·ably** \-blē\ *adj*

Synonyms and shades of meaning

Different forms of the word

above individual worth and that supports a centralized autocratic government headed by a dictator, severe economic and social regimentation, and forcible suppression of opposition [Italian *fascismo*, from *fascio* "bundle, fasces, group," from Latin *fascis* "bundle" and *fasces* "fasces"] — **fas·cist** \'fash-əst\ *n or adj, often cap* — **fas·cis·tic** \fa-'shis-tik\ *adj, often cap*

\ə\ abut	\aù\ out	\i\ tip	\ò\ saw	\ù\ foot
\ər\ further	\ch\ chin	\ī\ life	\òi\ coin	\y\ yet
\a\ mat	\e\ pet	\j\ job	\th\ thin	\yü\ few
\ā\ take	\ē\ easy	\ng\ sing	\th\ this	\yù\ cure
\ä\ cot, cart	\g\ go	\ō\ bone	\ü\ food	\zh\ vision

Pronunciation key: helps you say the word

Tools: Spell-Check

If you write on a computer, the program you use can check your spelling. If you misspell a word, that word will appear underlined. The program then gives you a choice of possible words you might want to use.

Look at the words the spell-check program shows you. Then choose the one that fits.

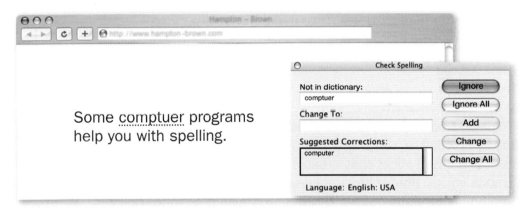

Don't trust spell-check completely, though! The program only looks at spelling, not word meanings. So if you used the wrong word, the spell-check program might not find it.

Even if you use a spell-check program, you still need to proofread your paper carefully.

Edit and Proofread, continued

Tools: Your Own Checklist

The English language can be tricky! It seems like there are a million different mistakes you could make. In fact, most people make the same mistakes over and over.

Look at your old papers to see which mistakes you make again and again. You could also ask your teacher about mistakes to look out for.

What kinds of mistakes does Vince make in these papers?

Vince Amalfi

Grade 7

2/14

    The last book I've read that I really liked ~~were~~ *was Goodbye, Robot*. It tells the story of a boy named Shaun. Shaun invents a small robot that creates songs by mixing notes of famous songs. Shaun becomes a successful musician, but then someone finds out his trick. Shaun also gets to know a girl who writes her own music, he realizes her music is much better than his own. It's a great story.

Vince Amalfi

Grade 7

4/10

    I've always been interested in video games, ever since I was a kid, I played them every chance I got. My uncle took me to see the Virtual World show at the museum. It's so cool. They had games about car racing, football, and boxing. I put on a special helmet and it was like I was in the game. The game's special effects were wonderful. The people who made this game really knew what they ~~was~~ *were* doing.

Make a list of the mistakes you make in your papers. Use this list to look out for those mistakes when you write. When you no longer make a mistake, take it off the list. Be sure to add new errors to look for!

Vince's Editing Checklist (4/20/08)

☑ Words I mix up:
- "its" and "it's"
  "It's" is short for "it is."

☑ Mistakes I make with verbs:
- I forget the apostrophe in "I've."
- I mix up plural and singular ("was" instead of "were").

☑ Mistakes I make with words:
- I add an extra "l" to words ending in –ful.

☑ Sentence problems to look out for:
- Run-on sentences
  To fix: break long sentences into two sentences

If you are writing your paper by hand, be sure to use good handwriting. After you fix your mistakes, rewrite your paper using your best handwriting.

Virtual-reality goggles make some video games very realistic. ▼

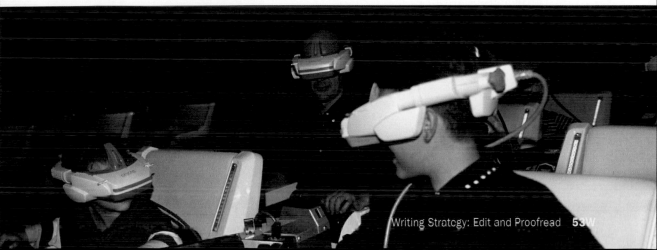

Edit and Proofread, continued

Correct Your Mistakes

When you proofread, it can be hard to find your mistakes. Errors in spelling, grammar, and punctuation are small details. They are easy to miss. Here are some tips to help you find your mistakes.

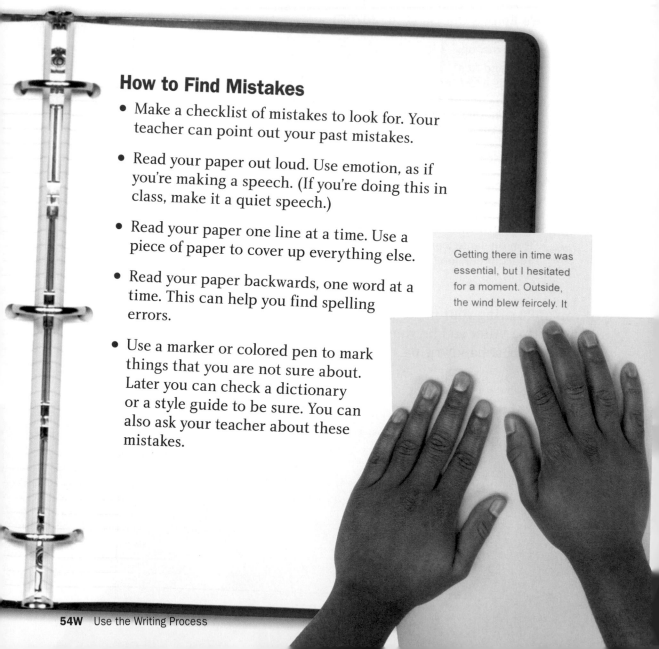

How to Find Mistakes

- Make a checklist of mistakes to look for. Your teacher can point out your past mistakes.

- Read your paper out loud. Use emotion, as if you're making a speech. (If you're doing this in class, make it a quiet speech.)

- Read your paper one line at a time. Use a piece of paper to cover up everything else.

- Read your paper backwards, one word at a time. This can help you find spelling errors.

- Use a marker or colored pen to mark things that you are not sure about. Later you can check a dictionary or a style guide to be sure. You can also ask your teacher about these mistakes.

Getting there in time was essential, but I hesitated for a moment. Outside, the wind blew feircely. It

Proofreading Marks in Action

This paper is edited using some common proofreading marks. Look at the model to see how these marks are used.

How I Learned to Prooofread

I used to think that editing my essay just meant running the computer's spell-check program and accepting whatever changes it suggested. Now I no know better. A computer will not catch mistakes like correctly spelled words that our are used incorrectly. In english class my teacher taught us how to use proofreader's marks to correct mistakes like words that need to be capitalized or made Lowercase. You can use a caret to insert any words that you forgot to put in.

My english teacher said Different kinds of carets are used to insert quotation marks apostrophes commas and semicolons however, dont use a caret to insert a colon. Here's how to insert a period or colon use a circle with one or two dots inside.

Also, if you accidentally type a word twice, use the delete mark to remove the extra extra word. You can use a similar mark to cross out replace words or phrases.

Finally, know what marks to use to insert a space, close up a space, and fix letters or words that are in the order wrong Practice your proofreading skills, and soon your writing will be letter-perfect.

Editing and Proofreading in Action

Read your paper again to fix language errors. This is what you do when you edit and proofread your work:

- **Check the Grammar** Make sure that you have used correct and conventional grammar throughout. In particular, make sure you used complete sentences. (See page 57W.)

- **Check the Spelling** Spell-check can help, but it isn't always enough. For errors in forming the plurals of nouns, you'll have to read your work carefully, and perhaps use a dictionary. (See page 58W.)

- **Check the Mechanics** Errors in punctuation and capitalization can make your work hard to understand. In particular, check that your sentences begin with a capital letter and end with a period, a question mark, or an exclamation point. (See page 59W.)

Use these marks to edit and proofread your problem-and-solution paragraphs.

Editing and Proofreading Marks

MARK	WHAT IT MEANS	MARK	WHAT IT MEANS
∧	Insert something.	╱	Make lowercase.
⩜	Add a comma.	℘	Delete, take something out.
⩙	Add a semicolon.	⁋	Make new paragraph.
⊙	Add a period.	⬭	Spell out.
⊙	Add a colon.	⌃	Replace with this.
ⱽ ⱽ	Add quotation marks.	∽	Change order of letters or words.
ⱽ	Add an apostrophe.	#	Insert space.
≡	Capitalize.	⌣	Close up, no space here.

Reflect

- **What kinds of errors did you find? What can you do to keep from making them?**

GrammarWorkout

Check for Complete Sentences

A complete sentence has a **subject** and a **predicate**.

Subject   Predicate
Many inventors build models of their inventions.

- The subject of a sentence is the person or thing the sentence is about.

- The **complete subject** includes all the words that tell about the subject. The most important word in the complete subject is usually a **noun**.

   EXAMPLE   Many inventors build models of their inventions.

- The **complete predicate** often tells what the subject does. The **verb** shows the action.

   EXAMPLE   Many inventors build models of their inventions.

Find the Trouble Spots

> I have always wanted to become an inventor.
> Last year, I started to think about a great invention
> that could change the world. I went to the library
> and looked for books about inventors. ∧Needed
>   *gave me a book*
> inspiration. The librarian at the desk ∧ It was about
> Thomas Edison and Benjamin Franklin. I really
> admire them. Invented so many things. They were
> so creative. The lightbulb, the lightning rod, and
> the phonograph.

Find two more incomplete sentences. Add a subject or predicate.

Editing and Proofreading in Action, continued

> ### SpellingWorkout

Check Plural Nouns

A plural noun names more than one person, place, or thing.

- To make most nouns plural, just add **-s**.

EXAMPLES	invention + s = inventions	problem + s = problems
	librarian + s = librarians	camera + s = cameras

- If the noun ends in *s, z, sh, ch,* or *x,* add **-es**.

EXAMPLES	coach + es = coaches	gas + es = gases
	flash + es = flashes	box + es = boxes

Find the Trouble Spots

A few ~~week~~ weeks ago I went to the science fair where my cousin Robin was showing her latest invention: a solar-powered leaf blower. Beautiful trees and ~~bushs~~ bushes surround the housees in Robin's neighborhood. In autumn, though, thousands of leaves blow from the tree branches onto her lawn. Her invention helps her get rid of those masss of leaves!

Find and fix two more errors with plural nouns.

MechanicsWorkout

Check Sentence Punctuation

Make sure every sentence ends with the right punctuation mark.

Sentence Type	End Punctuation	Mark
statement	period	.
question	question mark	?
exclamation	exclamation mark	!
command	period or exclamation mark	. or !

EXAMPLES The light in Sarah's room was off. (statement)

Was the light in Sarah's room off? (question)

The light in Sarah's room was off! (exclamation)

Turn the light in Sarah's room off. (command)

Find the Trouble Spots

I read that the ballpoint pen was an invention that changed the way we write. at first, I didn't believe it. What's the big deal about an ordinary plastic pen that we use every day. Then I tried to write with a fountain pen. It is really, really, hard? First of all, it is easy to drop ink all over the page. Then you need to train yourself to hold the pen correctly, because your letters can come out very thin or too thick. The ballpoint made writing easy

Find and fix three more errors in punctuation or capitalization.

Publish, Share, and Reflect

What's It Like

Your latest artwork is a sculpture made from old computer parts. You're very proud of it and you want to show it off. You set the sculpture inside a display box with a spotlight aimed right at it. This is what publishing is like. You "dress up" your writing so it will appeal to everyone who sees it.

Now you are ready to publish your problem-and-solution paper. The ideas that follow will help you with the finishing touches.

How Should You Share Your Writing?

Once you're done with your paper, what happens next?

- Collect your writing in a portfolio.

- Decide how to publish your writing. Decide who your audience will be. Do you want to share your writing with just a few people you're close to or with a wider audience?

- Keep thinking about your writing. This will help you improve over time.

You can share your writing with just a few people or with the whole world.

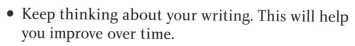

Sharing It with Friends

If you want to keep your writing "among friends," try these ideas:

- Write a letter to a friend or family member asking him or her to read your writing. Include a copy of your paper.

- Send your writing attached to an e-mail to someone you trust.

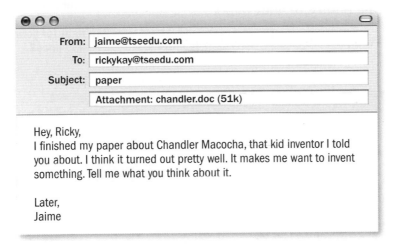

TechTIP

Keep safety in mind when publishing your work— especially when publishing online. Review the Acceptable Use Policy for your school before posting online.

- Another cool way to share your writing is to give it to someone as a gift. Suppose you've written a paper about your best friend. You could give her a copy of your paper, typed or carefully handwritten on nice paper. You could even frame it.

Making It Public

Sharing your writing with other people feels good! The feedback you get from them will help you become a better writer. Are you ready to share your writing with people you do not know as well? Here are some ways to make your writing public.

- Submit your work to your school newspaper or literary magazine.

- Read your writing to a class other than your own—perhaps kids in a younger grade.

- Look for writing contests in your local paper or online.

Publish, Share, and Reflect, continued

Adding Pictures to Your Work

Adding pictures to your paper can help people understand your ideas better. If you're using a computer, it's easy to add illustrations to your paper.

- Glue or tape interesting photos to your paper.

- Scan drawings, charts, or photographs into your paper.

Reflect
- How will you share your problem-and-solution paper?

- What can you do to make your paper especially right for your audience?

Ready for Publishing

An Easier Time for Wheelchair Users
by Jaime Rivera

The writer added a photograph that goes with the paper.

Thanks to 12-year-old Chandler Macocha, wheelchair users now have an easier time getting things out of backpacks. Chandler invented a swing-out backpack holder for wheelchairs.

The seed for this invention began with Chandler's young next-door neighbor who used a wheelchair. His neighbor always had problems reaching around the back of her wheelchair for her backpack. Sometimes she had to ask others for help. Chandler figured that a lot of people had this same problem.

Chandler had an idea for a solution, so he developed a working model. Then his neighbor tried out the model. By pulling a lever, she could make the backpack swivel forward. Chandler's idea worked.

Chandler's neighbor wasn't the only one who thought the swing-out backpack holder was a good idea. For this invention, Chandler received a Da Vinci Award, which is given for innovations that help people overcome physical limitations. In addition, the U.S. Patent Office gave Chandler a patent on the invention. Now, with Chandler's swing-out backpack holder, Chandler's neighbor and other wheelchair users no longer struggle to get their backpacks.

Keep Thinking About Your Writing

Finishing a paper doesn't mean you stop thinking about it. Looking back on your work can help you improve your writing. Ask yourself what worked in this paper and how you can improve your writing. Reflect on your writing by asking yourself questions.

Questions to Think About

1. What do I like most about my writing?

2. Did I get any unexpected questions or comments from readers?

3. How did this paper make me a better writer?

4. What was the hardest part about writing this paper?

5. What did I learn by working on this paper?

6. How can I improve my writing?

7. What other topics would I like to write about?

8. What other kinds of writing would I like to try?

Build Your Portfolio

Making a portfolio is a good way to store and organize your best work. You can use a file folder or binder to save your papers. You may also include drafts in your portfolio. This will help you see how your writing has improved.

You can make your portfolio public or keep it private. Many writers use portfolios to show off their work. If you do this, you should keep more personal papers, such as journal entries, in another place.

Use Multimedia

If you are making a presentation to a large audience, make it have a greater impact by using visuals, computer technology, and sound.

Enhance Your Presentation with Visuals

As the old saying goes, a picture is worth a thousand words. Add pictures and other visuals to your presentation to clarify reasons, strengthen claims and evidence, and add interest.

Backpack

- Show or project photos that relate to your topic. Make sure they are eye-catching and large enough for everyone to see easily.

- Show an illustration that will help your audience understand the claims you make.

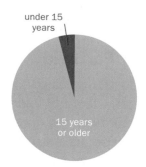

under 15 years

15 years or older

Ages of Wheelchair Users in U.S.

- Use charts or graphs to help your audience see the relationships among your claims, reasons, and evidence.

- Does your presentation include historical or geographical information? Consider displaying a map to help your audience visualize the location.

- Present a snippet of a video, using a DVD player, tablet, or computer.

" I can look up Chandler Macocha's patent online and print out a picture of his invention."

—Jaime

Enhance Your Presentation with Sound

Consider using sound recordings to really make your presentation come alive. Be imaginative and think of different sounds that will keep your audience interested and clarify your claims.

- Play the national anthem of the country that is the topic of your presentation. Or, play a recording by a musician described in your presentation.

- Play snippets of a speech by a famous politician, personality, or researcher.

> "Let us all hope that the dark clouds of racial prejudice will soon pass away and the deep fog of misunderstanding will be lifted from our fear-drenched communities."
>
> —*Martin Luther King, Jr.*

- Share parts of recorded interviews or comments by experts whom you quoted to provide evidence in support of claims you make in your presentation.

- Ring a bell or play a ring tone between major parts of your presentation to help your audience identify each of the claims you are making.

Remember: The goal of using media is to enhance your presentation—not to replace it. Use photos, charts, and graphics to convey only information that relates directly to your topic. Videos and sound recordings should also be used sparingly. Brief snippets are enough to keep your audience's attention.

THE Many Writers YOU ARE

Model Study

Personal Narrative

When was the last time you told someone a story about yourself? Maybe you shared an exciting trip you took or something funny that happened to you at the mall. When you tell about something that happened to you, you are telling a **personal narrative.**

Because a personal narrative is about you, you'll write it in the **first person.** That means you'll use *I, we, me* and *my* a lot. You'll also usually use **sequential order** so your readers can follow the events in the order in which they happen—from beginning to end.

Read the student model on page 69W. It shows the features of a good personal narrative.

PERSONAL NARRATIVE

A good personal narrative

☑ has a beginning, a middle, and an end

☑ includes real events, people, and places

☑ uses specific details that let the reader "see and feel" what's happening

☑ expresses the writer's feelings.

Feature Checklist

Hustle to the Hoop

by Angela Ross

I almost didn't want to get out of bed that morning, until I noticed my lucky red gym shorts folded neatly next to my backpack. Basketball tryouts were today! I threw on my clothes and dashed to the kitchen to grab breakfast. I could feel my stomach churning as I crunched on my corn flakes. I didn't expect to be so nervous.

On my walk to school, I imagined running onto the court, dressed in a shiny black and yellow jersey. I could practically hear my name over the PA: "And now, starting forward Angela Ross!"

During lunch, I practiced my jump shot while disposing of my empty lunch bag. Finally, my nerves settled and I felt prepared. I was ready for the challenge.

Everyone wanted to impress Coach Ward. For once, I was happy that my height helped me stand out in a crowd. I used my best moves and hustled down the court so fast I nearly wore all the rubber off my shoes. I hoped my performance was enough to get me on the team.

When the tryouts were over, the list of team members was posted in the girls' locker room. I ran my finger down the alphabetized names and stopped when I got to the Ks— Ross. "I made it!" I yelled. "Congratulations," said Coach Ward, as she handed me a shiny black and yellow jersey.

Student Model

Write a Personal Narrative

WRITING PROMPT Have you ever faced a challenge? Maybe you had to move somewhere new, or you stood up for something you believed in. Though it was tough at the time, the experience may have helped you discover strengths you didn't know you had.

Think of a time you faced a big challenge. Then, write a personal narrative that

- briefly explains what the challenge was
- tells what happened in the beginning, middle, and end
- describes what you experienced—what you saw, heard, and felt
- tells what the experience means to you.

Prewrite

Here are some tips for planning your personal narrative.

1 Gather Details About Your Experience

You know which experience you want to describe, so now collect as many sensory details as you can to *show*, and not just tell, your readers what the experience was like.

Matt wants to tell about the day he quit the track team. He took notes about that day in a **five-senses diagram.**

Matt's Five-Senses Diagram

I saw . . .	• the track—an endless circle • the backs of runners
I heard . . .	• my feet hitting the ground • my own breathing • Coach putting me down
I smelled . . .	• the hot asphalt pavement
I tasted . . .	• my own sweat
I touched or felt . . .	• my soaked shirt sticking to me • burning in my legs and lungs

② Organize Your Ideas

How can you build your narrative? Organize your details into a plot with a clear beginning, middle, and ending. Try using a **sequence chain** to show the series of events. Here's the plan Matt used to organize his **personal narrative.**

Matt's Plan for His Personal Narrative

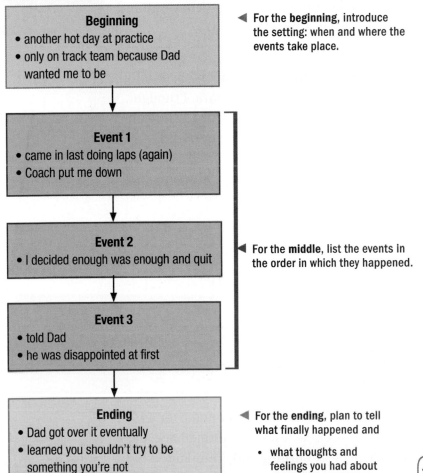

Beginning
- another hot day at practice
- only on track team because Dad wanted me to be

◀ For the **beginning**, introduce the setting: when and where the events take place.

Event 1
- came in last doing laps (again)
- Coach put me down

Event 2
- I decided enough was enough and quit

◀ For the **middle**, list the events in the order in which they happened.

Event 3
- told Dad
- he was disappointed at first

Ending
- Dad got over it eventually
- learned you shouldn't try to be something you're not

◀ For the **ending**, plan to tell what finally happened and
- what thoughts and feelings you had about the event
- why you find this experience memorable.

Reflect
- Do you know which details to include?
- Does your sequence chain show the sequence of events?

Draft

With a good plan in place, you're ready to start writing your draft.

- **Use Your Organizer** Use your sequence chain to keep the events in your narrative organized. Spend time crafting the beginning (so readers understand the situation) and ending (so they know what it meant to you).

> It was another long, hot, boring afternoon of running laps. *Even homework is more fun than this*, I thought. I was only on the track team because my dad wanted me to be, and it felt like this practice would never end.

- **Add Plenty of Details** Use a lot of sensory details to show rather than just tell what happened.

Five-Senses Diagram

I saw . . .	• the track—an endless circle • the backs of runners
I heard . . .	• my feet hitting the ground • my own breathing • Coach putting me down
I smelled . . .	• the hot asphalt pavement

From Matt's Draft

> My feet hit the hot, smelly asphalt over and over as I ran around the endless circle. I was breathing hard and I felt the muscles in my legs burning and cramping.

Reflect

- Read your draft. Is it clear what happened first, next, and last?

- How strong is your beginning? Your ending?

DRAFTING TIPS
Trait: **Organization**

If Your Writing Wanders . . .
Sometimes as you write you try to tell about too many ideas at once. Then your writing seems disorganized because it wanders all over the place.

Try Using an Idea Organizer . . .
An idea organizer can help you stay focused on the most important parts of your experience. Start by writing down what you learned from your experience, or your "truth." Then map how you arrived at that truth.

Here's an idea organizer Matt created:

Idea Organizer

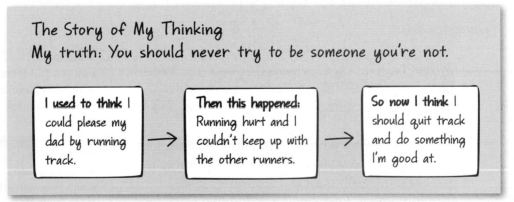

The Story of My Thinking
My truth: You should never try to be someone you're not.

| I used to think I could please my dad by running track. | → | Then this happened: Running hurt and I couldn't keep up with the other runners. | → | So now I think I should quit track and do something I'm good at. |

As Matt writes his draft all he has to do is fill in the details for each part, and his narrative will be focused from beginning to end.

Revise

As you consider how to revise your work, keep in mind your intended audience and your purpose for writing. Does your writing do what you want it to do? Will it connect with your audience?

❶ Evaluate Your Work

Read your draft to a partner. After you read, ask your partner questions:

- **About the Form** Can you picture the event? Can you tell how I felt about it and what it means to me?

- **About the Organization** Can you follow along with what happened? Is the order of events clear?

Revision in Action

From Matt's Draft

> My feet hit the hot, smelly asphalt over and over as I ran around the endless circle. I was breathing hard and I felt the muscles in my legs burning and cramping.
>
> No matter how hard I tried, I couldn't keep up with the other guys. I saw their backs as they pulled ahead of me. I heard Coach putting me down—again.
>
> At that moment, I decided I was through with track. I was through with sports, period. I didn't have to be here doing this.

Matt's partner says:

" Can you tell more about why running was so awful for you?"

" Maybe some dialogue would make your narrative more lively."

" This last detail is distracting. Do you need it?"

❷ Mark Your Changes

Add Text You might need to add more details to give your readers a clear and vivid picture of the event. Use this mark: ∧.

Delete Text Use ⌒ to take out details that aren't important.

Revising Marks	MARK	∧	⌒	⌒̣
	WHAT IT MEANS	Insert something.	Replace with this.	Take out.

Revised Draft

My feet hit the hot, smelly asphalt over and over as I ran around the endless circle. I was ~~breathing~~ gasping for breath ~~hard~~ and I felt the muscles in my legs burning and cramping. My shirt was plastered to my chest with sweat.∧

No matter how hard I tried, I couldn't keep up with the other guys. I saw their backs as they pulled ahead of me. I heard Coach putting me down—again. "Wake up, slow poke. Get a move on," he shouted.∧

At that moment, I decided I was through with track. I was through with sports, period. ~~I didn't have to be here doing this.~~

Matt added specific and more precise details to show what he was feeling.

Matt added some dialogue.

Matt took out an unnecessary and distracting detail.

Edit and Proofread

Are you happy with the content of your personal narrative? Read it over again to fix language errors. Here's what you do when you edit and proofread your work.

- **Check the Grammar** Make sure that you have used correct and conventional grammar throughout. In particular, check that you have used pronouns where possible to make your writing flow smoothly. (See page 77W.)
- **Check the Spelling** Spell-check can help, but it isn't always enough. To catch errors with plural nouns, you'll have to read your work carefully and perhaps use a dictionary. (See page 78W.)
- **Check the Mechanics** Errors in punctuation and capitalization can make your work hard to understand. In particular, check that you have capitalized all proper nouns. (See page 79W.)

Use these marks to edit and proofread your personal narrative.

Editing and Proofreading Marks

MARK	WHAT IT MEANS	MARK	WHAT IT MEANS
∧	Insert something.	/	Make lowercase.
∧,	Add a comma.	℘	Delete, take something out.
∧;	Add a semicolon.	¶	Make new paragraph.
⊙	Add a period.	◯	Spell out.
(:)	Add a colon.	∧‾‾	Replace with this.
∨" ∨"	Add quotation marks.	∼	Change order of letters or words.
∨'	Add an apostrophe.	#	Insert space.
≡	Capitalize.	⁀‿	Close up, no space here.

Reflect

- **What kinds of errors did you find? What can you do to keep from making them?**

Grammar Workout

Check Pronouns

Repeating the same nouns over and over can make your writing sound choppy and boring:

> **My dad** asked, "How was practice today?" My heart sank. **My dad** was the one who wanted me to join the team in the first place. **My dad** would never understand why I had quit.

Make your writing flow smoothly by replacing some nouns with pronouns:

> **My dad** asked, "How was practice today?" My heart sank. **He** was the one who wanted me to join the team in the first place. **He** would never understand why I had quit.

Make sure pronouns agree with the nouns they refer to: Singular pronouns refer to one person, place, or thing. Plural pronouns refer to more than one. For a complete list of pronouns, see page 466W.

Find the Opportunities

> My parents and I often disagree. But ~~my parents~~ *they* know me. My parents know I have to be my own person. Even Mike didn't give me a hard time about my decision. Actually, ~~Mike~~ *he* just seemed surprised. "I had no idea you felt that way," Mike said. My family understands a lot. My family can work through just about anything!

What other nouns can you replace with pronouns to improve the flow?

Spelling Workout

Check Plural of Nouns Ending in y

A plural noun names more than one person, place, thing, or idea.
Here are some rules for spelling plural nouns that end in *y*:

- Add **-s** to form the plural of a noun ending in a vowel and *y*.

  EXAMPLE   day + <u>s</u> = day<u>s</u>
                   play + <u>s</u> = play<u>s</u>
                   boy + <u>s</u> = boy<u>s</u>
                   decoy + <u>s</u> = decoy<u>s</u>
                   stingray + <u>s</u> = stingray<u>s</u>

- If a noun ends with a consonant and *y*, change the *y* to an
  i, then add **-es**.

  EXAMPLE   lady + <u>es</u> = lad<u>ies</u>
                   baby + <u>es</u> = bab<u>ies</u>
                   entry + <u>es</u> = entr<u>ies</u>
                   country + <u>es</u> = countr<u>ies</u>

Find the Trouble Spots

Other kids had hobb*ie*s like chess and singing, but I
was stuck at practice. As I jogged, I remembered how
relay*ie*s used to be fun. I sure wasn't having fun now. I
knew the guies were my buddys, but as they ran ahead
of me, they seemed almost like enemys.

Find and fix
three more
misspelled
plural nouns.

MechanicsWorkout

Check Capitalization of Proper Nouns

Proper nouns name a specific person, place, or thing. When you use proper nouns, always capitalize them. Here are a few examples:

- Capitalize people's names.

  EXAMPLES Coach Brown
  Jim
  Kira Jovanovich

- Capitalize months, days of the week, and holidays.

  EXAMPLES February
  Sunday
  Independence Day

- Capitalize the names of states, countries, and continents. Also capitalize names from geography, including geographic regions.

  EXAMPLES Indiana   Ireland
  Antarctica   the Swiss Alps
  the Northeast   the Deep South

Find the Trouble Spots

> Running has never been my favorite activity, especially in hot weather. As we did laps with coach johnson watching, I wished we had never moved to arizona from the midwest. I couldn't wait until saturday when I could sleep in.

Find and fix three more errors in capitalization.

4 | *Write as a* Storyteller

Model Study

Story About a Clever Character

You've probably read hundreds of stories from fables to folk tales to realistic fiction. What are your favorites? What kept you reading those stories?

Good writers use a lot of different techniques to grab and keep their readers interested. They start out right away by getting their readers involved with a main **character** and a **conflict**, or problem, the character needs to solve. Then they present events in order that lead to a **resolution**.

So, when you write a short story, you'll develop an interesting character. You'll describe the challenges that character faces as he or she tries to solve a problem. And, of course, you'll explain how things turn out in the end!

Read the student model on page 81W. It shows the features of a good short story about a clever character.

SHORT STORY

A good short story includes

☑ interesting **characters**

☑ details about the **setting**

☑ a **conflict** a character has to deal with

☑ a series of events that lead to a satisfying **resolution**, or ending.

Feature Checklist

Pierre and the Unwanted Roommates

by John Kirchner

The **beginning** introduces the **setting**, **characters**, and **conflict**.

With the first snowflake of winter, Pierre the mouse decided to move from the field to Farmer Leon's warm basement. He packed his things.

"Why are you moving, Pierre?" asked Claude.

Pierre saw that Claude wanted to come with him. Pierre did not want this. Claude was noisy and rude. Pierre replied, "I just want a little change."

"An excellent idea!" said Claude. "I'll come too."

The **middle** develops the plot. It shows how Pierre tries to solve his problem and what gets in his way.

Pierre could not refuse him. Claude was big and strong. So Pierre said, "I don't think there is room."

"Nonsense," said Claude. "That basement is big! I will invite Jaques and Jean-Luc to join us."

Now Pierre was alarmed. He could just imagine them eating all his food and leaving a mess.

"Oh, Claude," he said, "you would not like it there.

"I am old and weak," Pierre continued. "But young, healthy mice like you love to play outdoors."

The **ending**, or **resolution**, shows how the conflict was solved.

"You're right," said Claude. "We would not like to sit inside with you. How boring! Jacques, Jean-Luc, let's go roll in the snow." And he left Pierre to his packing.

Events in the plot are told from an outsider's **point of view**, but include how the character feels.

Dialogue keeps the plot moving.

Organization

A messy closet makes it hard to find what you need. But if you keep your closet neat and organized, you can instantly locate your favorite T-shirt or that new pair of pants. Organizing your writing is also important. It helps your reader know right away what's important in your story.

Why Does Organization Matter?

When writing is well organized, it's easy to see how the ideas go together. One idea flows right into the next.

Writers organize their ideas in a way that fits their purpose for writing. Below, the writer structures her story so it's easy to follow how a character tries to solve a problem.

> Long ago, the Norse gods needed a wall to protect their city from the giants. A giant who was skilled as a stonemason offered to build one within a year. What was his price? To marry the goddess Freya.
>
> But Freya refused to marry a giant, so the gods had to meet to discuss the matter. Freya said, "Tell the mason he has to finish in half a year. Surely he cannot work that fast. If he fails, he must give up his reward." The gods agreed, and the mason set to work.

Transition words link one plot event to the next.

Study the rubric on page 83W. What is the difference between writing with a score of 2 and writing with a score of 4?

Organization

	Does the writing have a clear structure, and is it appropriate for the writer's audience, purpose, and type of writing?	How smoothly do the ideas flow together?
4 Wow!	The writing has a structure that is <u>clear</u> and appropriate for the writer's audience, purpose, and type of writing.	The ideas progress in a smooth and orderly way. • The introduction is strong. • The ideas flow well from paragraph to paragraph. • The ideas in each paragraph flow well from one sentence to the next. • Effective transitions connect ideas. • The conclusion is strong.
3 Ahh.	The writing has a structure that is <u>generally</u> clear and appropriate for the writer's audience, purpose, and type of writing.	<u>Most</u> of the ideas progress in a smooth and orderly way. • The introduction is adequate. • Most of the **ideas** flow well from paragraph to paragraph. • Most ideas in each paragraph flow from one sentence to the next. • Effective transitions connect most of the ideas. • The conclusion is adequate.
2 Hmm.	The structure of the writing is <u>not</u> clear or <u>not</u> appropriate for the writer's audience, purpose, and type of writing.	<u>Some</u> of the ideas progress in a smooth and orderly way. • The introduction is weak. • Some of the ideas flow well from paragraph to paragraph. • Some ideas in each paragraph flow from one sentence to the next. • Transitions connect some ideas. • The conclusion is weak.
1 Huh?	The writing is not clear or organized.	<u>Few or none</u> of the ideas progress in a smooth and orderly way.

Organization, continued

Compare Writing Samples

A well-organized story presents events that lead logically to a **resolution** of a conflict or problem. It also includes **transitions** between events. Study the two samples of short stories on this page.

Well Organized

The Great Idea

The Great Dane and the Basset Hound shared a water bucket. Unfortunately, the Great Dane would always get to the bucket first and drink until the bucket was only half full. The Basset Hound was never able to reach the water at the bottom of the bucket, so he was left thirsty. He tried many times to stretch his neck and stick out his tongue, but he still could not get to the water.

Finally, a great idea came to the Basset Hound. He ran over to a pile of rocks and began carrying them over to the bucket and dropping them in one by one. Soon the water level rose to the top of the bucket, and the Basset Hound was able to quench his thirst.

The **conflict** is clear and the plot events follow in a logical order to a **resolution**.

Transitions help to show the order of events.

Not So Well Organized

The Great Dane and the Basset Hound

The Great Dane and the Basset Hound shared a water bucket. The Basset Hound was never able to reach the water at the bottom of the bucket, so he was left thirsty. The Great Dane would always get to the bucket first and drink until the bucket was only half full. He tried many times to stretch his neck and stick out his tongue, but he still could not get to the water.

A great idea came to the Basset Hound. He ran over to a pile of rocks and began carrying them over to the bucket. The water level rose to the top of the bucket.

The **conflict** is clear, but some events are out of order. The **resolution** could be clearer.

The story lacks transitions, so the events don't flow smoothly.

Evaluate for Organization

Now read carefully the story below. Use the rubric on page 83W to score it.

The Shoe Collection

by Gabriela Cortez

Is the conflict clear?

On the first day of school Hailey strutted into class in a new pair of leather shoes. All the girls oohed and aahed as usual.

Corrine did not wish to join the admiring crowd. "What's wrong, Corrine? Jealous?" Hailey scoffed.

"No, I have over 500 pairs of shoes at home that are just as nice as yours," said Corrine.

"Yeah, maybe in your dreams," Hailey snickered.

"I'll bring them tomorrow," Corrine declared.

What transitions can Gabriela add to improve the flow of events?

Corrine walked into school wearing the same old, scuffed shoes. Hailey laughed. "It was raining, and I didn't want to get my good shoes wet," Corrine claimed. "I'll bring them tomorrow."

Corrine again came to school without her new shoes. "It was too muddy out," explained Corrine.

On Thursday, Corrine came to class with a thick, binder. "What's that?" Hailey asked.

Does the resolution make sense? How could Gabriela improve it?

"My shoe collection," Corrine said proudly. She opened up her binder to reveal hand-drawn pictures of hundreds of pairs of shoes, each more beautiful than the last. All the girls gathered around and oohed and aahed at her unique creations.

Raise the Score

These papers have been scored using the **Organization Rubric** on page 83W. Study each paper to see why it got the score it did.

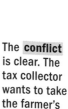

Overall Score: 4

The Clever Old Farmer
by Maggie Stoler

The **beginning** sets up the situation and the characters.

In a small village, an old farmer owned valuable property. It had vast fields, lush crops, and a sparkling freshwater spring. The local tax collector was most envious. He hoped the farmer would forget to pay his taxes. That way, he could seize the land. But the farmer always paid on time.

Fed up, the tax collector tried to fool him, declaring his taxes were two months overdue. "I have never missed a payment," the farmer insisted.

The **middle** develops the conflict. **Plot events** build to a turning point.

"It seems you've grown forgetful in your old age," snickered the tax collector. "Do you really think you can still make a living off of this farm?"

"Certainly," replied the farmer. "My land is very special. The more you take from it, the more it grows." Immediately the tax collector's eyes lit up with greed. "I'll give you part of my property if I never have to pay taxes again," the farmer offered. The tax collector accepted.

Right away, the farmer took the tax collector to a small ditch. "Here you are!" said the farmer, smiling. "Get a shovel and dig out as much dirt as you like. The more you take, the bigger the ditch will get." The tax collector sputtered with rage when he realized the farmer had fooled him.

The ending presents a satisfying **resolution** to the **conflict**.

The **conflict** is clear. The tax collector wants to take the farmer's land.

Transitions make the events flow smoothly together.

The Clever Old Farmer

In a small village, an old farmer owned valuable property. It had vast fields, crops, and a freshwater spring. The local tax collector was envious. He hoped the farmer would forget to pay his taxes. That way, he could seize the land. But the farmer always paid on time.

Fed up, the tax collector lied. He said the Farmer's taxes were overdue. "I have never missed a payment," the farmer said.

"It seems you've grown forgetful in your old age," snickered the tax collector. "Do you really think you can still make a living off of this farm?"

"Certainly," replied the farmer. "My land is very special. The more you take from it, the more it grows." The tax collector's eyes lit up. "I'll give you part of my property if I never have to pay taxes again," the farmer offered. The tax collector accepted.

"Here you are!" said the farmer. He took the tax collector to a small ditch. "Get a shovel and start digging. The more you take from it, the bigger the ditch will get." The tax collector was furious because the farmer had fooled him.

The **structure** of the story is still clear.

Some **transitions** are missing to connect one event to the next.

Most of the **plot events** follow a logical order, but the order here isn't clear.

▲ RAISING *THE SCORE*

How can the writer fix the order of events in the last paragraph? What transitions could she add to improve the flow of ideas?

Overall Score: 2

The Clever Old Farmer

The **structure** of the story is not clear.

The writing does have a **conflict** and a plot, but the **plot events** are jumbled.

An old village farmer owned valuable property. It had fields, crops, and a freshwater spring. The local tax collector wanted the land so he tried to trick the farmer.

"I'm not sure you can still make a living off of this farm," said the tax collector. "You can't even pay your taxes. You are overdue."

The farmer knew this wasn't true. He had a plan to get back at the tax collector.

So the farmer said, "My land has something special. The more you take from it, the more it grows." The tax collector was interested in his words. "I'll give you part of my property if I never have to pay taxes again," the farmer offered. "All right," said the tax collector.

The writer uses a few **transitions**, but they are not effective or meaningful.

The writing is missing a clear **resolution**.

Then the farmer said, "Here you are! Get a shovel and start digging." The old farmer pointed to a small ditch dug in a far corner of the land. "The ditch will get bigger and bigger."

RAISING *THE SCORE*

The writer needs to improve the order of events and add a resolution. What should she do?

The Clever Old Farmer

The story
lacks
structure.

A tax collector decided to lie to an old village farmer about his taxes. The farmer owned some valuable property and always paid his taxes on time.

The **conflict**
is not
explained.

"I'm not sure you can still make a living off of this farm. Maybe you should give it up," said the tax collector.

"Well," replied the farmer, "my land has something special. The more you take from it, the more it grows." The tax collector looked at him. "I'll give you part of my property if we can make a deal about the taxes," the farmer offered. The tax collector nodded.

There is no
resolution
because
there is no
apparent
conflict.

"Here's a fine ditch you can have!" said the farmer. The tax collector was mad. "Get a shovel and start digging," said the farmer.

Events are out
of order, and
transitions
are missing.

▲
RAISING *THE SCORE*
The writer needs to rearrange some
sentences and add details to tell when
things happen. What should she add?

How to Make Your Ideas Flow

When you're trying to get from point A to point B, it helps to have the trail clearly marked. Otherwise, you might get lost! When you write, transitions help you set up the path you want readers to follow. They're like signposts or markers that guide your reader through your story.

Use Transitions

A transition is any word or phrase that connects ideas. Add transitions to your sentences so they work together as a team to get your story across. Which of the examples is easier to follow?

Without Transitions

> The chicken and the dog lived on the farm. The wild coyote lived in the fields nearby. The coyote was always hungry. He tried to catch the chicken. The chicken knew that the dog did not like the coyote. The chicken became friends with the dog. The coyote never bothered the chicken.

The short, choppy sentences make the writing hard to follow. Ideas are not well connected.

With Transitions

> Once, a chicken and a dog lived on a farm. A wild coyote also lived in the fields nearby. The coyote was always hungry. All day long, he tried to catch the chicken. The chicken knew that the dog did not like the coyote. So, the chicken became friends with the dog. From that day forward, the coyote never bothered the chicken again.

With **transitions,** the writing flows smoothly from one idea to the next.

Choose the Right Transition

Transition words and phrases show how ideas are related.

Cause	Time	Order	Emphasize
as a result because since	afterward before earlier	finally first then	amazingly in fact more importantly
Examples	**Contrast**	**Comparison**	**Summary**
for example for instance	although however yet	also likewise similarly	all in all finally in the end

What transitions can you add to this passage to connect ideas?
Where will you add commas?

The chicken and the dog had been enemies for as long as anyone could remember. They shared fear and dislike of another animal. These former enemies formed a lasting friendship.

A repeated word links the sentences and ideas.

How to Connect Your Paragraphs

Just as transition words help you connect your sentences, they can also help you tie your paragraphs together. Effective transitions between paragraphs tell your reader what to expect next.

In this story excerpt, the writer explains the events in the story, but she does not use transitions.

Without Transitions

Zeus, the king of the Greek gods, once became very angry with a Titan named Atlas. Atlas had sided against Zeus in a war.

Zeus wanted revenge. He forced Atlas to hold up a pillar that supported the sky, stars, and planets. Soon poor Atlas longed for relief!

A man named Heracles approached Atlas. He explained that he wanted a few of the apples from Zeus's orchard. "Would you get some for me?" he asked.

Atlas saw the chance to get rid of his burden. "Of course I'll help you," he said. "But I will need a little favor from you in return. Just hold up this pillar while I'm gone. I'll be back in a little while."

Now look at how a few paragraph transitions connect the whole story, making it easier for the reader to follow. What transition could you use to connect the final paragraph?

With Transitions

Zeus, the king of the Greek gods, once became very angry with a Titan named Atlas because Atlas had sided against Zeus in a war.

Zeus wanted revenge, so he forced Atlas to hold up a pillar that supported the sky, stars, and planets. Soon poor Atlas longed for relief!

One morning, a man named Heracles approached Atlas. He explained that he wanted a few of the apples from Zeus's orchard. "Would you get some for me?" he asked.

Atlas saw the chance to get rid of his burden. "Of course I'll help you," he said. "But I will need a little favor from you in return. Just hold up this pillar while I'm gone. I'll be back in a little while."

This statue portrays Atlas, a well-known hero in Greek mythology. ▼

Write a Story About a Clever Character

WRITING PROMPT Interesting stories fascinate you with unexpected twists. The main character is up against impossible odds, but somehow he or she triumphs. Often, quick thinking—rather than power, beauty, or strength—is what solves the character's problem.

Think of a tricky problem and how a character might solve it. (You might draw on your own experiences or other stories for inspiration.) Write a story that includes

- details about the setting
- a clever main character who must solve a problem
- a character who stands in the way of the solution
- plot events that lead to a resolution.

Prewrite

Here are some tips for planning your story.

1 Think About Your Characters and Setting

Start by deciding who your story is about and where and when it takes place. Don't worry about planning all the details right away. Just get some ideas down.

Here's how Kristi began planning her story:

List of Characters

Setting: a village on a tropical island, hundreds of years ago

Characters	Description
Javi, age 13	smart, patient, poor, kind
Pando, age 13	strong, fast, confident
Naja, age 13	unpleasant, dishonest, always cheats
Village Chief (adult)	noble, powerful

2 Plan Your Plot—What's the Problem?

One way or another, good stories are always about problems. Think about who your characters are and where they live. What kinds of problems might they face? Choose a problem on which you can base your plot.

> The people in Javi's village eat fruit they catch as it falls from a tall tree. But if they don't catch the fruit, it gets smashed on the ground and it can't be eaten.

3 Plan Your Plot from Beginning to End

Next, think about what will happen in the beginning, middle, and end of your story. You might not have your whole plot figured out yet. That's OK—just make sure you have some rough ideas. Use a **plot diagram** like the one below to plan.

Plot Diagram

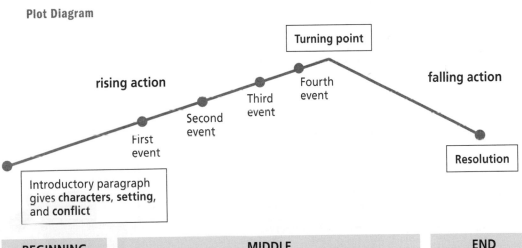

BEGINNING	MIDDLE	END
First, think through how you will introduce the main characters, setting, and conflict.	Next, think about the **rising action**. How will the plot events build toward a **turning point** when the conflict is resolved?	Finally, think about how to wrap things up. How will the **falling action** lead to a satisfying ending, or **resolution**?

4 **Flesh Out Your Plot**

Now that you've planned the overall structure of your story, flesh it out with details. You might like to use an organizer like the one Kristi used for her story about Javi's village.

Kristi's Plot Diagram for Her Story

> **Beginning**
> The Village Chief has a contest to see who can catch the most fruit.

↓

> **Events Before Turning Point**
> 1. Javi enters contest.
> 2. Javi studies how and when the fruit falls.
> 3. Other kids make fun of him (especially Naja).

↓

> **Turning Point**
> Javi figures out the secret of when the fruit falls. He wins the contest!

↓

> **Events After the Turning Point**
> The Village Chief gives Javi and his family a plot of land.

↓

> **Ending (Resolution)**
> Javi's family is no longer poor, and the village always has enough fruit.

5 **Get Feedback**

Got your ideas worked out? It's time to get feedback. Share your plot diagram with your friends or classmates.

6 Plan to <u>Show</u>, Not Tell

When you tell a story, try to show, not tell, what happens. Instead of saying, "It was a hot day," include details that show it was hot. Instead of saying, "So-and-so was smart," show it with dialogue and actions.

Sensory details are one way to show what happens. Kristi used a Five-Senses Diagram to plan:

Five-Senses Diagram

Javi saw . . .	• ripe fruit smashed on the ground • raindrops glistening on the tree branches
Javi heard . . .	• Naja saying that he will never win the contest
Javi smelled . . .	• the tropical flowers in the jungle
Javi tasted . . .	• the juices of the sweet fruit
Javi touched or felt . . .	• his legs go numb from standing so still

▲ Jackfruit is a staple food in India and other countries.

You don't need to tell readers everything about your characters. A few key details, along with dialogue, can pack a lot of meaning. Use a chart like Kristi's to plan:

Character Chart

Detail	What it means:
Javi spent many weeks studying the tree.	Javi is determined.
Naja stood under the tree two hours longer than she was allowed.	Naja is dishonest and sneaky.
Pando could out-run every person in the village and juggle five rocks in one hand.	Pando is fast and skillful.
The Chief's voice thundered, "The winner will receive a plot of land for farming."	The Chief is powerful and forceful, but also generous.

Reflect

• Do you know your character's problem and how he or she solves it?

• Have you thought of what obstacles stand in the character's way?

Draft

Now, it's time to draft your story. Don't worry about getting it perfect on the first try, but do follow your plan.

- **Use Your Organizer** Follow your writing plan so the events of your story will flow smoothly and the ending will be clear.

> On the small tropical island of Ratana, there was an extremely tall tree that produced sweet, delicious fruit. The tree was so tall, the villagers could only catch the fruit when it fell from the high branches. But the fruit fell fast and suddenly. The villagers had to be quick, for if the fruit hit the ground, it would be smashed and ruined.

Kristi used the beginning of her plot diagram to introduce the setting, characters, and conflict.

- **Add Details and Dialogue** Add sensory details, key details about characters, and dialogue to liven up your story.

Five-Senses Diagram

| Javi saw . . . | • ripe fruit smashed on the ground
• raindrops glistening on the leaves |
| Javi heard . . . | • Naja saying that he would never win |

From Kristi's Draft

> Every day, while the other children played games and rested in the sun, Javi watched the fruit tree. "You'll never win this stupid contest!" Naja would hiss, trying to distract him. Javi ignored her. He was looking at the smashed fruit on the ground and the raindrops on the tree's leaves.
>
> Soon Javi grasped the pattern of when and where the fruit fell. If it rained overnight, the fruit fell in the morning. If the night was dry, fruit fell in the afternoon. The wind determined where it fell.

TechTIP

Use the Find feature to look for a character's name in your story. Add dialogue or details relating to that character. Then repeat for other characters.

Reflect

- Read your draft. What details show that your main character is clever?

- Does your story have a strong ending?

DRAFTING TIPS
Trait: **Organization**

If Your Writing Is Not Connected . . .

Sometimes you get so focused on telling your story, you forget to show how events are connected. The result is that your writing feels jerky, like riding on a bumpy road.

Take Time for Transitions

Transitions can help you avoid those bumps and jerks. They let the reader know what to expect next. Time-order words are one kind of transition, but other kinds can also answer your readers' questions:

When did this happen?	Why did this happen?	Is this important?
After a while	As a result	As a matter of fact
Immediately	Because	In fact
Soon	Since	Most important

Kristi might use transitions in her story like this:

From Kristi's Draft

> Javi studied the tree even more closely. Soon he fully understood the pattern. In fact, he could predict exactly where and when fruit would fall. He gathered more fruit than anyone else, since he always knew when to watch for it.

As you write your story, think about how to use transitions to make your story flow smoothly.

Revise

As you revise your work, keep in mind your audience and purpose. Will your audience be entertained?

1 **Evaluate Your Work**

Read your story aloud to a partner. Have the partner sketch the scenes. Look at the sketches and ask yourself:

- **About the Form** Do the sketches show the setting? Do they show my story's key elements?

- **About the Organization** Do the sketches show events in a logical order? Are there any gaps? Does one show how the story ends?

Revision in Action

From Kristi's Draft

It was Naja's turn to catch fruit first. She stood under the tree in the afternoon, but nothing fell. She had slept late that morning. It had been a rainy night.

Then it was Pando's turn. It had been a dry night. He went to the tree in the morning and waited. When the fruit started falling, the wind blew the fruit over his head. He couldn't catch any. He had been there a long time and he was tired. It was afternoon.

Finally it was Javi's turn. After a dry night, he went to the tree in the afternoon. He checked the wind direction. He caught the fruit as they flew off the tree.

While Naja and Pando laughed at him, Javi had studied when and how the fruit fell. If it rained overnight, it fell in the morning. If the night was dry, it fell in the afternoon. The wind blew it down.

Kristi thinks:

" **It would be better to rearrange this.** "

" **This is confusing.** "

" **It would make more sense to explain this first.** "

2 **Mark Your Changes**

Rearrange Text To improve the flow of your story, you may need to change the order of sentences and paragraphs. Circle the text and draw an arrow to where you want to move the text.

You may also want to break your paragraphs up differently. Use the symbol ⁋ to show the start of a new paragraph.

Reflect

• Is your story clear to the reader?

• Do you need to add more details?

Revising Marks

MARK	∧	↶	⌐	ꟼ	⁋
WHAT IT MEANS	Insert something.	Move to here.	Replace with this.	Take out.	Make a new paragraph.

Revised Draft

It was Naja's turn to catch fruit first. She stood under the tree in the afternoon, but nothing fell. She had slept late that morning. It had been a rainy night.

Then it was Pando's turn. It had been a dry night. He went to the tree in the morning and waited. When the fruit started falling. the wind blew the fruit over his head. He couldn't catch any. He had been there a long time and he was tired. It was afternoon.

Finally it was Javi's turn. After a dry night, he went to the tree in the afternoon. He checked the wind direction. He caught the fruit as they flew off the tree.

While Naja and Pando laughed at him, Javi had studied when and how the fruit fell. If it rained overnight, it fell in the morning. If the night was dry, it fell in the afternoon. The wind blew it down.

Kristi rearranged several details in the first two paragraphs to make the events easier to follow.

Kristi moved the last paragraph to be first, for clarity.

Edit and Proofread

After you're satisfied with the content of your short story, read it again to fix language errors. This is what you do when you edit and proofread your work.

- **Check the Grammar** Make sure that you have used correct and conventional grammar throughout. In particular, check for subject-verb agreement. (See page 103W.)

- **Check the Spelling** Spell-check can help, but it isn't always enough. For errors with words that have tricky sounds, you'll have to read your work carefully and perhaps use a dictionary. (See page 104W.)

- **Check the Mechanics** Errors in punctuation and capitalization can make your work hard to understand. In particular, check your dialogue for correct punctuation and capitalization. (See page 105W.)

Use these marks to edit and proofread your short story.

Editing and Proofreading Marks

MARK	WHAT IT MEANS	MARK	WHAT IT MEANS
∧	Insert something.	╱	Make lowercase.
∧	Add a comma.	ℒ	Delete, take something out.
⌃	Add a semicolon.	⁋	Make new paragraph.
⊙	Add a period.	◯	Spell out.
⊙	Add a colon.	⌒	Replace with this.
⌄ ⌄	Add quotation marks.	∼	Change order of letters or words.
⌄	Add an apostrophe.	#	Insert space.
≡	Capitalize.	◡	Close up, no space here.

Reflect

- What kinds of errors did you find? What can you do to keep from making them?

Grammar Workout

Check Subject–Verb Agreement

- When the subject of a sentence is *he*, *she*, or *it*, or a noun that can be replaced by *he*, *she*, or *it*, the verb has a special form. For most verbs, just add *-s*.

  EXAMPLES   The villagers listen to the wind.
  The Chief listens, too.

- For the verb *have* there is a special form, *has*, that goes with *he*, *she*, or *it*, or a noun that can be replaced by them.

  EXAMPLES   The Chief **has** a good plan.
  The villagers **have** no idea what it is.

- The verb *be* has many special forms, not just for *he*, *she*, and *it*, but for other subjects as well.

  EXAMPLES   The Chief **is** smart.
  The villagers **are** glad.
  I **am** glad, too.

Forms of *be*	
I	am
he, she, it	is
we, you, they	are

Find the Trouble Spots

The villagers ~~is~~ are unhappy because no one has caught any fruit for days. The Village Chief is upset because he ~~have~~ has a birthday celebration planned. "The party are next week. My guests is expecting a magnificent spread. What shall I do?" the Chief asks his wife. Suddenly they has an idea. "We shall have a contest!"

Find three more subject-verb agreement errors to fix.

Edit and Proofread, continued

> ## Spelling Workout

Check Words with Tricky Consonant Sounds

One of the reasons spelling is tricky is that sometimes the same consonant sound can be spelled in different ways.

- The hard *c* sound heard at the beginning of *cat* can be spelled with *c*, *k*, or *ck*.

  EXAMPLES c̲amera   ki̲ss   speak̲   pick̲

- At the beginning of a word, this sound is most often spelled with a *c* before *a*, *o*, and *u*. It is most often spelled with a *k* before *e* and *i*. At the end of a word, use *k* after a long vowel sound and *ck* after a short vowel sound.

- The *j* sound heard at the beginning of *jam* can be spelled with *j*, *g*, or *dge*.

  EXAMPLES j̲ump   g̲enius   cag̲e   fudge̲

- At the beginning of a word, this sound is always spelled with a *j* before *a*, *o*, and *u*. Before *e* and *i*, sometimes it's spelled with *g* and sometimes with *j*—use a dictionary or spell-check. At the end of a word, use *ge* with a long vowel sound and *dge* with a short vowel sound.

Find the Trouble Spots

    Maya had set out to che_ck the forest to see what was making the _giant footprints—pawprints, actually—on the muddy path. Now the hairs on the bac of her neck stood up as she heard a howl from the center of the forest. She started to cross the brij over the creeck; the strange and chilling cry was getting closer.

Check for three more spelling errors to fix.

Mechanics Workout

Check Style with Dialogue

Here are a few simple rules for capitalization and punctuation with dialogue:

- Capitalize the first word of a quotation. Any punctuation that is part of what the speaker said comes before the ending quotation marks.

  EXAMPLE   Javi said, "I am going to win that contest."

- Dialogue often includes tags such as *Mike asked* or *Bella replied*. When a dialogue tag comes before a quote, include a comma between the tag and the opening quotation marks.

  EXAMPLE   The Village Chief explained, "Here are the rules."

When a dialogue tag comes *after* a statement in a quote, include a comma inside the ending quotation marks. If the quote ends in a question mark or exclamation mark, however, do not add the comma. These after-quote dialogue tags are not capitalized.

  EXAMPLES   "Now I understand why the rain is important," said Javi.

  "Javi, why are you still standing here?" asked Naja.

Find the Trouble Spots

"How did he do it?" ~~Cried~~ *cried* Naja. "I guess he watched the tree for many weeks," said Pando. "He watched the tree? That's the most foolish thing I ever heard" Said Naja. Pando sighed and said, "Well, he caught the fruit. Who are the fools now"?

Find and fix three more errors in punctuation or capitalization.

Publish, Share, and Reflect

You've worked hard to craft a short story that is organized, full of interesting details, and written well. Don't keep it to yourself— share it!

1 **Publish and Share Your Work**

One way to share your story is to read it out loud. This way, you can dramatize parts of your story and make them even more exciting than they are on paper. Here are a few ways to share your story aloud:

- Read it to your classmates or teacher.

- Read it to a children's group at a library or daycare.

- Organize a reading with other people you know who have written stories.

Here are some tips to make sure that everyone will stay wide awake and interested in what you have to say.

- Sound effects, like music, can really add to the atmosphere in the room during your presentation.

- Visual aids also boost your story. You can show your audience what happened, not just tell them about it.

- Practice, practice, practice! Once you're familiar with your story, you will be confident and ready to speak in front of an audience.

2 **Reflect on Your Work**

Publishing and sharing a piece of writing doesn't mean you can't alter or add to your story. Think back on what you have written. Ask yourself if there is anything you might change.

TechTIP

You can use a scanner to create an electronic version of a photograph or drawing. Scan a visual and then use the Insert feature to add it to your short story.

Reflect

- What did I learn about developing a plot?

- What was the hardest part about creating characters?

How to Read a Story Aloud

Reading your story aloud will help you bring it to life for your readers.

To give a successful oral presentation:

1. **Plan** Read your story aloud and on your own. Make notes about how you would like each part to sound. Underline or highlight places where you should read especially expressively.

2. **Practice** Focus on using a clear voice that will be heard and understood by your audience. To make sure your gestures look natural and relaxed, practice in front of a close friend beforehand, or videotape yourself and watch your performance.

3. **Deliver** Briefly introduce your narrative before you read. You might explain why you wrote it, or give a brief summary of the first events of the story. Then read your narrative to the audience, clearly and expressively. Remember:

   • Make eye contact with listeners while you read.

   • Vary the tone of your voice to fit different parts of your story. Don't tell your listeners what parts are sad or frightening or funny—show them.

   • Be an actor! Use gestures and facial expressions to communicate as you read.

" Sometimes it's not the strongest or the fastest person who wins—it's the smartest. Let me tell you a story about a clever guy who became a winner."

"I get good ideas for stories when I think about things that happen in my own life."

— Sayid

Model Study

Realistic Short Story

When you write a **realistic short story**, you tell about events that could really happen. The **characters** should remind readers of real-life people. The **setting** should also be believable, though the places and characters may be made up.

The **plot** of a realistic short story presents a **conflict**, or problem, that the main character needs to solve. The plot shows how the character tries to solve the problem and leads to a **conclusion**, or resolution, in which the problem is solved.

Pacing and dialogue develop the plot and the characters. **Pacing** is how quickly or slowly the plot moves from one event to another. **Dialogue** is the actual words that the characters say.

Realistic fiction is different from other kinds of fiction, such as science fiction. The setting is the real world. The characters solve everyday problems in believable ways.

REALISTIC SHORT STORY

A realistic short story

☑ has **characters** who are like real people in everyday life

☑ has a **setting** in the real world

☑ has a **plot** that presents a real-life conflict, or problem

☑ uses **pacing** and **dialogue** to develop characters and plot

☑ provides a believable **conclusion**.

Feature Checklist

The First Day
by Riley Nevil

The **setting** is realistic.

The **main character** is someone you could meet in real life.

Standing at the door of her new school, Julia took a deep breath, closed her eyes, and counted to ten. Opening her eyes, she stepped into a bustle of kids, all strangers. If Julia were at her old school, she'd be chatting and laughing with Mackenzie and Maddie on this first day. But no, her parents had to move. They promised that this new school would be better than her old one. But how could it be without her two best friends?

"Where is room 203?" Julia asked a boy standing nearby. But another boy ran up to him, and the two boys walked away, ignoring her.

A group of giggling girls bumped into Julia, knocking her bag off her shoulder. One girl turned. "Oh, sorry," she said and walked on.

"Do you know where room 203 is"? Julia asked after the girl.

"Upstairs," the girl called and then turned back to her friends.

"Hey," said a quiet voice next to Julia's shoulder. "I'm going to 203, too."

Julia turned to see a short, pale girl with gentle brown eyes that reminded her of Mackenzie.

"I'm Rana," she said. "You're new here."

"Yeah," Julia smiled shyly. "I'm Julia."

"Come on," said Rana. "We're going to be late."

Julia exhaled and beamed at Rana. "Let's go!" Julia's new school would be okay after all.

The plot presents a real-life **conflict.**

Dialogue helps develop characters and events.

Pacing moves the story along quickly.

The **conclusion** follows from and reflects on the story events.

Write a Realistic Short Story

WRITING PROMPT A writer of realistic fiction often shows how events can change a person's life. To do this, the writer creates a character who faces challenges that real people—like you!—also experience. Think about an event in your own or another person's life that would make a good story. Write a realistic short story that

- has **characters** who are like real people in everyday life
- has a **setting** that is like a real place
- has a sequence of realistic **plot** events that develop logically
- uses **dialogue** and **pacing** to develop characters and events
- provides a believable **conclusion** that follows from the events.

Prewrite

Here are some tips for planning your short story.

1 **Choose Realistic Story Elements**

Start by deciding on your characters and setting. Think about how you will use them to establish a realistic situation, or context, and develop a conflict that fits naturally into it. Don't worry about planning all the details right away. Here is how Angela began planning her story.

Story Elements

Setting: Ana's house, the hospital; a recent April morning

Characters:

Ana   youngest in the family, nervous

Dad   understanding, reassuring

Context: Ana's mom is going to have a baby

Conflict: Ana is nervous about how things will change after the baby is born.

---

2 **Organize Events**

Now that you have planned the story elements, it's time to plan the sequence and pacing of the events in your story. When you plan the pacing, you decide how quickly or slowly the events unfold. You might like to use an organizer like the one Angela used to write her story.

<u>Beginning</u>
Ana feels nervous about becoming a big sister. She is used to being the baby in the family.

↓

<u>Event</u>
Her new baby brother is born.

↓

<u>Turning Point</u>
Ana's dad talks to her about the responsibilities of being an older sister and reassures her. It makes her feel important and loved.

↓

<u>Event</u>
Ana meets baby Miguel.

↓

<u>Ending (resolution or conclusion)</u>
Ana no longer feels nervous. She feels proud and caring.

Reflect

- Are the events you have chosen to write about realistic?

- Does your plan show how the events unfold naturally and logically at a pace that makes sense for the story?

Draft

Now that you have planned each event in your realistic story, it's time to write your draft. Follow your plan, but don't worry about getting it perfect on the first try.

- **Introduce Characters, Setting, and Conflict** Use the beginning of your plot diagram to introduce the main character and to establish the context of the story. This helps your reader know who and what the story is about.

- **Pace the Events in the Story** How you pace your story depends on the events themselves. Speed up the pace to add excitement to events that have lots of action. As events wind down, slow down the pace.

> Ana was talking to her neighbor, Mrs. Gutierrez, when she heard her mom call, "The baby is coming! It's time to call Dr. Johan!" The family rushed to the hospital.

Angela used quick pacing to show the excitement of the coming baby.

- **Keep It Real** Use dialogue, precise words, and descriptive details to make story events more realistic.

> Ana's dad said, "Ana, being a big sister is an important job."
>
> Ana's eyes welled with tears. "How did you know how I felt?" she whispered.
>
> "I know it is hard for you right now," said her dad. "But you're going to be a great big sister."

Angela used precise words and realistic dialogue to help the reader picture the scene.

Reflect

- Read your draft. Does the pacing reflect the story events?

- Do you use details and dialogue to show your reader what is happening?

DRAFTING TIPS
Trait: **Organization**

If Your Writing Sounds Like a List . . .
When you include a lot of events in a story, it may start to sound like a list of unrelated ideas. Too many disconnected events can make your story seem unfocused and disorganized to your reader.

Zero In on a Part
Start by listing several key events on separate self-stick notes.

The baby is coming.	The baby is born.	Ana and her dad talk.	Ana meets her baby brother.

Then choose one event to zero in on. Expand it into several sentences. Here's how Angela focused on one event to expand and make her story more organized.

> ¶ Ana looked at her mom's tired face. She could smell her perfume. Her mom was holding Ana's brother on her lap, wrapped in a blanket.
>
> ¶ "Do you want to touch him?" she asked.
>
> ¶ Ana walked over and took her brother's hand in her own.

Revise

As you consider how to revise your work, keep in mind your intended audience and your purpose for writing. Does your writing do what you want it to do? Will it connect to your audience?

1 **Evaluate Your Work**

Read your story aloud to a partner. Ask your partner to sketch the story scenes. Look at the sketches and ask yourself:

- **About the Form** Do the sketches show realistic settings? Do they show main characters who are like real people in everyday life?

- **About the Organization** Do the sketches show the events in order? Are there any gaps? Does one show how the story ends?

Revision in Action

Angela's Draft

Ana was talking to her neighbor, Mrs. Gutierrez, when she heard her mom call, "The baby is coming! It's time to call Dr. Johan!" The family rushed to the hospital.

As Ana and her parents followed the sidewalk to the hospital doors, she wasn't feeling excited about her new baby brother. Ana was worried. After all, she was used to being the baby of the family. Ana wondered if her parents would still have time for her, too.

He said, "Ana, being a big sister is an important job." Ana's dad must have sensed how Ana felt.

> **"I should add a detail to tell more about when the story takes place."**

> **"I should add some more information about why Ana was worried to make these details more realistic."**

2 **Mark Your Changes**

Add Text To make the details more realistic, you may need to add text. Use a caret: ∧.

Rearrange Text Sometimes, ideas and sentences would fit better in other places in the story. In a realistic story, making sure that the sequence of events makes sense is especially important. To move text, circle it and draw an arrow where you want it to go: ↰.

Reflect

- Are the events arranged in an order that is logical?
- Do the details make the story seem more realistic?

Revising Marks	MARK	∧	↰	↰	⌢	¶
	WHAT IT MEANS	Insert something.	Move to here.	Replace with this.	Take out.	Make a new paragraph.

Revised Draft

> *that April morning*
> Ana was talking to her neighbor, Mrs. Gutierrez, ∧ when she heard her mom call, "The baby is coming! It's time to call Dr. Johan!" The family rushed to the hospital.
>
> As Ana and her parents followed the sidewalk to the hospital doors, she wasn't feeling excited about her new baby brother. Ana was worried. After all, she was
> *It seemed like for weeks, all Ana's parents talked about was the baby.*
> used to being the baby of the family. ∧Ana wondered if her parents would still have time for her, too.
>
> ∧He said, "Ana, being a big sister is an important job." Ana's dad must have sensed how Ana felt.

Angela added a detail about the setting.

Angela added realistic details about how her parents seemed more focused on the baby than on her.

Angela moved this sentence to make the sequence of events more logical.

Edit and Proofread

When you're happy with the content of your realistic short story, read your paper again to fix language errors. This is what you do when you edit and proofread your work.

- **Check the Grammar** Make sure that you have used correct and conventional grammar throughout. In particular, check the choices you have made for the words you use to describe things. (See page 117W.)

- **Check the Spelling** Spell-check can help, but it isn't always enough. Read your work carefully, checking any compound words. You can use a dictionary to check your work. (See page 118W.)

- **Check the Mechanics** Errors in punctuation and capitalization can make your work hard to understand. In particular, check that you have used commas correctly. (See page 119W.)

*Tech*TIP

Most word-processing programs have a built-in dictionary that you can check as you proofread your work.

Use these marks to edit and proofread your cause-and-effect paragraph.

Editing and Proofreading Marks

MARK	WHAT IT MEANS	MARK	WHAT IT MEANS
∧	Insert something.	/	Make lowercase.
∧	Add a comma.	℘	Delete, take something out.
∧	Add a semicolon.	¶	Make new paragraph.
⊙	Add a period.	◯	Spell out.
⊙	Add a colon.	⌃	Replace with this.
∨ ∨	Add quotation marks.	∽	Change order of letters or words.
∨	Add an apostrophe.	#	Insert space.
≡	Capitalize.	◡	Close up, no space here.

Reflect

- What kind of errors did you find? What can you do to keep from making them?

Grammar Workout

Check Adjectives

Adjectives are words that describe nouns—people, places, things, and ideas. You can even use them to describe things you can't see or touch, like someone's personality. Use adjectives to describe

- how something looks

    EXAMPLE   Sandra was wearing a **red** sweater.

- how something feels, tastes, or smells

    EXAMPLE   The apple was **crisp** and **juicy**.

- things you can't see or touch.

    EXAMPLE   I thought Bruce was in a very **grumpy** mood yesterday.

Adjectives will make your writing more colorful. Choose the best words to bring people, places, and things to life.

EXAMPLE   The flower has petals and a scent.

The flower has **delicate** petals and a **sweet** scent.

Find the Opportunities

After the talk with my dad, I felt a lot better. I took
a sip from the juice I was holding and looked at my
^ice-cold

mother's face. I could smell her perfume. She was
^tired

holding my brother on her lap, wrapped in a blanket.
"Do you want to touch him?" she asked. I walked over
and took my brother's hand in mine.

Add two
more colorful
adjectives to
this paragraph.

> ## Spelling Workout

Check Compound Words

Some longer words, called **compound words**, are made up of two smaller words.

EXAMPLES	basketball	= basket + ball		flashlight	= flash + light
	keyboard	= key + board		rainbow	= rain + bow
	sidewalk	= side + walk		toothbrush	= tooth + brush

To spell a compound word, say and spell the first smaller word. Then say and spell the other smaller word without putting a space in between.

A few compound words like the ones below are written with a space or a hyphen. Check the dictionary to be sure.

ice cream	hundred-meter dash
peanut butter	first-class ticket

Find the Trouble Spots

Before Miguel was born, I worried a lot about having a baby brother. What if I was watching him and some thing happened? What if I accidentally played too rough with him? Now I know how to be careful around him. I play with him all the time. I like to take him into our bac~k~yard. We play games, but we also help Dad with the garden. Together we have planted tomatoes and sun flowers *(sunflowers)*. My favorite time of the day is Miguel's after noon bath. You wouldn't believe the fun we have when he is in the bathtub!

Find two more compound words to fix.

MechanicsWorkout

Check Commas Between Adjectives

- Use a comma between two coordinate adjectives, or adjectives that modify a noun in the same way.

   EXAMPLES   Miguel peeked out of the **fluffy, striped** blanket.

- Use a comma if the meaning is still clear when you replace the comma with and, and reverse the order of the adjectives.

   CORRECT   His **enormous, sparkling** eyes looked right at me.

   CLEAR   His **enormous and sparkling** eyes looked right at me.

   CLEAR   His **sparkling, enormous** eyes looked right at me.

- Do <u>not</u> use a comma between adjectives that modify a noun in different ways. To check if you need a comma between non-coordinate adjectives, use the "reverse order" test. If the meaning is unclear, do not use a comma.

   SENTENCE   His **mischievous, brown** eyes made me smile.

   UNCLEAR REVERSED   His **brown mischievous** eyes made me smile.

   CLEAR, NO COMMA   His **mischievous brown** eyes made me smile.

Find the Trouble Spots

Now that Miguel is older, we read together after school. He loves looking at the colorful‸detailed illustrations. His favorite story is about some frisky little puppies. Often after we read awhile, we go outside to play. I roll a giant, bouncy ball to him and he rolls it back. Miguel tells everyone I'm his favorite⁄older sister. (That's funny because I'm his only sister!)

Find two more comma errors to fix.

"I write for my school newspaper, and I always try to tell why, not just what."

—Carol Ann

Model Study

Cause-and-Effect Essay

When you write a cause-and-effect essay, you explain what happened and why. You can focus more on the causes or on the effects, but you should organize your essay in a clear way.

1. Introduction

Gives the central idea of the essay.

2. Body

Explains causes and effects. You may want to arrange them in order of importance or in sequence.

3. Conclusion

Ends the essay and connects back to the central idea.

Read the student model on page 121W, which shows one good way to structure a cause-and-effect essay.

CAUSE-AND-EFFECT ESSAY

A good cause-and-effect essay

☑ presents one or more causes that lead to one or more effects

☑ includes an introduction, a body, and a conclusion.

Feature Checklist

Irish Immigration in the United States
by Diana Chadwell

The **introduction** states the central idea of the essay.

The **body** of the essay tells about the main causes and effects.

The **conclusion** wraps up the essay and ties back to the central idea.

In the mid-1800s, more than a million Irish people crossed the Atlantic Ocean. They were on their way to start a new life in the United States.

Irish people were escaping a major agricultural crisis. In 1845, Irish potato crops were wiped out by a blight, or plant disease. At that time, half of the Irish population depended almost completely on potatoes for their diet. As a result of the blight, more than a million people died of hunger. Another 1.5 million decided to immigrate to the United States.

When Irish immigrants arrived, they faced many challenges. Not only had they lost almost everything to the blight, they also found a great deal of prejudice in the United States. Because of this, they were forced to take low-paying jobs and live in cheap housing.

Though the new life in America was hard, the Irish community in the United States prospered and contributed a great deal to modern American culture.

The writer explains the **cause** first and then describes two effects.

The writer uses **signal words** to help the reader identify causes and effects.

Student Model

In the 1840s–1850s, Irish people came to the United States in search of a better life. ▼

Focus and Unity

What's It Like

After planting a young tree, landscapers might tie it to wooden poles and trim off extra branches. That's to make sure the tree grows straight and tall in one direction. You do the same thing when you focus your writing. You tie everything to one idea, and you cut off the parts you don't need.

How Can You Find a Focus?

When writing is focused, it's easy to understand the writer's main point. When it's unified, everything in the writing goes with the main point. Staying focused helps you achieve your purpose.

To give your writing focus, stick to your main topic, or central idea. To help make your writing focused:

- Figure out what your central idea is before you start to write.

- Start by explaining your central idea. Then give details that support it.

- Always ask yourself: Am I writing about my central idea, or am I writing off-topic?

- End with a conclusion that sums up your central idea.

Good focus is about clearly presenting your central idea. Study the rubric on page 123W. What is the difference between a paper with a score of 2 and one with a score of 4?

Focus and Unity

	How clearly does the writing present a central idea or claim?	How well does everything go together?
4 Wow!	The writing expresses a <u>clear</u> central idea or claim about the topic.	<u>Everything</u> in the writing goes together. • The main idea of each paragraph goes with the central idea or claim of the paper. • The main idea and details within each paragraph are related. • The conclusion is about the central idea or claim.
3 Ahh.	The writing expresses a <u>generally</u> clear central idea or claim about the topic.	<u>Most</u> parts of the writing go together. • The main idea of most paragraphs goes with the central idea or claim of the paper. • In most paragraphs, the main idea and details are related. • Most of the conclusion is about the central idea or claim.
2 Hmm.	The writing includes a topic, but the central idea or claim is <u>not</u> clear.	<u>Some</u> parts of the writing go together. • The main idea of some paragraphs goes with the central idea or claim of the paper. • In some paragraphs, the main idea and details are related. • Some of the conclusion is about the central idea or claim.
1 Huh?	The writing includes many topics and <u>does not</u> express one central idea or claim.	The parts of the writing <u>do not</u> go together. • Few paragraphs have a main idea, or the main idea does not go with the central idea or claim of the paper. • Few paragraphs contain a main idea and related details. • None of the conclusion is about the central idea or claim.

Focus and Unity, continued

Compare Writing Samples

In a focused essay, the main idea and details in each paragraph go with the central idea. Read the two samples of cause-and-effect essays on this page.

Focused

Learning a New Language

It can be difficult to adapt to the customs and language of a new country. One area that causes difficulty for immigrants to the United States is the English language.

Many communities have started English as a Second Language programs to teach English. Teachers and volunteers work together at special centers. Some volunteers are immigrants who have struggled with English. For that reason, they are some of the best teachers. As a result of these programs, many immigrants are able to communicate better in their daily lives.

Learning a new language is not easy. But community programs that teach English are making a big difference for people adapting to life in the United States.

The writer presents the **central idea** in the introduction.

The causes and effects are explained in the **body** of the essay.

The **conclusion** is also about the central idea.

Unfocused

Learning a New Language

It's often difficult to adapt to the customs and language of a new country. One area that causes difficulty for immigrants to the United States is the English language.

Many young people from other countries want to attend school here for awhile. To do this, they need to know English. To help out, some schools have started exchange programs. Some communities also offer English as a Second Language classes.

Learning a new language is not easy. But with the help of the community, many students and immigrants can successfully learn English.

The first paragraph suggests a **central idea,** but the body is about a different topic.

Evaluate for Focus and Unity

Now read carefully the cause-and-effect essay below. Use the rubric on page 123W to score it.

Know Where You're Going

Have you ever traveled to a foreign country? It can be a wonderful experience. However, if you don't know anything about your destination you might have a few problems.

Many people spend a lot of time traveling. When you travel, you should know the exchange rates for your money. Because every country is different, the exchange rates will be, too. Another problem you might have is getting around. In London, for example, if you just stand at the bus stop, the buses won't stop. That's because you need to raise your hand to show you want a ride. Double-decker buses are pretty fun to ride. Many of them are bright red. Think about your meals, too. You'll probably want to try some new things, so go ahead and order. But be careful. If you don't recognize the name of the meal, you might be surprised at what shows up on your plate.

When you travel, there is always someone around to help you. But it's good to be aware.

Does the introduction present the central idea?

How would you fix the main idea to go with the central idea? Are all the causes and effects clear?

Does the conclusion relate to the central idea? How would you fix it?

Raise the Score

These papers have been scored using the **Focus and Unity Rubric** on page 123W. Study each paper to see why it got the score it did.

Overall Score: 4

Farmers' Markets

Mike Cohen

The writer introduces the **topic** and **central idea.**

Would you like to try a strawberry pear, a custard apple, or an Indian fig? These are all fruits from faraway countries. Each has a strange shape and great taste. These great food choices are all available in your downtown farmers' market.

The **main idea** of each paragraph explains causes and effects that relate to the central idea.

Immigration from diverse countries to the United States has given us a great variety of foods to choose from. Many of the immigrants who moved here are farmers. They missed the kinds of foods they used to eat at home. So, they decided to import seeds from their home countries. They use the seeds to grow produce that is otherwise not available at the market. The farmers also discovered that some customers wanted foods they used to eat in their home countries. So more and more foods were added.

The conclusion repeats the **central idea.**

At the farmers' market, people can find a variety of foods from around the world. As they wander through the market, they'll also experience a taste of a lot of different cultures.

Farmers' Markets

Would you like to try a strawberry pear, a custard apple, or an Indian fig? These are all fruits from faraway countries. Each has a strange shape and great taste. These foods are all at your downtown farmers' market.

Immigration from different countries to the United States has given us a great variety of foods to choose from. Many of the immigrants who moved here are farmers. They missed the kinds of foods they used to eat at home. So, they decided to import seeds from their home countries. Many fruits and vegetables grow from seeds. The seeds are all shapes and sizes. They use the seeds to grow produce that is otherwise not available at the market. The farmers also discovered that some customers wanted foods they used to eat in their home countries. So more foods were added.

At the farmers' market, people can find foods from around the world. As they wander through the market, they'll also experience a taste of different cultures.

RAISING *THE SCORE*

The writer needs to state the central idea more clearly and take out unnecessary details. Which details should the writer take out?

Raise the Score, continued

Overall Score: 2

The paper has a **topic** but no central idea.

Farmers' Markets

Would you like to try a strawberry pear, a custard apple, or an Indian fig? These are all fruits from faraway countries. I love eating unusual foods from other cultures.

Many immigrants who live in the United States come from distant countries. Some immigrants who moved here are farmers. They grow certain foods themselves and sell them at a farmers' market. Because many people want foods from their home countries, they shop there. In San Francisco, where I live, there are many Chinese-American foods sold at the market.

This paragraph has many details, but they do not relate to one main idea.

Since the paper has no central idea, the conclusion does not feel like a summary.

Shoppers at the farmers' market are happy to find certain foods because they can't find them in their regular stores. They like finding new and exciting foods from other cultures at their downtown farmers' market.

RAISING THE SCORE

The writer needs to state a central idea about the topic, farmers' markets. What central idea could he include? How should he revise each paragraph?

Farmers' Markets

Do you like fruits from faraway countries? Some are strawberry pears, custard apples, and Indian figs. I love eating unusual foods from other cultures.

The writing has too many **topics** and no central idea.

Many immigrants who live in the United States come from distant countries. Some immigrants who moved here are farmers. They gave up things they were used to having every day. They sell all kinds of produce at farmers' markets. San Francisco's Chinatown has a lot of farmers' markets. Immigrants have to cope with new customs and a new language as well.

These paragraphs are about different topics.

This paragraph has a **main idea**, but doesn't relate to a central idea.

My grandmother likes to shop at the farmers' market. She came to the United States when she was just a little girl. It was difficult for her and my grandfather at first, but they made it. Their love for their home country made me appreciate my roots.

RAISING THE SCORE

The writer needs to choose one topic to write about. Suppose the writer focused the paper on farmers' markets. What details could be kept?

State a Central Idea

A tour guide will sometimes hold up a flag so the tourists following behind don't get lost or wander off in different directions. When you write, your central idea is like a flag. All of the other ideas and details must follow it.

Presenting a Central Idea

The central idea of an essay is the most important idea you want to tell about. It determines what other ideas and details you will include in your essay.

Usually, you address your central idea in your introduction:

> In karaoke, people sing along with their favorite songs by reading the lyrics on a screen. This type of entertainment was invented in Japan in the 1970s. Karaoke is becoming more and more popular in the United States, and today there are karaoke video games with which people can practice their singing.

The central idea is fairly clear in the paragraph above. To make your central idea perfectly clear, state it in a single sentence:

> Karaoke, in which people sing their favorite songs by reading the lyrics on a screen, is very popular today in the United States.

Look at additional examples on page 131W.

Your central idea shouldn't be too broad or too narrow.

Read the topic below. Then read the central ideas that follow.

Topic

I want to write about volunteers.

Too Broad

Volunteers can really make a difference.

This central idea is too broad. There are too many topics to write about.

Too Narrow

Leda Scola made a difference when she volunteered to teach Spanish at the Westlake Community Center.

This central idea is too narrow.

Just Right

Volunteers have really made a difference in the Westlake community.

The central idea is clear and expressed in one sentence.

State a Central Idea, continued

A focused cause-and-effect essay clearly establishes its central idea in the introduction. Study the two examples of introductory paragraphs on this page.

The first sentence states the central idea.

This detail supports the central idea.

Local radio stations can be really helpful to a community. Recently, many local radios have started broadcasting programs in Spanish. This way, they help inform the Spanish-speaking community about the city they live in.

Radio Shows in Spanish
- Local stations broadcast in Spanish.
- Spanish-speaking people have community involvement.

- The programs are so successful that local television stations are creating shows in Spanish.

This detail doesn't go with the rest of the paragraph.

The central idea is not clearly expressed.

Neighborhood kids and shop owners worked together. They wanted to save the Laotian Community Center. The center is downtown, near the schools. The center was going to be closed. But the kids in the neighborhood decided they couldn't let that happen. They wanted to keep a place where they could go play after school.

Saving the Laotian Community Center
- Why was it in danger?
- Why did people decide to save it?

- What was the effect of reopening the center?

TechTIP

Use the highlight tool in your word-processing program to highlight your central idea. The highlight will help you find it and check it as you write. Remove the highlight before you publish your work.

Now read the examples below. How well do they establish a central idea?

Most of the immigrants who came to the United States at the beginning of the nineteenth century lost contact with their home countries. Their connection to relatives back home faded over time. Many years later, the grandchildren of these immigrants are using Web sites to create family trees and discover more about their family history.

The Family Tree
- Many immigrants lose contact with their home countries.
- They use family trees to trace back their families.

  - Sometimes, they travel back to meet their relatives.

Many people come to the United States from other countries. A lot of times, they are escaping from a war-torn country or a cruel government. For example, many Vietnamese immigrants came to the United States after the Vietnam War. Also, the country's Cuban-American population increased after the Communist Party took over Cuba. Sometimes, it was very difficult for these people to adapt to their new lives. People also come to the United States to escape poverty.

Looking for Freedom
- Many people moved to the United States over the years.
- They moved to escape war.

  - They moved to escape discrimination.

Does the paragraph include a clear central Idea?

Stay Focused on the Central Idea

What's It Like ?

When you visit an unfamiliar city, you want to check out all of the sights. Chances are, you won't have time to visit all of the out-of-the-way places. You choose only the landmarks you most want to see. In the same way, when you write an essay, you focus on just a few important ideas.

Build on Your Central Idea

Once your central idea has been established in the introduction, stick to it as you write the body of your essay. Study the introduction and body paragraph for this essay.

> Local radio stations can be really helpful to a community. Recently, many local stations have started broadcasting programs in Spanish. This way, they help inform the Spanish-speaking community about the city they live in.
>
> Before the stations started broadcasting, many in the Spanish-speaking community were unaware of city services and special events. They had to rely on word-of-mouth from others at work and school. Not everyone received the same information. In particular, many people were confused about where to go for help during the recent storms.

The **central idea** is established in the introduction.

This **main idea** goes with the central idea.

All the **details** tell more about the main idea.

Now look at these paragraphs for an essay. Are they focused? What should the writer do to fix the body paragraph?

Many immigrants who came to the United States at the beginning of the twentieth century lost contact with their home countries. Now years later, the grandchildren of these immigrants are using Web sites to create family trees and discover more about their family history. They are also trying to regain a connection to the culture of their ancestors.

Many people in foreign countries have relatives who don't live with them. Although searching for relatives can take a lot of time and dedication, using the Internet has speeded up the process.

It's great for sending e-mail and communicating with your friends on blogs. But because there are so many Web sites to choose from, searchers need to be patient and plan blocks of time to do research. Some sites give directions for how to get started. Others provide more sites for lists of genealogy and ancestry records. And still others explain how to create a family tree.

The introduction establishes the **central idea**.

The **main idea** doesn't go with the central idea.

This **detail** doesn't belong. It doesn't tell about using the Internet to search for ancestors.

Write a Cause-and-Effect Essay

WRITING PROMPT Causes and effects shape your life and your world. Every community experiences changes over time.

Think of an important change in your community. Your cause-and-effect essay should

- tell what the change was in the introduction
- explain the causes and effects in the body
- wrap up the ideas in the conclusion.

Prewrite

Here are some tips for planning your essay.

1 **Choose a Topic**

Choose an event whose causes and effects are clear. Brainstorm ideas by asking questions.

Ideas	Cause-and-Effect questions	Possible causes and effects
When the new school was built	Why did this happen?	Many people had moved into the neighborhood.
When the city started picking up recycling	What happened because of this?	Everyone started recycling and cleaning up.
When we had a neighborhood cleanup day	Why did this happen?	There was too much garbage lying around on the sidewalks.

2 Write Your Central Idea

The central idea is the most important thing you have to say in your essay. You can state it in the first paragraph. That will help you focus on your topic.

> When the city began picking up recycling at people's houses, it led to many positive changes in the community.

Jamal states his central idea.

3 Organize Your Thoughts

Use a cause-and-effect chain like Jamal's to put your thoughts in order.

Jamal's Cause-and-Effect Chain

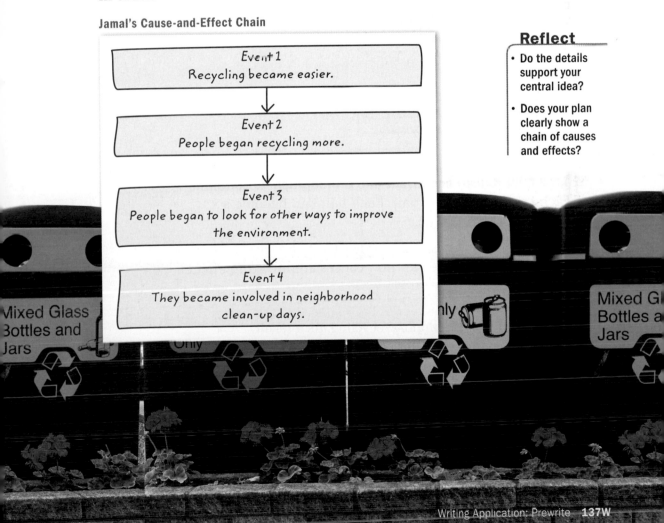

Event 1
Recycling became easier.

↓

Event 2
People began recycling more.

↓

Event 3
People began to look for other ways to improve the environment.

↓

Event 4
They became involved in neighborhood clean-up days.

Mixed Glass Bottles and Jars

Mixed Gl Bottles a Jars

Reflect

- Do the details support your central idea?

- Does your plan clearly show a chain of causes and effects?

Draft

Now that you have a topic to work on, it's time to draft! Remember, your draft doesn't have to be perfect. You will have time later on to make all the changes you need.

Use your cause-and-effect chart and your prewriting to make your first draft go smoothly.

- **Focus on One Cause and Effect at a Time** If you try to cover everything at once, you might lose your focus. Choose one cause and effect to work with at a time.

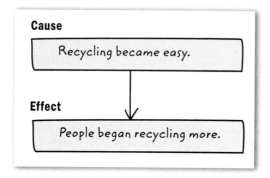

Cause

> Recycling became easy.

Effect

> People began recycling more.

- **Expand Each Cause and Effect into a Paragraph** Add details to each cause-and-effect pair. Each pair can become a paragraph in your essay.

- **Use Signal Words** Use signal words such as *because*, *since*, and *as a result* to show the reader how causes are linked to effects.

From Jamal's Draft

> The city began to support recycling. As a result, recycling became easier for people. People could put their recycling material out just like they did with garbage. As recycling became easy, many more people began recycling.

Reflect

- Does each paragraph show a clear cause and a clear effect?

- Did you use cause-and-effect signal words?

DRAFTING TIPS
Trait: **Focus and Unity**

If Your Writing Is Vague...
If you don't establish clear ideas and support your ideas with specific, relevant details, your readers won't understand what you're trying to say.

Try Drawing a Target Diagram First
You want readers to understand the importance of the event. When you develop your ideas effectively, your readers will be able to answer these questions:

1. What is the event mostly about?

2. What details do you remember?

3. What feelings are obvious in the piece?

4. What is a life lesson that you hear dawning on the writer?

To avoid vague writing, try completing a target diagram. Draw the diagram and fill in the rings with the answers you plan for your essay.

Event
Details
Feelings
Life Lesson

a community makes positive changes
city collects recycling
people recycle more, clean-up days
pride, happiness, joy
It feels good to take care of your city.

Jamal's Target Diagram

Revise

When you revise your work, you reread it to decide what changes you want to make. Think about your audience and purpose. Follow these steps.

1 **Evaluate Your Work**

Read your draft aloud to an adult—a relative, your teacher, or your librarian. Ask your listener the following questions:

- **About the Form** Are causes and effects clearly linked to each other? Can I better explain or connect my causes and effects?

- **About the Focus and Unity** Is my central idea clear? Try restating it. Do all of my details go with my central idea?

Revision in Action

Jamal's Draft

Have you heard of the ripple effect? When you drop a rock into water, ripples spread out. The city began supporting conservation efforts and positive changes started happening.

The city began collecting recycling materials from people's houses. People saw how easy it was to put out recycling materials along with their garbage. Many more people began recycling.

After the city removed trash from the creek, people became interested in doing more for the environment. We started clean-up days. People cleaned out common areas, like the old park.

Taking responsibility for our city has made everyone feel great. Now my community loves being involved in keeping their city clean.

Jamal's uncle says:

" The central idea could be clearer."

" It's hard to connect causes and effects. You need to add signal words."

" This seems like the most important effect. I'd say that first."

2 Mark Your Changes

Add Text To show where you will add sentences or ideas, use a caret: ∧. You can use this mark to

- add signal words to show causes and effects more clearly
- add text to clarify your central idea.

Rearrange Text Sometimes, ideas and sentences fit better in other places. To move text, use this mark: ⌒ .

Revising Marks MARK	∧	⌒	⌃	⌢	¶
WHAT IT MEANS	Insert something.	Move to here.	Replace with this.	Take out.	Make a new paragraph.

Revised Draft

Have you heard of the ripple effect? When you drop a rock into water, ripples spread out. ~~The city began~~ *Our city's decision to* supporting conservation efforts ~~and~~ *led to* positive changes ~~started happening~~ *in my community.* ∧

The city began collecting recycling materials from people's houses. People saw how easy it was to put out recycling materials along with their garbage. *As a result,* Many more people began recycling.

~~After the city removed trash from the creek,~~ people became interested in doing more for the environment. *So* We started clean-up days. People cleaned out common areas, like the old park.

Taking responsibility for our city has made everyone feel great. *(Now my community loves being involved in keeping their city clean.)*

Jamal clarified his central idea.

Jamal added signal words.

He deleted an unrelated detail.

Jamal rearranged sentences to put the most important effect first.

Revise, continued

You can revise your paper more than once. Every time you read it, look at it with fresh eyes. Find more things to improve.

③ Focus While You Revise

Delete Text When you edit your work, what you take out is just as important as what you write. To make your writing more focused and unified, use this mark ⟶ℓ to take out:

- details that are not related to the topic or central idea
- unnecessary repetitions of the same idea.

Revision in Action

Jamal's Draft

Have you heard of the ripple effect? When you drop a rock into water, ripples spread out. Our city's decision to support conservation efforts led to positive changes in the community.

The city began collecting recycling materials from people's houses. People saw how easy it was to put out recycling materials along with their garbage. As a result, many more people began recycling.

People became interested in doing more for the environment. So we started clean-up days. People cleaned out common areas, like the old park.

Now my community loves being involved in keeping the city clean. Taking responsibility for our city has made everyone feel great.

Jamal thinks:

" How could I make my central idea and main ideas even clearer?"

" Some of the details aren't very important to my central idea."

4 Test Your Focus

Read your paper aloud to yourself. Often you can hear problems you cannot see. Add a title and headings. Your headings should help readers understand the central idea.

Reflect

- Are your causes and effects clear and connected?

- What's the central idea? Is it clear? Does all the content connect to it?

Revising Marks	MARK	∧	↶	⌐	⟿	¶
	WHAT IT MEANS	Insert something.	Move to here.	Replace with this.	Take out.	Make a new paragraph.

∧ *Learning from Change*
Have you heard of the ripple effect? When you drop a rock into water, ripples spread out. Our city's decision to support conservation efforts led to positive changes in the community.
∧ *Start with Cleaning Up*
The city began collecting recycling materials from people's houses. People saw how easy it was to put out recycling materials along with their garbage. As a result, many more people began recycling.

People became interested in doing more for the environment. So we started clean-up days. People cleaned litter out of common areas, ~~like the old park.~~
∧ *Take Pride in Your Community*
Now my community loves being involved in keeping the city clean. Taking responsibility for our city has made everyone feel great.

Jamal added a title and section headings to make his central idea clearer.

Jamal took out unnecessary details.

Edit and Proofread

After you're satisfied with the content of your cause-and-effect essay, read your paper again to fix language errors. This is what you do when you edit and proofread your work:

- **Check the Grammar** Make sure that you have used correct and conventional grammar throughout. In particular, check for correct use of adverbs. (See page 145W.)

- **Check the Spelling** Spell-check can help, but it isn't always enough. Read your work carefully, especially words with prefixes and suffixes. You can use a dictionary to check. (See page 146W.)

- **Check the Mechanics** Errors in punctuation and capitalization can make your work hard to understand. In particular, check that your proper nouns are correctly capitalized. (See page 147W.)

Use these marks to edit and proofread your cause-and-effect essay.

Editing and Proofreading Marks

MARK	WHAT IT MEANS	MARK	WHAT IT MEANS
∧	Insert something.	/	Make lowercase.
∧	Add a comma.	℘	Delete, take something out.
∧	Add a semicolon.	¶	Make new paragraph.
⊙	Add a period.	⌒	Spell out.
⊙	Add a colon.	⌒	Replace with this.
ˇˇ	Add quotation marks.	∼	Change order of letters or words.
ˇ	Add an apostrophe.	#	Insert space.
≡	Capitalize.	⌣	Close up, no space here.

Reflect

- What kinds of errors did you find? What can you do to keep from making them?

GrammarWorkout

Check Adverbs

Adverbs are words that modify verbs, adjectives, or other adverbs. They can tell **how**, **when**, or **where**.

EXAMPLES   The boat sailed **west** into the sunset. *(tells where)*

I will call you **later** to talk about the party. *(tells when)*

Sharon lay **idly** on the couch. *(tells how)*

- Many adverbs are formed by adding **-ly** to an adjective. You can use these adverbs to make your writing more colorful.

EXAMPLES   The leaves fell **silently**.

The kitten looked **curiously** at the mouse.

The athlete proceeded **calmly** toward the starting line.

He commented **sadly** that there was nothing left to do.

- You can also use adverbs to make an adjective or another adverb stronger.

EXAMPLES   The child was **extremely** polite.

The child answered **very politely**.

Find the Trouble Spots

      Recycling_^ *quickly* became the main subject of conversation in my neighborhood._^ *Soon* Mrs. Gomez organized for a "recycling expert" to come and talk to the students. It was a interesting talk. The speaker explained the recycling process. He told us ways we can recycle school supplies.

Add two more adverbs to the paragraph to strengthen the language or make it more colorful.

Spelling Workout

Check Adverbs Ending in *-ly*

Follow these rules for adding the suffix **-ly** to an adjective to form an adverb:

- If the base word ends in **l** keep the **l**.

  EXAMPLE   real + -ly ⟶ really

- If the base word ends in a consonant plus silent **-e**, keep the **e**.

  EXAMPLE   late + -ly ⟶ lately

- For the adjectives *true* and *due*, drop the **-e** before you add **–ly**.

  EXAMPLE   true + -ly ⟶ truly

- For adjectives ending in **le**, drop the final **le** before adding **-ly**.

  EXAMPLE   possible + -ly ⟶ possibly

If you are not sure of the correct spelling, check the dictionary.

Find the Trouble Spots

Thanks to recycling, the governor spoke ~~favorablely~~ ^{favorably} of my city. We decided to ~~totaly~~ ^{totally} change our ways. Apparently, we are now inspiring many other cities. The governor praised us because for months we duely recycled paper, metal, and plastic. I am completly certain that my school played a big part in this.

Find and fix two more spelling errors.

Mechanics Workout

Check Capitalization of Proper Nouns

Proper nouns name a specific person, place, or thing. When you use proper nouns, always capitalize them. Here are some examples:

- Capitalize people's names and the names of organizations.

  EXAMPLES   Jill Wanaka

  Citizens Against Pollution

  Gloucester County School Board

- Capitalize the names of historical events and documents. Also capitalize the first word and any other important words in titles of books and articles.

  EXAMPLES   Civil War   Declaration of Independence

  Clean Air Act   Rachel Carson's *Silent Spring*

  "Caring for the Environment"

- Capitalize the names of days of the week, months, and holidays.

  EXAMPLES   Saturday   January   Earth Day

Find the Trouble Spots

In january, we started the second phase of our recycling project. Our teacher, Ms. Han, had asked us to prepare a poster titled "recycle!" Luckily, we can work in groups. I asked sarah to help me and we will meet next saturday to brainstorm some ideas. Sarah's mother is a member of the davis county environmental action group. I am looking forward to hearing her ideas.

Find and fix three more errors in capitalization.

Publish, Share, and Reflect

You've worked hard to craft a cause-and-effect essay that is organized, full of interesting details, and correctly written. Now it's time to share it!

1 **Publish and Share Your Work**

When you publish your writing, you put it in a final form and share it. How you publish it depends on your purpose and audience. You might choose to share your essay with just a few friends or classmates. Or, if you want to reach a wider audience, you might

- present it orally in your social studies class.
- post it on a blog or Web site. Invite readers to share their opinions and ideas.
- send it to your school or town newspaper.
- publish it in your school or class newsletter.

2 **Reflect on Your Work**

Even after you've published your work, you'll probably still keep thinking about it, and you might make additional changes later on. Ask yourself questions to decide what went well for this assignment and what areas you want to keep working on as a writer.

Reflect

- Is my writing clear and focused?

- Did writing about causes and effects help me understand my topic better? What did I learn from writing this essay?

How to Stay Focused

When presenting your essay orally, it is important to create and maintain a clear focus so your audience can follow and understand your ideas.

To give a successful presentation:

1. **Plan** Read your essay aloud and on your own. Make notes about the key details you want to stress. Think about how you want each part to sound. Mark the places where you should read with added emphasis. Add facts, descriptions, and examples that support your key points and make them more interesting.

2. **Practice** To make sure your presentation is focused, practice in front of a friend beforehand. Check that you made your key ideas clear by asking your friend to explain what you presented. You may also want to videotape yourself and watch your performance. See whether you look relaxed and whether your gestures are natural.

3. **Deliver** Before you read, briefly introduce your essay. You might explain why you chose your topic to write about, or summarize a few key points. Then present your essay to your audience. Remember to:

   • Read at a steady rate that your audience can easily follow and understand.

   • Pronounce each word clearly and correctly.

   • Speak at an appropriate volume and vary your tone to fit different parts of your essay. However, always make sure your audience can hear you.

   • Make eye contact with your listeners throughout your presentation.

" Sometimes a few small actions can lead to really big changes. I'm going to tell you about some simple actions our city took that led to very big and positive changes in our community."

"When I'm researching for a science report, I feel like I'm -already a scientist."

—Jennifer

Model Study

Research Report

Writing a research report involves three key steps:

❶ Gather Information

Choose a specific focused topic. After deciding what questions you want to explore, gather information from a variety of reliable sources and take notes to record important facts.

❷ Organize and Digest the Information

Now get organized. Be sure that you understand all your notes. Use them to create an outline—a plan for how to present your ideas.

❸ Present the Information

The last step is the most exciting—writing about your findings and presenting the facts in your own unique way.

Study the student model on pages 151W–153W. It shows the features of a good research report.

RESEARCH REPORT

A good research report

☑ is focused on a specific topic

☑ gives information from a variety of sources

☑ is well organized, with an introduction, body, and conclusion.

Feature Checklist

A Monster with the Power to Heal
Anita Hernandez

Can doctors use a reptile's venom to help treat a common disease? By studying a poisonous lizard called a Gila monster, researchers have been able to create a new drug to treat diabetes. The drug gives patients a new and different way to manage their diabetes.

Understanding Diabetes

Diabetes is a serious illness. Between 15 and 20 million people in the United States suffer from the disease (Michaels 16). Diabetes affects how your body makes and uses a chemical called insulin. Diabetes comes in two types. People with type I diabetes (5–10% of sufferers) cannot make insulin at all. People with type II diabetes cannot make enough insulin and/or may not be able to use the insulin their bodies make (Hikel 179).

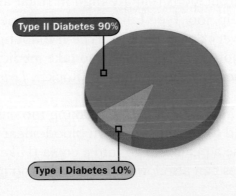

Type II Diabetes 90%

Type I Diabetes 10%

Introduction
The writer uses a question to introduce the topic.

The writer presents the **central idea** for her report.

Body
The writer uses **headings** to organize the paper.

The Gila monster is about 2 feet long. ▶

Research Report, continued

Each **main idea** is supported by facts and details from the writer's research.

Why is insulin so important? When you eat, your body turns food into a sugar called glucose. It is a special kind of sugar in your blood that your body uses for energy (Michaels 25). Normally, insulin helps the cells in your body absorb glucose from your blood (Patel 59). If your body doesn't make insulin, or if it doesn't use insulin well, cells can't absorb glucose the way they should. Cells don't get the glucose they need, and blood-sugar levels may become too high. This can cause many medical problems (Rocker, *Beating Diabetes* 15).

The writer gives **source information** for each fact.

People with diabetes often feel tired and hungry (Patel 60). Diabetics can also have other serious health problems. They may have problems with their eyesight. They may lose weight and have a higher chance of having a heart attack, too (Nigel 35).

Managing Diabetes

Each section relates to the writer's **central idea**.

Most diabetics need to watch their blood-sugar levels and stay away from foods that are high in sugar and fat. Exercise can help, too. Type I diabetics usually need insulin shots every day (Patel 65). Type II diabetics may need insulin shots, too. They may also take medicine to help their bodies make more insulin (Rocker, *Living with Diabetes* 20).

These medicines are not perfect. Taking too much insulin may lead to a sudden drop in blood-sugar levels, which can cause a person to go into a coma (Hikel 180). Other medicines can also lower blood sugar too much.

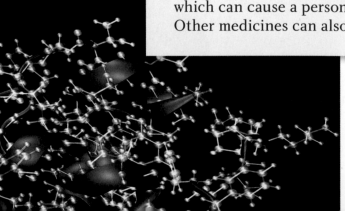

◄ 3-D computer-generated molecular model of human insulin monomeric form.

Medicine from a Monster

The Gila monster is a poisonous lizard that lives in the southwestern United States and Mexico. Though its bite hurts, it will not kill you. However, scientists noticed that its bite causes the body to make more insulin (Hikel 179–180)!

As Dr. John Eng analyzed Gila-monster venom, he discovered a chemical in it similar to the one that makes your body release insulin (Hikel 185). Based on his research, scientists made exenatide, a new drug to treat type II diabetes.

One advantage of exenatide is that it stays in the body longer, so diabetics don't need to take it as often. They don't have to check their blood sugar as often either. The drug can also help diabetics control their weight by reducing their appetite (Sampson 27). Diabetic John Davidson remarks, "As a chef at a busy restaurant, I found it hard to stay at a healthy weight. But ever since I started taking exenatide, my appetite has been under control. In fact, I've lost 15 pounds."

Thanks to the work of Dr. Eng and others with the Gila monster, diabetics have a better way to control their disease. Now researchers are looking into medical treatments that use the venom of sea snails and scorpions. Who knows what amazing medicines they will create next?

Direct quotes help make the report lively and interesting.

Conclusion Relates ideas to the central idea. Ends with a question to wonder about.

Write a Research Report

RESEARCH PROMPT Is there something or someone you wish you knew more about? Maybe something related to medicine or nutrition. Maybe a famous doctor or scientist.

Think of a specific topic you'd like to research. Then find out all you can about it and write a report. Your report should

- be about something that truly interests you
- be well organized, with a central topic, or idea, and lots of evidence to support it
- present information from at least five reliable sources. (Only one of your sources should be an encyclopedia.)

Develop a Game Plan

For some school assignments, you may not be entirely free to choose your topic. Your teacher will have an area in mind, for example: the Civil War. Still, you can suit your research to your interests:

- Focus and narrow your topic to a specific aspect of the general area you have been assigned.

- Write research questions to pinpoint what you want to know about the topic.

Once you have research questions down, check out a variety of different sources to answer them, and keep detailed notes of the information you find.

Look at the photo on the next page. Choose a research question. Name at least three places you could look for answers. Include at least one person who could serve as a source.

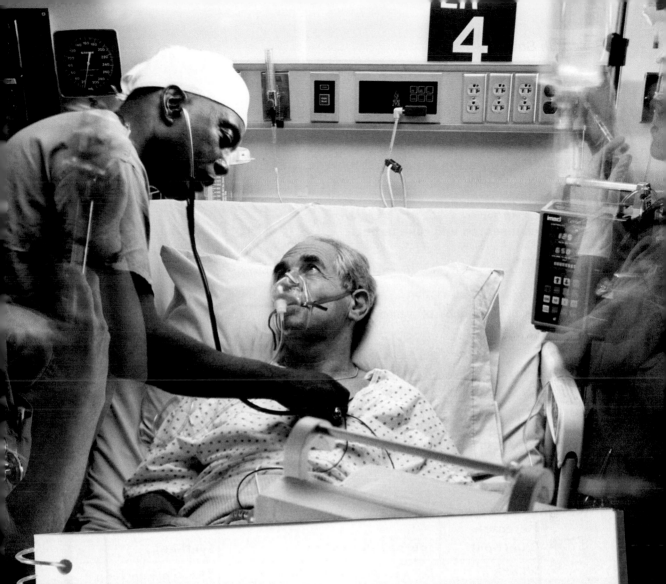

Research Questions

- What kind of training do you need to become a paramedic?

- What's it like to work in the emergency room of a hospital?

- How can research on animals help to save human lives?

- What are the latest advances in the field of organ transplants?

- How are rising medical costs affecting the average person?

Develop a Game Plan, continued

How to Get from A to B

As you investigate your topic, you take notes, put together your ideas, develop an outline, and use it to write your finished report. This diagram summarizes the path.

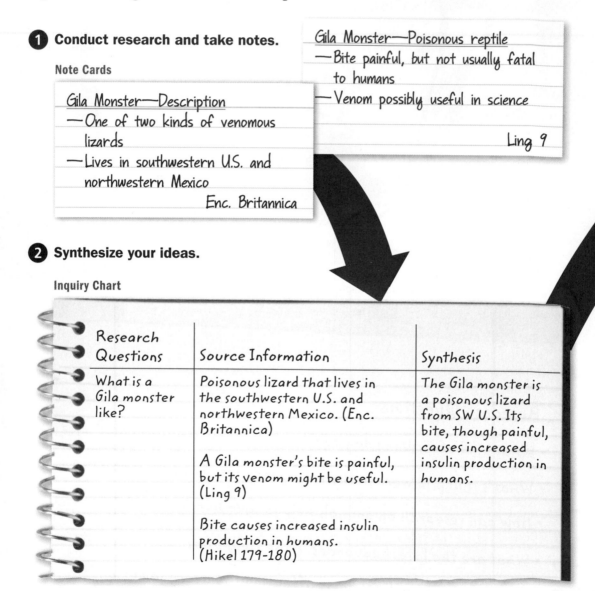

1 **Conduct research and take notes.**

Note Cards

> Gila Monster—Description
> —One of two kinds of venomous
>   lizards
> —Lives in southwestern U.S. and
>   northwestern Mexico
>   Enc. Britannica

> Gila Monster—Poisonous reptile
> —Bite painful, but not usually fatal
>   to humans
> —Venom possibly useful in science
>   Ling 9

2 **Synthesize your ideas.**

Inquiry Chart

Research Questions	Source Information	Synthesis
What is a Gila monster like?	Poisonous lizard that lives in the southwestern U.S. and northwestern Mexico. (Enc. Britannica) A Gila monster's bite is painful, but its venom might be useful. (Ling 9) Bite causes increased insulin production in humans. (Hikel 179–180)	The Gila monster is a poisonous lizard from SW U.S. Its bite, though painful, causes increased insulin production in humans.

Gila Monsters are one of
two species of seriously
venomous lizards. ▶

③ Develop an outline.

Outline

V. Medicine from Gila Monster
   A. Poisonous lizard in parts of U.S. and Mexico
      1. Bite hurts, but not harmful
      2. Poison in humans acts like insulin
   B. Dr. Eng analyzes venom
      1. Finds chemical that produces insulin
      2. Scientists make exenatide from venom

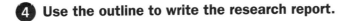

④ Use the outline to write the research report.

Research Report

Medicine from a Monster

   The Gila monster is a poisonous lizard that lives in
the southwestern United States and Mexico. Though
its bite hurts, it will not kill you. However, scientists
noticed that its bite causes the body to make more
insulin (Hikel 179–180)!

   As Dr. John Eng analyzed Gila monster venom, he
discovered a chemical in it similar to the one that
makes your body
release insulin (Hikel
185). Based on his
research, scientists
made exenatide, a
new drug to treat
type II diabetes.

Develop a Game Plan, continued

Choose and Focus Your Topic

You've made the right choice for a research topic if you
can answer "yes" to each of these questions:

- Does the topic interest you?

- Can you find enough information about the topic?

- Is your topic focused and specific?

Look at the planning chart that Anita prepared below.
How did she narrow her topic?

▲ A research
scientist at work

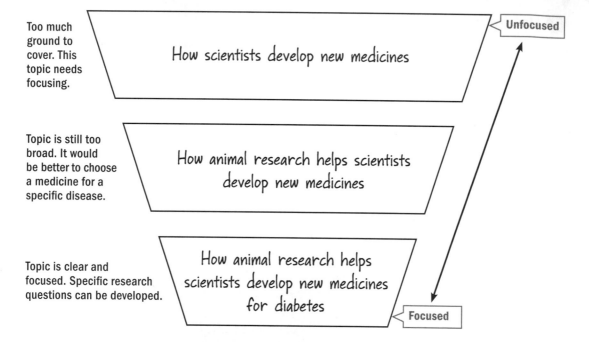

Too much ground to cover. This topic needs focusing.

How scientists develop new medicines

Unfocused

Topic is still too broad. It would be better to choose a medicine for a specific disease.

How animal research helps scientists develop new medicines

Topic is clear and focused. Specific research questions can be developed.

How animal research helps scientists develop new medicines for diabetes

Focused

Presearch and Put Together an FATP Chart

To really nail down your topic, and before diving into in-depth
research, it helps to do a little *presearch*—you don't know
what's out there until you look around a bit.

The Web is great for presearch. Time spent Web-surfing can help you choose an interesting topic about which there is enough information.

Through her Internet presearch, Anita found out about this new treatment for diabetes using Gila monster saliva! Now the research project came together in her head, and she was able to write her FATP Chart.

FATP Chart

Form: research report

Audience: my teacher and classmates

Topic: how studying the Gila monster helped scientists develop a new treatment for diabetes

Purpose: to inform readers about the new diabetes drug that scientists developed

Reflect

- Is your research topic specific and interesting enough?

- Do you need to write more questions to guide your research?

List Research Questions

Next put together some research questions for your report to "answer." Start out with a main research question, and then break it down into more specific sub-questions.

Vague

Main Question:
What is the best way to deal with having diabetes?

Sub-Questions:
1. What is diabetes like?
2. What can you do about it?
3. What are some treatments?

Specific

Main Question:
Is the new diabetes drug developed from Gila monster saliva better than traditional treatments?

Sub-Questions:
1. What is it like to live with diabetes?
2. How do doctors treat diabetes?
3. What did scientists discover about Gila monster saliva?

Locate Information Sources

A **source** is a place where you go to get something. Three kinds of sources are:

- the world around you—all you have to do is make a direct observation. This is not always possible (and, if you're researching rattlesnakes, may not be a good idea). But if you're researching the behavior of, say, butterflies in your backyard, open your eyes and look at your backyard!

- experts—people who know a lot about a topic, through study or through experience

- published materials which may be printed, transmitted electronically over the Internet, or captured in media such as films or sound recordings.

Getting Info from Experts

For Anita's paper on the new medicine for diabetes, an expert might be a doctor who specializes in diabetes or someone who has diabetes. Interviews are a great way to get first-hand information and eyewitness accounts.

How to Conduct an Interview

You can interview experts in person, by phone, or through e-mail.

1. Explain the purpose of the interview when you contact the person to set up an appointment.

2. Plan your questions in advance. Ask questions that will get more than just a "yes" or "no" response.

3. Always be respectful and courteous to the person you are interviewing.

4. Follow your plan, but be flexible. Your subject might bring up important issues you hadn't thought of before. Ask follow-up questions if you need to know more.

5. Tape-record your subject's responses or take detailed notes.

Getting Info from Published Sources

Most published research resources are available both in print and over the Internet. Different types of sources contain different types of information.

Type of Source	Print	Web	Description and Uses
almanac	√	√	An almanac summarizes information, such as facts and statistics. Use it to find facts about history, geography, and politics.
encyclopedia	√	√	The most important general information about a topic is in an encyclopedia. Use it to get a broad overview of a topic and verify facts.
magazines and newspapers	√	√	These periodicals contain current news and trends. Use them when you want to learn about recent local, national, and world events.
nonfiction books	√		Books include in-depth information on a topic. Use them to get deep knowledge of a topic.
online database		√	Databases give access to regularly updated facts, statistics, or a bibliography on a topic. Use them to check facts or to locate sources of information on a topic.
primary sources, such as a historical document, diary, letter, speech, etc.	√	√	Primary sources document past events as they were happening. Use them to gain first-hand information about historical or geographically distant people and events.
reference books	√		These books give detailed information on specialized topics. They are useful for gathering and checking facts.
Web sites		√	The Web offers a wide range of information, from general to quite specific. Locate sites that give an overview of your topic and link to other sites with more sources of information.

Locate Information Sources, continued

Libraries have Internet access and print materials. They also have reference librarians—they may not be experts in the topic you are researching, but they are all-around information experts.

Finding Printed Materials on the Shelves

Knowing where and how to find materials in the library is key to spending your research time wisely. Here's how research materials are arranged in most libraries:

- **Nonfiction books**—by subject area using call numbers based on the Dewey Decimal System

000–099	General Interest	500–599	Pure Sciences
100–199	Philosophy	600–699	Technology
200–299	Religion	700–799	The Arts
300–399	Social Sciences	800–899	Literature
400–499	Language	900–999	History and Geography

- **Biographies**—usually grouped with other nonfiction by the last name of the person the book is about

- **Periodicals**—alphabetically by title

- **Reference books**—in their own section or grouped with other nonfiction.

Searching on the Online Catalog

You can use the online catalog to search for print and multimedia resources by title, author, subject, or keyword. Follow these steps, if you decide to search by subject.

1 **Type in your subject to see what's available, and then click on an entry.**

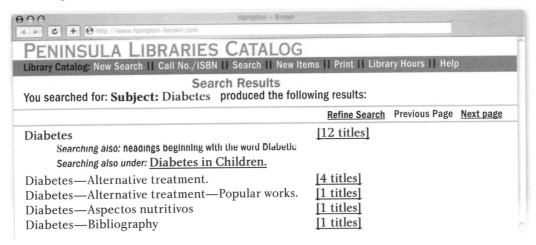

2 **Read the sources for that entry. Use the location and call number to find the source.**

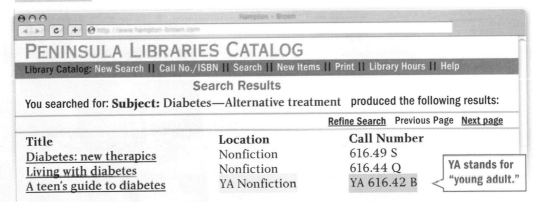

Locate Information Sources, continued

3 You can also click on the source to find a summary. Read the summary to see if the source looks promising, and check the status to see if it's available. Then write down or print out the information.

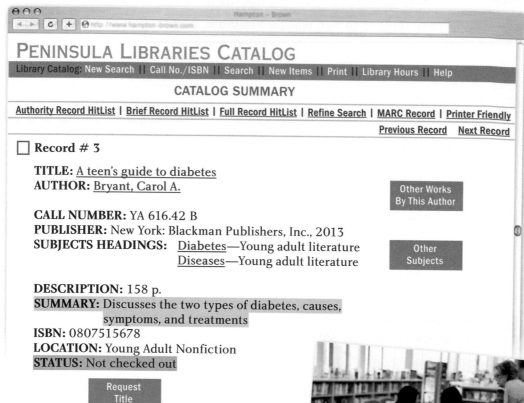

Beyond Paper: Electronic Sources

Books and periodicals are important in research, but you can
get a lot of information without ever opening a book! Just use
electronic sources, which store vast amounts of information
and include search tools to help you locate information quickly.
Electronic sources often include audiovisual information as well.

Some electronic sources are:

- **DVDs** Look for documentaries or educational
  programs that relate to your topic. Often
  programs originally on TV are available later
  on DVDs.

- **CDs** Listen to music, lectures, or books.

- **CD-ROMs** Compact discs can store
  a lot of data in one place, CD-ROMs
  often contain lengthy works, such
  as encyclopedias.

At the library, the reference
librarian can show you how to
use these specialized sources.

Locate Information Sources, continued

The Web: Time Saver or Time Waster?

The World Wide Web is your connection to unlimited information on every topic imaginable. And it's not all words, words, words on the Web. Many Web sites feature images, sound files, or video clips.

You can get onto this "information superhighway" from anywhere there is a computer with Internet access—the library, your classroom, or your home.

As with any highway, though, it will only be useful to you if you know how to drive safely in very heavy traffic.

The advantage of the World Wide Web is that it has more information than any library could possibly hold.

Unfortunately, doing research on the Web can also be difficult because there's so much information out there. Finding good sites can be like looking for a needle in a haystack.

If you waste hours online without finding anything useful, you'll end up feeling frustrated. That's why it's important to be a smart searcher.

Keeping Safe While You Search

The Internet makes it easy for people to find and exchange information—and information on the Web is available to anyone, anywhere. That's mostly a good thing, but it's important to be extra careful about protecting your personal information online. Here are some basics:

- **NEVER** give out your personal information to strangers online. Period. People can easily misrepresent themselves on the Internet, so don't take any chances.

- What if you want to make an online purchase or subscribe to a publication? Before you give out contact information and credit card numbers, check with an older relative. Also, check the site's security features.

- Don't give out personal information in chat rooms or on discussion boards, or when posting comments on a blog. These types of sites aren't reliable resources anyway.

- If you do stumble onto a Web site that looks fishy, just click the back button on your Web browser or, if necessary, close the browser window.

Get Information from the Web

If you know how, you can get information quickly from the Web.

Accessing a Database

A database is a huge computer file of information. Databases usually have search tools. You may find information of two types:

1. specific information about a particular topic

This site contains many types of information about Gila monsters.

2. references to other materials with information about a topic

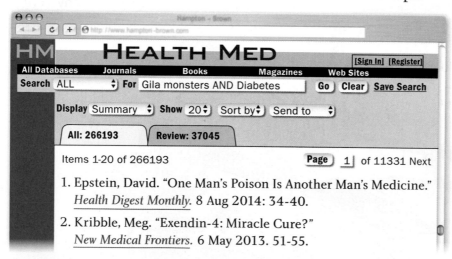

Search results show a bibliography of books and magazine articles about Gila monsters.

Here are some tips for smart searching with databases:

- Before you start, invest a little time in reading the guidelines for using the database.

- Do specific subject and keyword searches.

- If a bibliography-type database includes summaries, read the summaries carefully to see if the article looks promising.

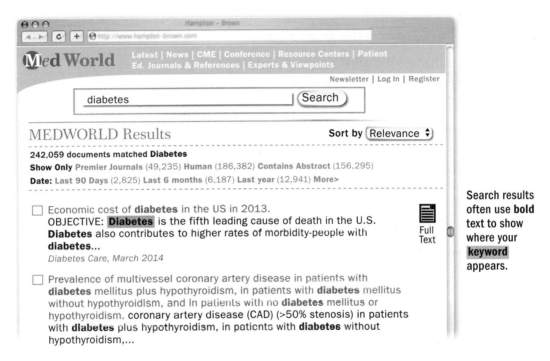

Search results often use **bold** text to show where your **keyword** appears.

- Save your searches to a separate document on your computer, so you know which subjects or keywords you have looked for.

- Finally, be sure to save any leads that look promising. You can save them within the database, print out articles or summaries, or e-mail search results to yourself.

Get Information from the Web, continued

Using a Search Engine

A search engine is a powerful computer program that can "read" *very* fast through the entire World Wide Web, and look for anything you tell it to.

Usually, the problem with these searches is that they return more information than you know what to do with. To focus your search, try these techniques:

- Make keywords as specific as possible.

- When searching for a phrase, like "diabetes symptoms," use quotation marks to group words together. That way you won't get results about other diseases.

- Don't type in questions. Type in the answer you want to find, such as "Gila monster's habitat." Then scan the results and click on a link to go directly to the site.

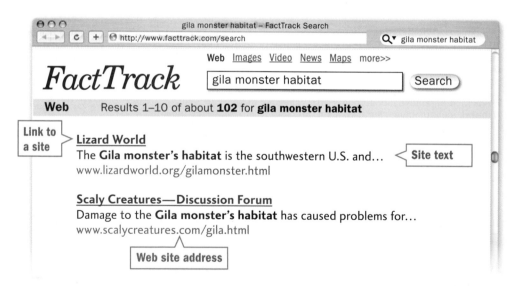

Saving Search Results

When you find a good Web site, you'll probably want to access it again. Keep track of useful sites using these techniques:

- Use your browser's "Bookmark" or "Favorites" feature to save good links. Organize your links in folders so you can find them easily.

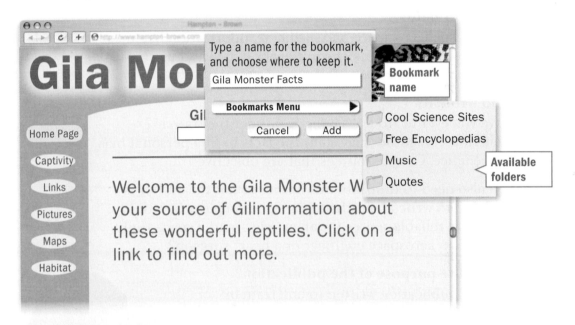

- Print out Web pages so you can refer to the paper copies when you're not at your computer.

Sort through the Information

Part of being a smart searcher is recognizing that not all sources are trustworthy. And also, that not all reliable information is useful.

Evaluating Print Sources

Carefully evaluate print sources by asking these questions:

1. **Is it up-to-date?**
   In fields such as science and medicine, information becomes quickly outdated. Check the publication date and use up-to-date sources to keep your facts accurate.

2. **Who wrote it?**
   Have you ever heard the saying "Consider the source"? Sometimes an author may slant the facts to fit a personal bias or prejudice. Choose sources that are objective.

   You also need to think about whether or not the author is qualified to write about the topic. For example, who would be a more reliable source for an article about a space flight to Mars: an aerospace engineer or a heart surgeon?

3. **What's the purpose of the publication?**
   Was the publication written to entertain or to inform? If you are researching facts about desert reptiles, an entertaining feature about pet lizards is probably not very useful.

Evaluating Web Sites

While many Web sites are carefully researched and accurate, others contain incorrect information. When you look at online sources, ask the same questions you ask for print sources, plus a few more:

1. **Does it look and sound professional?**
   Look for content that is well-written, organized, and free of obvious errors.

2. **When was it last updated?**
   Many sites include this information on the home page.

3. **What kind of site is it?**
   The last letters of a site's URL, or Web address, tell what kind of site it is.

If the URL ends in . . .	The site is maintained by . . .
.gov	a federal government organization
.mil	the U.S. military
.edu	a school, college, or university
.org	a professional organization
a state abbreviation (such as CA or TX) followed by .us	a state government
.biz	a business
.com or .net	a business or an individual

Generally, sites maintained by the government, colleges and universities, and professional organizations are more accurate than commercial or personal sites.

4. **Is the information confirmed by other Web sites?**
   Even if you're using a source that seems reliable, it's still a good idea to double-check your facts with other sources.

Sort through the Information, continued

Recognizing Relevant Information

When you skim and scan, you quickly read titles, headings, and key words in **bold** or *italics* to give you an idea of what the text is about. That way you can decide if the source will be useful.

Some of the information you find will be interesting or related to your topic, but just not relevant or important enough to include in your report. Just as you sort through sources, you'll need to sort through information.

To help you decide what's important:

1 **Think about your research questions as you read.**

Main Question:
Did the ancient Egyptians have medicines?

Sub-Questions:
1. What did they do when they got sick?

2. How did they treat common ailments?

Ancient Egyptians knew about medicines found in nature. ▶

2 Read the source carefully. Ask yourself questions like "Do the facts support the main points I want to explain in my report?"

Medicine—Egyptian Style

Thousands of years ago, ancient peoples had knowledge of many medicines found in nature. Dr. Louise Chen, an expert on ancient forms of medicine, explains, "People in ancient Egypt chewed willow bark to help with fever and headaches." The medicinal properties of the soft, flexible willow bark were also known to Native Americans and Greeks. Willow bark contains salicylic acid, from which aspirin is made. Chen's research also uncovered that ancient Egyptians chewed garlic before long journeys to keep "evil spirits" away. Today garlic is well known for its immunity-boosting properties, as well as its pungent, spicy flavor.

> "Here's a fact I can use in my report."

> "This detail about Native Americans and Greeks is interesting, but not relevant to my report on the ancient Egyptians."

Take Good Notes

As you gather information from a variety of sources, you're not going to be able to keep it all in your head! So, you'll need a system for recording and organizing what you learn:

- Write the important facts you find on index cards or in a computer file.

- Use a heading for each card or for each group of related notes.

- Identify the source (by title or author) and the page where you got the information.

- Separately, also record complete publishing information (title, author, publisher, etc.) for every source you use. You'll need this information for the Works Cited section of your report. (See pages 198W–199W for more details.)

Compare these note cards:

Disorganized

—Gilas are poisonous.
—They don't need to eat much.

　　　　I Am a Gila Monster, 37

Organized

Gila Monsters—Eating habits ◁ Heading
A Gila monster does not eat very often. Its digestive system processes food very slowly.

　　　　I Am a Gila Monster, 37 ◁ Source: book title and page number

Effective note-taking involves a mixture of **paraphrasing**, **summarizing**, and **direct quotation**.

Gila monsters live under rocks and in sandy soils with shrubs. ▶

Paraphrasing

When you paraphrase, you use your own words to restate what an author has written. To paraphrase:

1 **Read the source carefully.**

> ### I Am a Gila Monster
>
> Gila monsters are slow moving, non-aggressive lizards. Their venom is quite effective in subduing small prey and is delivered from grooves in the animal's teeth. Gila monsters eat only several times a year. The rest of the time their pancreases are turned off. When they eat, they secrete a hormone that turns their pancreases back on. Unlike poisonous snakes that "inject" their venom, Gilas have to chew on their prey to move the venom into the wound.

2 **Record the important information <u>in your own words</u>.**

Make sure each entry relates to the heading. In your note, do not use language that is too close to that of the source unless you decide to use a direct quote (see page 183W).

Too close to the source

> Gila Monsters—Eating habits
> Gila monsters eat only a few times a year. The rest of the time, the pancreas is turned off.
>   I Am a Gila Monster, 37

The researcher's own words

> Gila Monsters—Eating habits
> Gila monsters don't eat very often. They have a special digestive system that is only active when they eat.
>   I Am a Gila Monster, 37

Try to keep your paraphrase about the same length as the original text or a bit shorter.

About the right length

> Gila Monsters—Eating habits
> Gila monsters are poisonous lizards that live in the desert. They have a digestive system that becomes active only after they eat.
>   I Am a Gila Monster, 37

Take Good Notes, continued

Summarizing

When you summarize, you find and condense the most important ideas, leaving out many details. To summarize:

1 **Read Your Source Carefully**

To locate the most important ideas, look at titles, headings, and key words in *italics* or **bold** type. In an article or a longer passage, determine the main idea of each paragraph.

2 **Keep Track of Important Ideas and Details**

You can make notes in a graphic organizer to hold your thinking and then use it as a guide for your summary.

Main Idea: Animal hormones can be used to develop treatments for human diseases.

Detail: During the 1980s, Dr. Eng began studying the saliva of Gila monsters.

If you have your own copy of the source, you can highlight ideas. Or, use sticky notes to mark key points.

The Gila's Healing Hormone

Tricia Fitzpatrick

During the 1980s, Dr. John Eng did extensive research on hormones in a laboratory in New York. Eng hoped to discover how animal hormones could be used to develop treatments for human diseases. Dr. Eng began studying the saliva of the Gila monster, a venomous lizard native to the Southwest, after hearing that people who had been bitten by the monster produced extra insulin. Through his research, Eng discovered that the Gila monster's saliva contains a hormone that is similar to a human hormone that triggers insulin release. Eng's discovery was used to create a new drug to treat type II diabetes.

❸ Restate the Main Idea in Your Own Words

Try to get it all into one sentence, if at all possible.

> Dr. John Eng researched ways to use hormones from animals to treat human diseases.

❹ Condense the Important Details and Examples

In your summary, you will not include every detail that is in the original—just the most important points. The length of your summary will vary depending on how long your source is.

> Dr. Eng's Discovery
> Dr. John Eng researched ways to use animal hormones to treat human diseases. After learning that the bite of a Gila monster raised people's insulin levels, he studied the Gila's saliva. A hormone in it resembles a human hormone that helps release insulin. Eng's discovery resulted in a new drug for diabetics.
>   Fitzpatrick, 70

Source: author's name and page number

Don't forget to add a heading telling what the summary is about, and to identify the source and page number(s).

❺ Check for Accuracy

Once you've written your summary, read it over and compare it to the source material. Does your summary represent the source accurately? Are you sure you've captured the most important ideas? If necessary, revise your summary.

Dr. John Eng discovered the Gila monster's power to heal. ▶

Avoid Plagiarism

Plagiarism is the act of passing off someone else's words or ideas as your own. Some writers do this on purpose.

More often, writers plagiarize accidentally. If you haven't taken careful notes, it's easy to forget that you did not in fact come up with that great sentence yourself, but copied it straight out of a book and should have used quotation marks!

Either way, consequences can be harsh. Student writers might fail an assignment or get kicked out of school. Professionals can lose their jobs. Any writer who plagiarizes risks his or her reputation. The bottom line: never plagiarize intentionally, and keep careful notes to avoid doing it accidentally.

The Facts About Plagiarism

FICTION: It's easy to plagiarize without getting caught.
FACT: Teachers get to know different students' writing styles, so they can recognize unoriginal work. They can also use search engines to find writing that's plagiarized from the Internet.

FICTION: It's not plagiarism if you change the author's wording a little bit.
FACT: Any time you use an author's basic wording or ideas, you must credit the author by citing the source.

FICTION: Listing sources on your note cards is a waste of time. You can figure out that stuff later when you're writing your paper.
FACT: Sloppy, incomplete notes can lead to accidental plagiarism. **Always** keep track of sources and use quotation marks when necessary.

FICTION: Plagiarism is a great way to cheat the system.
FACT: If you plagiarize, you're cheating yourself.

What Does Plagiarism Look Like?

Compare the source article below with the student paper
based on that article. Notice words that are too-similar.

Source

> When my associates and I studied the chemical
> structure of exendin-4, we found it to be remarkably
> similar to that of the naturally occurring glucagon-
> like-peptide-1, or GLP1. This little-known hormone is
> produced in the human intestines and can stimulate
> beta cells in the pancreas to secrete insulin.

Student Paper

> Exendin-4 is remarkably similar to the
> naturally occurring glucagon-like-peptide-1. This
> hormone is known as GLP1. It is produced in the
> human intestines and can stimulate cells in the
> pancreas to secrete insulin.

How Can You Avoid Plagiarism?

First be sure to use quotation marks when you take
word-for-word notes from a source.

Note Card

> The structure of exendin-4 is "remarkably similar
> to that of the naturally occurring glucagon-like
> -peptide-1." This hormone, known as GLP1, is
> "produced in the human intestines and can stimulate
> beta cells in the pancreas to secrete insulin."

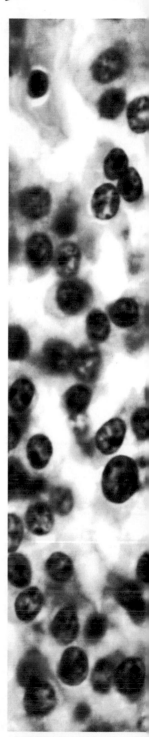

Pancreatic beta cells,
magnified 1000 times. ▶

Avoid Plagiarism, continued

When you write your paper, you can credit the source and show
the writer's exact words in quotations.

    Researchers have found that the chemical structure
of exendin-4 is "remarkably similar to that of the
naturally occurring glucagon-like-peptide-1" or GLP1,
a hormone found in the human intestines (Hikel 183).
GLP1 causes cells in the pancreas to produce insulin.

The original
writer's words
are in
quotations
and the **source**
is named.

Or, you can combine the information from the source with
other notes and your thoughts to put the information in
your own words.

    A research scientist, Frederick Hikel, M.D., has shown
an important connection between the structure of
exendin-4 and that of a human hormone called GLP1.
GLP1 encourages the human pancreas to produce insulin.

Research scientists look
for medical breakthroughs
every day. ▶

Using Direct Quotes

Usually it's best to paraphrase or summarize source material. However, including a few direct quotes can spice up your paper, especially if a writer's words are vivid or memorable.

New Treatments for Diabetes
Frederick Hikel, M.D.

Diabetics often take oral medications that are designed to lower blood-sugar levels. Unfortunately, sometimes these medications can be too effective, since they can lower blood-sugar levels to the point where the patient risks going into shock.

Keep these points in mind when you write down quotes:

- Record the exact words used in your source. If you need to add or change a word, either to make the meaning clear or to shorten or condense the quote, use square brackets [ ] to show where you made a change.

> Diabetes—Medication
> "Unfortunately, sometimes [older] medications can be too effective, since they can lower blood-sugar levels to the point where the patient risks going into shock."

- If you need to leave out part of a quotation, use an ellipsis [...] to show the omission. Make sure you don't alter the meaning!

> Diabetes—Medication
> "Unfortunately, sometimes these medications can . . . lower blood-sugar levels to the point where the patient risks going into shock."

Organize Your Notes

When you create a playlist of your favorite tunes, you probably organize the songs by artist or style. That makes it easier to find the one you want to hear. Organizing your research notes is like that, too. Once you get your notes in order, it's easier to find the facts you want to include in your research paper.

Why Organize?

If your notes are organized, your research paper will be, too. Organizing your notes will also help you discover if anything vital is missing:

After you've taken a lot of notes about your topic, you should

- put together, or synthesize, ideas from different sources
- decide if you have enough information on your topic or need to do more research
- use your notes to create an outline for your paper.

Gila monsters live in desert areas of Mexico and the United States.

Look at the outline below. How did the writer organize the information she gathered?

A Monster with the Power to Heal

I. Introduction—medicine from a monster
   A. Study of Gila monster led to a new medicine
   B. A new way to treat diabetes

II. Description of diabetes
   A. Type I diabetes
   B. Type II diabetes

III. Importance of insulin
   A. Helps body turn food into energy
     1. Body turns food into glucose
     2. Glucose—blood sugar, needed for energy
     3. Insulin—helps cells get glucose
   B. Diabetes—living with it
     1. High blood sugar causes health problems
     2. Insulin shots and medicine

IV. Medicine from the Gila monster
   A. Poisonous lizard in parts of U.S. and Mexico
     1. Bite hurts, but not harmful
     2. Poison in humans acts like insulin
   B. Dr. Eng analyzes venom
     1. Finds chemical that produces insulin
     2. Scientists make exenatide from venom
   C. Advantages of exenatide
     1. Stays in body longer
     2. Controls appetite and weight
     3. Davidson example

V. Conclusion
   A. Studying Gilas improved options for diabetics
   B. New ways to use animals in medicine

Title

Main topic, with roman numeral

Subtopic, with capital A, B, C, etc.

Supporting detail, with numeral 1, 2, 3, etc.

Organize Your Notes, continued

Synthesizing Ideas

Your research notes may have come from many different sources, but now you have to **synthesize** them, or pull them together, into one paper—the one you're going to write. Here's how:

1 **Start with a Chart**

Set up an **Inquiry Chart**. Once it's filled in, this chart will help you see how all the information you've gathered fits together and whether you've answered your research questions. First write your research questions.

Inquiry Chart

Research Questions	Source Information	Synthesis
What is it like to live with diabetes?		

2 **Group Note Cards by Related Ideas**

Use the headings and keywords on your note cards to decide which cards should be grouped together.

Problems with Diabetes

Diabetes—Problems
Ca_____
vis____
Diabetes—Managing
____
Diabetes—Problems
Often feel tired, hungry or thirsty.

Patel, 60

Treating Diabetes

Diabetes—Treatment
____
Diabetes—New drug
____
Diabetes—New drug
—Regulates blood sugar levels
—Lasts longer than other drugs

Nigel, 38

3 Fill In the Chart

Use your grouped note cards to fill in the Inquiry Chart. For the **Synthesis** column, review all the notes for a particular research question. What can you conclude from the information? Use your own words to write a statement that synthesizes the ideas.

Inquiry Chart

Research Questions	Source Information	Synthesis
What is it like to live with diabetes?	Diabetics are often hungry or thirsty. (Patel 60) Diabetics have to check their blood sugar often. (Rocker 15) Diabetics live with medical problems like impaired vision, blindness, and kidney damage. (Nigel 35)	Living with diabetes can be difficult because of the daily symptoms, and long-term health problems, as well as the need to check insulin levels frequently and to take medication.

If you have trouble synthesizing the ideas, try rereading your notes, or go back to your original sources. Still stumped? You may have to do additional research to get more information about the question that's puzzling you.

Organize Your Notes, continued

Checking for Completeness and Focus

Before you move on to creating a formal outline for your report, take some time to check your Inquiry Chart for

- completeness: Do you have all the information you need?

- focus: Is the information focused on your topic?

Maybe you need to answer a research question more fully, or you come up with another interesting question. If so, add notes like these in red to the chart.

Inquiry Chart

Research Questions	Source Information	Synthesis
What are the treatments for diabetes?	Diabetics follow a special diet. (Patel, 60) What is a good diet for diabetics? Can they eat sugar at all?	
	Some diabetics take a daily insulin shot. Others take pills. (Nigel, 35)	
	Diabetic patients have mixed feelings about the new Gila monster treatment. (Barry, 12) Find articles that include patients' responses.	

Interviewing an expert on your topic is a valuable source of information. ▶

Too Much Information

Not every note you take has to show up in your paper. Leave out information that

- doesn't relate to your research questions
- is contradicted by several other sources.

Inquiry Chart

Research Questions	Source Information	Synthesis
What is it like to live with diabetes?	Diabetics are often hungry or thirsty. (Patel, 60)	**"This doesn't tell what it's like to live with diabetes, so I'll leave it out."**
	~~Insulin was first used to treat diabetes in 1921. (Patel, 59)~~	
	Diabetics have to check their blood sugar often. (Rocker, 15)	**"All the other sources say that diabetics check their blood sugar 'daily' or 'often'. This is the only one that says 'three times a day.' I can't verify this in another source, so I'd better leave it out."**
	~~Check blood sugar three times a day (Franklin, 23)~~	

Good researchers follow their "gut" as they pursue their research. So if you don't have enough information, or if the information isn't focused enough, think of additional questions, and head back to the library or into the field.

Develop an Outline

Now you're ready to develop your outline—a final plan for your paper. Here's how:

1 Start with a Title

Use a title that tells readers what your paper will be about. You can use key words from your research questions or even ask a question.

Outline Title

> ## A Monster with the Power to Heal

2 Decide On Your Introduction

Your opening paragraphs should introduce your topic. Plan a central idea statement that summarizes your answer to your main research question.

Outline for Part I

> ### A Monster with the Power to Heal
>
> **I. Introduction—medicine from a monster**
>   A. Study of Gila monster led to a new medicine
>   B. A new way to treat diabetes
>
> Central idea

Main Research Question
Is the new diabetes drug developed from Gila monster saliva better than traditional treatments?

3 List Your Main Topics

List them in order, using Roman numerals, and see if you like the flow of your ideas.

Main Topics in the Outline

> **I. Introduction**
> **II. Description of diabetes**
> **III. Importance of insulin**
> **IV. Medicine from the Gila monster**
> **V. Conclusion**

These will become the subheads or section heads once you write your paper. Plan on a conclusion, too.

4 **Complete Your Outline**

Fill in subtopics and supporting details under each main topic. For example:

Outline for Part III

III. Importance of Insulin

B. Diabetes—living with it
  1. High blood sugar causes health problems
  2. Insulin shots and medicine

Draw subtopics for your outline from key words in your research questions. Your synthesis statements will give you a clue as to which supporting details go under each subtopic.

Inquiry Chart

Research Questions	Source Information	Synthesis
What is it like to live with diabetes?	Diabetics are often hungry or thirsty. (Patel, 60) Diabetics have to check their blood sugar often. (Rocker, 15) Diabetics live with medical problems like impaired vision, blindness, and kidney damage. (Nigel, 35)	Living with diabetes can be difficult because of the daily symptoms, and long-term health problems, as well as the need to check insulin levels frequently and to take medication.

Armed with your finished outline, you're ready to turn your hard-earned research and thinking into sentences and paragraphs for your research paper.

Draft

Work from Your Outline

Your outline provides the skeleton for your report. As you draft your report, you'll put some meat on those bare bones. (And, of course, you can change your "skeleton" as you write.) Use your outline to:

1 **Draft the introduction.**

Get your readers interested from the beginning. Try one or more of these techniques:

- Show how your topic relates to your readers' experiences.

- Ask the question you will answer in your paper.

- Present an attention-getting fact, quotation, or anecdote.

Be sure your introduction also includes some background about your topic and a central idea for your paper.

2 **Draft the body of your report.**

Look at the sections with Roman numerals in your outline. Turn each of those main points into one or more paragraphs.

3 **Sum up your ideas in the conclusion.**

In the final paragraph, relate your ideas to your central idea. Leave your reader with something to remember, such as a solution for a problem, a new question, or an amazing quote.

▼ Gila monsters live in places like Monument Valley in the Southwest.

Outline

A Monster with the Power to Heal

I. Introduction—medicine from a monster
A. Study of Gila monster led to a new medicine
B. A new way to treat diabetes

A Monster with the Power to Heal　　Question

Could doctors use poisonous reptilian venom to help treat common diseases? Scientists are developing new medications based on their study of certain plants and animals. By studying the venom of a reptile called a Gila monster, researchers have created a new drug to treat diabetes. The drug provides a convenient, effective alternative to traditional treatments for this disease.

Central idea

Draft of the Introduction

Outline

IV. Medicine from the Gila monster
A. Poisonous lizard in parts of U.S. and Mexico
  1. Bite hurts, but not harmful
  2. Poison in humans acts like insulin

The Gila monster is a poisonous lizard found in the Southwest. Its bite is very painful but usually not deadly. However, victims get a swollen pancreas and make more insulin!

Draft of Paragraph in the Body

Outline

V. Conclusion
A. Studying Gilas improved options for diabetics
B. New ways to use animals in medicine

Scientists are constantly looking at new ways that plants and animals can be used to cure our problems. Thanks to Dr. Eng's study of Gila monster poison, diabetics have more options available than ever. Now researchers are looking into medical treatments that use other animals. Who knows what's next?

Draft of the Conclusion

Draft, continued

Integrate Ideas from Your Research

One of the trickiest things to do when you write a report is to make sure your ideas and the information from your research flow together smoothly. As you write and revise your paper, try these techniques:

1 **Support general statements with facts from your research.**

Unsupported

Modern medicine probably uses lots of substances that come from animals and plants. But poison from a reptile? That's hard to believe, yet it's true. A new diabetes drug is based on the Gila monster's venom.

Supported

Modern medicine is making use of the Gila monster. For over 20 years, Dr. John Eng has been working on a new treatment for diabetes that's based on a chemical found in the Gila monster's saliva (Patel 45).

The writer supports a statement with a **fact**.

2 **Stay focused.**

Any quoted or paraphrased material within a paragraph should clearly connect to the **main idea**.

Unfocused

Diabetes interferes with the body's ability to regulate blood sugar. People with type II diabetes either can't produce enough insulin or can't use the insulin that their body produces (Patel 58). Between 15 and 20 million Americans suffer from diabetes (Michaels 16). Diabetes can also cause vision problems (Nigel 35).

Focused

Diabetes interferes with the body's ability to regulate blood sugar. People with type II diabetes may not produce enough insulin and/or may not be able to use effectively the insulin they do produce (Patel 58). If you have ever gone for a long time without eating, you probably noticed that you feel tired and weak. That's because your blood sugar is low.

In which paragraph do the details go with the main idea?

3 **Use your own ideas as the backbone of your paper.**

As you decide what details to include from your research, think about how you'll "connect the dots" for your readers.

Disconnected Facts/Too Many Citations

Dr. John Eng developed a new diabetes drug from Gila monster venom (Michaels 67). The Gila monster's venom contains a digestive enzyme (Barry 24). The Gila "probably uses its digestive enzymes to digest meals over a long period of time" (Barry 24). The Gila monster only eats a few times in a year (Barry 24).

Integrated Ideas and Citations

Scientists have developed a new treatment for diabetics by studying the Gila monster. The Gila monster, which eats only a few times a year, probably uses its venom as an enzyme to digest food (Barry 24).

4 **Cue the quotations.**

It's usually best not to leave a quotation standing alone; the mix of "voices" can make the writing sound awkward. The addition of transitional words (in red below) makes for a smooth connection.

Awkward Quotation, Fixed

The drug Dr. Eng developed has many advantages over older treatments for diabetes. John Davidson, a chef from Boston, was one of the first to try this new treatment. *He explains,* ∧

"Being a chef at a busy restaurant, I found it hard to control my cravings for food. But ever since I started taking this new drug, my appetite has been under control. I've lost 15 pounds and I feel great."

Reflect

- Do your introduction and conclusion give a good idea of what your report is about?

- Have you included enough details to support your central idea?

How to Cite Sources

You should briefly identify your source any time you refer to someone else's words or ideas in your paper. That way, you give other writers credit for their work and provide your readers with a way to learn more about your topic. At the end of your paper, provide a full list of your sources.

Keeping Track of Your Sources

If you record your sources right from the start, you won't have to spend hours figuring out where you found each fact.

- As you do research, list the following bibliographic information for every source. As you take notes, always write down the source's author or title (or both) and the page where you found the information.

Source Card

> Type: Book Source #1
> Title: Diabetes
> Author: Edward J. Michaels
> Publisher: Canton Press
> City: Baltimore
> Year: 2013

Note Card

> Dr. Eng's Research
> In the 1980s, Dr. John Eng began to study the effects of animal venom on humans.
>
> Michaels, 67

- Include information about sources in your draft. You don't have to worry about using the perfect format, but do add a note about where you found each fact or idea.

> Many diabetics are seeking out new remedies for diabetes. Researchers have recently developed a new drug treatment for people with type II diabetes. The treatment originated with the work of Dr. John Eng. Eng began studying the effects of Gila monster venom on humans in the 1980s. (MICHAELS PAGE 67)

How to Cite Sources in Your Final Draft

The point of including references in the body of your report is to help your reader find the full bibliographic information that appears at the end (see pages 198W–199W). The FAQ chart below outlines a system that most teachers will accept.

FAQ	Answer	Example
How do I cite a book or an article?	Give the author's last name and the page number where the information is found.	Dr. Eng began studying venom in the 1980s (Michaels 67).
What if the authors of two or more of my sources have the same last name?	Add an initial or a full first name to the reference.	Dr. Eng began studying venom in the 1980s (T. Michaels 67).
What if my source has more than one author?	If there are two or three authors, list them all. If there are more than three, use the first author's name followed by the abbreviation et al., which means "and others."	Gila monsters spend most of their time in burrows (Anderson and Jones 105). Gila monsters eat very infrequently (Carson et al. 105).
What if I used two different sources by the same author?	Mention the title also, in full or abbreviated.	The symptoms of diabetes can often be partly controlled through diet and exercise (Rocker, *Beating Diabetes* 67).
What if my source has an organization as its author?	Give the name of the organization, in full or abbreviated, just as you would with a person.	Many overweight Americans suffer from diabetes (Diabetes Help Network 12).
How do I cite a Web site?	Use the author's name, if known, or the name of the Web site.	Diabetes affects millions of Americans (Diabetes Information Site).

How to Create a List of Works Cited

You won't be finished with your research paper until you create your list of works cited. This is where you give your reader complete bibliographic information for each of the sources mentioned in the body of your report. The rules for putting together this list are many and complicated, so listen up:

1 **List all the publication details about each source you used.**

- For books:

  Michaels, Edward J. *Diabetes*. Baltimore: Canton Press, 2013.

  Author with   **Title, in**   **City of**   **Publisher**   **Year of**
  last name first   *italics*   **publication**   **publication**

- For newspaper articles:

  Barry, Todd. "New Hope For Diabetes Sufferers." *Youngstown Times*. 6 April 2014: B4.

  Section and
  page number

- For an article in an online magazine:

  Ling, Tara. "Gila Monsters." *Lizard World*. 15 Oct. 2013. 26 Aug. 2014.
  <http://www.lizardworld.org/gila.html>.   **Issue date**   **Date of access**

  Page URL, underscored
  and in angle brackets

Head spinning yet? And these are only some of the rules! If you need to know more, click on myNGconnect.com.

2 **Then list all sources alphabetically. The finished list should look something like this:**

Works Cited

Barry, Todd. "New Hope for Diabetes Sufferers." *Youngstown Times.* 6 April 2014: B4. — Newspaper article

Hikel, Fredrick. "New Treatments for Diabetes." *Diabetes and You.* Ed. Monique Jones. Los Angeles: Medline Press, 2014. 179–186. — Article or essay from a book

Ling, Tara. "Gila Monsters." *Lizard World.* 15 Oct. 2013. 26 Aug. 2014. <http://www.lizardworld.org/gila.html>. — Article from a Web site

Michaels, Edward J. *Diabetes.* Baltimore: Canton Press, 2013. — Book

Nigel, Roberto. "Great Gila Monsters." *Nature Weekly.* 2 May 2012: 30–39. — Magazine article

Patel, Nora. *Surviving With Diabetes.* Arizona: Southwestern Free Press, 2014.

Rickard, Ryan, M.D. 2014, Interview by Anita Hernandez. MP3 recording. February 6. Pennsylvania Hospital, Philadelphia. — Interview

Rocker, Brandon. *Type II Diabetes.* Newport, CT: Greens Press, 2012.

---. *Beating Diabetes.* Newport, CT: Greens Press, 2014. — The symbol --- means the author is the same as for the previous entry.

Revise

1 Evaluate Your Work

One of the best ways to get ideas for improving your paper is to get other students to read it. They can give you feedback about your writing during a peer conference. Here are a few questions you might ask your classmates:

What to Ask during a Peer Conference

- Is my introduction interesting?
- Does my paper have a clear central idea?
- Does each main idea relate to the central idea?
- Are there any parts that are confusing or don't belong?
- Do I need to add or take out anything?

Revision in Action

Amy's Draft

Have you ever been stung by a scorpion? The venom from some scorpions can cause severe pain and swelling. But doctors have found that a scorpion's venom can be helpful.

A protein in the yellow Israeli scorpion's venom shows promise in treating brain tumors (White 40). Not only are scorpions found in Israel, but you can find these ugly creatures in Arizona and Mexico as well. Patients treated with the protein can live for years instead of months. The injected protein attacks only the tumor's tissue, leaving the healthy tissue alone.

One student's response:

"I'm not sure exactly what you want to explain. Maybe you can make your central idea more specific."

"I thought I'd be reading about the scorpion's venom, but this detail confused me."

"This sentence doesn't flow from the one before. Can you rearrange them?"

❷ Mark Your Changes

Think about your classmates' comments as you review your draft. Then make your marks.

Add Text You may need to add

- a question or interesting fact to your introduction
- details to make your central idea specific
- source information you left out

Move Text Are all your sources in the right place? Does your paper have the best organization? Use ↶◯ to show the text you want to move.

Take Out Text To keep your paper focused and unified, take out the text that doesn't go with your central idea or tell more about a paragraph's main idea.

Reflect

- **Does your final draft have a clear central idea?**
- **Does everything in your report tell about that idea?**

Revising Marks

MARK	∧	↶◯	↖―	―ℓ	¶
WHAT IT MEANS	Insert something.	Move to here.	Replace with this.	Take out.	Make a new paragraph.

Revised Draft

Have you ever been stung by a scorpion? The venom from some scorpions can cause severe pain and swelling. But doctors have found that a scorpion's venom can ~~be helpful.~~ *help patients with brain tumors.*

A protein in the yellow Israeli scorpion's venom shows promise in treating brain tumors (White 40). ~~Not only are scorpions found in Israel, but you can find these ugly creatures in Arizona and Mexico as well.~~ Patients treated with the protein can live for years instead of months. The injected protein attacks only the tumor's tissue, leaving the healthy tissue alone.

Amy added details to make her central Idea clear and specific.

Amy took out this detail because it didn't relate to the main idea of the paragraph.

Amy moved this sentence to improve the flow of ideas.

Edit and Proofread

After you're satisfied with the content of your research report, read your paper again to fix language errors. This is what you do when you edit and proofread your work.

- **Check the Grammar** Make sure that you have used correct and conventional grammar throughout. In particular, check for correct use of possessive adjectives. (See page 203W.)

- **Check the Spelling** You may want to have a dictionary on hand to help you check for errors in words with more than one syllable. (See page 204W.)

- **Check the Mechanics** Errors in punctuation and capitalization can make your work hard to understand. In particular, check that you've used apostrophes for possessive nouns correctly. (See page 205W.)

Use these marks to edit and proofread your research report.

*Tech*TIP

If you have Internet access, you might try using an online dictionary to check your spelling.

Editing and Proofreading Marks

MARK	WHAT IT MEANS	MARK	WHAT IT MEANS
∧	Insert something.	/	Make lowercase.
∧	Add a comma.	ℰ	Delete, take something out.
∧	Add a semicolon.	¶	Make new paragraph.
⊙	Add a period.	◯	Spell out.
⊙	Add a colon.	⌃	Replace with this.
⌄ ⌄	Add quotation marks.	∼	Change order of letters or words.
⌄	Add an apostrophe.	#	Insert space.
≡	Capitalize.	◡	Close up, no space here.

Reflect

- What kinds of errors did you find? What can you do to keep from making them?

GrammarWorkout

Check Possessive Adjectives

To tell that someone owns or has something, use a possessive adjective: *my, your, his, her, its, our,* or *their.*

- The possessive adjective always comes before a **noun**.

  EXAMPLES   **my** mom   **her** report   **their** books

- The possessive adjective matches the noun or pronoun it goes with.

  EXAMPLES   I am interested in medical research. **My** report is about new discoveries.

  Do **you** think we can cure cancer? Maybe **your** research will tell us.

  Uncle Zeb is a researcher. **He** works in a lab. Is that **his** work area?

  The lab is neat. **It** is very clean. Someone scrubs **its** equipment every day.

Find the Trouble Spots

Their
Bees often sting people. ~~Its~~ bites can hurt, but heal quickly. Dad showed me what to do. Her job is as an EMT. When a bee bites, it can leave behind a stinger. *Its* ~~It's~~ stinger is attached to a venom sac. You can try to pull the stinger out. But that'll release more venom into my skin. So, gently scrape it out. Then wash the area and apply baking soda.

Check the possessive adjectives. Which ones still need to be fixed?

Edit and Proofread, continued

> # Spelling Workout

Check the Spelling of Long Words

A syllable is a word part that is spoken as one uninterrupted sound. Some words have one syllable while others have more than one.

One syllable	Two syllables	Three syllables
bite	reptile	poisonous
crawl	rep + tile	poi + son +ous

Use these tips to spell words that have more than one syllable:

- Read aloud the sentence in which the word is used. Does it sound and look right?

- Say the word. Listen for word parts you know to spell, such as a suffix or a prefix.

- Say each syllable slowly. How many sounds do you hear? Spell the sounds in the syllable.

- Repeat to spell the word syllable by syllable.

- Look up the word in a dictionary if you're still not sure about the spelling.

Find the Trouble Spots

An unlikely hero, the Gila monster is a venmous lizard *venomous* with bright pink and black coloration. This reptile's skin is covered with bony scales that look like beads. It has a stocky body with a large head and a short, fat tail. The Gila monster hides in burrows for much of its life (Sampson 23), hibernting during the winter and shelteing itself from the sun during the summer. *sheltering*

What other word is misspelled? How would you fix the error?

Mechanics Workout

Check Apostrophes in Possessive Nouns

To show who owns, or possesses, something, use a possessive noun. To make a noun possessive, add an apostrophe (') and *s* or just an apostrophe.

One owner even if it ends in **-s**:	Add **'s** A **researcher's** work is interesting. **Thomas's** job is in research.
More than one owner does not end in **-s**:	Add **'s** Some **people's** jobs can be dangerous.
More than one owner ends in **-s**:	Just Add **'** **Scientists'** findings are important.

Find the Trouble Spots

Researchers jobs can be a little dangerous, especially if they need to extract venom from an animals mouth. To obtain venom from a snake, for example, a worker grasps the snake firmly and holds its mouth over a beaker. Next, the reptiles fangs are forced through a latex cover. Then the worker squeezes the glands behind the snakes' head—and the venom squirts into the beaker.

Can you find the problems with the apostrophes in the passage?

Publish, Share, and Reflect

Now that your research is done and you've written a report that focuses on an interesting topic, you're ready to share the information with your readers.

❶ Publish and Share Your Work

Because you've taken special care to be sure your report is focused, well organized, and correctly written, your audience will certainly learn something from it.

Think about publishing your report by

- creating a special binding for it and leaving it in the library for the whole school to read

- posting it on your blog or e-mailing it to friends and family

- sending it to a popular teen magazine

- desk-top publishing it, enhancing it with photos and graphs to display in your classroom

- doing a multimedia presentation (see page 207W).

❷ Reflect on Your Work

After you publish and present your report, take some time to think about it. What went well? What do you think you could do differently for your next research report?

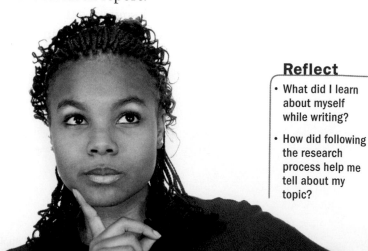

Reflect

- What did I learn about myself while writing?

- How did following the research process help me tell about my topic?

Use Multimedia

Multimedia presentations are great because adding sounds, graphics, and computer technology to your report helps you clarify information and make a greater impact on your audience.

Be sure to choose multimedia components that will add to, and not distract from, your report. For example:

Show Images and Graphics

- Display large, eye-catching photographs that relate to your topic.

- Include illustrations and diagrams to help explain complex information.

- Use charts or graphs to present a lot of data.

- Show maps to highlight a location.

- Play a short clip from a video related to your topic.

Add Music and Sound

- Play music from the time period of your report.

- Share parts of recorded interviews or audio clips from experts on your topic.

- Present a part of a speech by a famous personality.

Use Presentation Software or the Internet

- Make a computer slide show with images, sound, and text to tie together all the information for your audience.

- Use the Internet to find and display resources that demonstrate and explain complex concepts.

- Create an original Web site or blog with information and links your audience can use to learn more.

Research
RESOURCES

Resource Books

Parts of a Book

Title Page

Copyright Page

Table of Contents

Chapter Headings

Index

Glossary

Types of Resource Books

Atlas

Maps

Almanac

Dictionary

Thesaurus

Encyclopedia

Other Print Resources

Newspapers

Magazines

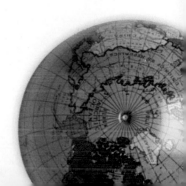

Resource Books

Parts of a Book

When you hear the word *print*, what do you think of? Books!
There are many different kinds of books. All books share some
features that make it easier for readers to find what they need.
Let's look at the parts of a book.

Title Page

The **title page** is usually
the first page in a book.

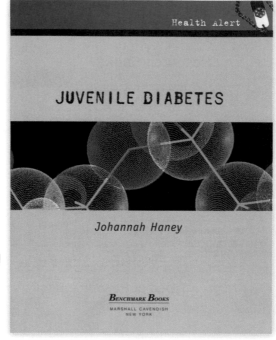

It gives the **title**
of the book and
the **author**.

It tells the
publisher and
often names
the cities
where the
publisher has
offices.

Copyright Page

The **copyright (©) page**
gives the year when the
book was published.

Check the
copyright
to see how
current the
information is.

Haney, Johannah
    Juvenile Diabetes / by Johannah Haney
        p.cm. — (Health alert)
    Includes bibliographical references and index.
    ISBN 0-7614-1798-2
        1.Diabetes in children—Juvenile literature.   2. Diabetes—Juvenile literature.
    I. Title. II.   Series: Health alert (Benchmark Books)

RJ420.D5H355 2005
616.4'62—dc22   2004005969

Copyright © 2011 Marshall Cavendish Corporation
All rights reserved
Printed in China
6 5 4 3 2

Table of Contents

The **table of contents** is in the front of a book. It shows how many chapters, or parts, are in a book. It tells the page numbers where those chapters begin. Look at the chapter names to see which ones might be useful to you.

A table of contents can be much more detailed than the one shown here. For example, it might list sections within chapters, important visuals, or special sections found in the book.

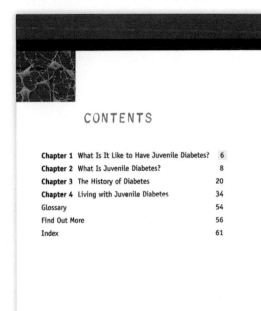

CONTENTS

A **chapter title** tells what the chapter is mostly about.

The **page number** tells where the chapter begins.

Chapter Headings

Once you have found a chapter you are interested in using from the table of contents, you will turn to the chapter. The first page in the chapter will contain a header describing what you will find in the chapter. Often, chapters are numbered.

[1]

WHAT IS IT LIKE TO HAVE JUVENILE DIABETES?

When Kathleen was six years old, she was just like other kindergartners. She enjoyed learning new things in school and she loved playing on the swings at recess. But by the end of the school year, Kathleen was thirsty all the time, had to ask the teacher for a lot of bathroom breaks, and sometimes fell asleep during class. Children can often become thirsty and tired, but Kathleen seemed to be thirstier and more tired than other children her age.

Her parents were worried so they took her to the doctor. The doctor examined Kathleen and had her go to the hospital to have some tests done. One of the tests checked Kathleen's **blood glucose**—or the sugar in her bloodstream. Abnormal blood glucose levels are often a sign of juvenile diabetes. When the test results came back, the doctor found out that

Parts of a Book, continued

Index

The **index** is usually found at the back of a book. It lists all the important subjects that are discussed in the book in alphabetical order. Use the index to see if the information you seek can be found in the book. After you read a book, the index can also be helpful when you want to locate a particular piece of information again.

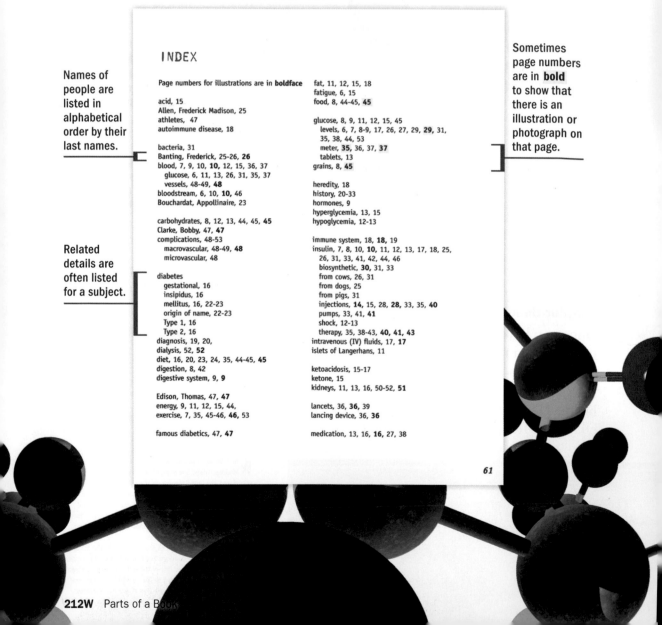

Names of people are listed in alphabetical order by their last names.

Related details are often listed for a subject.

Sometimes page numbers are in **bold** to show that there is an illustration or photograph on that page.

Glossary

A **glossary** lists important words used in the book and their meanings. It is found at the back of the book. Use the glossary to help understand specific vocabulary in a book.

GLOSSARY

Words are listed in alphabetical order.

autoimmune disease—a condition in which the body attacks its own normal healthy cells

bacteria—very small living cells which can only be seen using a microscope

blood glucose—the amount of glucose in the bloodstream

blood glucose meter—a device that measures the amount of glucose in the bloodstream

carbohydrates—chemical compounds found in food, such as starches and sugars

dialysis—a treatment for kidney failure that rids the body of toxic material

glucose—a type of sugar

The **definition** defines, or gives the meaning of, a word.

Types of Resource Books

Atlas

An **atlas** is a book of maps. There are several types of atlases, which are used for different purposes.

A **road atlas** is designed for drivers to use in deciding how to get from one place to another. The maps in a road atlas feature highways, streets, and other driving routes. Places such as cities, towns, and bodies of water are also shown on the road maps. The content of a road atlas might be limited to a small area such as one state, but a road atlas can also cover a huge area like a continent.

A **reference atlas** includes maps and information about every country in the world. Usually, a map of a country is shown on one page, and a second page shows facts and visuals about the country.

Historical atlases are filled with maps that show how people have explored and changed the world through time. These atlases also include interesting facts about history and often have time lines and other related visuals.

▼ Historical Atlas

▼ Road Atlas

▼ Reference Atlas

Since there are several types of atlases, it makes sense that you can find different types of maps inside them, doesn't it? You can use the different maps for different purposes. Let's see what some of them look like.

Physical Maps

A **physical map** shows the geographical features of a place, such as bodies of water and landforms.

Mapmakers often use techniques that make mountains look like they are rising off the page.

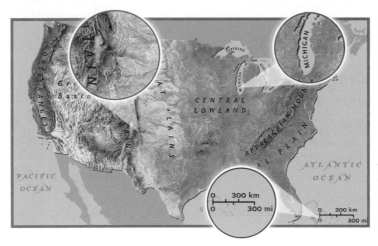

Landforms, like mountains or lakes, are often labeled.

The **scale** shows that this distance on the map is equal to 300 miles on land.

Product Maps

A **product map** uses pictures and symbols to show where products come from or where natural resources are found.

The **compass rose** shows the directions north, south, east, and west.

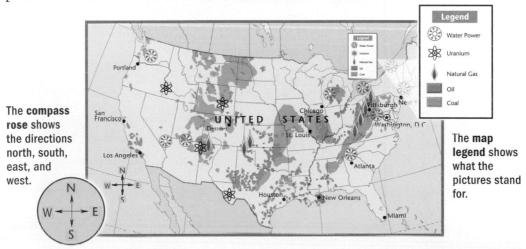

The **map legend** shows what the pictures stand for.

Types of Resource Books, continued

Political Maps

A **political map** shows the boundaries between countries, states, and other areas. It also shows capitals and other major cities. **Road maps** are usually set up like political maps.

A **grid system** is used on these maps to make it easy to find a particular place. Look up the place name in the index to find the right map and a code to the exact location on the map. For example, L-6 for this map is the square at which the row L and the column 6 intersect. Can you find Orlando somewhere in the square?

Historical Maps

A **historical map** shows when and where certain events happened.

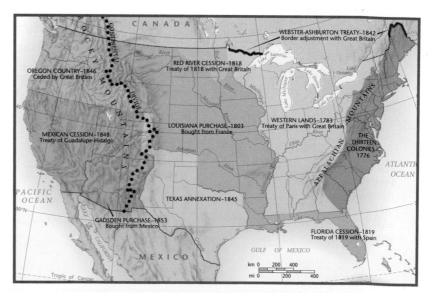

Almanac

An **almanac** is an up-to-date book filled with facts about interesting topics such as inventions, awards, trends, weather, movies, and television. A new almanac is published each year, which is why the information is so current. You can use an almanac to find quick facts about a topic.

Because almanacs tend to present information on a vast number of topics, you will find the **index** particularly useful in locating what you need.

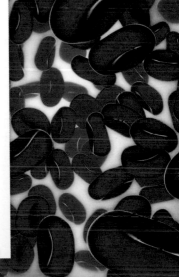

DIABETES

Diabetes is a condition that affects millions of people around the world. In most people, the pancreas produces a hormone called insulin. Insulin helps the body break down sugars, starches, and other foods. For people with diabetes, the pancreas often does not produce enough insulin or the insulin that is produced is not properly used by the digestive system.

There are several types of diabetes. People with type 1 diabetes do not produce insulin. Current estimates indicate that 5-10 percent of Americans with diabetes have type 1 diabetes. People with type 2 diabetes produce insulin, but their bodies do not properly use the insulin that is produced. In addition, they often do not have enough insulin. Most Americans with diabetes have Type 2 diabetes. Gestational diabetes is a form of the disease that affects pregnant women. Doctors report over 100,000 case of gestational diabetes in the United States each year. There are over 50 million Americans who have a condition known as pre-diabetes. Pre-diabetes, as the name suggests, describes a condition where a patient's blood-glucose levels are higher than normal but are not high enough to warrant a diagnosis of type 2 diabetes.

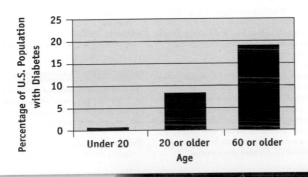

Types of Resource Books, continued

Dictionary

Think of the **dictionary** as a tool you can use to learn everything you need to know about a word. Dictionaries tell you how to spell, say, and use words.

Use the **guide words** at the top of each page to help you find the entry word you are looking up. The guide words are the first and last words on the page.

 detour ▸ diabetes

nated the gasoline pumps. **det·o·nate** (det′ən āt) *verb*, **detonated, detonating. detonation** *noun*.

detour A longer way to get somewhere: *We had to take a detour because the main highway was being repaired.* Noun.
　○ To cause to make a detour: *The police detoured the traffic because of the accident.* Verb.
de·tour (dē′tùr) *noun, plural* **detours;** *verb,* **detoured, detouring.**

detract To take away from the value or beauty of something: *The noisy people detracted from our enjoyment of the movie.* **de·tract** (dit rakt′) *verb,* **detracted, detracting.**

detrimental Harmful: *Smoking is detrimental to your health.* **det·ri·men·tal** (de′trə ment əl) *adjective.*

devastate 1. To destroy; ruin: *The hurricane devastated the small towns along the coast.* 2. To shock; distress: *My brother was devastated when his girlfriend broke up with him.* **dev·as·tate** (dev′ə stāt′) *verb,* **devastated, devastating.**

develop 1. To bring or come gradually into being: *I developed an interest in computers while in the third grade.* 2. To grow or cause to grow: *You can develop your muscles by exercising.* 3. To put to use; make available: *That country has not developed its natural resources.* 4. To treat photographic film with a chemical so that an image appears. **de·vel·op** (di vel′əp) *verb,* **developed, developing.**

development 1. The act or process of developing: *The development of a spacecraft that could reach the moon took many years.* 2. An event or happening: *New developments in the story were broadcast every hour.* 3. A group of houses or other buildings on a large area of land. The houses often look alike and are built by one builder. **de·vel·op·ment** (di vel′əp mənt) *noun, plural* **developments.**

deviate To do something in an unusual way: *Sometimes it's fun and exciting to deviate from one's plans on a trip.* **de·vi·ate** (dē′vē āt) *verb,* **deviated, deviating. deviation** *noun.*

device 1. Something made or invented for a particular purpose. A can opener, a toothbrush, and a clock are devices. 2. A plan or scheme; trick: *Clearing the throat is sometimes just a device for getting attention.* **de·vice** (di vīs′) *noun, plural* **devices.**

devil 1. the Devil. The chief spirit of evil. 2. A wicked, mischievous, or very energetic person: *That sister of yours is a little devil.* **dev·il** (dev′əl) *noun, plural* **devils.**

devious Sneaky; untrustworthy: *a devious mind.* **devious** (dē′vē əs) *adjective.*

devise To think out; invent; plan: *We devised a secret code that no one could decipher.* **de·vise** (di vīz′) *verb,* **devised, devising.**

devote To give effort, attention, or time to some purpose; dedicate: *I want to devote all my energy to studying dancing.* **de·vote** (di vōt′) *verb,* **devoted, devoting.**

devoted Loyal; faithful: *My devoted friend would do anything for me.* **de·vot·ed** (di vō′tid) *adjective.*

devotion A strong affection; faithfulness: *They felt great devotion to their grandparents.* **de·vo·tion** (di vō′shən) *noun, plural* **devotions.**

devour 1. To eat; consume: *The hungry child devoured the sandwich.* 2. To destroy: *The flames devoured the house.* **de·vour** (di vour′) *verb,* **devoured, devouring.**

devout 1. Very religious: *devout church members.* 2. Sincere; earnest: *You have my devout wishes for your success in the school play.* **de·vout** (di vout′) *adjective.*

dew Moisture from the air that forms drops on cool surfaces. Dew gathers on grass, plants, and trees during the night.
Other words that sound like this are do and due. **dew** (dü or dü) *noun, plural* **dews.**

dewlap The skin that hangs loose under the throat of cattle and certain other animals. **dew·lap** (dü′lap or dü′lap) *noun, plural* **dewlaps.**

dexterity Skill in using the hands: *Both magicians and pianists need great dexterity.* **dex·ter·i·ty** (dek ster′i tē) *noun.*

WORD HISTORY

The word **dexterity** goes back to a Latin word meaning "right" or "right hand." Since most people are right-handed, the right side used to be associated with strength, skill, and ability.

diabetes A disease in which there is too much sugar in the blood. A person with diabetes either

 200

Look for examples of all of these types of information on these dictionary pages.

- How to divide a word into syllables
- What part of speech a word is
- Different forms of a word
- The history of a word

 diabetic ⇒ **diaper** **D**

cannot make or cannot use enough insulin, the substance the body needs to use sugar properly. The word *diabetes* is used with a singular verb. **di•a•be•tes** (dī′ə bē′tis *or* dī′ə bē′tēz) *noun.*

diabetic Having or having to do with diabetes. *Adjective.*
○ A person who has diabetes. *Noun.*
di•a•bet•ic (dī′ə bet′ik) *adjective; noun, plural* **diabetics.**

diabolic Very wicked or evil: *a diabolic scheme to conquer the world.* **di•a•bol•ic** (dī ə bol′ik) *adjective.* **diabolical** *adjective.*

diagnosis An opinion about what is wrong with a person or animal formed after looking at the patient and studying the symptoms: *a diagnosis of chicken pox.* **di•ag•no•sis** (dī′əg nō′sis) *noun, plural* **diagnoses** (dī′əg nō′sēz).

diagonal Having a slant: *The dress had a pattern of diagonal stripes. Adjective.*
○ A straight line that connects the opposite corners of a square or rectangle. *Noun.*
di•ag•o•nal (dī ag′ə nəl) *adjective; noun, plural* **diagonals.**

diagram A plan or sketch that shows the parts of a thing or how the parts are put together: *We'll use this diagram of the model airplane when we build it. Noun.*
○ To show by a diagram; make a diagram of: *It's easier to diagram my house than to explain where all the rooms are. Verb.*
di•a•gram (dī′ə gram) *noun, plural* **diagrams;** *verb,* **diagramed, diagraming.**

dial 1. The face of an instrument. A dial is marked with numbers, letters, or other signs that show time, quantity, or some other value. A clock, a compass, and a meter usually have dials. 2. The disk on a radio or television set that is turned to tune in a station or channel. 3. The disk on some telephones that is turned by the finger when the caller is selecting the number being called. *Noun.*
○ 1. To tune in by using a radio or television dial: *Dial another channel and find a better program.* 2. To select numbers when making a telephone call: *The caller dialed a wrong number. Verb.*
di•al (dī′əl *or* dīl) *noun, plural* **dials;** *verb,* **dialed, dialing.**

dialect A form of a language that is spoken in a particular area or by a particular group of people. **di•a•lect** (dī′ə lekt) *noun, plural* **dialects.**

dialogue Conversation, especially in a play, movie, or story: *That play is full of funny dialogue.* **di•a•logue** (dī′əlôg′) *noun, plural* **dialogues.**

dial tone The sound you hear when you first pick up a telephone.

diameter 1. A straight line passing through the center of a circle or sphere, from one side to the other. 2. The length of such a line; the width or thickness of something round: *The diameter of the earth is about 8,000 miles.* **di•a•me•ter** (dī am′i tər) *noun, plural* **diameters.**

diameter

diamond 1. A mineral that consists of pure carbon in the form of a clear or pale crystal. It is the hardest natural material known. 2. A figure having four sides and four angles that is shaped like this. 3. A playing card marked with one or more red diamonds. 4. **diamonds.** The suit of cards marked with this figure ♦. 5. The space on a baseball field that is inside the lines that connect the bases. **di•a•mond** (dī′mənd *or* dī′ə mənd) *noun, plural* **diamonds.**

A baseball field is called a diamond because of its shape.

diaper A baby's underwear made of soft, folded cloth or other material. **dia•per** (dī′pər *or* dī′ə pər) *noun, plural* **diapers.**

PRONUNCIATION KEY:
at ā ape fär câre end mē it ice pierce hot ōld song fôrk
oil out up ūse rūle pull tûrn chin sing shop thin this
hw in white; zh in treasure. The symbol ə stands for the unstressed vowel sound in about, taken, pencil, lemon, and circus.

Thesaurus

A **thesaurus** is similar to a dictionary, but instead of giving word meanings, it lists synonyms and antonyms. A thesaurus can be especially useful when you are looking for just the right word to use. For example, you might want to describe how *helpful* the new treatment for diabetes is—but without using that tired, overworked adjective. You could look up *helpful* in a thesaurus and find an entry that looks like this:

Synonyms are words with almost the same meanings.

> assistive
>
> **helpful**   *adjective*   accommodating, advantageous, assistive, beneficial, convenient, cooperative, eager to please, effective, fruitful, good for, handy, obliging, of service, of use, productive, useful, valuable, willing to help, worthwhile.
> ANTONYM   inconvenient; unhelpful; unobliging; useless
>
> useless

Antonyms are words with opposite meanings.

Which synonym would you decide to use?

A thesaurus can also be helpful when you are trying to decide how to express your thoughts about a big idea or topic. If you can't seem to come up with the right words, look up the subject—for example, *cure*—and see what you find.

> **cure** *noun*   **1** alleviation, antidote, elixir, fix, healing, help, medicine, remedy, restorative, therapeutic, treatment.

These are only a few of the words listed in one thesaurus for that subject. Just think about how helpful these words might be.

A thesaurus might give more information than simple lists of words.

This thesaurus looks very similar to a dictionary. It includes a definition for each **entry word**. The definition is followed by a **sample sentence** featuring the word. This thesaurus also includes **guide words** at the top of the page.

baby

baby *n.* a very young child or animal: The *baby* is only ten months old.
Synonyms
infant a child too young to walk or talk: You need to carry an *infant*.
newborn a baby that has just been born: The *newborn* and her mother go home from the hospital.

beautiful

beat *n.* a repeated sound, usually with a regular occurrence: Tap your foot to the *beat*.
Synonyms
pounding I could feel the *pounding* of my own heart.
rhythm The *rhythm* of the rain put me to sleep last night.

This thesaurus does not include definitions, only sample sentences.

wakeful adjective **1** *he had been wakeful all night* AWAKE, restless, restive, tossing and turning. ANTONYM asleep.

2 *I was suddenly wakeful* ALERT, watchful, vigilant, on the lookout, on one's guard, attentive, heedful, wary. ANTONYM inattentive.

walk verb **1** *they walked along the road* STROLL, saunter, amble, trudge, plod, dawdle, hike, tramp, tromp, slog, stomp, trek, march, stride, sashay, glide, troop, patrol, wander, ramble, tread, prowl, promenade, roam, traipse; stretch one's legs; *informal* mosey, hoof it; *formal* peram-

Types of Resource Books, continued

Encyclopedia

An **encyclopedia** is a series of books with articles that give facts about many different topics. Each book is called a **volume**. The volumes and articles are arranged in alphabetical order. You can use an encyclopedia for a broad overview of a subject.

An article about Diabetes would be in this volume.

This is where you would find information about gila monsters.

Most encyclopedias have a volume called an **index**. The index lists other related subjects to look up.

Some encyclopedias are on a computer disk. You can read the information from the disk on your computer screen.

Guide words are used on encyclopedia pages to make it easy to flip through and find the specific article you want to read.

Gila Monsters   223

The **entry word** of an article is its title.

Headings tell what each section in an article is about.

The Gila monster is one of only two species of venomous lizards in the world. Unlike venomous snakes, Gilas do not inject venom through hollow fangs. Instead, the Gila monster has a set of large, grooved teeth in their lower jaw. The venom enters their prey through these grooves when the Gila monster chews. Very little venom is actually introduced in a Gila monster's bite. Most Gila bites are non-fatal for humans.

The **Gila monster's physical features** are very distinctive. Some species of Gila monsters have pink or orange markings appearing as an unbroken band across their back.

The Gila monsters are known for their distinct markings. Most Gilas are black with pink or orange markings. They are also the largest lizards in the United States. Gilas measure up to about 22 inches (56 cm) in length. Capable of eating relatively large meals, the Gila monster stores fat in its tail and body to conserve energy. Since this ability keeps them from having to search constantly for food, Gila monsters spend much of their lives underground.

The contributor of this article is Alan Huffman, Professor of Zoology at the University of Virginia.

Distribution and Habitat

Gila monsters are primarily located in the southwestern region of the United States and northern Mexico. Areas with the highest concentration of Gila populations include Arizona, southeastern California, southern Nevada, southwestern Utah, and southwestern New Mexico. Though they are not listed as endangered by the United States Endangered Species Act, Gilas are still a threatened species. Many of the states that are home to Gilas have their own laws protecting the reptiles.

Gilas live primarily in the desert. They prefer to reside in areas with just enough moisture to support a few shrubs. They also like rocky foothills and grasslands. Most of the time, they can be found hiding in burrows or under rocks. They have also been found in areas with elevations up to 5,000 feet. Unfortunately, human beings are the greatest threat to their habitats. Overgrazing, truck farming, and cotton planting are destroying the Gila's natural habitat.

Gila Monsters' habitat at a glance
Named after the Gila River in Arizona, Gila Monsters can be found throughout the American Southwest and Mexico.

The **author** of each encyclopedia article is chosen because he or she is an expert on the topic.

Other Print Resources

Newspapers

A **newspaper** is a daily or weekly series of publications that presents news of interest on the local, state, national, and world levels. People read newspapers to get information. You can use newspapers to find information about current events. You can look at old newspapers to help you write about something that happened in the past.

News Articles

Newspapers contain **news articles**. These are factual accounts of current events. As you read a news article you should find the answers to five key questions (sometimes referred to as the "Five Ws") about the event it describes: *Who? What? When? Where? Why?*

New Hope for Diabetics

The headline grabs readers' attention and gives a quick idea of the story content.

The lead paragraph gives a summary of the story.

MAY 9, 2014   It's long been established that diabetics have to walk a fine line when treating their condition. Insulin has to be injected in precise amounts. Too much could send a person into a coma from a sudden drop in blood-sugar levels. Not enough would fail to keep blood sugar under control. A new kind of drug could be the answer.

It's called exenatide, made from the hormone exendin-4. Dr. John Eng discovered the hormone in his research with animal venom. He studied the Gila monster, a poisonous lizard found in Mexico and the southwestern United States. People bitten by the Gila monster often suffered from an inflamed pancreas, causing an increase in the production of insulin.

Thanks to the Gila monster's venom and Dr. Eng's research, diabetics now have a new medication that's superior to older drugs used for treatment. Exenatide remains in the bloodstream longer, so it doesn't have to be taken as often as other medications. It can also help people manage their weight, as it helps control appetite.

Diabetes is a very serious condition, and Type II diabetes is becoming more common. "As a clinician working with diabetics," Dr. Eng says, "the struggle is to try and achieve as much glucose (blood sugar) control as you can to prevent bad complications like kidney failure, retinal disease that can cause blindness, and nerve damage that causes loss of sensation in the feet." His new drug can help diabetics control the illness, instead of the illness controlling them.

News stories often quote experts, eyewitnesses, and other voices of authority.

Editorials

Most newspapers also usually include **editorials**. These are opinion-based pieces of writing on topics of interest to readers. Editorials often appear in their own section of a newspaper and look different from news stories. This is so that readers will know that editorials present opinions in addition to facts. You can use editorials to give you ideas to write a persuasive essay or to present the opinions of other people.

Stopping the Diabetes Epidemic

Medical professionals used to refer to type II diabetes as adult-onset diabetes, because people over the age of 40 were most at risk for developing it. The term "adult-onset" is no longer appropriate because more and more children and teens are being diagnosed with type II diabetes. We have to stop the rise of this disease before it gets even worse.

Between 1997 and 2012, the incidence of type II diabetes increased by 27%. In 1997, research showed that 5.1% of American adults were diagnosed, compared with 6.5% in 2012. It's not just adults who are suffering. Studies have shown that, among diabetic children, 30-50% have type II diabetes, compared with less than 5% before 1994.

This rise in type II diabetes is linked to a rise in obesity and an unhealthy lifestyle. Americans today are eating more and exercising less. This is especially a problem for children. Overweight children are likely to suffer from health problems later in life. Early intervention is the key to preventing and treating type II diabetes. If children learn early on to eat healthy and stay active, they'll maintain those healthy habits through adulthood.

Elementary and middle schools should improve their physical education programs. Many of them are not rigorous or goal-oriented. School programs should encourage children who do not like team sports to pursue other exercise activities, like jogging, biking, or swimming. Schools should also teach nutrition through high school and offer healthy meals at lunchtime. As a society, we need to look after our children and ensure that they grow up with healthy habits and lead healthy lives.

*The author's **opinion** is clearly stated.*

Facts are used to support the opinion.

*Editorials often end with a specific **call to action**.*

Other Print Resources, continued

Magazines

A magazine is a special collection of articles. Some magazines are written about one interest or hobby, such as sports or music. Others are targeted for one group of people—teens or children, for example. Still other magazines, including news and entertainment magazines, are published to appeal to a wide variety of readers.

Magazines are published on a schedule such as monthly or weekly. For example, a monthly magazine publishes a new issue every month. Magazines are sometimes called periodicals. A period is a span of time. You can use magazines for a variety of writing purposes. Past issues of magazines are also helpful in writing about events that happened in the past.

NATIONAL PROGRAM
for DIABETICS

The headline and lead paragraph of a magazine article are designed to draw readers' attention.

Headings help to break up the text of magazine articles, which can be several pages long. The headings also tell what the sections are about.

With diabetes on the rise and many Americans overeating and not exercising enough, it's clear that something has to be done about this national health problem. The National Diabetes Education Program (NDEP) was developed to intervene with the growing diabetes crisis. Part of the National Institutes of Health located in Bethesda, Maryland, the NDEP provides valuable support and services to diabetics and their families.

WHAT DOES THE NDEP DO?

Raising awareness and educating the public on diabetes are the primary goals of the NDEP. Its objectives are to teach people about the dangers of diabetes and the lifestyle choices that can put people at risk, and to help diabetics improve their diet and exercise habits so they can manage the disease. The NDEP also promotes health care policies that make quality diabetes care accessible to patients.

They do all this by building partnerships with health

organizations that are concerned with diabetes and related conditions. The NDEP is partly sponsored by the National Institute of Diabetes and Digestive and Kidney Diseases, as well as the Division of Diabetes Translation of the Centers for Disease Control and Prevention. Over 200 other organizations work together to help the NDEP meet its goals.

This program pays special attention to high-risk groups, including African Americans, Hispanics, Native Americans, and Alaska natives. People belonging to these ethnic groups have a higher risk for developing diabetes. The NDEP also runs diabetes education campaigns for doctors and other health care professionals so they can better treat diabetic patients.

WHY IS THIS NECESSARY?

Diabetes affects approximately 20.8 million people in the United States. Of those, it is estimated that 6.2 million are undiagnosed. Diabetes can have serious complications, especially if it goes untreated. Heart attack, stroke, and kidney disease are among the most common consequences of diabetes. In the U.S., diabetes is one of the leading causes of disability and death.

Type II diabetes is often preventable. With information and resources, even people who are at risk can adopt healthy habits that will prevent or delay the onset of diabetes. A healthy diet and regular exercise will help people maintain a normal weight, which in turn decreases the likelihood of developing diabetes. If a patient is diagnosed with type II diabetes, it can be controlled with diet, exercise, and medication. The NDEP makes this information and health care available to the people who need it the most.

Most magazines use color and plenty of visuals to make the pages more attractive and interesting to readers.

Write a
Story Scene

Model Study

Story Scene

Did you try a new restaurant or go to the park this weekend? What was it like? To help readers imagine what you did, you can write a **story scene**.

A good story scene uses lively, specific words to present a clear image. It tells where and when the action takes place. It also includes **sensory details** to describe the events.

Vivid, memorable story scenes are often included in stories and novels. But a good story scene can also stand on its own. It paints a picture with words so readers can imagine they are there!

Read the student model on page 229W. Look for the features of a good story scene.

STORY SCENE

A good story scene

☑ helps readers imagine something that has happened

☑ uses vivid and precise language to tell where and when the action takes place

☑ includes sensory details to describe the events.

The San Felipe
by Eva Martens

Eva introduces
**where and
when** the
scene takes
place.

The ship sailed from Spain in 1690. Powerful and majestic, it stood nearly ten stories high and stretched out for over seventy feet. Its three giant masts stood proudly. Together they supported five enormous sails. On the very top flew a colorful flag. Its shades of deep red and bright yellow formed a vibrant design. The flag whipped and cracked as it waved in the wind.

**Sensory
details** help
readers know
what sailing on
a tall ship was
like.

The ship's massive body looked strong and sturdy. Squeaky planks of wood formed the main deck. Inside were layers of narrow decks used for sleeping and storing supplies. Each level smelled of gunpowder and salted meats.

**Vivid and
precise words**
paint a clear
picture of the
ship and its
journey.

The ship sailed grandly through the frigid ocean water. Waves crashed against its strong bow. With each wave, salty water drenched the deck. Soon the San Felipe would be in America.

Student Model

The front of a ship is called
the bow. The rear is called
the stern. ▼

Write a Story Scene

WRITING PROMPT What events or people in history do you find fascinating? Have you experienced anything that reminds you of the past or how people lived back then? Can you imagine tall ships sailing for the New World or what it was like when Native Americans first encountered European explorers?

Think about a person or event from the past, or an experience that taught you more about the past or about your place in history. Then write a story scene that

- makes the person, event, or experience "come alive"
- includes vivid and precise words
- uses details that appeal to the senses.

Prewrite

Here are some tips for planning your story scene.

1 Choose a Good Topic

Choose a topic that interests you. You should also choose a topic that you remember well or can find enough information about. Jot down several ideas, and then select the best one. Ryan used a chart to help him choose a topic.

Ideas	Good Topic for a Story Scene?
outfits worn by Spanish explorers	probably not enough information for a whole scene
early European sailing ships	I could not include any personal experiences
traditional Native American feast	I have been to a feast with my friend Shawn, so I could write details I know about

2 Complete Your Writing Road Map

Your story scene of a meal will sound a whole lot different if you're writing it to make your kid brother laugh than if you're writing it to teach an adult how to cook it! Get clear on your audience and purpose with an FATP chart.

FATP Chart

Form: _story scene_

Audience: _classmates_

Topic: _a Native American feast_

Purpose: _to tell what it was like at the feast and describe the foods I ate_

TechTIP

List details as phrases or sentences. Then use cut and paste from the Edit menu to move details around as you need to.

3 Gather Your Details

Think about your topic. What is there to see, hear, smell, feel, and taste? Trap the sensory details in a **five-senses diagram**. At the same time, you can gather some vivid, precise words.

I see . . .	• fire <u>leaping</u> in a pit • people <u>swirling</u> around me
I hear . . .	• a <u>crackling</u> fire • lively conversation • <u>crispy</u> pumpkin seeds
I feel . . .	• <u>squishy</u> soft fry bread • smooth squash
I smell . . .	• <u>pungent</u> garlic • spicy onions
I taste . . .	• <u>tender</u> deer meat • sweet pudding

Five-Senses Diagram

A Native American dish might include wild onions. ▼

Draft

Now that your plan is in place, it's time to start writing.

- **Grab Your Reader's Interest** Start out with vivid sensory words, a snippet of dialogue, a question, or an unexpected fact to get your reader's attention right away.

> Fresh, spicy, sweet, and absolutely delicious! That's how I'd describe what I ate during a Native American feast last week.

Ryan uses sensory words in the beginning to spark the reader's curiosity.

- **Add Details to Develop Your Description** Adding a lot of details to your writing will make it interesting and help your story scene "come to life." Think about how to use details to describe events.

From Ryan's Draft

> When my friend Shawn and I arrived, everyone was talking, laughing, and telling stories. Cooks were busy over an open-pit fire, cooking large slabs of fresh deer meat. I could hear sizzling and popping as hot grease dripped into the flames.

Ryan adds details to tell more about the feast—what he saw, heard, and smelled.

◄ These young Apache women are baking different kinds of corn bread.

Reflect

- Do you have a first sentence that hooks the reader?

- Do you have enough details to give a full picture of your topic?

DRAFTING TIPS
Trait: **Focus and Unity**

If Your Writing Sounds Like a List . . .

Sometimes using too many disconnected details can make your writing repetitive and choppy. To keep your story scene from sounding like a list, focus in on one part of the person or thing you are describing.

Zero In on a Part

Start by listing on index cards various parts of the experience on which you could focus your description.

the people	the food	the dances	the stories

Then, choose the card with the idea that is the most interesting to you. Zero in on that idea by expanding it with details and examples. Mention the other ideas only in passing, if at all. Ryan chose to focus his story scene on the food.

From Ryan's Draft

> The smell of deer meat flavored with garlic and onions made my stomach growl. The wood smoke and mix of aromas tickled my nostrils.

Revise

As you revise your work, keep in mind your audience and purpose. Will your writing make the subject come alive for your readers?

1 **Evaluate Your Work**

Read your story scene aloud to a partner. Have your partner draw sketches based on the story scene. When you're done reading, look at the sketches. Ask yourself:

- **About the Form** Do the sketches show what I was trying to paint with words?

- **About the Sensory Details** Do I need to add more vivid details to give the reader a sense of being there?

▲ Tribal dress might be worn at a Native American powwow.

Revision in Action

Ryan's Draft

When my friend Shawn and I arrived, everyone was talking, laughing, and telling stories. Cooks were busy over an open-pit fire, cooking large slabs of fresh deer meat. I could hear sizzling and popping as hot grease dripped into the flames. The smell of deer meat flavored with garlic and onions made my stomach growl. The wood smoke and mix of aromas tickled my nostrils.

"Here, try some fry bread," said Shawn. "That'll help until the rest of the meal is ready." Finally, someone handed me a plate of food.

Ryan thinks:

"This paragraph could use a few more vivid words to liven it up."

"Will everyone know what fry bread is like?"

"I have to add some details here!"

2 **Mark Your Changes**

Clarify To make your story scene clearer, you may have to add more details. Use a ∧ mark to

- add more sensory details

- add information to elaborate on or support your ideas.

Delete Text To take out unimportant details, use a delete mark: ⟿ .

Rearrange Text Move sentences around if you need to improve the flow of ideas.

Reflect

- How could you change parts of your story scene to make them more sensory?

Revising Marks	**MARK**	∧	⤺	⌐	⟿	¶
	WHAT IT MEANS	Insert something.	Move to here.	Replace with this.	Take out.	Make a new paragraph.

Revised Draft

When my friend Shawn and I arrived, everyone was talking,
                              sweating over a crackling
laughing, and telling stories. Cooks were ~~busy over an~~ open-pit

fire, cooking large slabs of fresh deer meat. I could hear sizzling

and popping as hot grease dripped into the flames. The smell
                    pungent
of deer meat flavored with∧garlic and onions made my stomach

growl. The wood smoke and mix of aromas tickled my nostrils.

    "Here, try some fry bread," said Shawn. ⅄That'll help until the

rest of the meal is ready." Finally, someone handed me a plate

~~of food.~~∧ filled with tender deer meat, wild rice, fresh beans,
      ∧acorn squash, and pumpkin seeds.

    Fry bread is like a doughnut, but thinner and
    without the hole in the middle.

Ryan added vivid words and sensory details.

Ryan added an explanation to clarify.

Ryan fleshed out his story scene with specific details.

Edit and Proofread

Does your story scene paint a vivid picture? If so, you're now ready to fix language errors. This is what you do when you edit and proofread your work:

- **Check the Grammar** Make sure that you have used correct and conventional grammar throughout. In particular, check that you are using verbs correctly. (See page 237W.)

- **Check the Spelling** Spell-check can help, but it's not enough. For errors with suffixes, you'll have to read your work carefully, and perhaps use a dictionary. (See page 238W.)

- **Check the Mechanics** Errors in punctuation and capitalization can make your work hard to understand. In particular, check that you use commas correctly in lists. (See page 239W.)

Use these marks to edit and proofread your story scene.

Editing and Proofreading Marks

MARK	WHAT IT MEANS	MARK	WHAT IT MEANS
∧	Insert something.	╱	Make lowercase.
∧	Add a comma.	℘	Delete, take something out.
∧	Add a semicolon.	⊄	Make new paragraph.
⊙	Add a period.	⬭	Spell out.
⊙	Add a colon.	⌒	Replace with this.
⋎ ⋎	Add quotation marks.	∼	Change order of letters or words.
⋎	Add an apostrophe.	#	Insert space.
≡	Capitalize.	⌣	Close up, no space here.

Reflect

- What kinds of errors did you find? What can you do to keep from making them?

GrammarWorkout

Check Frequently Misused Verbs

- **Lie and Lay** Use *lie* to describe what people or animals do when they sleep. Use *lay* to describe what you do *to* something—for instance, laying a book down.

  EXAMPLES John needs to **lie** down because he's very tired. Please **lay** the compass on the table.

Lie and *lay* are especially tricky because *lay* is the past tense form of *lie!*

  EXAMPLE Yesterday, I **lay** down for a quick nap and slept five hours!

- **Sit and Set** To *sit* you need a chair. But, you can *set* something down by putting it on a flat surface.

  EXAMPLES Roger, please **sit** in this chair. I **set** the box down on the ground.

- **Rise and Raise** When something *rises,* it goes up by itself. But if you make something else go up, you *raise* it.

  EXAMPLES The sun will **rise** at six o'clock. Can you **raise** the flag?

Find the Trouble Spots

I'm so glad we were able to ~~rise~~ raise people's interest in foods from other cultures. Our social studies class prepared a Native American feast at school. My friends and I helped lie the food on the table. As we ~~sat~~ set each different dish down, we inhaled the delicious aromas raising from the pots and bowls.

Find two more verb errors to fix.

Edit and Proofread, continued

Spelling Workout

Suffix	Meaning
-ful	full of
-hood	quality of
-ive	having qualities of
-less	without
-ly	in a certain way
-ment	an action or process
-ness	state of
-y	having the quality of

Check Words with Suffixes

A suffix is added at the end of the word. It changes the word's meaning. Study the suffixes in the chart.

When you add a suffix to a base word, the spelling of the base word may change. If you are not sure about the spelling, check the dictionary. Here are some rules that generally apply to the spelling of a base word:

- When you add the suffix *-ful* to a base word that ends in a consonant plus *y*, change the *y* to *i* and then add *-ful*.

  EXAMPLE   beauty + *-ful* ⟶ beautiful

- When you add the suffix *-y* to a base word that ends with silent *e*, drop the *e* before adding *-y*.

  EXAMPLE   spice + *-y* ⟶ spicy

- When you add the suffix *-ness* or *-less* to a base word ending in a consonant plus *y*, change the *y* to *i* before adding the suffix.

  EXAMPLES   happy + *-ness* ⟶ happiness
  pity + *-less* ⟶ pitiless

Find the Trouble Spots

The smells of different foods cooking mingled together in the smoke̶y air. Soon Shawn and I sat down to a bounty̶ful feast. (We knew it hadn't been easey to prepare!) The servings were plentyful, and everyone commented on the tastyness of the meal.

Find three more spelling errors to fix.

Mechanics Workout

Check Serial Commas

When you list more than two things in your writing, you need to separate them with commas. Without commas, the list will be confusing or unclear.

CONFUSING   Good squash is **creamy moist rich and smooth.**

CLEAR   Good squash is **creamy, moist, rich, and smooth.**

Be sure to use a comma between the next-to-last item in the list and the word *and*. This comma is called a **serial comma**. Without it, your meaning may be unclear.

CONFUSING   I greatly admire **my parents, George Washington and Abraham Lincoln.**

CLEAR   I greatly admire **my parents, George Washington, and Abraham Lincoln.**

Find the Trouble Spots

The guests arrived looking tired͜ weak͜ and weary. We had prepared roasted pork seasoned with peppercorns, salt͜ and sage. We also made a stew with potatoes, wild onions and squash. We hoped everyone would rest relax and replenish their bodies.

Find three more places to add a comma.

Model Study

Literary Response

When you read a good story, you probably want to recommend it to as many people as possible. You can share your thoughts by writing a **literary response.**

When you write a **literary response**, you explain why you liked—or didn't like—a story. You write your opinion about different parts of it and support your opinions with evidence from the text.

Read the student model on page 241W. It shows the features of a good literary response.

LITERARY RESPONSE

A good literary response

☑ quickly summarizes what you read

☑ states your ideas and claims about the literature

☑ expresses your personal response to the literature

☑ uses evidence from the text to support your opinions

☑ may mention what you learned from the text.

Feature Checklist

Monsoon Summer
by Mitali Perkins
Reviewed by Angela Acevedo

The writer introduces the work. She includes her name as the person who reviewed it.

Do you know what a monsoon is? It's a really heavy tropical rainstorm. That word in the title of the book made me want to read it. I always like books that take me to faraway places, and this one did not disappoint me.

The writer gives her **personal response** to the work.

Monsoon Summer is about a young girl named Jasmine Gardner—"Jazz" for short. Her mother is from India. Jazz is supposed to go to India for the summer and work with her mother in an orphanage there. That is the place where her mother grew up before she came to California. Jazz has a hard time settling in at first, but the place starts growing on her.

The writer gives a **brief summary** of the story.

I think this book is mostly about friendship and traditions. In the orphanage, Jasmine meets a girl named Danita, who becomes her friend. Danita takes her through the cluttered streets of the city of Pune in the state of Maharashtra. She helps Jazz appreciate her heritage.

The writer supports **opinions** with **evidence** from the book.

I can identify with Jazz. My family came from Paraguay many years ago, before I was born. My family is thinking of taking a trip there next summer. Like Jazz, I am scared to go. Like Jazz, I think I will learn a lot about myself.

The writer sums up why she liked the story and tells what she learned from it.

Student Model

Development of Ideas

What's It Like?

A good news report about a football game does more than just tell the final score. It also shows a few of the best plays and tells something about how the game felt. To keep your writing interesting and satisfying, you also need to add details and examples to develop your ideas.

How Do You Develop Ideas?

When writing is well-developed, it has plenty of details to support the writer's ideas. It leaves readers feeling satisfied.

For a literary response, a writer wants readers to understand his or her opinions about a poem, story, or novel. So, the writer supports each idea or claim with evidence and specific examples from the literature. Below, Zeke wants readers to understand how he feels about a book he read.

> Worlds Apart by Kathleen Larr is about the first English settlers of the Carolinas. I've always wondered what Native Americans thought of settlers, because their cultures were so different. I think the book shows how two people can learn to accept and appreciate their differences. In the book, some young people, like the English teenager Christopher and the Sewee Indian Asha-po, become friends.

The writer uses **evidence** from the book to support his claim.

Study the rubric on page 243W. What is the difference between a paper with a score of 2 and one with a score of 4?

Development of Ideas

	How thoughtful and interesting is the writing?	How well are the ideas or claims explained and supported?
4 Wow!	The writing engages the reader with meaningful ideas or claims and presents them in a way that is interesting and appropriate to the audience, purpose, and type of writing.	The ideas or claims are fully explained and supported. • The ideas or claims are well developed with important details, evidence, and/or description. • The writing feels complete, and the reader is satisfied.
3 Aaah.	Most of the writing engages the reader with meaningful ideas or claims and presents them in a way that is interesting and appropriate to the audience, purpose, and type of writing.	Most of the ideas or claims are explained and supported. • Most of the ideas or claims are developed with important details, evidence, and/or description. • The writing feels mostly complete, but the reader still has some questions.
2 Hmmm.	Some of the writing engages the reader with meaningful ideas or claims and presents them in a way that is interesting and appropriate to the audience, purpose, and type of writing.	Some of the ideas or claims are explained and supported. • Only some of the ideas or claims are developed. Details, evidence, and/or description, are limited or not relevant. • The writing leaves the reader with many questions.
1 Huh?	The writing does not engage the reader. It is not appropriate to the audience, purpose, and type of writing.	The ideas or claims are not explained or supported. The ideas lack details, evidence, and/or description, and the writing leaves the reader unsatisfied.

Development of Ideas, continued

Compare Writing Samples

A good literary response presents the writer's feelings. It develops the writer's ideas with evidence and interesting examples. Study the two examples of a literary response on this page.

Well-Developed

Behind the Mountains
by Edwidge Danticat
Reviewed by Eunji Yeong

This book tells about a Haitian girl named Celiane and her two brothers, Mo and Aline. Their father is in New York City. He is trying to earn money to bring the family there to live. Celiane misses her father, but she isn't sure that she could ever leave Haiti, where she has grown up.

I can identify with Celiane because I left my home country, too. It's hard to be a family when your mother or father is far away. The book does not tell how Victor, Celiane's father, felt in New York. But he must have felt lonely for them. He must have felt frightened, too, because the book takes place when there were riots in Port-au-Prince, Haiti's capital.

The writer supports her ideas with **evidence** from the story.

The writer gives a **personal response** and explains her feelings.

Not Developed

Behind the Mountains
by Edwidge Danticat
Reviewed by Ania Banerjee

This is a good book. I enjoyed it very much. It's about a girl in Haiti named Celiane. Her father wants her to come live with him in New York.

The book takes place during a tough time in Haiti. Everyone is fighting in the streets of the main city.

The writer gives a **personal response**, but doesn't explain it.

The writer gives little evidence to support ideas. The reader will have a lot of questions.

Evaluate for Development of Ideas

Now read carefully the literary response below. Use the rubric on page 243W to score it.

▲ Many Cuban immigrants have settled in Miami, Florida.

Flight to Freedom
by Ana Veciana-Suarez

Reviewed by John Langley

I don't really know what it means to leave your home country to find freedom. However, when I read *Flight to Freedom,* I understood why so many Cuban people came to the United States. I also feel for the teenage girl, Yara, who has to say goodbye to her home and adapt to a new country.

Yara's father tries to hold on to the family's Cuban identity. He hopes they will be back in Cuba soon. She and her older sister, Ileana, have to be Cubans at home but Americans in school. I think every young person growing up feels pressure like this. You don't know who you are.

Yara's lucky. She becomes friends in school with Jane. Jane and her family show respect for Yara's family's customs. I can see how that could be good for Yara. She would not have to choose. She might be able to live in both worlds.

Flight to Freedom is written as a diary. I don't usually like that kind of book. I prefer stories like on TV. But in this book I got a chance to get inside Yara's head and see America and her new life through her eyes.

One thing she said was very interesting to me. She asked what her life would have been like if Fidel Castro had not come into power. One event can change the lives of many people. What big event like that could change mine?

Does the writer cite evidence from the book to support his ideas?

How well does the writer explain his personal response to the book?

Does the writing seem complete? Has the writer answered all your questions?

Raise the Score

These papers have been scored using the
Development of Ideas Rubric on page 243W.
Study each paper to see why it got the score it did.

▲ Esperanza grows up in a
neighborhood like this.

Overall Score: 4

The House on Mango Street
by Sandra Cisneros
Reviewed by Kari Desai

The **questions** get readers interested. Then the writer gives a **brief summary** of the book.

What's it like growing up? Do you like where you live? When you read this book, you can compare your feelings to those of a young girl named Esperanza. It tells her feelings about growing up on Mango Street in a Mexican neighborhood in Chicago.

The writer presents her **personal response** to what she read.

I like how Cisneros divided the book into small parts. Each part describes one experience. That helped me focus on one thing at a time. In one part, for example, she talks about not liking her name. That made me think of a time when I wanted to change mine.

The writer develops and supports her ideas with **evidence or examples** from the book.

Sometimes I felt sad while reading the book. Esperanza seemed so disappointed about her life and where she lived. But then I thought about how your experiences can change who you become— they help you know what you want and don't want.

The ending sums up the writer's response so the writing feels complete.

The House on Mango Street is a very thoughtful book. I felt as if I understood Esperanza and what she went through. Because of the way it's written, I can easily find my favorite parts to reread.

The House on Mango Street

The **questions** get readers interested. Then the writer gives a **brief summary** of the book.

What's it like growing up? Do you like where you live? When you read this book, you can compare your feelings to those of a young girl named Esperanza. It tells her feelings about growing up on Mango Street in a Mexican neighborhood in Chicago.

I liked how Cisneros divided the book into small parts. In one part, she tells how her Mama's hair smells. In another part, she talks about not liking her name.

The writer includes some **evidence** to support her opinion, but leaves the reader with a few questions.

Sometimes I felt sad while reading the book. Esperanza seemed so disappointed about her life and where she lived. But then I thought about how your experiences can change who you become—they help you know what you want and don't want.

The ending wraps up the writer's **personal response** to the book, but could be more complete.

The House on Mango Street is a very thoughtful book. I felt as if I understood Esperanza and her feelings.

▲ RAISING *THE SCORE*

The writer should add details to the second paragraph and the conclusion to support her opinion. What questions should she answer for the reader?

Raise the Score, continued

Overall Score: 2

The House on Mango Street

The beginning is not very interesting. The writer needs to condense the ideas to create a **brief summary** of the book.

This book tells about a young girl's thoughts and feelings. Her name is Esperanza. Esperanza lives on Mango Street in a Mexican neighborhood in Chicago. She tells about her parents, brothers, and sister. She even tells about a junk store in the neighborhood and the man who owns it. She describes all the different things that happen as she grows up.

I really liked the way the book is divided into small parts. Each part tells what Esperanza thinks about her family and neighbors.

The writer gives her **personal response**, but it's not clear why she feels this way. The **evidence and examples** are vague and uninteresting.

The ending is incomplete. It leaves the reader wondering how the writer relates to Esperanza.

Sometimes I felt sad while reading the book. Esperanza seemed upset. But then I thought about how even things you don't like can change for the better.

The House on Mango Street is a good book. I can relate to Esperanza.

RAISING *THE SCORE*

The writer needs to develop her ideas with clear examples and interesting details. What can she do to better support her opinions? How can she fix the conclusion?

The House on Mango Street

This book is about a girl who lives on Mango Street. Her family lives in a Mexican neighborhood in Chicago.

I like how the book has short parts. Sometimes a part tells about something she does. Other times it tells about something she's thinking about.

I liked the different descriptions. She tells about her family and neighbors. Everything is told through Esperanza's eyes. You really get to know her.

I liked reading this book. It describes some of the things about growing up I'm familiar with. I can relate!

RAISING *THE SCORE*

The writer needs to give specific details about the book and support her ideas with evidence and examples. What kinds of details and evidence could she add?

Good Beginnings and Endings

What's It Like ?

A good beginning and a good ending are like bookends that hold up your writing. A good beginning makes readers want to read more. A good ending wraps up what you've said and helps your readers remember.

Starting Out Right

Here are some ideas for grabbing your reader's interest right away:

- Start with a question.

> What would you do if your family made you pack up, get on an airplane, and fly to a new country? In Ana Veciana-Suarez's novel Flight to Freedom, people do exactly that. I am very impressed by the main character's strength. Yara is one powerful girl.

- Start with a statistic.

> About 50,000 Cubans came to the United States between 1959 and 1962. This was right after Fidel Castro took over Cuba. Cubans wanted to be free. Ana Veciana-Suarez's novel Flight to Freedom tells the story of one Cuban family who came to America.

- Start with a quotation.

> "We have to be either here or there. . . . We must choose," says Yara at the start of Ana Veciana-Suarez's novel *Flight to Freedom*. Is Yara García a Cuban, like her parents want her to be, or an American, as her friends want her to be? I don't envy her choice.

- Start with a personal connection.

Many Cuban Americans have settled in Miami's Little Havana. ▼

> When I read Ana Veciana-Suarez's novel *Flight to Freedom*, so much seemed familiar. No, it wasn't the Latino names. My family is from Kosovo. What was familiar was the issue of being both from here and from back there. I have to deal with that, too.

The sample below shows a boring beginning. How could you improve it using one of the techniques you've just learned about?

> Well, I read a book by a really good author, and it was awesome. I got so much out of it. I liked it. I think you will, too. The main character is our age. The problems seemed very real to me.

Good Beginnings and Endings, continued

Finishing Strong

A good ending scores major points with readers. You worked hard to share your ideas. Now the ending should help them remember what you've said. Here are some ways to do that:

- End by going back to your main point.

> Yara in Flight to Freedom proves that overcoming problems can make you stronger. Yes, you can live in both worlds. And you can enjoy the best parts of each.

- End by summarizing your ideas.

> In conclusion, Flight to Freedom has taught me important lessons about life. Some people can adjust to new situations. Other people just put up with new things, but in their hearts they never give in. Like Yara's father, their stubbornness is at the heart of who they are.

Traditional Cuban dishes are often served at outdoor festivals. ▼

- End with a question, or answer a question you asked at the start. The following model does both!

> Why does Yara's father believe that someday he will go back to Cuba? Maybe we all like to believe in dreams and miracles. We like to believe that our luck will change. We'll have winning teams in every sport. Our dreams keep us going. What's your dream?

- End with a personal example.

> *Flight to Freedom* has deep personal meaning for me for one last reason. My family moved here from the other side of the United States. That's not a foreign country, but it is far away. We moved from a place where everyone knew everyone to a place where we knew no one. Yara reminds me of me.

- End with a quote. It can be from a famous person or from someone you admire.

> I once heard a song with the line "Freedom is just one more word." That certainly isn't true for the García family. They cherish their freedom.

The sample below shows a weak ending. How could you improve it using one of the techniques you've just learned about?

> This was a really good story. I liked it. It made me think about what's important to me. You should read it, too.

Explain and Support Your Ideas

What's It Like ?

If you're shopping for a cell phone, you want the salesperson to say more than just "Buy this one." You want to hear reasons, details, and explanations. When you write, you're trying to "sell your ideas." Like a good salesperson, you need to support and explain them.

Backing Up What You Say

When you write a literary response, your purpose is to tell how the book made you feel and what you took away from it. If you don't include enough evidence to support your ideas, you won't get your points across.

So, what can you do to meet your purpose? Once you have a beginning that captures your readers' interest, keep your audience reading by adding enough specific details to explain and support your ideas.

Try some of these techniques to explain and support your ideas:

- Include facts and specific details.

> Naming Maya is the title of a book by Uma Krishnaswami. The book tells about the summer Maya spends visiting relatives in India with her mother. Maya explores the city of Chennai. She finds it very different from home.

These **specific details** come straight from the story.

- Add examples from the literature.

> As she tries to adjust to a foreign culture, Maya makes some blunders. For example, one day she takes pictures of a statue of Ganesha, an Indian god. A policeman stops her. He says taking pictures is forbidden.

- Add direct quotations from the literature.

> Maya befriends Kamala Mami, the family's elderly housekeeper. Mami defends Maya. She argues with the policeman who scolds her. "There are thugs and bandits breaking the law all over the city ," she says. "And here you are, harassing a child."

The writer uses a **quotation** from the story to show how Mami defends Maya.

Idols of elephant-headed Hindu God Danesha. These idols are used in festivals in India. ▼

Explain and Support Your Ideas, continued

- Explain your own thoughts in more detail.

> Maya isn't the only person who has trouble adjusting to a new place. We all do. When it seemed like it had been a terrible mistake for my family to move here, my aunt said to give it time. Good things can happen. Now I have friends, and I like my school. I play on the basketball team, and we may even be league champions. If I hadn't moved here, none of this would have happened.

Evaluate for Support

Read carefully the literary responses below. Decide how you could make them better.

Naming Maya provides an interesting look at the culture of modern India. The reader learns about the city of Chennai as Maya explores it. It's a crowded city. The streets are alive with "pedestrians, cyclists, occasional cars, and auto rickshaws." There are many interesting sights. Maya takes pictures of a lot of cool stuff.

The writer uses a **quotation**. Where else would you like to see the novelist's own words?

The writer uses **general words** to describe the city. What specific details or examples could you replace them with?

Maya feels like she's in her mother's way. She says, "Mom seems relieved when I tell her I'll go shopping with Mami. She's probably been wondering what to do with me." Maya feels sad. That's why she makes friends with Kamala Mami. They do a lot of things together.

What could you add or change to develop ideas in this paragraph?

◀ An elephant leads a procession in India.

Write a Literary Response

WRITING PROMPT What is your favorite book or story? Is there a particular character in it that you relate to really well? Did you learn something important from the book?

Think of a book that's important to you. Then write a literary response that includes

- a beginning that captures the reader's interest
- a brief summary of the book
- your personal response or opinions about the book
- an explanation of why it's important to you
- evidence and examples to support your ideas
- a satisfying conclusion.

Prewrite

Here are some tips for planning your writing.

1 Choose a Book That Means a Lot to You

Write about literature that is important to you. If you feel strongly about your subject, your writing will be more interesting. Jot down a few possibilities.

My Favorite Books

Taking Sides by Gary Soto
Hoot by Carl Hiaasen
Code Talkers by Joseph Bruchac

❷ Record Your Thoughts About the Book

Reread or review the book. Record your overall opinion, favorite parts, and important ideas.

Try summarizing all your ideas like Miguel did:

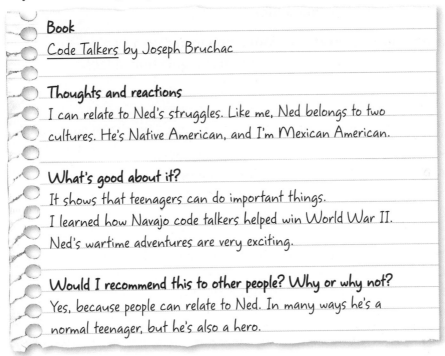

Book
Code Talkers by Joseph Bruchac

Thoughts and reactions
I can relate to Ned's struggles. Like me, Ned belongs to two cultures. He's Native American, and I'm Mexican American.

What's good about it?
It shows that teenagers can do important things.
I learned how Navajo code talkers helped win World War II.
Ned's wartime adventures are very exciting.

Would I recommend this to other people? Why or why not?
Yes, because people can relate to Ned. In many ways he's a normal teenager, but he's also a hero.

Miguel's Notes for His Paper

❸ Gather Support for Your Opinions

Look at the text carefully. Use an **opinion chart** to help you organize and support your opinions.

Opinion Chart

Opinion Chart
I don't think adults realize the important things teenagers can do.

Support
When Ned is little, he's forbidden to speak Navajo. — As a teenager, Ned joins the Marines to fight in World War II. — He uses his language to talk in code. — Ned and other Navajos become heroes.

Reflect

• Do your notes tell how *you* feel about the work?

• Can you support your opinions with evidence and examples?

Draft

Once you know what you want to say, start writing your draft. Use your notes and charts to make your first draft go smoothly. Keep the story or book that you are writing about nearby. That way you can refer to it while you write.

- **Start with a Good Beginning** Think of a way to get your reader's attention right away. You might use a question, a fact, or a quotation.

> What if your country looked down on your people— but also depended on you to win a war? That's what happened to Navajo Marines. Joseph Bruchac's *Code Talkers* tells their story— and the story of Ned, one of those brave Marines.

Miguel used a thought-provoking question to hook the reader.

- **Develop Your Ideas** Use your graphic organizer to guide your writing as you develop your ideas with evidence and examples. If you feel "stuck," stop and look through the book again for inspiration.

From Miguel's Draft

> Sometimes I think adults don't realize the important things young people can do. If they read Ned's story, I'm sure they would change their minds. Not all teenagers just sit around and play video games. Do you? Ned was young when he joined the Marines to fight in World War II. And although he was forbidden to use any words from the Navajo language in school, he and the other Navajo Marines used their language to send top-secret messages. They were heroes.

Miguel used his opinion chart to organize and support his ideas.

Reflect

- Does your draft explain what the book or story means to you?

- Do you support your ideas with evidence?

DRAFTING TIPS
Trait: **Development of Ideas**

If You Can't Write Enough...

Do you suffer from "skimpy" writing? If you don't use enough details to support your ideas, your readers won't understand what you want them to.

Try Getting into an Argument... with Yourself

When you are challenged to prove your ideas, you can usually think of a lot more to say! To come up with support for your ideas, imagine what you might say if you were in an argument.

To argue with confidence, though, you have to know **how** you know things.

Ways You Know Things

1. You go places and experience things.	**5. You read things in newspapers.**
2. You have feelings and thoughts.	**6. People tell you things.**
3. You see things on television.	**7. You hear things on the radio.**
4. You read things in books.	**8. You learn things online.**

In a real argument, you tell how you know things to prove your ideas. In an imaginary argument to help you develop your ideas, you can use your "proof" to add details.

Revise

As you revise your work, consider your audience and purpose. Will your writing spark people's interest in the book?

1 **Evaluate Your Work**

Share your draft with friends or classmates. Ask for feedback:

▲ Navajo Marines sent secret messages during World War II.

- **About the Form** Is it easy to tell how I feel about the book? Did I state my opinion clearly?

- **About the Development of Ideas** Do you have unanswered questions about my response? Do I need to add more evidence to make my ideas clear?

▸ *Revision in Action*

from Miguel's Draft

    Sometimes I think adults don't realize the important things young people can do. If they read Ned's story, I'm sure they would change their minds. Not all teenagers just sit around and play video games. Do you? Ned was young when he joined the Marines to fight in World War II. And although he was forbidden to use any words from the Navajo language in school, he and the other Navajo Marines used their language to send top-secret messages. They were heroes.

    I really admire Ned and others like him because of what they overcame. The book describes many of Ned's experiences that I'm not sure I'd be able to cope with.

Miguel's friend says:

" This interrupts what you say about Ned. I'd take it out. "

" Exactly how old was Ned when he joined up? "

" Maybe you could tell about some of Ned's experiences from the book. "

2 Mark Your Changes

Clarify You might need to add more evidence to clarify your opinion for your readers. Use this mark: ∧ to add:

- specific details about the plot, characters, or setting

- direct quotations from the text

- a stronger statement of your opinion and reactions.

Delete Text You may also need to take out details that aren't important or that don't address your opinion or reactions to the book. Use the delete mark: ⟶℘.

Reflect

- Have you included enough support for your opinions?

- How could you change your conclusion to make it more effective?

Revising Marks

MARK	∧	↶	⌐	⟶℘	⁋
WHAT IT MEANS	Insert something.	Move to here.	Replace with this.	Take out.	Make a new paragraph.

Revised Draft

Sometimes I think adults don't realize the important things young people can do. If they read Ned's story, I'm sure they would change their minds. ~~Not all teenagers just sit around and play video games. Do you?~~ Ned was ~~young~~ only sixteen when he joined the Marines to fight in World War II. And although he was forbidden to ~~use any words from the Navajo language~~ speak Navajo in school, he and the other Navajo Marines used their language to send top-secret messages. They were heroes.

I really admire Ned and others like him because of what they overcame. The book describes many of Ned's experiences that I'm not sure I'd be able to cope with. ∧ For example, in school they washed out his mouth with soap for speaking Navajo.

Miguel took out unnecessary details and condensed a few.

He changed some details to make them more specific.

Miguel added evidence from the book to clarify and support his ideas.

Edit and Proofread

Once you know that your literary response gets your point across, read it again to fix language errors. This is what you do when you edit and proofread your work.

- **Check the Grammar** Make sure that you have used correct and conventional grammar throughout. In particular, check for past tense verbs. (See page 265W.)

- **Check the Spelling** Spell-check can help, but it isn't always enough. Read your work carefully, especially when adding endings like *–ed* and *–ing* to verbs. (See page 266W.)

- **Check the Mechanics** Errors in punctuation and capitalization can make your work hard to understand. In particular, check the use of italics, underlining, and quotation marks in the titles of literary works. (See page 267W.)

Use these marks to edit and proofread your literary response.

Editing and Proofreading Marks

MARK	WHAT IT MEANS	MARK	WHAT IT MEANS
∧	Insert something.	⁄	Make lowercase.
∧	Add a comma.	ℯ	Delete, take something out.
∧	Add a semicolon.	¶	Make new paragraph.
⊙	Add a period.	◯	Spell out.
⊙	Add a colon.	⌒	Replace with this.
ʾʾ ʾʾ	Add quotation marks.	∼	Change order of letters or words.
˅	Add an apostrophe.	#	Insert space.
≡	Capitalize.	◡	Close up, no space here.

Reflect

- What kinds of errors did you find? What can you do to keep from making them?

Grammar Workout

Check Past Tense Verbs

- To form the **past tense form** of most verbs, you simply add **-ed**.

  EXAMPLES
  walk + **-ed** = walk**ed**
  talk + **-ed** = talk**ed**
  watch + **-ed** = watch**ed**

- Some verbs are **irregular**. They don't follow the same rules as regular verbs. The list contains just a few common irregular verbs. For more about verbs, see pages 480W–481W in the Grammar Handbook. If you're not sure if a verb is regular or irregular, check the dictionary.

Some Irregular Verbs

Present Tense	Past Tense
see	saw
do	did
think	thought
know	knew

Present Tense	Past Tense
get	got
give	gave
tell	told
write	wrote

Find the Trouble Spots

     I ~~thinked~~ *thought* what happened to Ned after the war was unfair. He ~~seed~~ *saw* how lots of other Marines getted jobs based on what they had done as soldiers. But Ned couldn't discuss what he had done. He telled no one about his experience as a code-talker. No one knowed about his heroism, but he never gived up.

Find four more verb errors to fix.

Edit and Proofread, continued

> ### SpellingWorkout
>
> # Check Verbs with Endings
>
> When you add endings such as -**ed** and -**ing** to verbs, you may need to make a change to the base word. Follow these rules:
>
> - If a verb ends with one vowel and one consonant, double the consonant before you add -**ed** or -**ing**.
>
>   **EXAMPLES**   hum   +   -ed   =   humm**ed**
>   beg   +   -ing   =   begg**ing**
>
> - If a verb ends with a silent *e*, drop the *e* before adding -**ed** or -**ing**.
>
>   **EXAMPLES**   hope   +   -ed   =   hop**ed**
>   have   +   -ing   =   hav**ing**
>
> ### Find the Trouble Spots
>
> >   I ~~loveed~~ *loved* reading about Ned's adventures during the war. Because they were secret, he couldn't go around ~~braging~~ *bragging*, so he decideed just to live his life. He spent years educateing people on his reservation. Finally, in 1969, the government said the story wasn't classified anymore. People startted diging for more information about it.
>
> Find and fix four more spelling errors.

Mechanics Workout

Check Titles of Literary Works

Different types and genres of literary works require different styles and punctuation.

- As a general rule, the titles of shorter works will have quotation marks.

  EXAMPLES "Jabberwocky" (poem)
  "The Black Cat" (short story)
  "Code Talkers in World War II" (article)
  "The Role of Navajo Code Talkers in World War II" (essay)

- The titles of longer works, such as books and plays, will be italicized if you are writing on a computer. If you are handwriting your paper, underline the titles.

  EXAMPLES *Geronimo* (novel)
  The Navajo Code Talkers (nonfiction book)
  Myths from Around the World (collection of stories)
  Romeo and Juliet (play)
  Engine Grease (magazine)

Find the Trouble Spots

Joseph Bruchac's book "Code Talkers" really got me interested in this subject. I went to the library to find out more. I found an article called "Code Talkers—The Secret Weapon." I also found a short story titled Speak the Language. I am thinking about writing an article on this topic. Maybe I can publish it in War Stories magazine.

Find and fix two more errors in titles.

Publish, Share, and Reflect

Your final draft expresses your thoughts and feelings about a story or other literary work that matters to you. Why not share your thoughts with other readers, too?

1 Publish and Share Your Work

You might want to make your response public, just as professional book reviewers do. Here are a few ways to share it with a wide audience:

- Post it on a blog or personal Web site. This option lets you use cool fonts to express your individuality.

- Submit your work to your school newspaper or literary magazine.

- Look for Web sites that publish essays and reviews by teens, and send your work in.

- If your town has a community TV channel, you can present your work on the air!

Since the subject of your work is personal, you might prefer to keep it closer to home. If so, you might

- give a copy to a close friend or family member

- read it aloud in a book group.

2 Reflect on Your Work

Keep thinking about your work after it's finished. Did you get your message across? Does your writing say something about *you* as well as about the book?

Reflect

- Did I learn more about why this book means a lot to me?

- Did I express my feelings well in my response?

How to Conduct a Book-Club Meeting

To share your writing with a few classmates or friends, you might arrange a book-club discussion. Members of a book club decide in advance what books they want to read. They all read the same book on their own. Then, they come together to share their thoughts about it.

To conduct a book-club meeting:

1. Work with your group to decide on a book, as well as a date, time, and place to meet. (You might have it at your house, or ask a teacher if you can reserve a classroom after school.)

2. Schedule the meeting at least two weeks in advance. That way, everyone will have time to read.

3. Be prepared! Read the book (or reread it) beforehand. Write down your thoughts and responses.

4. Plan a relaxed, fun gathering. If it's at your house, you might provide snacks and arrange chairs in a circle.

5. Begin the discussion by asking a question about the book. You might ask about people's overall reactions or about a particular point you found interesting.

6. Be courteous. Allow time for everyone to share their responses. Don't interrupt, even if you disagree.

7. Share your own response. Don't be shy about expressing your opinions!

8. Encourage the group to ask and answer each other's questions.

" My favorite scene in this book is when Jed startles Annie in the forest. Annie is so scared, but then Jed smiles and they have an instant bond. "

Model Study

Summary Paragraph

What was the last movie or book you told a friend about? Did you describe the events word for word? Probably not. You probably gave your friend a **summary** of the events, or a shortened version of the story—a version that included only the most important parts.

In the same way, when you do research for a project or study for an exam, you often need to summarize what you read. You need to read closely and evaluate which ideas are important and which are not.

To summarize a paragraph or a short passage, you might write a one-sentence **summary statement**. To summarize an article or a book, you might write a **summary paragraph**.

Read the student model on page 271W. It shows the features of a good summary.

SUMMARY PARAGRAPH

A good summary

☑ states the original writer's ideas in your own words

☑ includes all of the main ideas and important details

☑ leaves out details that are not important.

Feature Checklist

Smoky, the War Hero Dog

by Wendy Hall

Smoky wasn't much to look at when soldiers found her at the bottom of a battlefield foxhole. But one soldier, Bill Wynne, befriended her and made Smoky his unit's mascot. This tiny Yorkshire terrier is one of the best-known dogs of World War II.

Smoky went everywhere with Bill. She flew 12 missions and won eight awards. She did dangerous duty on the ground, too. In 1945, she dragged a telephone wire through a pipe under a runway. That way, she kept the airbase connected and aware of possible enemy attacks.

Bill taught Smoky many tricks. In hospitals from Korea to Australia, she entertained the patients.

When World War II was over, Bill took Smoky to Cleveland, Ohio. There she got her own TV show. After she died in 1957, the city built a monument to her. Smoky was the war's smallest soldier and most famous war dog.

Good Summary

Wendy Hall's "Smoky, the War Hero Dog," is about a Yorkshire terrier who was a World War II hero. With a soldier named Bill Wynne, she flew many dangerous missions, protected the troops on the ground, and entertained the wounded with her tricks. After the war, she had a TV show in Cleveland. She died in 1957.

Student Model

Four-pound Smoky was a Yorkshire terrier like the dog shown here. ▶

Write a Summary Paragraph

WRITING PROMPT A good summary folds the ideas of a longer piece of writing into a small packet that is easy to carry in your brain. Try it: Find a story or a news article that interests you. Read it carefully and then write a summary paragraph that

- gives the title and author of the work
- restates the most important ideas in your own words
- includes only the most important details
- leaves out unimportant details.

Prewrite

Here are some tips for planning your summary paragraph.

❶ Keep Track of the Important Ideas

Read carefully. Think about the title and any headings. They usually name the key ideas. If you have a copy you can mark up, underline or highlight the main idea of each paragraph. (Often the main idea is stated in the first or last sentence.)

❷ Ask Yourself Questions

As you read, keep a conversation going with yourself:

- What's this about?
- What's the point of this part?
- How could I say this part in just one sentence?

Tech*TIP*

Open a document and take informal notes as you read. Later, you can rework your notes to draft your summary.

❸ Note Key Details

If a detail seems particularly important, you can highlight it (with a color different from the one you used for the main ideas) or write it on a sticky note or a separate sheet of paper. Look at the ideas Janet highlighted.

TERRY, THE ACTOR DOG
by Anthony Sydnor

"We're off to see the Wizard," sang Dorothy in *The Wizard of Oz*. Behind her ran Toto, her faithful dog. The role of Toto was played by a dog called Terry. Terry may be the first famous actor dog in movie history.

A SEASONED PRO

Terry was a female Cairn terrier. When she was picked for her big role in *The Wizard of Oz*, she was only five years old and already a movie star. In fact, that was her fifth movie.

By the time her film career ended in 1942, she had acted in 12 movies. After *The Wizard of Oz*, Terry's owner officially changed her name to Toto.

Janet highlighted **important ideas** and **key details** in different colors.

❹ Organize Your Notes

However you keep track, you should end up with an organized list like Janet's.

Important Ideas	Key Details
—First famous actor dog in movie history	—female Cairn terrier
—Played Toto in Wizard of Oz	—was in 12 movies

Reflect
- Which method for finding the most important information works best for me?

- Do I have all the key details, but not too many?

Draft

With your prewriting notes in hand, it's time to get drafting! Here are some suggestions:

- **Start with a One-Sentence Summary** Try summing up the main idea in just one sentence. That will get you to focus on the most important idea. Then develop and expand the sentence into a paragraph.

    Janet's One-Sentence Summary

    > Anthony Sydnor's "Terry, the Actor Dog" tells about the famous dog who played Toto in The Wizard of Oz.

- **Trim and Squeeze** Your prewriting notes probably contain many important ideas and details—too many for a good summary. See how many you can just leave out without making your summary inaccurate.

    Some ideas you just can't leave out. But can you maybe combine a couple into one? Or can you express it using fewer words? The idea is to get things down to the least number of words, while still being clear and accurate.

    From Janet's Notes

    > —Oz was Terry's 5th movie
    > —acted in a total of 12 movies

    From Janet's Draft

    > Terry acted in several movies before and after Oz

- **Use Your Own Words** Putting ideas in your own words is often the best way of combining and condensing. It's also a good way to make sure you understand what you're saying, and not just parroting the author.

Reflect
- Did I include all the main ideas?
- What details can I leave out?
- Did I use my own words?

DRAFTING TIPS

Trait: **Focus and Unity**

If Your Writing Sounds Choppy . . .

It's a good idea to read your writing aloud. Hearing your writing helps you know whether it flows or sounds choppy. Choppy writing can result from too many simple sentences that are the same length.

Short, Choppy Sentences

Sharon Guynup's "Brooklyn Dog a Rising Star in New York Art Scene" is about a Jack Russell terrier. The terrier is named Tillie. Tillie scratches on special paper to make images. Tillie has had her images shown in art galleries. Tillie has even appeared on television.

Try Combining Sentences

Combining sentences will help your writing flow better and make it more interesting. There are many ways to combine sentences. Look for places to use conjunctions or to make sentences into dependent clauses. Here are two ways to combine sentences and improve the paragraph above.

One Way to Combine the Sentences

Sharon Guynup's "Brooklyn Dog a Rising Star in New York Art Scene" is about a Jack Russell terrier. ~~The terrier is~~ named Tillie. *who* Tillie scratches on special paper to make images. Tillie has had her images shown in art galleries. *and* ~~Tillie~~ has even appeared on television.

This writer combined sentences 1, 2, and 3 and sentences 4 and 5.

Another Way to Combine the Sentences

Sharon Guynup's "Brooklyn Dog a Rising Star in New York Art Scene" is about a Jack Russell terrier. *Tillie,* ~~The terrier is named Tillie.~~ Tillie scratches on special paper to make images. *which have been* ~~Tillie has had her images~~ shown in art galleries. Tillie has even appeared on television.

This writer combined sentences 1 and 2 and sentences 3 and 4.

Revise

As you start revising your summary, don't lose sight of your audience and your purpose for writing. Does your writing do what you want it to do? Will it connect with your audience?

1 **Evaluate Your Work**

Read your summary aloud and see what can be improved. As you read, ask yourself:

- **About the Form** Did I include all the main ideas? Are all the details important?

- **About the Focus and Unity** Did I stick to my topic? Can I improve my summary by taking something out?

Revision in Action

Janet's Draft

> Anthony Sydnor's "Terry, the Actor Dog" tells about the famous dog who played Toto in *The Wizard of Oz*. Terry was a Cairn terrier and an actor. When she was five years old, she played Toto. Terry was chosen because she looked exactly like the dog in the novel's original drawings. She made more money than some of the actors in the movie. One day she got hurt on the set. She played in many movies in her lifetime. Thanks to Terry, Cairn terriers became the darlings of dog lovers in the U.S.

Janet thinks:

" This has too many words. I'm repeating myself too much."

" I don't need the detail about her being hurt on the set."

" I didn't use my own words in the last sentence."

2 Mark Your Changes

Consolidate Text You might need to make your writing shorter and more concise. You can consolidate text by

- deleting unnecessary or unimportant details
- using fewer words to say the same thing
- taking out repetitive words or phrases
- combining sentences.

Reflect

- Have you included all the important ideas?
- What sentences could you combine to make your summary shorter?

Revising Marks	**MARK**	∧	↶	⌐	‿	¶
	WHAT IT MEANS	Insert something.	Move to here.	Replace with this.	Take out.	Make a new paragraph.

Revised Draft

Anthony Sydnor's "Terry, the Actor Dog" tells about the famous dog who played Toto in *The Wizard of Oz*. Terry was a Cairn terrier and an actor. ~~When~~ ^was chosen when she^ she was five years old, ~~she played Toto. Terry was chosen~~ because she looked exactly like the dog in the novel's original drawings. ~~She made more money than some of the actors in the movie. One day she got hurt on the set.~~ ^Because of^ She played in many movies in her lifetime. ~~Thanks to~~ Terry, Cairn terriers became ^very popular^ ~~the darlings of dog lovers~~ in the U.S.

Janet took out repeated information and combined sentences.

Janet took out unnecessary details.

Janet rewrote the last sentence in her own words.

Edit and Proofread

After you're satisfied with the contents of your summary paragraph, read it again to fix language errors.

- **Check the Grammar** Make sure that you have used correct and conventional grammar throughout. In particular, check for correct use of object pronouns after verbs. (See page 279W.)

- **Check the Spelling** Spell-check can help, but it isn't always enough. Pay special attention when adding endings to words ending in **-y**. (See page 280W.)

- **Check the Mechanics** Errors in writing contractions can make your work look careless. This kind of error can also cause confusion. Be sure to check that you have used apostrophes correctly. (See page 281W.)

Use these marks to edit and proofread your summary.

Editing and Proofreading Marks

MARK	WHAT IT MEANS	MARK	WHAT IT MEANS
∧	Insert something.	/	Make lowercase.
∧	Add a comma.	ℒ	Delete, take something out.
∧	Add a semicolon.	¶	Make new paragraph.
⊙	Add a period.	⬭	Spell out.
⊙	Add a colon.	⌐	Replace with this.
ᵛᵛ ᵛᵛ	Add quotation marks.	∼	Change order of letters or words.
ᵛ	Add an apostrophe.	#	Insert space.
≡	Capitalize.	⌣	Close up, no space here.

Reflect

- What kinds of errors did you find? What can you do to keep from making them?

Grammar Workout

Check Object Pronouns

- **Pronouns**, like nouns, can be the **subject** of a sentence or the **object** of a verb in the predicate.

  EXAMPLES   My teacher played the movie.
  He played **it** twice.

- Subject and object pronouns often have different forms. Make sure you use the correct form.

Subject Pronouns	I	you	he	she	it	we	they
Object Pronouns	me	you	him	her	it	us	them

  EXAMPLES   **I** went to see *The Wizard of Oz.*
  My father picked **me** up afterward.

- When a pronoun is used together with a noun or with another pronoun, it must still be in the correct form.

  INCORRECT   My sister and me went to the movies.

  CORRECT   My sister and **I** went to the movies.

  INCORRECT   My father drove my sister and I home.

  CORRECT   My father drove my sister and **me** home.

Find the Trouble Spots

Noises often startled Terry on the set. It wasn't easy
for ~~she~~ her sometimes. The wind machines scared she,
too. But ~~her~~ she and the other actors got along great. My
sister and I wished we could have watched they all.

Find and fix two more pronoun errors.

Edit and Proofread, continued

> ## Spelling Workout

Check Words Ending in -y

Follow these rules to form the plural of nouns ending with *y*:

- For nouns that end with a vowel plus *y*, just add *-s*.

  EXAMPLE   tray + -s = trays

- For nouns that end with a consonant plus *y,* change the *y* to *i* and then add *-es*.

  EXAMPLE   duty + -es = duties

Follow these rules to add *-s*, *-ed*, or *-ing* to verbs ending with *y*:

- For verbs that end with a vowel plus *y*, just add *-s* or *-ed*.

  EXAMPLES   obey + -s = obeys
  destroy + -ed = destroyed

- For verbs that end with a consonant plus *y*, change the *y* to *i* before adding *-es* or *-ed*.

  EXAMPLES   fry + -es = fries   rely + -ed = relied

- Keep the *y* at the end of a verb when adding *-ing*.

  EXAMPLES   obey + -ing = obeying
  carry + -ing = carrying

Find the Trouble Spots

Studios ~~emploied~~ employed dog actors for many movies last year. It is not easy to train dogs to act. They usually have to start as puppyes, so they can learn tricks more easily. When a dog ~~studyes~~ studies, it thinks it is plaiing!

Find and fix two more spelling errors.

MechanicsWorkout

Check Apostrophes with Contractions

- Many contractions are formed with a pronoun and the verb forms *am, is, are,* or *will.* In these contractions, an apostrophe replaces the first letter of *am, is,* or *are,* or the *wi* in *will.*

  EXAMPLES   they + are ⟶ they're   she + is ⟶ she's

                 they + will ⟶ they'll   we + will ⟶ we'll

- *You're* and *your* are sometimes confused. Use *you're* only when you can replace it with the words *you are* without changing the meaning.

  EXAMPLE   **You're** walking **your** best friend's dog.

- Use *it's* only when you can replace it with the words *it is* without changing the meaning.

  EXAMPLES   **My** dog's collar fell off. **Its** buckle was broken.

                   It's time to buy a new one, I guess.

Find the Trouble Spots

You'll
~~You'ill~~ have a hard time believing what I'm about to tell
you. A photographer in my neighborhood says ~~hes~~ *he's* going to
put my chihuahua in a magazine! He saw Mindy standing
on her hind legs and jumping up and down. Its not the first
time she has done that. He thinks sh'is really cute. He is
working on an ad for dog food. Your going to be surprised
when you open a magazine one of these days!

Find and fix three more errors with contractions.

> Writing a letter to the editor is a way to share an idea or opinion you care about.
>
> —Caroline

Model Study

Letter to the Editor

Have you ever wanted your friends or neighbors to know what you think about something, such as adopting shelter dogs or building a new firehouse? A good way to let others know your opinions is to write a letter to the editor of a newspaper or magazine.

A **letter to the editor** tells your opinion, or what you think about a subject. It also gives reasons and evidence to support your opinion. When you write a letter to the editor, you use a formal tone so that readers will take your opinion seriously.

The student model on page 283W shows the features of a good letter to the editor.

LETTER TO THE EDITOR

A good letter to the editor

☑ clearly states an opinion about a subject

☑ includes reasons and evidence to support the opinion

☑ uses a formal style and the proper format

☑ includes a closing statement that restates the opinion

Feature Checklist

Dec. 29, 2014

Molly included **the date** in the upper right corner.

Dear Editor,

The letter includes a formal **greeting**.

Your recent article "Can Teens Come to the Rescue?" (December 28) asks whether young people can help their communities. The answer is certainly yes! Teenagers can act as volunteers in many different ways.

Molly clearly **states her opinion** in the first paragraph.

The story of my dog Scruffy and the Dragon Slayers shows one example of what I mean. When my house caught fire, we had to leave our dog Scruffy behind. Luckily, teenager Jill Trudeau was there to save him. Jill crawled through the smoke and heat to get him, and they both got out safely. Jill and some other girls from my school are "Dragon Slayers." The Dragon Slayers help fight fires, rescue people in accidents, and search for missing people.

Molly gives **evidence** to support her opinion.

Many teenagers "come to the rescue"—nearly 60% of teenagers volunteer each year (National Survey of Children's Health). A few fight fires, but many more help in hospitals, senior centers, animal shelters, and other places. Their volunteering helps rescue themselves, too. According to the *Journal of Primary Prevention*, teenagers who volunteer do better in school and have higher self-esteem.

Molly uses **formal language** to tell her opinion.

Jill Trudeau, the Dragon Slayers, and all teenage volunteers show that teenagers can "come to the rescue."

Sincerely,
Molly Jones

Molly uses a formal **closing**. She gives her full name in the signature.

◀ The Dragon Slayers are a teenage firefighting and emergency medical group in Aniak, Alaska.

Letter to the Editor, continued

Whether you write and mail your letter or send an e-mail, write it in a formal style. You want editors and readers to take your opinions and claims seriously, so the style should show that you also take your writing seriously.

- **Introduction** Editors receive many letters, so it is important to get right to the point. Clearly state your opinion or claim in the first paragraph. If you are writing in response to an article, it will help the editor if you cite the title of the article and the publication date.

June 5, 2014

To the Editor,

In response to your article "Why Designer Dogs Cost Top Dollar" (June 3), I would suggest that people could save money by adopting dogs from a local shelter. Adopting costs much less than buying "designer" dogs from a breeder or even a pet store.

Many shelter dogs are healthier than purebreds, and some are already spayed or neutered, so you will save even more money in the future.

- **Body** Other people can have opinions that are different from yours, and you should briefly restate those points of view in your letter. Then support your opinion by presenting clear reasons and evidence in a logical order. In this letter, for example, the writer might cite facts from a reliable source, such as a local animal shelter or national dog rescue society.

Some people claim that expensive "designer" dogs are better because you get what you pay for, and that costly dogs have better health and temperament. They believe that breeders who sell purebred dogs are all trustworthy.

Some purebred dogs come from so-called "backyard" breeders. And, according to AdoptAPet.com, shelter dogs are actually less likely to suffer from health problems than purebred dogs bought from these breeders. Shelter dogs are screened for temperament and often receive training. In addition, shelters may have purebred dogs. According to the ASPCA, about 25% of shelter dogs are pure breeds.

Dogs make loving, healthy pets no matter what they cost, so it's a good idea to rescue one instead of spending lots of money.

Sincerely,
Alex Morales

- **Closing** In a letter to the editor, you want the closing to sound formal. You might use a closing like, "Sincerely" or "Thank you." Capitalize the first word of the closing, and use a comma after the last word.

Write a Letter to the Editor

WRITING PROMPT You write a letter to the editor to tell your opinion or respond to something you read. Maybe you think the community should support a raise in pay for ambulance drivers or build a new animal shelter. Or maybe you read that the mayor wants to cut funding for firefighters, and you disagree.

Think about something that you heard or read lately and have a strong opinion about. Then write a letter to the editor that

- gives your opinion about that subject
- cites facts and evidence that support your opinion
- uses formal language
- includes a closing statement that restates your opinion
- uses the proper format.

Prewrite

Here are some tips for preparing and planning before you write your letter to the editor.

① Choose a Topic to Write About

To keep your letter focused, choose a topic that lets you form an opinion and defend it. Think about events you have read about, heard about in the news, or that happened in your town. Here's how Lydia decided on her topic:

> **Ideas**
> It might be hard to find reliable evidence.
> —The Neighborhood Watch does good work.
> —Our community should organize a food drive.   This is perfect!
> —How my cousin works as a paramedic.
> I don't have an opinion about this.

❷ Plan Your Letter to the Editor

As you plan your letter to the editor, keep in mind that sometimes people will disagree with your opinion. You need to consider other points of view. Then you can plan a response that supports your opinion with clear reasons and relevant evidence.

Before you start writing, you might want to jot down some views that people who oppose your opinion might have and think of a logical response for each one.

Lydia thinks that her community should organize a food drive to help people who are out of work because of recent job losses in her town. Here's how she organized some opposing views and responses to her idea.

Lydia's T Chart

Opinion: Because of recent job losses, our community should start a food drive to help people who are out of work.

Opposing View	Logical Response
We should all take responsibility for our own lives.	Sharing and helping each other is what builds a community.
Buying food for everyone who needs it is expensive and will put a burden on many people.	Many small contributions add up. If many people pitch in, no one takes on too much responsibility.

Reflect
- Did you think of opposing points of view?
- Did you write a response to each idea that opposes yours?

Draft

Once you know what you want to say, you can start writing.

- **Use the Right Form** Set up your letter with the date and a greeting.

From Lydia's Draft

> November 26, 2014
>
> To the Editor,
>   Many people in our area have lost their jobs and making ends meet is tough for some of them. To help, I think our community should organize a food drive.

- **Use Your Notes** Focus on the reasons and evidence that support your opinion and respond to people who disagree with you. Use a formal and polite style so that your readers will pay attention to what you say.

From Lydia's Draft

> Some people will say that we should all be responsible for taking care of ourselves. I disagree. Tough times can fall on anyone at anytime, and you can't always manage on your own. Sharing and helping each other builds a community and keeps it strong. A caring, healthy, happy community is good for everyone who lives here.
>   Others might think that a food drive will cost them too much. It doesn't have to, because many small contributions add up. If everyone pitches in, no one has to spend too much, and we can make a big difference.

Reflect

- Does your draft have all the parts of a letter to the editor?

- Did you offer clear reasons and evidence to support your opinion?

DRAFTING TIPS

Trait: **Development of Ideas**

If Your Writing Is Vague. . .

If you don't support your opinion with clear reasons and relevant evidence from reliable sources, your readers won't understand what you're trying to say.

Try Drawing a Target Diagram First

You want readers to understand and agree with your opinion. To develop your ideas, answer these questions on a **target diagram**.

1. What is your opinion?

2. What reasons and evidence support your opinion?

3. What opposing points of view are there?

4. What logical responses do you offer to those points of view?

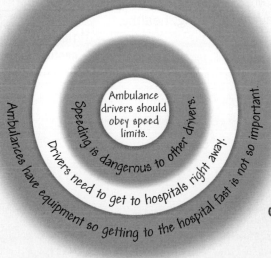

Oded's Target Diagram

Revise

As you think about how to improve your letter, keep in mind your audience (the editor and readers of the newspaper or magazine) and your purpose for writing.

1 Evaluate Your Work

You might want to show your draft to a friend via e-mail, and ask for a response. Ask:

- **About the Form and Tone** Is my letter formatted properly? Does it sound formal and serious?

- **About the Development of Ideas** Should I add more reasons and evidence to support my opinion?

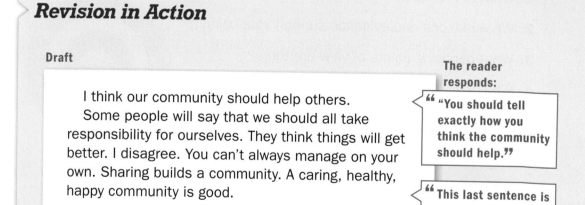

Revision in Action

Draft

> I think our community should help others.
> Some people will say that we should all take responsibility for ourselves. They think things will get better. I disagree. You can't always manage on your own. Sharing builds a community. A caring, healthy, happy community is good.

The reader responds:

" "You should tell exactly how you think the community should help."

" This last sentence is confusing. You need to clarify."

② Mark Your Changes

Clarify If you find things in your first draft that are unclear or confusing, you'll need to make changes to clarify what you mean. This could mean

- adding details to explain or to give more information
- deleting phrases or sentences that are confusing.

Revising Marks

MARK	∧	↶	⌐	ℯ	¶
WHAT IT MEANS	Insert something.	Move to here.	Replace with this.	Take out.	Make a new paragraph.

Revised Draft

Many people in our area have lost their jobs. To help,

I think our community should ~~help others~~. *organize* *a food drive.*

Some people will say that we should all be responsible for taking care of ourselves. ~~They think things will get better.~~ I disagree. You can't always

Sharing and helping each other builds a community and keeps it strong.

manage on your own. ~~Sharing builds a community.~~

A caring, healthy, happy community is good. *for everyone who lives here.*

The writer added information to make the opinion clearer.

The writer deleted a confusing sentence and added details to clarify.

Edit and Proofread

After you are satisfied with the content of your letter to the editor, read it again to fix any language errors. This is what you do when you edit and proofread your work:

- **Check the Grammar** Make sure that you have used correct and conventional grammar throughout. In particular, check for your use of prepositional phrases. (See page 293W.)

- **Check the Spelling** Spell-check can help, but it isn't always enough. For errors with sound-alike words, you'll have to read your work carefully, and maybe use a dictionary. (See page 294W.)

- **Check the Mechanics** Errors in punctuation and capitalization can make your work hard to understand. In particular, check that your commas and dashes are correct. (See page 295W.)

Use these marks to edit and proofread your letter.

Editing and Proofreading Marks

MARK	WHAT IT MEANS	MARK	WHAT IT MEANS
∧	Insert something.	╱	Make lowercase.
∧	Add a comma.	ℰ	Delete, take something out.
∧	Add a semicolon.	¶	Make new paragraph.
⊙	Add a period.	◯	Spell out.
⊙	Add a colon.	⌒	Replace with this.
ⱽ ⱽ	Add quotation marks.	∿	Change order of letters or words.
ⱽ	Add an apostrophe.	#	Insert space.
≡	Capitalize.	◡	Close up, no space here.

Reflect

- What kinds of errors did you find? What can you do to keep from making them?

Grammar Workout

Check for Prepositional Phrases

Prepositions are words that serve to indicate location, direction, or time. Here is a list of common prepositions.

about	behind	by	near	over
above	below	for	of	to
ahead of	beside	in	on	toward
at	between	inside	outside	under

You can use **prepositional phrases** to add details to your writing. A prepositional phrase always begins with a preposition.

EXAMPLES   I read a book **about volunteer organizations**.
(describes the book)

The volunteers organized a food drive **in our city**.
(tells where the volunteers organized the drive)

The volunteers worked **for seven hours**.
(tells how long the volunteers worked)

Find the Opportunities

There are millions of people ∧who don't have enough to
        in this country
eat. Fortunately, there are organizations providing food∧
        to people in need.
They help by raising awareness and collecting funds and
supplies. My school, for example, is collecting canned
goods door to door. We found many people ready to help.
It is a wonderful experience, and we are happy to help our
community.

Where else
could you add
prepositional
phrases to
add details?

Edit and Proofread, continued

> # Spelling Workout

Check Sound-Alike Words

If you hear the following sentence read aloud, you'll have no trouble understanding it:

When the firefighters got their, they could smell the cent of smoke.

But if you see it written, it's likely that you'll be confused. That's because there are problems with sound-alike words.

Word	Meaning
their	belonging to them
there	at or to a certain place
cent	unit of money
scent	smell

To find and fix problems with sound-alike words, you have to know which words are the troublemakers. Study the list of common sound-alike words on page 522W of the Writer's Files.

Find the Trouble Spots

Mrs. Kennedy's students went out ~~two~~ *to* collect food ~~too~~ *two* days a week. They kept track of all donations the (hole) time. Our class (knows) the battle against hunger isn't (one) by a single person. It takes the entire community working together. I'm proud of how we worked as a team.

Check the circled words. Are they spelled correctly? If not, how should they be spelled?

MechanicsWorkout

Check Use of Commas and Dashes

- At the beginning of a letter to an editor or a friend, set off the greeting with a comma.

  EXAMPLES   Dear Editor,
  Hi, Enid,

- At the end of a letter to an editor or a friend, set off the closing with a comma.

  EXAMPLES   Yours truly,
  Your friend,
  Sincerely,

- A dash can be used in a letter to an editor or to a friend to add information or a personal comment or reaction.

  EXAMPLES   People should help the hungry—both locally and globally.

  You said that no one would support our food drive—you were wrong!

Find the Trouble Spots and Opportunities

Dear Neil

  How are you? I'm really tired because we were up all night preparing boxes for the food bank. The delivery truck slid on the icy road and almost went down a hill! Luckily, nothing bad happened.

  Your friend
  Aaron

Add the missing commas in the greeting and closing. Where could you add a comment with a dash?

"Learning how to write an effective business letter made me feel confident and powerful."

—Lynn

Model Study

Business Letter

When you buy a CD, a snack, or a pair of jeans, you are functioning as a **consumer**. As a consumer, you might need to write to a company to

- ask for information about an item you plan to buy

- make a claim about a product that left you unsatisfied and support your claim with evidence

- request a missing part or a replacement

- thank someone for especially good service.

In all of these cases, you would write a **business letter**. In a business letter, you use a polite tone, formal language, and a set format to get your point across.

Study the model on page 297W. It shows the features of a business letter.

BUSINESS LETTER

A good business letter

☑ makes a claim and states the situation clearly

☑ provides evidence that develops and supports the writer's claim

☑ uses formal language and a polite tone

☑ follows the standard business-letter format.

Feature Checklist

---

729 Springer Street
Chicago, IL 60614
March 28, 2014

The letter includes the writer's address and the date.

The letter includes the address of the person to whom it is being sent, and a **formal greeting**.

John Green, Director, Customer Service
Pet Choice, Inc.
111 Grandview Avenue
Chicago, IL 60601

Dear Mr. Green:

The writer uses a polite tone to make the claim that she deserves a refund.

On December 11, 2013, I bought a coat for my dog, Pepi, from your catalog. I now believe that I should receive a refund for that coat. It is one of your "Warm and Cozy" fleece coats in dark green. The coat arrived by mail on December 15. On December 17, I put the coat on Pepi and went for a stroll in the park. It was raining lightly, but we kept on walking for a full hour. When I got home, though, I had a surprise. The dye from the coat had stained Pepi's fur green. After many baths, I still cannot completely remove the stains.

The writer gives **information** about the purchase and explains the problem in detail.

The writer proposes a remedy for the situation and provides evidence for why she deserves a refund.

I'm returning the coat along with copies of the receipts for the coat and the two bottles of dog shampoo I used. According to your website, you provide refunds to any customers who are not completely satisfied with their purchases. Therefore, I think I am entitled to a refund for my expenses.

Please feel free to call me at (773) 555-7797 if you have any questions. Thank you for your attention to this problem.

The writer ends with a **closing** and a **formal signature**.

Sincerely,

Joanna Haan

Joanna Haan

Student Model

Write a Business Letter

WRITING PROMPT Have you ever had a problem with something you bought?

Think of a problem you might want to contact a business about. Then plan and write a business letter that

- makes a claim and explains the problem or situation clearly
- provides evidence to support the claim
- suggests a possible solution
- uses formal language and a polite tone
- uses the proper format of a business letter.

Prewrite

Here are some tips for planning your letter before you start writing.

1 Plan What You'll Say About the Problem

Organize your facts. Use a list of questions and answers to help you remember all the details.

Sarita's Planning for Her Letter

Question	Answer
What did I buy?	a rechargeable flashlight
When did I buy it?	April 11, 2014
Where did I buy it?	Goldman's Sporting Goods, Deep Creek, South Dakota
What was the problem?	The battery did not last eight hours.
Why was it a problem?	My family and I got lost at night while hiking.

TechTIP

If you prewrite on the computer, you can easily cut and paste from your notes as you write your first draft.

❷ Find Out Whom to Contact

To get the best results, contact a specific person. Call the company's service department or use the Internet to find out who is responsible for customer service.

❸ Decide on the Solution You Want

What can the company do to help solve the problem? What will it take to fix the situation? Before you write your letter, be clear on what you want to ask.

POSSIBLE SOLUTIONS

1. *The company could give me a new flashlight.*
2. *The company could refund my money.*
3. *The company could remove the 8-hour guarantee from the box.*

ULTRA BEAM

CUSTOMER SERVICE DEPARTMENT
6312 Circle Court
Springfield, IL 62701
(217) 555-BEAM

Refunds and Exchanges
Contact:
Samuel Resnick
Customer Service Representative
Extension 4117

Reflect

- Do you know what you want to say about your problem?

- Are you clear on the solution you want?

Draft

With a plan in hand, you're ready to write an effective business letter. Follow these steps:

- **Make Your Letter Look Neat and Formal** Type your letter on a computer. Use a business-letter template if your word-processing program has one.

- **Make Your Letter Sound Professional** Most consumer letters of complaint follow an organization similar to the one shown below. Follow this organization as you draft and you'll get a good start on a crisp, effective business letter.

Include the name, title, and address of the person you're writing to.

Use a formal greeting followed by a colon (:).

Start with your address and the date. Don't include your name here.

Sender's address
Date

Recipient's name
Recipient's address

Formal Greeting(:)

Body Paragraph 1
Explains the problem in detail, but not too much detail! Gives information about date and place of purchase. States a claim about what you think the company should do about the problem.

Body Paragraph 2
Explains in more detail what the company can do to solve the problem or to satisfy you as a consumer. Gives reasons and evidence to support your claim that the company should do this.

Use a formal closing such as *Sincerely*. Leave space for your handwritten signature, and then type your full name.

Conclusion
Politely thanks the reader for reading your letter and addressing your problem.

Formal closing

Space for signature

Sender's name

Reflect

- Does your letter look neat and professional?

- Have you clearly explained both the problem and your suggested solution?

DRAFTING TIPS
Trait: **Development of Ideas**

If You Need More Details . . .
Sometimes your writing doesn't seem complete. You've followed your plan, but somehow your writing isn't clear.

Try Adding Snapshots and Thoughtshots
- Read your writing to yourself. Picture the details in your mind. What did I see, hear, and feel? Write down these details to create a snapshot of the moment.

- What did I think? Write down your thoughts. This is called a thoughtshot.

Snapshots	Thoughtshots
What time of day was it?	How did I feel about walking in the dark?
What sound did the bulb make?	How do I feel about the flashlight?
What happened to the flashlight?	

Sarita used these answers to her questions to add details to her letter.

> Recently I bought a flashlight from your company, and it did not work as you advertised. My family and I used it on a nighttime hike through a beautiful state park. We had hiked for two hours when we noticed the beam was getting weaker and weaker. Then I heard a loud pop. The flashlight bulb had burned out! It was pitch black, and my family and I had to shuffle back to our campsite along a steep, rocky road without any light. It was a dangerous journey, and I was very frightened.
>
> I am very disappointed in your product. According to your website, the bulb is supposed to last for eight straight hours, but it only lasted for two.

Revise

Keep your audience and purpose in mind as you revise your letter. What impression will you make on the person receiving the letter? Is the letter likely to get the results you want?

1 **Evaluate Your Work**

Have a trusted adult read your letter and suggest ideas for how to make it better. Ask questions:

- **About the Form** Is my tone polite? Are there parts of my writing that should be made more formal?

- **About the Development of Ideas** Are the problem and solution clear? Did I provide clear reasons and evidence for my complaint? Were any parts of the letter confusing?

Revision in Action

From Sarita's Draft

I am writing to inform you of a problem I have with one of your flashlights. It is in the Camper's Companion series. The model number is IX63. I bought this flashlight on April 11, 2014, at Goldman's Sporting Goods in Deep Creek.

According to the guarantee, the battery is supposed to last eight hours. During a recent night hike in the beautiful Badlands State Park, the battery died after only four hours! My family and I had to hike back to our campsite in the dark. It was very dangerous.

I am enclosing the faulty flashlight. I have also included a photocopy of my receipt. I put in the guarantee too. Please send me a full refund.

Sarita's reader says:

" The first paragraph seems too wordy."

" You could probably state these ideas in fewer words."

" Maybe you should combine some of these sentences."

2 Mark Your Changes

Consolidate Business letters shouldn't be chatty and newsy. You want to give as much information as necessary while also getting to the point quickly. You can consolidate ideas in your letter by

- deleting unnecessary words and information
- saying things in fewer words
- combining sentences to pack more information into less space.

Reflect

- Do you need to add any additional details?

- Did you use a formal and polite tone?

Revising Marks

MARK	∧	↶	⌐	ℓ	⁋
WHAT IT MEANS	Insert something.	Move to here.	Replace with this.	Take out.	Make a new paragraph.

Revised Draft

I am writing to inform you of a problem I have with ~~one of~~ your ~~flashlights. It is in the~~ Camper's Companion ~~series. The model number is~~ flashlight. 1X63, I bought this flashlight on April 11, 2014, at Goldman's Sporting Goods in Deep Creek.

According to the guarantee, the battery is supposed to last eight hours. During a recent night hike ~~in the beautiful Badlands State Park,~~ the battery died after only four hours! My family and I had ~~to~~ a dangerous hike back to our campsite in the dark. ~~It was very dangerous.~~

I am enclosing the faulty flashlight, ~~I have also included~~ a photocopy of my receipt, and ~~I put in~~ the guarantee ~~too.~~ Please send me a full refund.

Sarita combined sentences to consolidate ideas.

Sarita moved a detail into a previous sentence.

Sarita combined sentences to make her conclusion less wordy.

Edit and Proofread

After you're satisfied with the content of your business letter, read your paper again to fix possible errors. This is what you do when you edit and proofread your work.

- **Check the Grammar** Make sure that you have used correct and conventional grammar throughout. In particular, check for correct use of subject and object pronouns. (See page 305W.)

- **Check the Spelling** Spell-check can help, but it isn't always enough. Read your work carefully, especially words with Greek and Latin roots. Use what you know about word roots to check the spelling. (See page 306W.)

- **Check the Mechanics** Errors in punctuation and capitalization can make your work hard to understand. In particular, check that you have correctly used the colon and semicolon. (See page 307W.)

Use these marks to edit and proofread your letter.

Editing and Proofreading Marks

MARK	WHAT IT MEANS	MARK	WHAT IT MEANS
∧	Insert something.	/	Make lowercase.
∧	Add a comma.	ℰ	Delete, take something out.
∧	Add a semicolon.	¶	Make new paragraph.
⊙	Add a period.	⬭	Spell out.
⊙	Add a colon.	⌃	Replace with this.
ᵛ ᵛ	Add quotation marks.	∼	Change order of letters or words.
ᵛ	Add an apostrophe.	#	Insert space.
≡	Capitalize.	⌣	Close up, no space here.

Reflect

- What kinds of errors did you find? What can you do to keep from making them?

Subject Pronoun	Object Pronoun
I	me
you	you
he	him
she	her
it	it
we	us
they	them

GrammarWorkout

Check Subject and Object Pronouns

- Most pronouns have different forms, depending on whether they are used as the **subject** of a sentence or as the **object** of a verb in the predicate.

  EXAMPLES   The salesman was nice to Megan.
  He helped **her** find some beautiful shoes.

- The object form of a pronoun is also used when it follows a **preposition**—words like *of,* *with,* *for,* and *about.*

  EXAMPLES   I'll write a letter to the owners.
  I'll explain to **them** how helpful the salesman was.

- When a pronoun is used together with a noun or with another pronoun, it must still be in the correct form.

  INCORRECT   Megan and me went shopping for shoes.

  CORRECT   Megan and **I** went shopping for shoes.

  INCORRECT   That day shopping was fun for Megan and I.

  CORRECT   That day shopping was fun for Megan and **me**.

Find the Trouble Spots

    The flashlight was fully charged before my family and
    ~~me~~ I took it on our hike. ~~Us~~ We hikers need reliable equipment.
    My little brother and sister were excited when we left. But
    it was scary for he and she when the flashlight failed. It
    wasn't pleasant for we older folks either.

Find and fix three more pronoun errors.

Edit and Proofread, continued

> ## SpellingWorkout

> # Check Words with Greek or Latin Roots

> Many words in English come from Greek or Latin roots like these:

> | Latin Root | Meaning | Common Words |
> |---|---|---|
> | cent | one hundred | century, centipede |
> | luna | moon | lunar |
> | ques | ask, seek | quest, question, inquest |
> | scrib, script | to write | script, inscribe, scribble |

> | Greek Root | Meaning | Common Words |
> |---|---|---|
> | chrono | time | chronic, chronological |
> | logo | word, reason, study | logo, dialogue, biology |
> | phono | sound | phonograph, phonics |
> | psych | mind, soul | psychology, psychic |

> Knowing Greek and Latin roots can often help you spell a word correctly—or help you know when it's spelled incorrectly.

> **EXAMPLE**   There will be a ~~looner~~ *lunar* eclipse next Saturday.

> ### Find the Trouble Spots

> I am writing to ~~rekwest~~ *request* a refund for my new ~~telefone~~ *telephone*. The written deskripsion says it's guaranteed for 5 years. I was really siked about it. But it stopped working in a month for no lojical reason. I'd like a one hundred persent refund.

> Find four more misspelled words. Which Greek or Latin root can help you to spell each correctly?

MechanicsWorkout

Check Colons and Semicolons

Colons (:) and semicolons (;) are often misused. Here are some useful rules for these tricky punctuation marks.

Use a colon (:)	Examples
to introduce a list	We found all of the materials at the store: nails, lumber, and masking tape.
to draw attention to an explanation, summary, or quote	Your product did not fulfill its guarantee: to provide eight hours of battery life.
to follow the salutation of a business letter	Dear Mrs. Tamaka: To whom it may concern:
to separate hours and minutes	I left at 9:30.

Use a semicolon (;)	Examples
to join two related sentences	Some of your products may live up to your guarantees; this one certainly did not.
to separate items in a list when the items contain commas	Your other products include fishing gear; poles, reels, and tackle; camping equipment; and outerwear.

Find the Trouble Spots

Dear Mr. Goldman ⊙

    I bought the Camper's Companion IX63 on April 11. It was sitting in your front display. The flashlight box stated a guarantee. To give eight hours of intense light. Well, I turned the flashlight on at 505 p.m. By 912 p.m. it was dead, I couldn't get it to light.

Find four more places to insert a colon or a semicolon.

Model Study

Paragraphs in Chronological Order

What happened at the last football or basketball game? How did you become interested in playing the guitar or volunteering at the animal shelter? To answer those questions, you'd probably tell about the actions or events in the order in which they occurred.

When you write to tell about events in order, you'll be using **chronological order.** You'll use words like *before, after, then,* and *finally* to show the sequence of events. To describe events that take place over a long period of time, you might include dates as well.

Read the model on page 309W. It is written in chronological order.

PARAGRAPHS

Paragraphs in chronological order

☑ each have a main idea and supporting details

☑ describe events in the order in which they happened

☑ use sequence words and dates to show the order of events.

Feature Checklist

from Play Ball!
by Michael Ruscoe

Each paragraph includes a **main idea** and details.

World War II erupted just twenty years after World War I. The U.S. entered the conflict several years later, in 1941. Baseball officials offered to stop playing the game for as long as the war lasted. They felt this would help support the country.

But President Franklin D. Roosevelt didn't want the national pastime to stop. In a letter to baseball officials, he wrote, "I honestly feel it would be best for the country to keep baseball going." The games continued.

Within each paragraph, events are in chronological order.

The writer presents events in sequence. The paragraphs flow in chronological order.

Many players did go from ball fields to battlefields. Their absence gave women a chance to play ball professionally. Many other women went to work, too. They filled the jobs men left to go fight in the war.

The All-American Girls Professional Baseball League formed in 1943. Some of its players were as good as the men they replaced. One pitcher even struck out Babe Ruth. He was one of baseball's greatest male stars.

The writer includes **sequence words** and **dates** to show the order of events.

The league proved so popular that it continued after the war. It didn't fold until 1954. By then, more than 600 women had played professional baseball.

Professional Model

▼ Elise Harney, pitcher for the Kenosha Comets, refreshes her makeup between innings.

Write Paragraphs in Chronological Order

WRITING PROMPT In the world of sports, action-packed events happen all the time. Think about a sport you like to play or watch. You might consider a major change in that sport, a landmark event, or your own participation in the sport. Then write two to four paragraphs that

- each have a main idea and supporting details
- present a series of events in chronological order
- use sequence words to show the order of events.

Prewrite

Before you start writing, make a plan. Here's how:

1 **Choose and Narrow Your Topic**

If you want to tell about a popular sport such as basketball or baseball, it's best if you focus on one thing about that sport and avoid including information that is general knowledge.

Try writing down as many ideas as possible, then choose the best one. Here's how Derrick narrowed his topic.

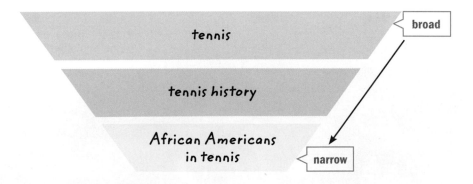

tennis — broad

tennis history

African Americans in tennis — narrow

❷ Gather Your Facts and Get Organized

Are you focusing on one major event? If so, try using a sequence chain to organize your ideas.

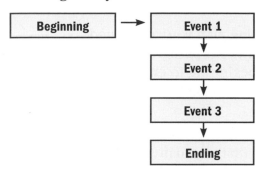

Or, use a time line if you want to tell about events that span a longer period of time.

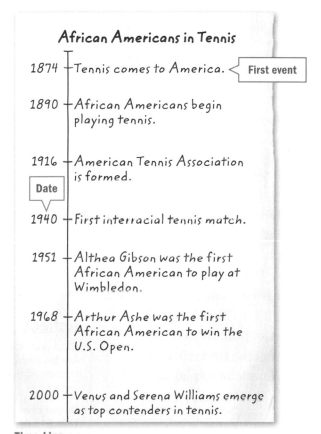

Time Line

▲ Althea Gibson grew up in Silver, South Carolina. She began playing tennis as a child.

Reflect

- Did you include the most important facts about your topic?

- Does the order of events make sense?

Draft

Now that you've got your facts in order, you're ready to start writing.

- **Use Your Organizer** Follow the writing plan you've outlined on your graphic organizer. That way, your paragraph will flow in chronological order, from beginning to end. Just turn the facts and details into sentences and paragraphs.

From Derrick's Draft

> In 1874, the game of tennis was first played in America. Over a decade later, tennis spread to the African American community. By 1916, the sport was so popular that the American Tennis Association was formed. The association is commonly known as the ATA.

Derrick uses sequence words and dates from his time line to show the order of events.

- **Add Plenty of Details** Your paragraph might be dull if you simply list event after event. As you write, add interesting details.

Dull

> In 1940, the first interracial tennis match was played. In 1951, Althea Gibson was the first African American to play at Wimbledon.

Interesting

> In 1940, the first interracial tennis match was played. In the following years, more interracial matches took place.
>
> During this time, African American Althea Gibson gained attention. In 1951, she was the first African American to play at Wimbledon.

Reflect

- Read your draft. Are the events in chronological order?

- Do you have enough details?

DRAFTING TIPS
Trait: **Development of Ideas**

If Your Writing Wanders . . .
Sometimes you get your writing going, and it starts going too many places. You have so many ideas that you don't know which one to stick with. The result is that your writing wanders and appears disorganized.

Try Writing a Skeleton Essay First
This is not an essay about a skeleton! A **skeleton essay** is a super-quick pre-draft that shows just the main points of your essay, without any details.

Here's an example for Derrick's paper.

Skeleton Essay

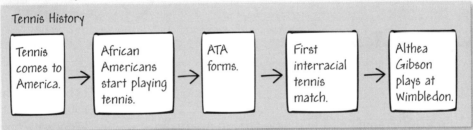

Then, for his actual draft, Derrick "exploded" each sentence by adding details about each event.

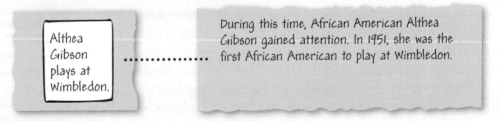

Revise

As you revise, think about your audience and purpose for writing. Does your writing do what you want it to? Will it connect with your audience?

1 **Evaluate Your Work**

Read your draft. Write out the events as a numbered list to see if you need to change the order. Ask yourself:

- **About the Form** Do I tell about something that happened? Do I have enough details about the events?

- **About the Development of Ideas** Are my paragraphs in chronological order? Did I include sequence words or dates to clarify when things happened?

Revision in Action

From Derrick's Draft

In 2000, tennis had two new African American superstars. Sisters Venus and Serena Williams impressed everyone in the tennis world. By the 1980s, tennis was open to all ethnicities. Thanks to the achievements of champions such as Gibson and Ashe, African American athletes had a chance in this sport. Venus won the U.S. Open and Wimbledon many times. Serena also won the U.S. Open and Wimbledon titles many times. Sometimes they played against each other in the finals. Today the Williams sisters continue to win major tennis titles. They keep the door open for future African American tennis stars.

Derrick thinks:

" I should tell why people were impressed."

" The order here is confusing. How earlier players affected the sport should be first."

" I say the same thing twice. I should combine the ideas into one sentence."

2 **Mark Your Changes**

Clarify Text To make your ideas clearer, you may need to add details. Use this mark: ∧.

You can also clarify the order of events by drawing a circle around text you want to move and drawing an arrow to show where the text should be: ↶⌢ .

Consolidate Text Combine text that says the same thing. Use ⟋ᵉ to take out repetitive or unnecessary words.

Reflect

- Are events in order?

- Do you have enough details?

- Can you consolidate any text?

Revising Marks

MARK	∧	↶⌢	↖	⟋ᵉ	⁋
WHAT IT MEANS	Insert something.	Move to here.	Replace with this.	Take out.	Make a new paragraph.

Revised Draft

In 2000, tennis had two new African American superstars. Sisters Venus and Serena Williams
They were powerful and competitive athletes. impressed everyone in the tennis world. By the 1980s, tennis was open to all ethnicities. Thanks to the achievements of champions such as Gibson and Ashe, African American athletes had a chance in this sport. *Both Venus and Serena* Venus won the U.S. Open and Wimbledon many times. ~~Serena also won the U.S. Open and Wimbledon titles many times.~~ Sometimes they played against each other in the finals. Today the Williams sisters continue to win major tennis titles. They keep the door open for future African American tennis stars.

Derrick rearranged ideas to follow a clear chronological order.

Derrick added details to make ideas clearer and more interesting.

Derrick consolidated two repetitive sentences.

Edit and Proofread

After you're satisfied with the content of your paragraphs, read your essay again to fix language errors. This is what you do when you edit and proofread your work:

- **Check the Grammar** Make sure you have used correct and conventional grammar throughout. In particular, check for consistent verb tenses in sentences that tell about the same event. (See page 317W.)

- **Check the Spelling** Spell check can help, but it's not enough. Double-check to make sure you've spelled correctly two-syllable words with the /uh/ sound. (See page 318W.)

- **Check the Mechanics** Errors in punctuation and capitalization can make your work hard to understand. In particular, check that you use a comma before the conjunction in a compound sentence. (See page 319W.)

Use these marks to edit and proofread your paragraphs.

Editing and Proofreading Marks

MARK	WHAT IT MEANS	MARK	WHAT IT MEANS
∧	Insert something.	╱	Make lowercase.
⌃	Add a comma.	ℰ	Delete, take something out.
⌃	Add a semicolon.	¶	Make new paragraph.
⊙	Add a period.	◯	Spell out.
⊙	Add a colon.	⌢	Replace with this.
⌄ ⌄	Add quotation marks.	∼	Change order of letters or words.
⌄	Add an apostrophe.	#	Insert space.
≡	Capitalize.	‿	Close up, no space here.

Reflect

- What kind of errors did you find? What can you do to keep from making them?

Grammar Workout

Check Verb Tenses

The tense of a verb shows when an action happens.

- The present tense shows that the action is happening now or happens all the time.

- The past tense tells about something that happened earlier or in the past.

- The future tense tells about an action that will happen later, or in the future.

When you write sentences about the same topic, keep your verbs all in the same tense. That way your readers won't get confused about when things happen.

CONFUSING   Althea Gibson won the women's ATA championship
            many times. She even beats some of the male players.

CORRECT   Althea Gibson won the women's ATA championship
            many times. She even beat some of the male players.

Find the Trouble Spots

> In 1940, the first interracial tennis match in ^was
> played. World champion Don Budge plays ^played against
> African American tennis star Jimmy McDaniel. The
> match will be held at the Cosmopolitan Tennis Club in
> New York. Budge beats McDaniel 6-1 and 6-2.

Find two more verb tense errors to fix.

Edit and Proofread, continued

> ## Spelling Workout

> # Check Words You Have to Know or Look Up

Some words you can figure out how to spell; others you just have to know.

For example, if you were hearing the word *dragon* for the first time, chances are you could figure out how to spell the first syllable, *drag-*. But how could you figure out that second syllable? How could you know that the correct spelling is *dragon* and not *dragan* or *dragun* or *dragin*?

You might know the spelling is *dragon* because you've seen the word many times before and have memorized the spelling. If you had not seen it before, you'd have to look up the correct spelling in a dictionary.

That's because the sound that the **o** makes in *dragon* (sounds kind of like *uh*) can be spelled with any vowel in English.

> **EXAMPLES**   ar**ou**nd   pix**e**l   lim**i**t   poss**u**m

This sound happens very often in the unstressed syllable of a two-syllable word, and it can give you spelling nightmares. So, do whatever it takes to learn those tricky spellings. For example, to learn *dragon*, you might imagine the **o** as the eye of a dragon.

Find the Trouble Spots

> It was hot as an ~~ovin~~ *oven* the day Ann and her cousun Jill tried out for the baseball team. Umong the girls, a dozon looked like good players, but Ann stood out ~~obove~~ *above* the others.
>
> Ann and Jill made the team, yet they were worried. Could a women's league sicceed?

Find and fix four more misspelled words with the *uh* sound.

Mechanics Workout

Check for Commas before Conjunctions

An **independent clause** contains a subject and a verb and can stand alone as a sentence.

EXAMPLES   Althea Gibson lived in South Carolina.
She learned to play tennis as a child.

A compound sentence contains at least two independent clauses joined by **and, but,** or **or.** When you use a conjunction to join two independent clauses, place a comma before that conjunction.

EXAMPLES   Althea Gibson was a great tennis player, **and** people in her community were inspired by her.

Jimmy McDaniel lost the match, **but** the significance of the tournament was groundbreaking.

Would the Budge-McDaniel match change the rules, **or** would tournaments continue to be segregated?

Find the Trouble Spots

Tennis was popular in African American neighborhoods and some families built new courts. Many African American athletes became great tennis players‚but they were not allowed to play in major tournaments. Did tennis stay segregated or did people change this? Players like Althea Gibson and Arthur Ashe did‚and the sport became better because of them.

Find two more places to add missing commas.

"Finding out how others
became who they are
inspires me."
—Rosale

Model Study

Biography

On the surface, some people's lives seem exciting, while other people's lives might seem pretty ordinary. But when you look beneath the surface, everyone's life includes some interesting stories. When you write a **biography,** you tell the story of someone else's life. You can choose to write about someone famous or someone you know.

A biography is different from an **autobiography.** A biography is about someone else's life and uses the **third-person pronouns** *he* or *she.* An autobiography is the story of your own life. It uses the **first-person pronouns** *I* and *me.*

Biographies and autobiographies have many things in common. They both give dates and facts and describe the things that make that person's life unique.

Read the student model on page 321W. It shows the features of a good biography.

BIOGRAPHY

A good biography

☑ gives background information about the person

☑ tells about important events in the person's life

☑ presents events in chronological order.

Feature Checklist

Satchel Paige
by Lawrence Paddock

The writer includes many **important events** in Paige's life and presents them in chronological order.

Pitcher Leroy Robert "Satchel" Paige was born in Alabama in 1906. His childhood was difficult. At 12, he was sent to reform school for truancy and shoplifting. But there he learned how to pitch from his supervisor, Eddie Byrd. After finishing school in 1923, he joined the Mobile Tigers, a semi-pro baseball team.

In 1926, Paige was hired to play for the Chattanooga Black Lookouts. During one game, Bill "Plunk" Drake taught Paige his famous "Hesitation Pitch." Soon after, Paige joined the Birmingham Black Barons. In 1929, he got 184 strikeouts—a season record for the Negro League.

Paige married Janet Howard in 1934. During the wedding reception, he signed a new contract with the Philadelphia Giants, then pitched for them during his honeymoon. He divorced Janet in 1943. In 1947, he married Lahoma Brown. They had four children.

Paige played on many teams during his career. He pitched for the Philadelphia Giants, the El Paso Mexicans, the Cleveland Indians, and other teams. He also played in Cuba, the Dominican Republic, Mexico, and Puerto Rico.

In 1966, Paige pitched his last game. He died on June 8, 1982 at his Kansas City home.

The writer gives background information about the subject's life.

The writer includes **sequence words** and **dates** to make the order of events clear.

Student Model

Satchel Paige became one of the best-known pitchers of all time. ▶

Voice and Style

Would you wear the same clothes to a school dance that you wore to your team's playoff game? What about to your cousin's wedding? Of course not! They're totally different events, with different people attending. Writing is similar. What you write—and how you write it—changes depending on why you are writing, and who will read it.

Make Your Writing Sound Like You

You may talk differently to your parents, coach, and kid sister, but you always sound like yourself. That's what you want to do with your writing. You want to create your own personal style by the words you choose and the way in which you put them together.

When your writing sounds "real," people will want to read it. Even though you need to tailor your writing for different audiences and purposes, you still want to show who you are as a writer.

Friendly and Informal

> My favorite baseball player of all time is Satchel Paige. He's incredible, because his family was poor and he didn't even have formal baseball lessons. But he still became one of the most talented pitchers in the big leagues. What an amazing athlete!

Formal, but not Stiff

> A baseball player whom I greatly admire is Satchel Paige. His family was working-class, and he never had formal baseball lessons. Yet he rose to become one of the most talented pitchers in the big leagues. As an African American, he also had to overcome discrimination in his sport.

Study the rubric on page 323W. What is the difference between a paper with a score of 2 and one with a score of 4?

Voice and Style

	Does the writing have a clear voice and is it the best style for the type of writing?	Is the language interesting and are the words and sentences appropriate for the purpose, audience, and type of writing?
4 Wow!	The writing <u>fully</u> engages the reader with its individual voice. The writing style is best for the type of writing.	The words and sentences are interesting and appropriate to the purpose and audience. • The words are precise and engaging. • The sentences are varied and flow together smoothly.
3 Ahh.	<u>Most</u> of the writing engages the reader with an individual voice. The writing style is mostly best for the type of writing.	<u>Most</u> of the words and sentences are interesting and appropriate to the purpose and audience. • Most words are precise and engaging. • Most sentences are varied and flow together.
2 Hmm.	<u>Some</u> of the writing engages the reader, but it has no individual voice and the style is not best for the writing type.	<u>Some</u> of the words and sentences are interesting and appropriate to the purpose and audience. • Some words are precise and engaging. • Some sentences are varied, but the flow could be smoother.
1 Huh?	The writing does <u>not</u> engage the reader.	<u>Few or none</u> of the words and sentences are appropriate to the purpose and audience. • The words are often vague and dull. • The sentences lack variety and do not flow together.

Voice and Style, continued

Compare Writing Samples

Good writers use colorful and precise language, and vary their sentences to engage their readers. Study the two examples below.

Engaging

Baseball's First

One of the first African American men to succeed in professional baseball was Bud Fowler. He joined a white pro team in 1878. At the time, he was the only black player competing in the league. By the late 1800s, as many as 50 black players were on white teams.

Fowler was born John Jackson in Fort Plain, New York, in 1858. Why was he known as Bud Fowler? Rumor has it that he was nicknamed "Bud" because he cheerfully called other players that.

He played for teams in Ohio, Massachusetts, Minnesota, and Canada. He also supported himself as a barber. After a long illness, he died in Frankfort, New York, in 1913.

Precise words make the writing lively and interesting.

The writer mixes short and long sentences and different sentence types, including a question.

Not Engaging

Bud Fowler

Bud Fowler was the first African American to play professional baseball. He began playing in a white league in 1878. He was the only black player. There were more by the late 1800s. By the late 1800s, there were 50 black players.

Fowler was born John Jackson. He was born in a small town in New York in 1858. No one knows why he was called "Bud". Some say because he called other players that.

He played for teams in Ohio, Massachusetts, Minnesota, and Canada. He also worked as a barber. He died in Frankfort, New York, in 1913.

Too many **repeated words** make the writing sound dull.

The sentences sound very similar. Using too many statements makes the writing boring.

Evaluate for Voice and Style

Now read carefully the biography below. Use the rubric on page 323W to score it.

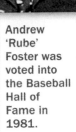

Founder of the Negro Leagues

Andrew "Rube" Foster was one of the most important African Americans in baseball. He was born in Texas in 1879. He played for the Waco Yellow Jackets in 1897. He was a star by 1903, after success with the Otsego Independents and the Cuban X-Giants.

He joined the Chicago Leland Giants in 1907. Foster helped them win 110 games. In July of 1909, he broke his leg. He recovered in time for a series against the Chicago Cubs, which the Lelands lost.

In 1911, the Lelands became the Chicago American Giants. By 1915, Foster was playing very little. In 1917, he pitched his last game. Then he became a bench manager. He was known as a strict manager and a great teacher.

In 1920, Foster met with seven other owners of midwestern clubs to form the Negro Leagues, a professional league for African American players. The American Giants won the first three seasons. In 1923, the Kansas City Monarchs emerged as their rival, beating them two years in a row.

Foster was almost killed by a gas leak in 1925. Soon, he began to have mental problems. Halfway through the 1926 season, he couldn't work and was sent to an asylum. Foster died in 1930.

Are the sentences varied? Do they flow well together?

Andrew 'Rube' Foster was voted into the Baseball Hall of Fame in 1981.

Is the writer's word choice engaging and interesting? Which words would you replace?

Raise the Score

These papers have been scored using the Voice and Style Rubric on page 323W. Study each paper to see why it got the score it did.

Overall Score: 4

Babe Ruth: A Baseball Legend
by Anthony Calabrese

The **informal tone** fits the writer's subject and purpose.

George Herman Ruth, Jr. was a sports hero and an American icon. You might know him as "The Babe." Ruth was born to a working-class family in Baltimore, Maryland. At age 19, he was discovered by Baltimore Orioles owner Jack Dunn. Within a few months, Ruth was playing for the Boston Red Sox.

Babe Ruth was discovered by Baltimore Orioles owner Jack Dunn at the age of 19.

The writer mixes short and long sentences and includes different sentence types.

Ruth won several World Series championships and soon dominated the game as the Red Sox's best pitcher. Was his flair for pitching his only talent? Hardly! He was also a skilled home run hitter. His phenomenal talents made him a superstar.

After six successful years in Boston, Ruth was sold to the New York Yankees. In his first season in New York, Ruth shattered his own home run record. Then in 1923, Ruth led the Yankees to their first-ever World Series title.

Specific, precise words make the writing come alive.

Ruth retired in 1935. By then he was considered the greatest player of all time. Although Ruth passed away in 1948, his mark on sports is still felt today.

Babe Ruth: A Baseball Legend

The informal tone fits the writer's subject and purpose.

George Herman Ruth, Jr. was a sports hero and an American icon. You might know him as "The Babe." Ruth was born to a working-class family in Baltimore, Maryland. At the age of 19, Ruth was discovered by Baltimore Orioles owner Jack Dunn. Within a few months, Ruth was playing for the Boston Red Sox.

The writer mixes short and long sentences, but all the sentences are statements.

Ruth won several World Series championships. He soon dominated the game as the Red Sox's best pitcher. He was also a good home run hitter. These combined talents made Ruth a rising superstar.

The writer uses some spooifio, precise words, but could use more.

After six successful years, Ruth was sold to the New York Yankees. In his first season in New York, Ruth beat his own home run record. Then in 1923, Ruth led the Yankees to their first-ever World Series title.

Ruth retired in 1935. By then he was already considered the greatest playcr of all timc. Even though Ruth passed away in 1948, his mark on sports is still felt today.

RAISING THE SCORE

The writer needs to use different kinds of sentences and precise words to make the writing livelier. Which words and sentences could the writer changc?

Raise the Score, continued

Overall Score: 2

The writer's voice and style aren't unique.

Babe Ruth

George Herman Ruth, Jr., "The Babe," was a sports hero. He was born in Baltimore, Maryland. Baltimore Orioles owner Jack Dunn found him at age 19. Soon he was playing for the Boston Red Sox.

Ruth played so well, he won several World Series championships. He was a great pitcher and a good home run hitter. He was a superstar.

Too many sentences start the same way, and most are short. The flow is not smooth.

Then Ruth was sold to the New York Yankees. Ruth beat his own record. Ruth led the Yankees to their first-ever World Series title. He was their greatest player.

Ruth stopped playing in 1935. He was considered the greatest player of all time. Ruth passed away in 1948. He made his mark on sports.

A few of the words are engaging, but too many are vague.

The writer repeats the same words too many times.

RAISING THE SCORE

The writer needs to vary the sentences and use specific, precise words. What words should be replaced with more powerful ones?

Babe Ruth

George Herman Ruth, Jr. was a good athlete. He was born in Baltimore, Maryland. The owner of the Baltimore Orioles found him when he was 19. He started playing for the Boston Red Sox.

Ruth became a very successful player. He won several World Series games. He was a good pitcher. He was also a good batter. He was one of the best players ever.

Ruth was sold to the New York Yankees. As a Yankee, he continued to be a successful player. Ruth beat his own record in his first season. Thanks to Ruth, the Yankees would become very successful.

Ruth stopped playing in 1935. He passed away in 1948.

The writing is not very interesting. The writer uses too many short, simple sentences that start the same way.

The writer uses too many **vague words.**

The writer **repeats the same dull words** over and over.

RAISING THE SCORE

The writing is vague and boring. What can the writer do to fix the language and sentences to make it lively and colorful?

Choose the Right Voice

What's It Like

What kind of music do you listen to? Do you listen to different songs according to your mood? Choosing a voice when you write is like picking the right music. A writer's voice changes depending on the topic, audience, and purpose.

Adapt Your Voice to Your Form and Topic

To decide which voice you will use, think about your writing form. If you write a poem, for example, you'll probably use powerful, colorful language to show strong emotion. If you write a report, you'll present facts in an unemotional way. How is the voice of the poem different from the ad?

Baseball

Smack, crack

The ball

whizzes

Up, up, up

Over the field

Into the stands

A poem uses short lines to create colorful images.

Little League Starts Soon!

Little League is more than just hitting the ball and rounding the bases. It's also a time to have some fun with your friends. If you're at least five years old, join today!

▲ An ad presents information in a brief and inviting way.

You can adapt your voice for your topic, too. The voice you use for a serious topic, such as segregation in sports, would be different from the voice you use for an account of your favorite team winning the championship.

Adapt Your Voice for Different Audiences

When you're writing to a friend, it's okay to use an informal voice. For other audiences, like your teacher or the editor of local paper, a formal voice is better.

Formal

> Baseball players report for spring training in February. Pitchers and catchers arrive first. Everyone else arrives a week later. But the best baseball players don't wait until February. Many of them train all year long.

Informal

> I can't wait until the season starts. Too bad there's no preseason games in our league! I heard about some of the pros' off-season training routines. My dad said he'd work out a training program with us if we wanted him to.

The writer expresses emotion and addresses the reader directly.

Adapt Your Voice to Your Purpose

When you write to inform, you use a different voice than you use to persuade. How does the writer change the voice to fit the purpose?

To Inform

> Baseball teams play 162 games from March to September, with as many as 6 games a week. Each team carries many players. But there can only be nine men on the field at any given time.

To Persuade

> Everyone in the school must come to the baseball game. Our team will play to raise funds to restore the city library damaged after the flood. Be there on time—5 p.m. sharp!

The writer uses words like "must" and includes a command.

Choose the Right Voice, continued

The writer below was asked to write a persuasive piece about how baseball is a more demanding sport than football. Compare the essay with the writer's FATP chart. Does the writing fit the form, audience, topic, and purpose?

FATP Chart

Form: _essay_

Audience: _my classmates_

Topic: _differences between baseball and football_

Purpose: _to persuade_

Baseball vs. Football
by Lavar James

Which is harder: a season that lasts eighteen weeks, or one that lasts seven months? How often would you like to play a sport? Once a week, or three to six days a week? Those are just some of the differences between football and baseball. As you can see, baseball is the harder sport to play.

Baseball players play 162 games over a seven-month season. That's more than ten times the number of games that football players play.

Baseball players also have to play both offense and defense, so most of them play all nine innings. Football teams, however, are made up of three different teams: the defense, the offense, and "special" teams like those that return punts or kick field goals. That's why a football player's playing time is measured in minutes. He might play for only minutes out of an hour-long football game!

I hope you'll agree with me that baseball is more demanding. How could you not?

Is the writer's tone appropriate for his classmates?

How effectively does the writer persuade readers? What words might make the paper more convincing?

This sports column for the school paper should highlight the players and their accomplishments. Did the writer meet the goal? What changes would you recommend?

Form: _newspaper column_

Audience: _students and teachers_

Topic: _school team and its accomplishments_

Purpose: _to inform_

The Doubledays Double the Score
by Rita Henderson

Down 3–6 in the ninth inning, the Doubledays did not lose heart. Instead, the players did everything they could to even the score.

Rodriguez stepped to the plate and swung hard at the first pitch. She scorched the ball! It was right to the second baseman, but Rodriguez didn't care. As soon as the ball left the bat, she left home plate. Running hard right out of the box, she beat the throw to first base. With one runner on, the team now had a chance.

Childs was the next batter. Four pitches later, Childs walked to first base, moving Rodriguez to second. Kelly was next up. What with Kelly's wildness at the plate, as she swung hard at everything, the pitcher focused on her. The pitcher never even noticed Rodriguez's lead until she had safely stolen third base! Kelly struck out, but she had done her job. The lead runner had advanced.

Lee's single brought Rodriguez home, and moved Childs to third—she reached the base right under the tag! A walk and a single later, the Doubledays had doubled the score and tied the game. But would it be enough?

Did the writer use strong verbs and colorful language?

Is the writing informative?

Did the writer vary her sentences?

Use Figurative Language

At first, this may look like a photo of a bee. But look again. It's a flower. Sometimes writers can use words and phrases in ways that go beyond what they literally mean.

Writers use figurative language—idioms, similes, and metaphors—to say things in vivid and imaginative ways. Use figurative language to make your writing fun and colorful.

Figurative Language: Idioms

In an idiom, the phrase as a whole means something different from what the words mean by themselves. See how this writer used an idiom to make his explanation more interesting.

> The pitcher is on the mound. She starts the wind-up. Here comes the snap. Keep your eyes peeled or you might miss the ball! In fast-pitch softball, pitchers use special techniques to deliver a ball with incredible speed.

Include idioms here and there, but don't overuse them. Too many idioms can make your writing sound too informal.

Idiom	What You Really Mean
The coach was really steamed.	The coach was very angry.
Winning was a piece of cake.	Winning was easy.
She put her heart into the game.	She put all her effort into the game.
The team gave it their all.	The team tried as hard as they could.

See how the idioms emphasize this writer's point:

The All-American Girls League

The All-American Girls Professional Baseball League formed in 1943. The women had their work cut out for them because many people believed women couldn't play sports. Those fans ate their words when a female pitcher struck out Babe Ruth, one of baseball's greatest male stars. The league was so hot that it continued after the war. It didn't fold until 1954. By then, more than 600 women had stepped up to the plate—literally and figuratively!

Where can this writer add idioms to spice up his biography of Jackie Robinson?

Jackie Robinson

In 1947, Jackie Robinson became the first African American player in the big leagues. He helped lead the Brooklyn Dodgers to the World Series. They tried as hard as they could but they lost the World Series to the New York Yankees. Still, Robinson showed that African Americans could do as well as white players.

Use Figurative Language, continued

Figurative Language: Similes

A simile compares two unlike things using the words *like* or *as*. Which paragraph gives a more vivid impression of a catcher and his uniform?

Without Similes

Who is that crouched behind home plate? It's the catcher. Of all the players, the catcher has to wear the most equipment. His uniform consists of a heavy wire mask and chest protector. And, completing the outfit are leg guards which need to be strong enough to protect his knees and shins.

With Similes

Who is that crouched like a tiger behind home plate? It's the catcher. Of all the players, the catcher has to wear the most equipment. Like a suit of armor, his uniform consists of a heavy wire mask and chest protector. And, completing the outfit are leg guards which need to be as tough as nails to protect his knees and shins.

Read the similes in the passage below. Then look for places where the writer could add more similes.

Have you ever attended a baseball game? Watching the game is only part of the action. As fans settle into their seats, they greet their neighbors like long-lost relatives. Each time their favorite team makes a successful play, they pop up suddenly. They cheer, shout, and yell. During all this, vendors wander up and down the bleachers offering all kinds of treats. You can buy hot dogs, popcorn, cotton candy, and drinks. A day at the ball park is as noisy a rock concert, but enjoyed by thousands of baseball fans.

Figurative Language: Metaphors

Like a simile, a metaphor compares two things, but it does not use the words *like* or *as* to make the comparison. Instead, it says that one thing is the other thing. How does the paragraph with the metaphor help you better "see" Wrigley Field?

Without metaphors

> Wrigley Field in Chicago, Illinois is where the Chicago Cubs play, and it has been since 1916. The stadium is an irregular shape and surrounds a field of bluegrass and clover. Over 41,000 fans at once can watch their favorite team play ball. And to check the score all they need to do is check the scoreboard that juts 85 feet above the field.

Women's teams played in Wrigley Field during World War II. ▼

With metaphors

> Wrigley Field in Chicago, Illinois is home for the Chicago Cubs, and it has been since 1916. The stadium is an ancient coliseum surrounding a field of bluegrass and clover. Over 41,000 fans at once can watch their favorite team play ball. And to check the score all they need to do is check the scoreboard, a city block jutting 85 feet above the field.

Read the metaphors in the passage below. Then look for places where the writer could add more metaphors.

> The Smithsburg Lions were mighty warriors, and the only undefeated football team in the league. Each player was huge and cranky. How could the Jackson Jaguars possibly beat them? The Jaguars did have a few secret weapons, though. Their linemen were big and strong. They could push through the Lions. And, their running backs were fast wild horses that no one could catch.

Write a Biography

WRITING PROMPT A biography is the story of a person's life. Who has an interesting life that you would like to share with others? Think of a person whose life you'd like to write about for your classmates. Research your subject. Then, write a biography that includes

- background information about your subject
- the important events from your subject's life, in chronological order
- sequence words and dates to show the order of events.

Prewrite

Here are some tips for planning your biography.

1 **Choose Your Topic, Audience, and Purpose**

Decide whom you will write about. Will you write about a famous athlete? You might also write about a person you know well, such as a family member or local legend.

Think about who will read your biography and what you want your audience to learn from it. That will be your purpose, or reason, for writing. Your audience and purpose will determine the style you use. Lena used an FATP chart to get clear on her audience and purpose.

Dottie Schroeder was a star in the All-American Girl's Professional Baseball League. ▼

FATP Chart

Form: _biography_

Audience: _my classmates_

Topic: _female baseball star Dottie Schroeder_

Purpose: _to inform my classmates about Dottie Schroeder's life_

② Decide What's Most Important

Because there's so much to say about a person's life, focus in on the most important ideas. You may already know a lot about your subject, but do research to check your facts and fill in the missing details.

③ Organize Your Thoughts

A good biography presents events in chronological order. Use a graphic organizer, such as a sequence chain or time line, to organize events.

Lena's Plan for Her Biography

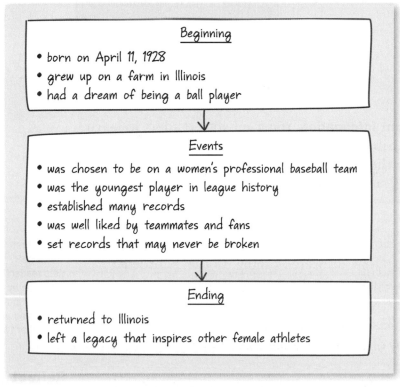

Beginning
- born on April 11, 1928
- grew up on a farm in Illinois
- had a dream of being a ball player

Events
- was chosen to be on a women's professional baseball team
- was the youngest player in league history
- established many records
- was well liked by teammates and fans
- set records that may never be broken

Ending
- returned to Illinois
- left a legacy that inspires other female athletes

Reflect

- Did you research your subject's life carefully?

- Did you organize events in chronological order?

Draft

Now that you've gathered and organized your facts, it's time to start writing!

- **Use Your Organizer** Follow your writing plan. If you used a sequence chain to get organized, expand each box into a paragraph. Remember to start out with a good beginning.

Beginning	→	Include:
		• **opening sentence that hooks readers**
		• **introduction of your subject**
		• **date and place of birth**
		• **description of early life**

- **Include Important Information** You want your readers to learn all about your subject when they read your biography. So be sure to include the facts they need. Hook your reader with a good opening sentence.

From Lena's Draft

> The expression "you throw like a girl" would have a whole new meaning if that girl were Dorothy "Dottie" Schroeder. Schroeder was one of the greatest female baseball players of all time. She was a standout in the All-American Girl's Professional Baseball League (AAGPBL). Her example inspired many other female athletes.

Lena's first sentence gets readers' attention by giving a familiar expression an unfamiliar twist.

◄ Dottie Schroeder could play different positions on the field.

Reflect

- Does your opening sentence hook the reader?

- Did you include the important events of your subject's life?

DRAFTING TIPS
Trait: **Voice And Style**

If Your Writing Is Too Vague . . .
Vague or repetitive language can make your writing sound dull and boring.

Use an Intensity Scale to Spice It Up!
"Weigh" your words on an Intensity Scale like this:

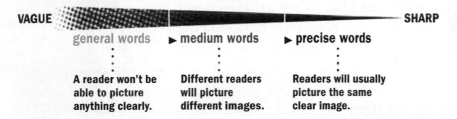

VAGUE ════════════════► **SHARP**

general words ▶ **medium words** ▶ **precise words**

| A reader won't be able to picture anything clearly. | Different readers will picture different images. | Readers will usually picture the same clear image. |

When you use words that fall toward the right end of the scale, your writing will be clear, sharp, and interesting!

VAGUE ════════════════► **SHARP**

good ▶ **talented** ▶ **extremely gifted**

Try it. Use an Intensity Scale to find the most colorful, vivid words to tell about your subject's life.

Lena's Intensity Scale

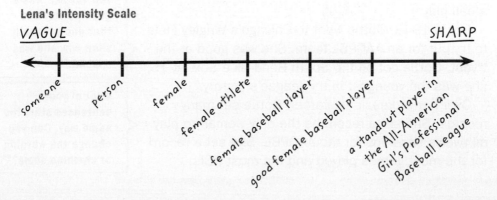

VAGUE ◄─────┼─────┼─────┼─────┼─────┼─────┼─────► *SHARP*

someone · person · female · female athlete · female baseball player · good female baseball player · a standout player in the All-American Girl's Professional Baseball League

Revise

As you revise, remember your audience and purpose. Will your writing do what you want it to? Will it connect with your audience?

1 **Evaluate Your Work**

Let a partner read your biography and give you feedback. Ask your partner questions about your writing:

- **About the Form** Is my writing well-organized? Are all the events about the person's life important?

- **About the Voice and Style** Is my writing interesting to read? Are there any places where I could use more precise or colorful language?

Dottie Schroeder played 12 years in the AAGPBL. ▼

Revision in Action

From Lena's Draft

> The expression "You throw like a girl" would have a whole new meaning if that girl were Dorothy "Dottie" Schroeder. Dottie was a good player in the All-American Girl's Professional Baseball League (AAGPBL). She was born April 11, 1928 in Sadorus, Illinois. She grew up on a farm. Dorothy wanted to be a ball player.
>
> So, in 1943, Dottie went to Chicago's Wrigley Field to try out for an AAGPBL team. She was good at the tryout. Dottie got on the South Bend Blue Sox. At 15, she was the youngest in the league's history.
>
> Over her professional career, Dottie set many records. She set a record as the only woman to play all twelve sessions for the AAGPBL. She set a record for the most games played and the most RBIs.

Josh thinks:

" The opening sentence is good, but the rest are all short and a little boring."

" You say she was a good player, but that doesn't really show why she was special."

" A lot of your sentences start the same way. Can you change the wording or combine some?"

2 Mark Your Changes

Add and Clarify Text To make your writing lively and clarify ideas, add colorful language, precise words, and details. Use this mark: ∧

Consolidate Text When you consolidate text, you make it shorter by

- taking out unnecessary details or repeated ideas
- saying the same thing with fewer words
- combining sentences.

Reflect

- Did you vary your sentences?
- Did you use precise, interesting words and details?

Revising Marks	MARK	∧	↶	⌐	⌣	⌐ℓ
	WHAT IT MEANS	Insert something.	Move to here.	Replace with this.	Take out.	Make a new paragraph.

Revised Draft

The expression "You throw like a girl" would have a whole new meaning if that girl were Dorothy "Dottie" Schroeder. Dottie was a good ^standout player in the All-American Girl's Professional Baseball League (AAGPBL). She was born April 11, 1928 in Sadorus, Illinois. ^Dorothy She grew up on a farm. Dorothy wanted to be a ball player. But, she had always dreamt about playing baseball.

So, in 1943, Dottie went to Chicago's Wrigley Field to try out for an AAGPBL team. Would her unusual talent shine? Yes, if certainly did. She was good at the tryout. Dottie got on ^was chosen for the South Bend Blue Sox. At 15, she was the youngest in the league's history ^—and one of the best!

Over her professional career, Dottie set many records. She set a record as ^was the only woman to play all twelve sessions for the AAGPBL. She set a record ^also held the for the most games played and the most RBIs.

Lena changed the length of some sentences and replaced vague words with more precise ones.

Lena used different sentence types to make the writing more lively.

Lena replaced repetitive words and phrases.

Edit and Proofread

After you're satisfied with the content of your biography, read your paper again to fix language errors. This is what you do when you edit and proofread your work:

- **Check the Grammar** Make sure that you have used correct grammar throughout. In particular, check that you've kept verb tenses consistent when you are working with compound and complex sentences. (See page 345W.)

- **Check the Spelling** Spell check can help, but it isn't enough. For errors with silent consonants, you'll have to read your work carefully. (See page 346W.)

- **Check the Mechanics** Errors in punctuation and capitalization can make your work hard to understand. In particular, check that you've correctly used semicolons. (See page 347W.)

Use these marks to edit and proofread your biography.

Editing and Proofreading Marks

MARK	WHAT IT MEANS	MARK	WHAT IT MEANS
∧	Insert something.	╱	Make lowercase.
∧	Add a comma.	ℰ	Delete, take something out.
∧	Add a semicolon.	¶	Make new paragraph.
⊙	Add a period.	◯	Spell out.
⊙	Add a colon.	⌒	Replace with this.
⌄ ⌄	Add quotation marks.	∿	Change order of letters or words.
⌄	Add an apostrophe.	#	Insert space.
≡	Capitalize.	◡	Close up, no space here.

Reflect

- What kinds of errors did you find? What can you do to keep from making them?

> ## GrammarWorkout

Check Consistency in Verb Tenses

When you combine ideas to form compound or complex sentences, always be sure to keep your verbs consistent.

Watch for consistency when forming compound sentences:

CONFUSING	Dottie **tries** out for a baseball team, and the South Bend Blue Sox **selected** her. *(mixes present- and past-tense verbs)*
CONSISTENT	Dottie **tried** out for a baseball team, and the South Bend Blue Sox **selected** her. *(past-tense verbs)*

Watch for consistency when forming complex sentences:

CONFUSING	Although baseball **is** her favorite, she **loved** all sports. *(mixes present- and past-tense verbs)*
CONSISTENT	Although baseball **is** her favorite, she **loves** all sports. *(present-tense verbs)*

Find the Trouble Spots

    She joined the farm league when she ~~is~~ ^{was} only ten. The kids on the team are bigger than her, but that didn't stop Dottie. She showed them how fast she could move, and she demonstrated how well she ~~threw~~ ^{could throw}. She becomes a standout player while she was still very young.

Find two more verb-tense errors to fix.

Edit and Proofread, continued

> ## SpellingWorkout

Check Words with Silent Consonants

Some words have consonants that are not pronounced. Get to know words with silent consonants. If you are not sure about a word, circle it and check the dictionary. If the silent consonant comes at the beginning of the word, you may need to look in two places!

Some common silent consonants are **k**, **w**, and **b.** If you've used words that have a silent consonant, make sure you haven't left it out.

Silent Consonant	Examples
k	know, knight, knee, kneel, knowledge, knife
w	write, wrong, wrist, wrap, wrestle
b	thumb, crumb, comb

Find the Trouble Spots

Ever since she was little, she knew that she wanted to be a professional baseball player. Unfortunately, there were not a lot of opportunities for women. Things changed after the start of World War II. Nowing that a number of male baseball players would be deployed overseas, baseball owners restled with a new problem. Who could they get under their thumb Who would play in their fields?

Find two more places where silent consonants should be added.

> ## Mechanics Workout

Check Semicolons

A **semicolon** indicates a pause slightly longer than a comma. Like the conjunctions **and, but,** and **or,** it can be used to join two independent clauses. Use it when the ideas in the two clauses are related.

EXAMPLES   The Kenosha Comets played well this season; they hope to make it to the championship.

The crowd roared as she stepped up to the plate; everyone was rooting for her.

She hit a home run in the ninth inning; however, it was not enough to win the game.

Find the Opportunities

The AAGPBL ended in 1954. However, Dottie continued to play baseball. She played three sessions on a touring team. Altogether Dottie played 15 sessions of professional baseball. No other woman has broken this record yet. Dottie's picture was placed in the National Baseball Hall of Fame. She was one of the few women individually featured. Dottie passed away in 1996. However, her legacy will continue to inspire others.

Find two other places where you can use a semicolon to combine sentences.

Publish, Share, and Reflect

Are you satisfied with the content of your biography? Does it share the details of someone else's life in an interesting way that gets your voice across, too? If so, you might like to share it with someone else.

❶ Publish and Share Your Work

Whether you write about someone famous or someone you know, other people might be interested in reading what you have to say. Here are a few ways you might share your biography with others:

- Desktop-publish your biography. A local copy shop will help you make duplicates to hand out.

- Send your biography in to a local newspaper or magazine for teens.

- Post your writing on a personal blog or Web site.

- Read your biography aloud to family or friends. See page 349W for tips on how to give a successful oral presentation.

However you choose to share it, including photos can help your readers connect with the person you write about.

❷ Reflect on Your Work

Just because you published and shared your work doesn't mean you're finished with it. Reflect on what you have written. Ask yourself what you learned from writing about someone else's life.

Reflect

- Does my biography show why my subject's life is important?

- Did my own voice come through in my writing?

Emphasize Your Points

Read your biography to your classmates to get their reactions.

To give a successful oral presentation:

1. **Plan** Read your biography aloud on your own. Map out what you are going to say. Decide the order in which you will present your ideas. Underline or highlight the main events or key points that you want to emphasize. Use key words to signal those ideas.

2. **Practice** Practice what you'll say before you speak. Also think about your delivery. Focus on using a clear voice that can be heard by your audience. Be sure to pronounce your words distinctly so that important events don't get lost. Use natural-looking gestures and eye contact to help emphasize your main ideas or themes. Practice your delivery in front of a mirror or make a video and watch your performance.

3. **Present** Briefly introduce your biography before you read. You might explain why you wrote it or why the person is important to you. Then read your biography to the audience, clearly and expressively. Remember:

   - Make eye contact with your listeners while you read so that you can monitor their reactions and confirm their understanding.

   - Speak loudly enough so that your audience can hear you, but change the volume of your voice to show different emotions. A softer voice can convey fear or deep feeling, for example, and a louder voice can show excitement. Slow down and speed up when it makes sense for the events in the biography.

   - Don't be afraid to "ham up" your presentation a little. It will help keep your audience's attention.

" **Writing a biography really puts me into the world and adventures of another person and helps me learn the lessons of his or her life.** "

Model Study

Public Service Announcement

What do you care about? A new city park? An after-school arts
program? Recycling? You can become an advocate for your cause.
An **advocate** is someone who publicly supports a cause or issue.
You can be an advocate in your everyday life. You can, for example,
wear an "Adopt-a-Pet" baseball cap to show your support for a local
pet shelter. You can also write as an advocate. One way to do this is
to write a public service announcement.

A **public service announcement** is a short message or position
statement that is delivered to an audience. Most public service
announcements are broadcast on radio, television, or other media. Like
other kinds of speeches, a good public service announcement engages
the audience and tries to persuade people to agree with a position.

Read the student model on page 351W. It shows the features of a
good public service announcement.

PUBLIC SERVICE ANNOUNCEMENT

A good public service announcement

☑ captures the listener's interest with a clearly stated position

☑ tells how the position differs from alternate or opposing positions

☑ supports the position with logical reasons and relevant evidence

☑ uses transition words and phrases

☑ concludes with a call to action that supports the position.

Feature Checklist

Let's Take Care of Our Air!

by Bruce Ansill

If you have ever choked on hot, polluted, summer air or seen the gray cloud hanging over some of our biggest cities, then you know that we have a smog problem. In my city last summer, we had twelve "red alert" smog days when it was recommended that the sick and the elderly stay indoors. To make our air cleaner and safer for us all, our state needs to pass regulations that will reduce smog.

When California faced a similar smog problem, lawmakers there created regulations controlling emissions from new cars and requiring oil companies to produce cleaner-burning gasoline. As a result, their biggest city had only three "red alert" smog days in 2010.

Some people argue that it will cost our state too much to check whether the new rules are being followed. Although there might be a short-term cost, the long-term savings in health-care expenses will more than offset that increase. Also, what price are we willing to pay for better health and quality of life?

California has been able to greatly reduce smog through regulations. The positive outcome in California makes it clear that our state needs to pass laws to control smog and take care of our air.

Student Model

*The writer presents his **position** on the issue.*

*The writer cites reliable **evidence**.*

*The writer tells an **opposing position** and addresses it.*

*The writer uses **transition words** to connect ideas.*

*The writer's **conclusion** follows from the position he presented.*

Write Effective Sentences

Combine Sentences

Good writing has a rhythm to it. The sentences are varied and interesting to read. If your writing sounds choppy, try to combine some sentences.

Short, Choppy Sentences

Our town's sanitation trucks should make their collections early in the day. They won't block traffic that way. Regular trash can be picked up first. Then another truck can pick up the recycling.

One Way to Combine the Sentences

Our town's sanitation trucks should make their collections early in the day. They won't block traffic that way. Regular trash can be picked up first. Then another truck can pick up the recycling.

so they ... *After* ... *is*

This writer combined sentences 1 and 2 and sentences 3 and 4.

Another Way to Combine the Sentences

Our town's sanitation trucks should make their collections early in the day. They won't block traffic that way. Regular trash can be picked up first. Then another truck can pick up the recycling.

because ... *followed by* ... *employed for picking*

This writer combined sentences 2–4.

Vary Your Sentences

Your writing will be livelier if you make some sentences short and others long. That way you can create a nice rhythm and flow. Use different kinds of sentences, too.

We Should Recycle More Materials

Many people recycle. We recycle cans. We recycle paper. We recycle metal. However, more things can be recycled. We should recycle them. We should recycle old batteries. They should not go in landfills. We should recycle old computers. You can use the parts again. Dryer lint can be recycled too. It can be used as insulation. We should recycle as many materials as we can.

All the sentences are statements, and most are about the same length.

Rev Up Your Recycling!

You probably know that newspapers, glass, and metal find uses as other products. But did you know that you can also recycle batteries, computers, and even dryer lint? Used batteries can and should be recycled, because they are hazardous in a landfill. Many parts of old computers can be used again. Dryer lint? It works as insulation and compost. So the next time you put a glass bottle in a blue bin, think about what else you can recycle!

The writer uses different kinds of sentences, and the sentences vary in length.

Write Effective Sentences, continued

Streamline Your Sentences

To keep your readers interested, avoid using too many words.
Readers shouldn't get lost between the beginning and the end of
a sentence.

Overloaded Sentence, Streamlined

Camping is a great activity that lets you get outdoors ~~and~~
enjoy nature ~~because you are close to the land and it is when~~
~~you can~~ experience life without all the usual distractions.
If you do go camping, though, it is important to follow the
rules of good camping. You always want to leave the land as
natural and clean as possible.

Don't write three or four words where just one will do.

Wordy Sentences, Streamlined

Campers should wash and
brush their teeth at least 200
feet away from lakes and streams
~~due to the fact that~~ soap and
toothpaste can harm living things.
Even a small amount of detergent
can harm ~~a large number of~~ fish
and other animals.

Instead of . . .	Use . . .
a large number of	many
at the present time	now
due to the fact that	because
in this day and age	today

◀ Campers who
cook on a stove
do less land
damage than
when they build
a campfire.

Another way to streamline sentences is to combine them with **appositives**. An appositive renames a noun or pronoun.

Choppy Sentences

A campsite should be treated with care. A campsite is a suitable place for people to spend time in nature. A good choice would be somewhere with existing campsites. Existing campsites are places that already have been used to set up tents and other equipment.

Streamlined with Appositives

A campsite, a suitable place for people to spend time in nature, should be treated with care. A good choice would be somewhere with existing campsites, places that already have been used to set up tents and other equipment.

Keep Your Sentences Parallel

When you compare or list more than one item, use similar, or parallel, grammatical forms.

Not Parallel

The campers knew to put water on the campfire rather than letting it die out on its own.

Parallel

The campers knew to put water on the campfire rather than to let it die out on its own.

Not Parallel

Carry out extra food, equipment, and what you see left by others.

Parallel

Carry out extra food, equipment, and litter.

How would you edit this sentence to make it parallel?

Not Parallel

Not only was the campsite too close to the river, a trail ran right by it.

Write a Public Service Announcement

WRITING PROMPT   What cause or issue in your school or community do you care about? What can you do to support the cause or resolve the issue? How can you get others involved?

Think about a cause that you support. Write a public service announcement that

- captures your audience by giving your position on the cause up front
- supports your position with logical reasons and relevant evidence
- addresses opposing views
- provides transition words and phrases to show how your ideas are related
- concludes with a call to action that supports your position.

Prewrite

Here are some tips for planning your public service announcement.

1 Choose a Good Topic

Brainstorm issues or causes that you would like others to support. Try to think of causes that you really care about so that your writing will sound sincere. Jot down a few possibilities, and then choose the best one. Rayna made a chart to help her choose a topic.

Ideas	Good and Bad Points
putting birdhouses in the park	too narrow; not everyone will be interested
building a wind farm to create energy for our town	too broad—would have to do a lot of research
recycling more things to help the environment and save money	people will be interested in this topic, and I can find the information I need

❷ Get to the Point

A public service announcement needs to engage the audience quickly. It's all right to begin with an attention-getting question or statement, but then you need to reveal your position.

Rayna's purpose for writing her public service announcement is to convince her audience that recycling can save money. She starts with a thought-provoking question and then moves right to her position.

> Do you want to save money and help preserve the environment at the same time? If so, you should recycle as many different materials as you can.

❸ Organize Your Ideas

A public service announcement is a way to express your ideas about public issues. Sometimes people will disagree with your position. So it's important to plan how to respond to possible opposing views.

Reflect
- Do you state your position clearly and up front?
- Do you respond to possible objections to your position?

Rayna's Plan for Her Public Service Announcement

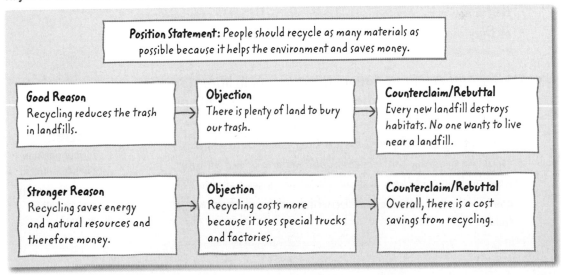

Position Statement: People should recycle as many materials as possible because it helps the environment and saves money.

Good Reason Recycling reduces the trash in landfills.	→	**Objection** There is plenty of land to bury our trash.	→	**Counterclaim/Rebuttal** Every new landfill destroys habitats. No one wants to live near a landfill.
Stronger Reason Recycling saves energy and natural resources and therefore money.	→	**Objection** Recycling costs more because it uses special trucks and factories.	→	**Counterclaim/Rebuttal** Overall, there is a cost savings from recycling.

Draft

Now that you've organized your ideas for a public service announcement, it's time to start writing!

- **State Your Position** Remember, hook your reader's attention and then get to the point.

- **Prove Your Point** Add your reasons and evidence.

> Recycling is easy to do and has many benefits for both the local community and the entire planet. Cities and states can actually earn money by selling recycled materials to factories that make them into new products. The environment as a whole benefits because recycling reduces the demand for landfill space, energy, and natural resources.

Rayna gives reasons and evidence to support her position.

- **Address Opposing Views** Respond to possible objections.

> Some people think that recycling just isn't worth the trouble. In fact, it saves energy and natural resources. Making an aluminum can from recycled metal uses only 5% of the energy that a can from new ore would need. Recycled paper saves millions of trees each year.

Rayna responds to possible objections.

- **Ask for Agreement or Action** In your conclusion, state what you want your audience to do. Be clear and specific.

> Recycling is really very easy. Most communities have a recycling program that collects your materials, and all you have to do is sort them and put them into a separate bin. The community and entire planet benefit, so keep, or start, recycling today!

Reflect
- Is your position clearly stated?
- Did you end with a clear call to action?

DRAFTING TIPS
Trait: **Voice and Style**

If Your Writing Sounds Boring . . .
Boring writing lacks punch. If you don't get your listener's attention with vivid words, you won't be able to sell your opinion in a public service announcement.

Try Picking Verbs with a Punch
When you replace bland, overused verbs with vivid and precise ones, you can spice up your writing.

Here is an example of how you can punch up the verbs to change bland writing to interesting writing.

Bland

> Many electrical appliances use electricity even when they are turned off. Check that those appliances are unplugged.

Interesting

> Many electrical appliances consume electricity even when they are turned off. Verify that those appliances are unplugged.

The following chart shows a few verbs that can make your writing more interesting. A thesaurus Is a great resource for finding precise, vivid verbs.

Instead of...	Try...
eat	munch, gulp, devour, consume
give	present, donate, provide, supply, grant
protect	defend, guard, shield, safeguard, shelter
pull	drag, haul, tug, yank
say	shout, reply, exclaim, whisper, holler
write	record, scribble, scrawl, inscribe

Revise

As you revise your public service announcement, remember your audience and purpose. Will your writing do what you want it to do? Will it connect with your audience?

1 Evaluate Your Work

Let a partner read your public service announcement and give you feedback. Ask your partner questions about your writing:

- **About the Form** Is my writing well organized? Is my position, or opinion, clear? Did I provide strong support for my position, or opinion?

- **About the Voice and Style** Does my announcement hook your interest? Are the word choices precise? Are there places where I could write with more punch?

Revision in Action

From Rayna's Draft

What's a good reason to recycle? It's a good way to limit pollution. Many people think that recycling just saves materials. It does a whole lot more. The EPA estimates that if each family recycled half of its waste each year, 2,400 fewer pounds of carbon dioxide would enter the atmosphere.

It is important to recycle materials other than paper, glass, and metal in order to keep them out of landfills. Batteries release metals into the soil and water that harm people and other animals. Over 200 million gallons of used motor oil are improperly thrown away each year. Recycling them instead would reduce pollution. People can and should recycle car and bicycle tires, too. Many materials put in landfills can pollute our land and water.

Hector thinks:

" You used the word *good* in the first two sentences."

" You could combine sentences here."

" Your conclusion should follow the position you gave."

② Mark Your Changes

Add Text You may need to add text to make your public service announcement more persuasive. Use this mark ∧ to add:

- facts, examples, and other evidence to support your position

- clear reasons to support your position

- text to make the opening sentence or conclusion more interesting.

Replace Text Use this mark ⌒ to replace bland words with words that are more vivid or precise.

Reflect

- Do you need to add reasons or evidence to support your position?

- Do you need to replace bland words with words that will make your writing more interesting?

Revising Marks	MARK	∧	⌒	⌒	⌒	⌐
	WHAT IT MEANS	Insert something.	Move to here.	Replace with this.	Take out.	Make a new paragraph.

Revised Draft

What's a good reason to recycle? ~~It's a good way to~~ *It limits*
limit pollution. Many people think that recycling just saves
materials, *but* It does a whole lot more. The EPA estimates
that if each family recycled half of its waste each year,
2,400 fewer pounds of carbon dioxide would enter
the atmosphere.

It is important to recycle materials other than paper,
glass, and metal in order to keep them out of landfills.
Batteries release metals into the soil and water that harm
people and other animals. Over 200 million gallons of used
motor oil are thrown away improperly each year. *so* Recycling
them instead would reduce pollution. People can and
should recycle car and bicycle tires, too. ~~Many materials
put in landfills can pollute our land and water.~~

∧ Recycling has the great benefit of reducing pollution so
everyone should recycle as many different materials as
they can.

Edit and Proofread

When you've made your public service announcement as strong as possible, the last step is to fix your language errors. This is called editing and proofreading your work.

- **Check the Grammar** Make sure that you have used correct grammar throughout. In particular, check for correct use of the present perfect tense. (See page 363W.)

- **Check the Spelling** Spell-check on a computer can be helpful, though it won't catch all your spelling mistakes. You should read carefully for the spelling of words ending with *-y.* (See page 364W.)

- **Check the Mechanics** Mistakes in punctuation can make your work hard to understand. In particular, check that you have used commas between adjectives correctly. (See page 365W.)

Use these marks to edit and proofread your announcement.

Editing and Proofreading Marks

MARK	WHAT IT MEANS	MARK	WHAT IT MEANS
∧	Insert something.	╱	Make lowercase.
⋀	Add a comma.	℘	Delete, take something out.
⋀̇	Add a semicolon.	⁋	Make new paragraph.
⊙	Add a period.	⬭	Spell out.
⊙̈	Add a colon.	⌒	Replace with this.
ⱽ ⱽ	Add quotation marks.	∼	Change order of letters or words.
ⱽ	Add an apostrophe.	#	Insert space.
≡	Capitalize.	‿	Close up, no space here.

Reflect

- What kinds of errors did you find? What can you do to keep from making them?

> ## Grammar Workout

Check Present Perfect Tense

The present perfect tense is formed with the helping verb **has** or **have** plus the past participle.

- Use the present perfect tense when the time period you are referring to is not finished.

  EXAMPLES I **have studied** a lot about global warming.
  My science teacher **has helped** me understand it.

- The past participle of regular verbs ends in **-ed.** However, many verbs have irregular past participles. For a listing of some irregular verbs, look in the Grammar Handbook

  EXAMPLES

Regular Verbs	Past Participle	Irregular Verbs	Past Participle
warm	warmed	freeze	frozen
melt	melted	spend	spent

- Make sure you use the correct form of the helping verb. With **he**, **she**, or **it**, or with nouns that can be replaced by **he**, **she**, or **it**, use **has**. For all other nouns and pronouns, use **have**.

  EXAMPLES I <u>have</u> spent the last two summers doing research.
  The Earth <u>has</u> **warmed** a lot in the last two centuries.

Find the Trouble Spots

The environment ~~have~~ **has** suffered ever since plastic was invented. Plastics have ~~consumpted~~ **consumed** a lot of energy for many years. Many scientists have gave detailed warnings about the dangers of plastic. They seen evidence that the plastic filling up our landfills will not go away any time soon!

Find and fix two other present perfect tense errors.

Edit and Proofread, continued

> ## SpellingWorkout

Spelling Words Ending with -y

Follow these spelling rules to add endings to words that end with **-y.**

- If a word ends in a consonant + **y,** change the **y** to **i** before you add **-es, -ed, -er,** or **-est.**

  EXAMPLES story stories   try tried
  silly sillier   happy happiest

- For words that end with a vowel + **y,** just add **-s** or **-ed.**

  EXAMPLES play played   key keys   boy boys

- If you add **-ing** to a verb that ends in **-y,** do not change the **y** to **i.**

  EXAMPLES studying emptying crying

Find the Trouble Spots

A few days ago, I read an article about the amount of trash different neighborhoods recycled. I was worried when I saw that our neighborhood was last on the list. Many familes on our street do recycle, but apparently that's not enough. So, I'm tring to change that. Along with my best buddyes, we are giving the neighbors lessons on playng a positive role in the environment. We'll show them the easyiest ways to recycle!

Find five more spelling errors to fix.

Mechanics Workout

Check Commas Between Adjectives

- Use a comma between two coordinate adjectives, or adjectives that modify a noun in the same way.

  EXAMPLE   Behind me, I heard Sam's **clear, friendly** voice.

- To check if you should use a comma between the adjectives, try the following two tests. If the meaning is still clear, use a comma.

  EXAMPLE   Sam has an **amazing, delicious** meal planned for today.

  Test 1:   Use a comma if the meaning is still clear when you replace the comma with the word **and**.

  Sam has an **amazing** <u>and</u> **delicious** meal planned for today.

  Test 2:   Use a comma if the meaning is still clear when you reverse the order of the adjectives.

  Sam has a **delicious, amazing** meal planned for today.

Find the Trouble Spots

Sam loves to fix tasty‿unique meals for all his family. When his hungry boisterous relatives come over, they have a great time. After the meal, though, there are a lot of leftovers! But Sam reuses the sturdy plastic containers that butter and soft cheeses come in. He never throws away old white containers. He fills the clean empty containers with the leftovers. That way, everyone gets to take some food home.

Find three more places where there should be a comma.

Model Study

Persuasive Essay

Are there issues that you care deeply about? Well, writing as a citizen is one way to share your opinions. You try to persuade readers to agree with you. With a good persuasive essay, you may even convince your readers to take action.

PERSUASIVE ESSAY

A good persuasive essay

- ☑ states the writer's position on the issue
- ☑ appeals to logic using evidence
- ☑ appeals to emotions using persuasive language
- ☑ addresses the opposing argument
- ☑ ends with a call to action.

Feature Checklist

Read the persuasive essay on the following pages. The writer opens by acknowledging the opposing arguments. She goes on to address those concerns one by one.

She states her position. Later you will find that she repeats or restates it.

Lake McDonald in
Glacier National Park ▶

Climate Change

by Maria Nguyen

Many people think that we aren't in danger from climate change. They think that global warming doesn't affect us. I disagree. Climate change is an issue that affects everyone. It's a danger to all the plants, animals, and people on Earth. If each person made small changes, it would be a big help to the planet.

Climate change is a big problem. Scientists have been studying climate change for years. They say that the world is getting warmer every year. Even a change of a few degrees can make ice melt. Glaciers in Montana have been melting. Today there are only 27 glaciers in Glacier National Park. In 1910, there were 150.

Temperatures have been going up for many reasons. One reason is higher levels of carbon dioxide, a gas that traps heat. When the sun's rays reach the surface of the Earth, part of their energy is reflected back into the atmosphere. The other part is absorbed and heats up the surface. The warmed surface then radiates heat in the form of infrared rays. Carbon dioxide and other gases in the atmosphere trap this heat, warming up the Earth in what scientists call the "greenhouse effect."

The writer provides background on the issue and states her **position**.

The writer gives **reasons** to support her position.

The writer appeals to logic with **facts and statistics**.

Student Model

Persuasive Essay, continued

The greenhouse effect, which occurs naturally, has intensified in the last two centuries. Carbon dioxide in the atmosphere has been increasing dramatically. Many factors have led to this increase. There are more factories now. More people have cars, and they drive farther to work and school. These factors and many others have led to the increase in carbon dioxide.

Plants all over the world use carbon dioxide and water to make food through a process called photosynthesis. Oxygen is given off as a byproduct. But developers have cut down trees, and cities have expanded without replanting trees. This has made the problem worse. Plants have been unable to help reduce the increased levels of carbon dioxide.

Even though it seems hopeless, it is not. The damage done by climate change is not permanent. We should do everything we can to stop the damage now. Each person can begin by becoming more energy-efficient. We could walk or ride bikes more, and we could plant trees. We could talk to our friends and neighbors about making changes. If every person made a small change, imagine what that would do! We could make the world safer for the future.

The writer gives additional **reasons** supported by **facts**.

The writer includes **appeals to reader's emotions**.

The writer lists **ways for readers to take action**.

But it isn't just individuals who need to change. There are changes to be made by governments, too. Governments should start taxing companies that produce too much carbon dioxide. They should also spend money researching alternative energy sources. There are forms of energy, such as wind and solar generation, that don't produce as much carbon dioxide. The government should give money to car companies for research into engines that are more energy-efficient. Cars represent 31 percent of all the carbon dioxide pollution. Can't you see we need to take action?

Changes have to happen. Every person can make small adjustments to help slow down climate change. We can write letters to our representatives to ask for responsible action. We all have to do whatever we can. Our planet is being damaged by processes that we could reverse or at least slow down. Change your own life, and write to your elected representative to demand that the government get involved.

Additional **facts and statistics** support the writer's argument.

The writer ends by restating her **position** and including a **call to action**.

Appeal to Logic

When you're having an argument with a friend, you try to convince the person that you are right. You do this by giving reasons for your opinions. You do the same thing when you write persuasively. You appeal to your reader's logic with solid reasons supported by facts and evidence.

Build Strong Arguments

Include the following to appeal to your reader's sense of logic.

Solid Reasons

Back up your point of view with two or three solid reasons. You can start with your strongest reason, or begin with your weakest and build up.

Most Convincing Reason
↓
Less Convincing Reason
↓
Least Convincing Reason

Facts and Statistics

Adding facts and statistics makes your argument more convincing.

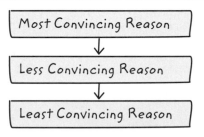

> Climate change has been happening for years. It has been getting warmer and warmer. The average temperature has increased 1.4 degrees since 1880. Eleven of the last twelve years have been recorded as the hottest since 1850.

With Examples

To make your reasons more convincing, you can add supporting examples.

Global climate change has negative effects on the environment. The Arctic ice is disappearing, which raises water levels. Glaciers are disappearing. Coral reefs are dying off. Higher temperatures lead to more extreme weather events like hurricanes and tropical storms.

Backup from an Expert

You can also include an expert's opinion to support your own.

Are humans causing climate change? A United Nations panel has said yes. UN scientist Mike Jambur said that humans have contributed the most to make the Earth warmer.

Read the example below. How could the writer include appeals to logic to make the argument more convincing?

Endangered Species

Part of caring for the environment is protecting species that are in danger of becoming extinct. Many species of animals are endangered. When a species becomes extinct, everyone loses. Keeping endangered species alive and healthy is important for people all over the world. We should do everything we can to stop organisms from dying out. Having many different kinds of animals on Earth makes our planet a better place for humans and all animals.

Where could the writer add facts, statistics, or expert opinions?

Appeal to Emotion

Have you ever watched a movie with suspenseful music? In the movies, the music often gives you cues as to what is happening on the screen and how you should feel. Appeals to emotion are like music in movies. They can affect the reader's feelings and motivate the reader to take action.

Use Persuasive Language

Use words that show you believe in your opinion. Try not to sound extreme, though. Show that you care about the issue, but make sure you sound reasonable. Check out the examples below. What makes the middle one the most effective?

Not Enough Emotion

> Global climate change concerns everyone. We should do something about it.

Effective Appeal to Emotion

> Global climate change is a very important issue. Everyone has the ability to make small changes. Small changes will lead to big effects that could save our planet.

Too Emotional

> You are ridiculous if you think climate change is not a problem. We need to do something quickly or else. Our planet is in terrible danger!

Use Personal Examples

You can appeal to emotions by including personal stories. These stories can come from people affected by an issue. Remember that these examples don't replace facts and statistics. But they're a great way to make readers care more about what you're saying.

Personal Example

> Climate change affects everyone. "I am afraid that the water level in the lake will keep rising," says homeowner Marcus Wells.

Personal Example

> Climate change causes more extreme weather events. The Jones family lost their home in Hurricane Katrina.

Read the model below. How could it be improved?

Hurricane Katrina

Hurricane Katrina was one of the worst storms ever to hit the United States. The hurricane formed over the Atlantic Ocean in late summer of 2005. On August 29, this storm made landfall in Louisiana and Mississippi. It caused major flooding in many wild areas and in many places where human beings live.

Hurricane Katrina destroyed animal habitats and property all over the Gulf Coast of the U.S. The storm wrecked oil platforms and refineries. This has had a big economic impact on the Gulf states. The forestry industry was also negatively affected. The storm flattened millions of acres of forest.

How could the writer change the language to appeal to readers' emotions? Where could he add a personal example?

Support Your Arguments

It is always important for lawyers to have evidence to support their case. If they don't have evidence, their case could get thrown out. A persuasive essay is like a case in court. If you don't include enough evidence to support your opinions, your readers won't be convinced.

Gather Evidence

Evidence supports your opinions. Use evidence from various sources to convince your audience of your argument. You might include evidence based on your own experience, facts and statistics, or even expert opinions.

Use a chart like the one below to organize your evidence. It will also show whether you need more ideas.

Argument	Evidence
Climate change affects everyone.	Animals' habitats are being destroyed. Animals are becoming extinct. People who live near the coast are in danger. If climate change continues, people may lose their homes.
Making change in your life is easy.	Bicycling and walking save energy and keep you fit. Most people can plant trees. Energy-efficient lightbulbs save money and are easy to install.
The situation is not hopeless.	Scientists have said that we can reverse climate change. If each person changed a small thing, big changes would happen.

As you write, use your list of arguments and evidence. Make sure you include appeals to readers' logic and to their emotions. Use these techniques:

- Support your reasons with facts.

> Many countries have taken action. They charge companies that produce too much carbon dioxide.

- Develop your reasons with details.

> More than 100 million people live close to sea level. If the water level rose, they might lose their homes.

- Use persuasive language to get readers on your side.

> Shouldn't each of us do what he or she can? Together, we can stop climate change!

Read the example below. How could the writer improve it?

Climate Change

Climate change is a major issue in today's society. Many people think that climate change will alter human society completely. It is also bad for plants and animals.

Some businesses and companies are not doing very much to help prevent climate change. They do not realize what a problem it is. Changes in the climate are a problem that everyone should do his or her best to prevent.

How could the writer make this argument more convincing by adding support?

Use Charts, Tables, and Pictures

As we go to school or work, we see thousands of images. These images could be on billboards or bus stops. They could even be road signs. Visuals get our attention in a way that words can't. In a persuasive essay, visuals can convince readers by showing them at a glance why your position is valid. They communicate ideas in a simple way, and they can grab readers' attention.

Strengthen Your Argument with Visuals

You can develop your ideas by adding visuals. Some examples of visuals are charts, tables, and pictures. Graphics get readers' attention. They can also help make complicated ideas clear.

- Use a graph or a pie chart to present data or statistics.

- Present information or statistics in a table like the one below.

Rising Global Temperatures

Year	Average Temperature
1960	57.6°F
1970	58.3°F
1980	58.1°F
1990	59.8°F

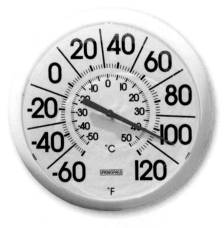

- Another way to strengthen your arguments is to include pictures. Pictures can show your reader exactly what you mean.

Mount Kilimanjaro

Mount Kilimanjaro is a well-known mountain in Tanzania. It is especially famous for its snowy summit. Unfortunately, a warming climate has caused the snows of Kilimanjaro to melt.

The image below on the left shows Mount Kilimanjaro in 1993. The image on the right shows the same view in 2000. In seven short years, almost the entire snow cap disappeared. Some scientists think that by 2020, the snows of Mount Kilimanjaro will be gone completely.

TechTIP

Use a scanner to turn photographs or other images into digital files you can insert in your paper.

▼ The peaks of Mount Kilimanjaro were once covered in snow, but now the snow is melting.

1993   2000

Write a Persuasive Essay

WRITING PROMPT The environment affects everyone. People have different opinions about how best to deal with environmental issues. Maybe you feel strongly about stopping climate change or reducing greenhouse gases. How would you persuade others to agree with your position?

Think of an environmental issue you feel strongly about and know something about. Then write a persuasive essay that includes

- background about the issue
- a clear statement of your position on the issue
- reasons and evidence to support your position
- a call to action asking readers to do something about the issue.

Prewrite

Here are some tips for planning and preparing before you start writing.

1 Choose an Issue and a Position

It's important to write about an issue you care about. Think about environmental issues that affect you or your community. Choose one you know a little about.

Next, decide what your position on the issue is—and what you want people to do about it. Ricky thought of a specific way people could cut down on the amount of plastic in the environment.

Issues I care about

Climate change—We should drive less or drive cars that use less gas.

Air pollution from factories—They should reduce pollution.

People using too much plastic—We should not drink so much bottled water.

2 Gather Evidence to Support Your Position

Learn more about your topic. It's the best way to find evidence to support your arguments. Do research to make sure that you know the issue well. Then write down evidence based on personal experience, facts and statistics, or expert opinions. Use a chart to organize your evidence.

Argument	Evidence
People should drink tap water instead of bottled water.	Tap water is free. Plus, drinking it doesn't lead to lots of plastic bottles lying around.
Plastic bottles are bad for the environment.	They last for years in landfills. They are not biodegradable, so they don't break down.

TechTIP

Start a file with reasons, facts, and examples. Write them as phrases or sentences. Then **cut** and **paste** them to move them around as you draft.

3 Organize Your Main Supporting Points

Now that you've done the research, what are the best reasons that you have to support your position? What reasons will you give to convince others to agree with you?

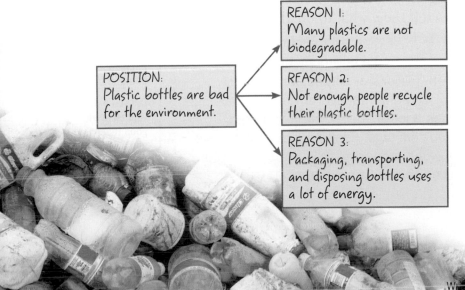

POSITION:
Plastic bottles are bad for the environment.

REASON 1:
Many plastics are not biodegradable.

REASON 2:
Not enough people recycle their plastic bottles.

REASON 3:
Packaging, transporting, and disposing bottles uses a lot of energy.

Reflect

• Do you have a clear position on your issue?

• Is there enough evidence to support your opinion?

Draft

You've thought about the issue, done some research, and organized your reasons and evidence. Now it's time to start writing. Use your planning to create a strong argument.

- **Write an Introduction** Start off by giving your readers a little background about the issue. Then, state your position clearly in **one sentence**.

From Ricky's Draft

> Many people enjoy their favorite beverage by sipping it from a plastic bottle. We carry these bottles everywhere because they seem convenient. Unfortunately, our convenience is actually a burden. Plastic bottles are bad for the environment, so we should cut down on using them.

Ricky introduces readers to the issue and then clearly states his opinion.

- **Build Your Case** Present your arguments and your supporting evidence to the reader. Use your list of reasons and evidence to write the essay. Appeal to your reader's logic and emotions.

- **End with a Strong Conclusion** In your last paragraph, restate your position and main supporting reasons. Then, end with a **call to action**! You've gotten readers to care about the issue—now tell them what to do about it.

> The plastic bottle's toll on the environment is obvious. Landfills are filled with millions of bottles, because few people recycle them. Creating, transporting, and disposing of plastic bottles uses a lot of energy. Try to limit the amount of plastic you consume. Even if it's difficult to give up drinking bottled water, at least recycle the bottles you use. Everyday choices can make a difference!

Reflect

- Did your introduction provide enough background information?

- Did you build your case with good reasons and evidence?

- Did you end with a strong call to action?

DRAFTING TIPS
Trait: **Voice and Style**

If Your Writing Isn't Convincing Enough...
In a conversation, communication is back and forth. You say your opinion, hear what others think, and have a chance to respond. When you're writing, you can't hear your readers' thoughts. That's why it's important to consider how readers will respond to your arguments. Then you can be prepared with answers.

Try Taking The Other Side
You've taken a side on the issue. Chances are, not everyone will agree with you! Try looking at it from another point of view. How would someone who disagrees with you challenge your arguments? How could you respond?

Argument	Challenge	Response
Americans should consume less bottled water.	Drinking water is healthy. If Americans give up bottled water, won't they just drink more sugary beverages?	Bottled water is not the only source for healthy drinking water. The tap in your kitchen also provides safe, clean drinking water.

Once you have predicted what some possible objections might be, you can prepare your response. Use a calm, reasonable tone. By including this in your essay, you show your reader how well-thought-out your argument really is.

Revise

Think about your audience and purpose as you revise. Will your writing persuade your readers and motivate them to take action?

1 **Evaluate Your Work**

Exchange drafts with a partner and read his or her essay. Try to find points that you could argue with, and have your partner do the same for you. Ask questions:

- **About the Form** Are the arguments clear, convincing, and well-supported? How might someone challenge my position?

- **About the Voice and Style** Does my voice come through? Do my sentences sing?

Revision in Action

From Ricky's Draft

Many people drink beverages from plastic bottles. We carry these bottles everywhere. They are used for all kinds of beverages. They seem convenient. People just throw them out when they are done. But plastic bottles are bad for the environment. We should recycle them.

One of the reasons that plastics are bad for the environment is that they are not biodegradable. That means they last for a very long time. There are lots of plastic bottles in garbage landfills. There are also lots of plastic bottles in rivers and streams. There are plastic bottles on the ground too. Americans drink more than 8 million gallons of bottled water annually.

Ricky's partner says:

" You have a lot of short sentences. That makes your introduction dull."

" What does 'a very long time' mean? Be specific."

" You're repeating the same ideas a lot. Maybe you could combine some sentences."

2 **Mark Your Changes**

Clarify To make your text clearer, you may need to

- add details to support or explain your position
- replace vague words or dull phrases with more precise or colorful language.

Consolidate Streamlining your text can make your arguments clearer and more convincing. You may need to

- delete repetitive or wordy phrases and dull words
- combine sentences to make your writing more sophisticated.

Reflect

- Are your arguments convincing? How could you add more support?
- Does the writing in your essay sound like you?

Revising Marks	**MARK**	∧	↶	↱	↝	¶
	WHAT IT MEANS	Insert something.	Move to here.	Replace with this.	Take out.	Make a new paragraph.

Revised Draft

Many people drink ^their favorite^ beverages from plastic bottles ^—juice, soda, and of course, water.^ We carry these bottles everywhere. ~~They are used for all kinds of beverages.~~ They seem convenient. People just throw them out when they are done ^B~~b~~ut plastic bottles are bad for the environment. We should recycle them.

~~One of the reasons that~~ ^because^ plastics are bad for the environment ~~is that~~ they are not biodegradable. That means they last for ^centuries^ ~~a very long time~~. There are lots of plastic bottles in garbage landfills ^. There are also lots of plastic bottles~~ ^and^ In rivers and streams ^. There are plastic bottles~~ on the ground too. Americans drink more than 8 million gallons of bottled water annually.

Ricky consolidated some sentences. He also added more colorful language.

Ricky consolidated ideas so his writing wouldn't sound repetitive.

Ricky replaced vague words with more precise words to clarify.

Edit and Proofread

When you've made your argument as strong as possible, the last step is to fix your language errors. This is called editing and proofreading your work.

- **Check the Grammar** Make sure that you have used correct grammar throughout. In particular, check for the placement of participial phrases. (See page 385W.)

- **Check the Spelling** Spell-check on a computer can be helpful, though it won't catch all your spelling mistakes. Read carefully to check words spelled with *q, ie,* or *ei.* (See page 386W.)

- **Check the Mechanics** Mistakes in punctuation can make your work hard to understand. In particular, pay attention to how you have used commas with participles and appositives. (See page 387W.)

Use these marks to edit and proofread your essay.

Editing and Proofreading Marks

MARK	WHAT IT MEANS	MARK	WHAT IT MEANS
∧	Insert something.	╱	Make lowercase.
∧	Add a comma.	ℒ	Delete, take something out.
∧	Add a semicolon.	¶	Make new paragraph.
⊙	Add a period.	◯	Spell out.
⊙	Add a colon.	⌒	Replace with this.
∨ ∨	Add quotation marks.	∼	Change order of letters or words.
∨	Add an apostrophe.	#	Insert space.
≡	Capitalize.	◡	Close up, no space here.

Reflect

- What kinds of errors did you find? What can you do to keep from making them?

Grammar Workout

Check Participial Phrases

When you write, be sure to place participial phrases near the words they describe. Otherwise, you might create a "dangling participle."

- Always place a participial phrase near the word it describes. Sometimes you can just move the phrase to fix the problem.

  Not OK: **Mom put several in her cart reaching for the reusable bottles.**

  OK: **Reaching for the reusable bottles, Mom put several in her cart.**

- Sometimes you need to rephrase the sentence and include a word for the phrase to describe.

  Not OK: **Concerned about the plastics problem, reusable bottles would help.**

  OK: **Concerned about the plastics problem, Mom knew that reusing bottles would help.**

Find the Trouble Spots

Mom did something good for the environment ⟨buying⟩ ⟨reusable drinking bottles⟩ Having reusable bottles is really convenient, too. Filling the bottles with water, they go just about anywhere. We often get thirsty and ask Dad to stop traveling for a long time. But we don't have to stop because we have water. I never miss a play by going to the snack bar watching a football game. My drink is right there by my side. My bottle is ready for the next time I go somewhere, cleaned after each use.

Find and fix four other misplaced or dangling participles.

Edit and Proofread, continued

> # Spelling Workout

Check Words with *q*, *ie*, and *ei*

There are some spelling rules in the English language that are pretty reliable. Here are a couple of them.

- The letter *q* nearly always has the letter *u* right after it. Some proper nouns are exceptions.

EXAMPLES	quit, quarter, quest
EXCEPTIONS	Iraq, Qatar

- When the letters *i* and *e* appear together, *i* usually comes before *e*. However, this changes when the letters come after the letter *c*, or when *ei* make the sound of long *a*.

EXAMPLES	friend, relief, achieve
EXCEPTIONS FOR C	ceiling, conceited, perceive
EXCEPTIONS FOR LONG A SOUND	sleigh, freight, neighbor

Find the Trouble Spots

You might not beli**ev**e your eyes, but they aren't decieving you. There is no q~~u~~estion: parts of some landfills look like feilds of plastic bottles. Take a qick visit to your local landfill, and think about how all that plastic affects the qality of our environment.

Find four more spelling errors to fix.

Mechanics Workout

Participial Phrases and Appositives

Regular Verbs	Past Participle
warm	warmed
melt	melted

Irregular Verbs	Past Participle
freeze	frozen
spend	spent

The **present participle** of a verb is the form that ends in *-ing*.

> **EXAMPLE**   The Earth is **getting** warmer.

The **past participle** of regular verbs ends in *-ed*. However, many verbs have irregular past participles. For a listing of some irregular verbs, look in the Grammar Handbook.

A **participial phrase** is a group of words that contains either a present participle or a past participle and can be used to tell more about a noun or pronoun. Set off participial phrases with commas.

> **EXAMPLE**   The new law, **written in 1985,** has helped a lot.

An **appositive** is a noun or noun phrase that tells more about a noun or pronoun. Set off appositives with commas.

> **EXAMPLES**   Renee, **my oldest sister,** helped our community recycle its plastic bottles.
> She'll be working with the city council president, **Mr. Sykes.**

Find the Trouble Spots

Concerned about the environment‸activists have formed a new organization‸Recycle Now. Plastic bags unfortunately used by most supermarkets and department stores can at least be recycled. My neighbor Mr. Robinson reuses his plastic shopping bags.

Find two phrases to set off with commas.

Publish, Share, and Reflect

By now your persuasive essay is organized and convincing, and it lets your voice come through. The next step is to share it with readers.

1 Publish and Share Your Work

Your essay won't persuade anyone if you don't share it! When you publish your writing, think about the best way to present your ideas to your audience.

You might want to make your essay public, especially if it addresses an issue that affects your community. To share your essay with a wide audience, consider these ways of publishing:

- Post it on a blog or Web site.
- Publish it in your school newspaper.
- Send it as a letter to the editor of your local newspaper.
- Send it as a letter to your local politician.
- Present it on a local radio program.

Alternatively, you may share your essay by reading it aloud to a smaller audience, such as your family, your friends, or your class. However you choose to share it, think about ways to make it clear and informative. For instance, you might

- use tables to present detailed information
- use bulleted lists to summarize major points.

2 Reflect on Your Work

Keep thinking about what you wrote! You took the time to research and write about an issue that matters to you. Stay informed about the topic, and revisit your essay if you want to make changes.

Reflect

- What did I learn about the issue from writing about it?

- Has my position on this issue changed at all?

How to Give a Persuasive Speech

Is there a project at school or in your community that you would like to see happen? It could be something fun (like a comedy club) or that people need (like a literacy center). You can give a persuasive speech that tells why your project is a good idea and convinces school or community leaders to make it happen.

Here is how you present a persuasive speech:

- **Pick a subject.** Choose a topic that you feel strongly about. You will be expressing an opinion, or your point of view about the subject.

- **Support your opinion.** Even though an opinion tells what you think, it should be supported by clear reasons and evidence, such as facts, examples, or statistics. Choose information from reliable sources that best shows your audience why your project is important. Expect that some people will disagree with you and prepare ways to answer their objections respectfully.

  " Giving a good speech about a subject I care about is important. I can explain why the topic matters and try to convince others to think about the issue another way. "

- **Plan your speech.** Present your ideas in an order that is easy to follow and convincing. Begin by stating your opinion, use effective transitions, and end with a powerful conclusion. Include persuasive words such as *must* and *should*. Make graphics or find photos that enhance your speech.

- **Practice and give your speech.** Speak clearly and loudly enough so that everyone can hear and understand you. Make eye contact with individuals in the audience. Use natural gestures to emphasize the key ideas. Use a confident and convincing tone of voice. Stay relaxed and on topic.

Writing
FORMS

Advertisements

Autobiography

Biography

Book Review

Character Sketch

Description

Directions

E-mail

Essays

Interview

Job Application

Letters

Literary Response

Newspaper

Personal Narrative

Play

Poetry

Procedure

Story

Web site

Workplace and
Consumer Resources

Advertisements

Print Ad

Advertisements are a powerful form of persuasion. They can be used to "sell" almost anything—food, clothes, vacation spots, even political candidates. Print ads appeal to readers by combining text with eye-catching visual images.

"Whistle" was a soft drink popular in the 1920s. ▼

Attracts readers' attention with images

Uses descriptive words to appeal to consumers

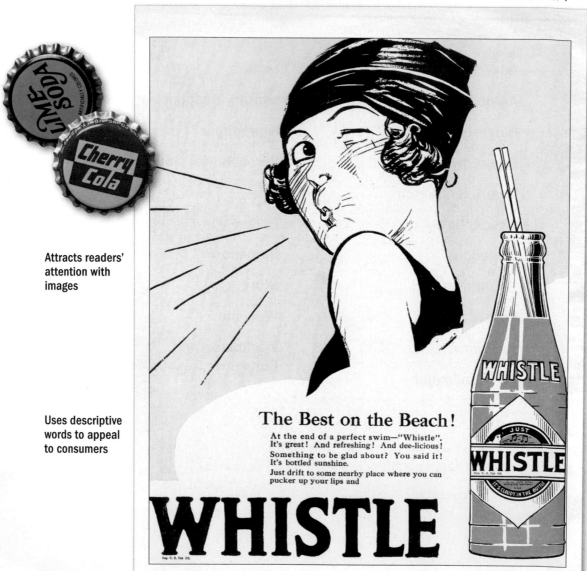

The Best on the Beach!

At the end of a perfect swim—"Whistle".
It's great! And refreshing! And dee-licious!
Something to be glad about? You said it!
It's bottled sunshine.
Just drift to some nearby place where you can
pucker up your lips and

WHISTLE

TV Ad Script

Advertisements on television get viewers' attention and present a brief, persuasive message, often with catchy phrases and vivid images. Some ads try to sell a product. Others, like the public service announcement (PSA) below, try to persuade viewers to take action on a community concern.

Crushed aluminum cans ready for recycling ▶

"Recycling" PSA

Scene: A living room with doorway to the kitchen visible in background. JAMAL is taking a nap on the couch in the living room.

KEVIN begins wrestling a heavy garbage bag from the trash can in the kitchen. JAMAL wakes up.

JAMAL (*annoyed*): Why does taking out the trash have to make so much noise?

KEVIN: It's all these soda cans.

JAMAL: What are those doing in the garbage?

KEVIN: Making noise, I guess.

KEVIN puts the heavy bag down. It drops loudly.

JAMAL: No, I mean, why are they in the trash when they aren't garbage? Those cans could be melted down and reused. Recycling metal cans saves energy and resources.

Cut to a recycling bin full of cans.

VOICE-OVER: If it clinks, it's not garbage. Recycle.

Cut to CCFEA logo and URL.

VOICE-OVER: For more information about recycling in your neighborhood, visit our Web site. Paid for by Concerned Citizens for Environmental Activism.

Stage directions tell what happens on-screen.

Dialogue defines what the actors will say.

A clear persuasive message often uses brief, memorable language.

Autobiography

An autobiography is the story of someone's own life. When you write an autobiography, you tell about the experiences that made you who you are today.

At age 7, Firoozeh Dumas moved to the U.S. from Iran. ▶

Often includes background about family history and childhood experiences

Moving to America was both exciting and frightening, but we found great comfort in knowing that my father spoke English. Having spent years regaling us with stories about his graduate years in America, he had left us with the distinct impression that America was his second home. My mother and I planned to stick close to him, letting him guide us through the exotic American landscape that he knew so well. We counted on him not only to translate the language but also to translate the culture, to be a link to this most foreign of lands. . .

Uses first-person pronouns.

Once we reached America, we wondered whether perhaps my father had confused his life in America with someone else's. Judging from the bewildered looks of store cashiers, gas station attendants, and waiters, my father spoke a version of English not yet shared with the rest of America. His attempts to find a "vater closet" in a department store would usually lead us to the drinking fountain or the home furnishings section. Asking my father to ask the waitress the definition of "sloppy Joe" or "Tater Tots" was no problem. His translations, however, were highly suspect. Waitresses would spend several minutes responding to my father's questions, and these responses, in turn, would be translated as "She doesn't know." Thanks to my father's translations, we stayed away from hot dogs, catfish, and hush puppies, and no amount of caviar in the sea would have convinced us to try mud pie.

Tells about specific memorable events.

Biography

A biography tells the story of someone else's life. Long biographies can appear in books. Shorter ones may appear in magazines, encyclopedias, or Web sites.

▲ This engraving shows pioneers traveling West in the 1800s.

Laura Ingalls Wilder
born Feb. 7, 1867,
Lake Pepin, Wis., U.S.;
died Feb. 10, 1957,
Mansfield, Mo.

Laura Ingalls grew up in a family that moved frequently from one part of the American frontier to another. Her father took the family by covered wagon to Minnesota, Iowa, Missouri, Kansas, Indian Territory, and Dakota Territory. At age 15 she began teaching in rural schools. In 1885 she married Almanzo J. Wilder, with whom she lived from 1894 on a farm near Mansfield, Missouri. Some years later she began writing for various periodicals.

Prompted by her daughter, Wilder began writing down her childhood experiences. In 1932 she published *Little House in the Big Woods,* which was set in Wisconsin. After writing *Farmer Boy* (1933), a book about her husband's childhood, she published *Little House on the Prairie* (1935), a reminiscence of her family's stay in Indian Territory. The "Little House" books were well received by the reading public and critics alike.

Wilder continued the story of her life in *On the Banks of Plum Creek* (1937), *By the Shores of Silver Lake* (1939), *The Long Winter* (1940), *Little Town on the Prairie* (1941), and *These Happy Golden Years* (1943). Her books remain in print.

Laura Ingalls Wilder

Often describes the subject's life and work, using chronological order

Time words and dates cue the order of events.

450

Book Review

Sometimes you read a book that you just have to tell others about. You can tell about it by writing a book review.

The *Circuit*
by Francisco Jiménez

Reviewed by Vicente P.

The first paragraph tells what the book is mostly about, or its main idea.

The Circuit is about a boy, Panchito, from a family of poor migrant farmworkers. He loves school. But Panchito works in the fields, and his family moves from town to town, so he can't go to school very often. When he does go to school, sometimes he has to start in the middle of the school year. It's hard for him because he is a stranger in the class and he doesn't speak or understand English well.

The next section tells how you feel about the book and why.

I like this book. My dad is in the army, so my family moves a lot. I know how Panchito feels being the new kid in class. I feel sorry for him because just when he starts to like a place and he makes friends there, he has to leave. I know how that feels, too.

The final paragraph tells the most important idea you learned from the book.

This book makes me thankful that I don't have to work hard like Panchito. And, even though my family moves a lot, I'm thankful that I always have a home and enough to eat. I also realize that I'm lucky because I speak English and I get to go to school.

Character Sketch

A character sketch may appear in fiction or nonfiction writing. It's like a quick word portrait of another person. A character sketch may portray a real person or a fictional character.

THIS BOY'S LIFE | Tobias Wolff   15

Dwight was a short man with curly brown hair and sad, restless brown eyes. He smelled of gasoline. His legs were small for his thick-chested body, but what they lacked in length they made up for in spring; he had an abrupt, surprising way of springing to his feet. He dressed like no one I'd ever met before—two-tone shoes, hand-painted tie, monogrammed blazer with a monogrammed handkerchief in the breast pocket. Dwight kept coming back, which made him chief among the suitors. My mother said he was a good dancer—he could really make those shoes of his get up and go. Also he was very nice, very considerate.

I didn't worry about him. He was too short. He was a mechanic. His clothes were wrong. I didn't know why they were wrong, but they were. We hadn't come all the way out here to end up with him. He didn't even live in Seattle; he lived in a place called Chinook, a tiny village three hours north of Seattle, up in the Cascade Mountains. Besides, he'd already been married. He had three kids of his own living with him, all teenagers. I knew my mother would never let herself get tangled up in a mess like that.

Includes **descriptive details** about appearance, actions, and personality

The writer tells his opinion of the character.

Description

A description uses specific details to help readers picture whatever is being described. Use words that appeal to the reader's senses.

Includes vivid sensory details

It was one of those super-duper cold Saturdays. One of those days that when you breathed out your breath kind of hung frozen in the air like a hunk of smoke and you could walk along and look exactly like a train blowing out big, fat, white puffs of smoke.

It was so cold that if you were stupid enough to go outside your eyes would automatically blink a thousand times all by themselves, probably so the juice inside of them wouldn't freeze up. It was so cold that if you spit, the slob would be an ice cube before it hit the ground. It was about a zillion degrees below zero.

Word pictures create a memorable image of this very cold day.

It was even cold inside our house. We put sweaters and hats and scarves and three pairs of socks on and still were cold. The thermostat was turned all the way up and the furnace was banging and sounding like it was about to blow up but it still felt like Jack Frost had moved in with us.

Directions

Directions tell how to play a game, how to get somewhere, or how to make something. When you write directions, the most important thing to do is to put the steps in order.

Game Directions

The **beginning** tells how many people can play.

The **middle** tells how to play the game.

The **end** tells how to win the game.

Rock, Paper, Scissors

Number of players: 2

How to Play: First make a fist with one hand. Next, shake your fist three times as you say *rock, paper, scissors*. Then do one of these:

–Keep a fist for *rock*
–Put two fingers out for *scissors*
–Put your palm down for *paper*

Finally, look at your hands to see who wins.

Who Wins: Rock beats scissors, scissors beats paper, and paper beats rock. Play again if both players have the same hand position.

Order words show the steps.

Directions to a Place

Direction words tell people which way to go.

To get to the theater, turn left out of the parking lot. Go four blocks past the school, to Citrus Street. Turn Right. The theater is on the left. It's a yellow building with a big, white sign.

Describing words help someone find the correct place.

Directions, continued

Directions for Making Something

The title tells the name of the food.

The ingredients and amounts of each thing you need are listed.

The steps are in order.

What's Cooking

Shrimp and Vegetable Stir Fry

Ingredients

3/4 pound shrimp

2 tablespoons canola oil

3/4 cup sliced mushrooms

1/2 cup sliced onion

1/2 cup sliced green pepper

1/4 cup chopped cabbage

1/4 cup teriyaki sauce

1 cup quick-cook brown rice

2 cups water

1. Boil water in a pot. Add the rice and cook for 20 minutes.
2. Heat oil in a large skillet.
3. Place vegetables in the skillet. Cook 5 minutes or until tender, stirring frequently.
4. Remove vegetables from the skillet.
5. Place shrimp in the skillet and cook 3 minutes.
6. Add vegetables back in with the shrimp.
7. Add teriyaki sauce and heat until the sauce is warm.
8. Spoon the stir fry over the rice. Serves 10.

E-mail

People write e-mail messages for many different reasons—to chat with friends and family, communicate with coworkers, sometimes even to apply for a job. Therefore, they can be as informal as a note left on the fridge or as formal as a business letter—make sure you get the tone right!

To: hfarlow@klm.com
From: jackier@teenswrite.net
Sent: June 3, 2014, 3:30 p.m.
Subject: Dog Sitting Opportunity

Dear Mr. Farlow:

I am writing in response to your recent advertisement seeking someone to take care of your dogs over the summer. I love dogs and would like the opportunity to take care of yours. I have two dogs of my own, and they are both well-trained and happy dogs due to my training and care. I can apply the same training and care to your dogs over the summer.

I am available to work from June 21 until September 1. Thank you for your consideration. I look forward to hearing from you.

Regards,

Jake Rider

The **Subject line** states the **purpose** of the message.

The writer gets to the point right away and keeps the message short.

Essays

Cause-and-Effect

A cause-and-effect essay tells why something happened. When you write a cause-and-effect essay, you may focus mainly on causes or mainly on effects, or you may discuss both.

The introduction in column 1 introduces the topic.

The first section of the body explains the effects the car wash had on the team.

THE CAR WASH

I'm on the Stingrays Softball team. We're a club team made up of girls from different schools in this area.

Last spring our team hoped to go to the club team tournament up in Pleasanton. But there was a big entry fee, plus we needed money for travel and a weekend hotel stay.

Someone suggested we have a car wash to make money. Someone else suggested a bake sale. We decided to do both at the same time, on two weekends.

Family members, coaches, and volunteers helped organize the event and prepare food for it. But we girls did all of the car washing!

What We Got, Besides Money

We had the car wash/bake sale at the side of the grocery store in town. Lots of cars came, so we really had to work hard—and it was hot! It was good exercise, though. It actually made us stronger and fitter.

We worked together and took turns doing different

tasks. This made us feel more like a team, which helped us play better later.

We sacrificed our free time for the car wash, but even before that we hardly ever went out to shop, eat, or see movies. We needed to save up for our trip. This experience made us realize what time and money are really worth.

We all love softball. After all we had to go through, we really appreciated that we got the chance to play it.

THE COMMUNITY IMPACT

People were generous. Some even paid extra, more than the price of the car wash or the food.

Because of the car wash, more people found out about our team and started coming to our games to support us. The stands were usually packed with fans!

It made us realize how much people care. We wanted to do well for all the fans who supported us, so we tried even harder to win.

I almost forgot. The "event" was a huge success. We made more than enough money for the trip, so we were able to buy some new equipment we badly needed.

We didn't win the tournament, but we came in second, which was amazing for a team just starting out. We had a great season. Now we can't wait for this season to begin. And it all started with a car wash!

The second section explains other effects of the car wash, including the effect on the community.

The conclusion leaves the reader with something to think about.

Comparison-Contrast

A comparison-contrast essay describes how two things are alike and different. You may choose to describe one item completely before you move on the next. Or, you might organize your essay according to the specific points you're comparing.

The introduction names the **two things** being compared.

The body has section heads and point-by-point organization.

Each section covers the main similarities and differences.

RECREATION

TWO CHOICES, NO EXCUSES

We all know we need to exercise. What can we do when school's out? Of course, if the weather's nice, you can always walk your dog, or play tennis or basketball on the outdoor courts at school. In our town, we can go to the Community Center or Teen Center, too. What's the difference, you ask?

INSIDE AND OUT
The Community Center has a large multi-purpose room, which serves as a gym, a dance hall, theater, and banquet room. You can play basketball or table tennis, or take karate, dance, and other classes there. There's another room with a pool table. Outside, there's a playground for younger kids, but older kids can exercise on the equipment, too.

The Teen Center has a music room, and a pool table and table-tennis table in separate rooms.

Outdoors, there's one basketball hoop, a sand volleyball court, and the main feature: a huge skate park.

ATMOSPHERE
All ages are welcome at the community Center, so you never know who you might run into there. Special classes and activities are offered for kids ages 5–12 and senior citizens ages 55 and up.

The Community Center gym

Depending on the activity in the main room, it may be "quiet time" for kids or seniors, there may be music playing for a dance or singing class, or there may be a basketball game or table tennis tournament going on.

In contrast, all the posters, bulletin-board information, games, and activities at the Teen Center are for kids ages 13–18. Music isn't permitted out in the skate park, but teens can share their music in the music room.

WHERE YOU SHOULD GO

The Community Center offers lots of activities, but not all at the same time. If you want to play a game on a wood court, check the schedule for basketball hours, or join the Youth Basketball League.

However, if you're a teen, and you just want to shoot baskets and hang out with kids your age, go to the Teen Center. It is always open after school and on weekends. If you want to skate, it's the *only* place to go.

These **transition words** show a contrast.

The conclusion sums up the major differences to help the reader make a decision.

The skate park is open to all ages.

Persuasive Essay

Writing as a citizen often involves writing to persuade. In a persuasive essay, you try to convince others to agree with your position on an important issue—and to take action.

What position does Mike take in his essay? What arguments does he use to try to convince his readers?

End the Curfew Now
Mike Bozarth

The opening provides background on the issue. States the writer's position.

The city officials in San Antonio believe that imposing a curfew on teenagers makes our city a better place. I disagree. Lifting the curfew would help local businesses by encouraging people to visit downtown stores at night. Furthermore, it would help make our city safer and reduce crime. It would also reward the city's hard-working students by allowing them to hang out with their friends at more comfortable times of day. Ending the curfew would improve life in San Antonio.

The body gives reasons for the writer's position and provides supporting evidence.

Ending the curfew would benefit our city's economy. Right now, our town is nearly empty at night because there aren't any teenagers around. But if the curfew were lifted, more people would spend time shopping downtown at night. That would help local businesses to grow and encourage stores to stay open longer. Longer store hours, in turn, would lead to better wages and more jobs available for retail workers.

Furthermore, although many people think the curfew reduces crime, it actually doesn't. In fact, since the curfew began last year, vandalism and theft have been on the

A view of San Antonio, Texas, at sunset ▶

rise. Officer Cheryl Williams of the San Antonio Police Department says that most of these crimes occur in quiet areas when no one's around. So, if more people were outside during the evenings, our town would be safer. People would think twice about committing a crime, since more potential witnesses, including teenagers, would be around to report it.

Finally, dropping the curfew would benefit the city's students. Right now, by the time they finish their homework and want to see their friends, it's too late to do anything. Some people say, "Why can't teenagers hang out downtown after school?" The problem with that suggestion is that it's really hot here in Texas. In the daytime, when it's 100 degrees outside and super sunny, people just want to stay in. At night, it's cooler, and the sun isn't hurting your skin. Students should be allowed to enjoy a nighttime social life.

The curfew law penalizes good kids and does nothing to benefit local businesses or to make our city safer. People should write to the mayor and urge her to lift the curfew on teens. It's the right thing to do.

Persuasive essays often include a response to an anticipated objection.

The conclusion includes a **summary** of the writer's ideas and a **call to action**.

Interview

An interview presents a conversation in question-and-answer format. When you write an interview, prepare your questions beforehand and record carefully the answers of the person you are interviewing.

Molding Troubled Kids into Future Chefs
An Interview with Neil Kleinberg
by Kathy Blake

Neil Kleinberg is the culinary-arts training manager at a tiny, 12-seat, takeout cafe operated by Covenant House, a shelter for runaway teenagers in New York City. Kleinberg says his job at Ezekiel's Cafe involves being father, mother, brother, counselor, teacher, and adviser, as well as a tough boss to the 17- to 21-year-old trainees who work with him.

Starts with background information about the person interviewed

How do you work as executive chef and culinary-arts trainer?

A place this small doesn't need an executive chef. My real job is teaching. Ezekiel's Cafe exists to give kids who live at Covenant House hands-on training in food service so they can get good jobs. Of course, when you say Covenant House, you know that these are kids with troubled pasts who need a lot of training in life skills, not just job skills. We screen the kids to try to get the ones who really have the desire to work in the industry, because to work this hard takes a lot of commitment.

When did you know you wanted to cook?

I always wanted to be a chef, and this was before it was trendy. When I was a kid growing up in Brooklyn, I'd go to Lundy's, which was the largest restaurant in the world at one time, and I'd think, "I want to be the chef here someday." That's why I tell the kids to be careful what they wish for! I got my wish, and it was really hard work. We did 1,500 dinners on Saturday nights. I essentially gave up my life for two years.

Was that immediately before you went to Ezekiel's?

Yes. I'd worked really hard my whole career; and when I left Lundy's, I needed some soul-searching time. So I took about a month and a half off and traveled to Australia, Thailand and Europe. When I got back, I wanted to teach but I still wanted to cook. I knew I'd always been good at directing people.

Lists the interviewer's questions and the interviewee's responses

Job Application

Many companies ask job candidates to fill out applications before they can be considered for a position. When you fill out a job application, make sure that the information is clear, accurate, and easy to read.

Application For Employment

WE ARE AN EQUAL OPPORTUNITY EMPLOYER

We consider applicants for all positions without regard to race, color, religion, sex, national origin, age, marital or veteran status, the presence of a non-job related medical condition or handicap, or any other legally protected status.

(PLEASE PRINT)

Date of Application: **5/15/14**

Position(s) Applied For: **Camp Counselor**

Name: **Torres** (Last Name) **Maria** (First Name) **A.** (Middle Name)

Address: **17 Redwood Rd.** (Number and Street) **Baxter** (City) **IA** (State) **50028** (Zip Code)

Phone Numbers: **(641) 555-8384** (Home) (Cell) (Other)

Social Security Number: **200 / 00 / 0000**

If you are under 18, can you provide required proof of your eligibility to work? ☑Yes ○No

Have you ever filed an application with us before? ○Yes ☑No   *If yes, give date*

Have you ever been employed with us before? ○Yes ☑No   *If yes, give date*

Are you currently employed? ☑Yes ○No

May we contact your present employer? ☑Yes ○No

Are you prevented from lawfully becoming employed in this country because of Visa or Immigration Status? ○Yes ☑No
(Proof of citizenship or immigration status will be required upon employment.)

On what date would you be available for work? **6/21/14**

Are you available to work: ☑Full Time ○Part Time ○Shift Work ○Temporary

Have you been convicted of a crime? *(Conviction will not necessarily disqualify an applicant from employment.)* ○Yes ☑No
If yes, please explain: _____

EDUCATION:

	Elementary	High School	College/University	Graduate
School Name and Location	Baxter Elementary	Baxter High School	N/A	
Years Completed	K-8	9-11		
Diploma/Degree	N/A	N/A		

EMPLOYMENT EXPERIENCE: Start with your present or last job. Include job-related military service assignments and volunteer activities. You may exclude organizations which indicate race, color, religion, gender, national origin, handicap or other protected status.

Employer **Baxter Tutoring Center**   Phone Number **(641) 555-1240**

Address/City/State/Zip **2 W. Klondike Ave., Baxter, IA 50028**

Job Title **Tutor**   Supervisor **Robin Hedding**

Duties **Tutor elementary-school students in math and science**

Dates of Employment **9/12 — present**   Hourly Rate/Salary **$6/hr**

Reason for Leaving **Tutoring center is closed from June through September.**

Provides personal information

Writes "N/A" in any section that does not apply

Tells about past work experience

Letters

Friendly

In a friendly letter, you write to someone you know, using an informal tone. A friendly letter often tells about recent events in the writer's life.

August 31, 2014

Dear Amber,

    How are you? My family and I just got back from our vacation late last night. We had such a great time out west. It was like nothing I had ever seen before.

    We traveled all over Colorado and Arizona. First we went to a National Park near the Rocky Mountains in Colorado. We hiked all day until I thought my legs were going to fall off. I was really surprised by how many deer we saw along the trails. The mountains themselves were incredibly beautiful. Some of them are over 12,000 feet high!

    Believe it or not, Arizona was even more amazing. We went to see the Grand Canyon. I'd seen pictures of it before, but looking at pictures is nothing like seeing it in person. The pictures don't show all the different colors in the rocks and soil, and they definitely don't show how huge the canyon really is. It's truly an awesome sight.

    Write to me and tell me about your summer. Hopefully we can get together sometime before school starts.

Your "best pal,"
Kelsey

Include the date. It is not necessary to include your address.

Tell your news in an informal tone.

Use an affectionate closing.

Inquiry/Request

When you write a letter of inquiry or request, you ask for specific favors, materials, or information. Use business-letter format.

242 Crescent Ln.
Oceanside, CA 91147
July 14, 2014

Mr. Nelson Tatupu
Recreation Dept.
Fallbrook City Hall
27 Leatherneck St.
Fallbrook, CA 92648

Dear Mr. Tatupu:

    I am writing to request information about your city's Youth Football team, the Rebels. I will be moving to Fallbrook soon, and I have heard that your community has an excellent Youth Football program. I would like to learn more about it.

    Please send me more information about the program, including age and weight requirements for players. Please also send me an application to join the team.

    Thank you very much for your time. I look forward to hearing from you.

Sincerely,

Robert Truitt

Robert Truitt

Includes your address as well as the date

States the reason for writing

Requests specific information or materials

Closes formally with full signature

Praise

A letter of praise expresses appreciation for the actions of a person. When you write to offer praise, be specific about why you are pleased.

37 Scotson Road
Parkville, OR 97086
October 6, 2014

Mr. Fred Simms
Parkville Youth Athletic League
1100 Carey Lane
Parkville, OR 97086

Dear Coach Simms:

Thank you so much for your patience, caring, and hard work this summer. Your efforts have made my teammates and me into better players and made this year's baseball season one to remember.

When the season started, most of us didn't know each other and we didn't work together very well. In only a few weeks, you brought us together and taught us how to play as a team. Under your coaching, my skills greatly improved. Even when I made a bad play in the field, you didn't get upset. Instead, you taught me how I could learn from my mistakes and do better next time.

Thanks again for making this baseball season so memorable. I can't wait to play on your team again next year!

Sincerely,
Tony Lopez
Tony Lopez

Tells why the person mattered to the writer

Provides specific details

Problem-Solving

Consumers write problem-solving letters to inform a company or organization about a problem. State your complaint and explain how the problem can be solved.

714 Almond Road
Fresno, CA 93707
August 1, 2014

Mr. Gary Zimmer, Chairman
Green Grass Teen Craft Fair Committee
43 Howard Avenue
Fresno, CA 93707

Dear Mr. Zimmer:

    On June 23, 2013, I paid to reserve a table to sell my handmade jewelry at the upcoming Green Grass Teen Craft Fair. However, I recently read on your website that the date of the fair has been moved forward a week. Unfortunately, I will be out of town during the festival's new date, and I will not be able to attend.

    I am enclosing a copy of my approved reservation application and my receipt. I would like you to send me a refund for the price of my reservation.

    Thank you for your time and attention. Please feel free to call me at 555-6784 with any questions.

Sincerely,
Beth Vaden
Beth Vaden

Politely states the complaint

Tells how the writer wants the problem resolved

Often includes contact information

Literary Response

A response to literature is similar to a literary analysis, but it focuses more on the writer's personal, individual reactions to the work. You still need to support your response with concrete details from the text.

When I Was Puerto Rican

by Esmeralda Santiago

Reviewed by Jennifer K.

States opinion and summarizes the book

This is a delightfully woven story of immense passion and unconquerable spirit. In this extraordinary autobiography, Santiago, an immigrant to New York from rural Puerto Rico, tells the story of her trials and triumphs, defeats and heartaches, in vivid detail.

Santiago grew up in what her *mami* calls "savage" conditions, dutifully obeying her parents as they constantly moved. Her greatest relocation occurred when a "metal bird" flew her, her mother, and two of her siblings to the rough city of New York. . . .

Using words as her medium, Santiago paints a beautiful picture of her life. I smelled the spices and herbs emanating from the special Puerto Rican dishes her *mami* prepared. Mesmerized, I watched as her *abuela* delicately stitched her needlework. . . . Santiago writes with such clarity and fierceness that it is impossible for any person not to see, feel, and understand what she went through in her remarkable journey.

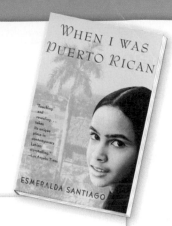

Santiago's unique style is easy to follow. When I read the book, I was immediately hooked and could not stop until I read the last word. The stories are interesting and full of insight. Santiago addresses fears and trials of all people. I especially related to her conflicts with her cultural identity. Anyone who has lived in between two cultures can relate to her story. Santiago wrote, "When I returned to Puerto Rico after living in New York for seven years, I was told I was no longer Puerto Rican. . . . In writing the book I wanted to get back to that feeling of Puertoricanness I had before I came here. Its title reflects who I was then, and asks, who am I today?"

Describes the writer's emotional response to the book

Santiago's book provides a sense of hope. The narrator is transformed from a confused and frightened child into a spirited woman full of courage and hope. Her success in life— acceptance into New York City's High School of Performing Arts and graduating from Harvard with highest honors—proves she is capable of achieving her dreams.

Santiago's strong will and courage are evident throughout her story. *When I Was Puerto Rican* describes the remarkable journey that her life has been.

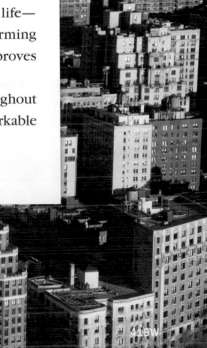

Newspaper

Editorial

An editorial is a newspaper or magazine article that is written to persuade people to believe the same way you do. When you write an editorial, tell how you feel about something. That's your opinion. Give facts to support your opinion.

Opinions about the subject are in the first paragraph.

Next, facts expand on the opinion.

February 6, 2014

Save the Gentle Manatees

Our manatees need protection from speeding boats. If we don't keep boat speeds slow, more and more of these gentle beasts will die.

A few members of the City Council want to pass a law that will increase boat speeds in some waterways where manatees live. When boats go too fast, the manatees can't get out of the way of the dangerous boat propellers in time.

We need to tell the City Council that saving the manatees is important to us. Increasing boat speeds is not. You can take action no matter where you live. Call, write, fax, or e-mail City Council members. Ask them to support protection for manatees and their home, and to *keep existing slow speed zones in our waters*! Any type of letter or call helps!

The end tells what people can do to help, and states your opinion again.

News Article

A news article tells about a recent event. It covers the "5 Ws": who, what, where, when, and why. A news article uses an "inverted pyramid" structure: it states the main points in the beginning, and then provides less important details in later paragraphs.

Tropical Storm Florence Forms in Atlantic

Weather system intensifies but poses no immediate threat to land

States the main point

MIAMI, FL—Tropical Storm Florence formed today in the open Atlantic, becoming the sixth named storm of the 2014 hurricane season.

Tells what happened and when

Florence had top sustained winds near 40 mph, 1 mph over the 39 mph threshold for a tropical storm, and it was expected to slowly intensify over the next few days, according to the National Hurricane Center.

Tells where and who might be affected

Its tropical storm force winds extended 115 miles from its center, but posed no immediate threat to land.

At 11 a.m., the storm was centered 935 miles east of the Lesser Antilles and was moving west at about 12 mph, forecasters said.

Florence follows Tropical Storm Ernesto, which was briefly the season's first hurricane before hitting Florida and North Carolina last week as a tropical storm.

At least nine deaths have been attributed to Ernesto, and the aftereffects were still being felt early today. About 75,000 people remained without power in New York's Westchester County.

Last year's Atlantic storm season set a record with 28 named storms and 15 hurricanes.

Often connects the story to a broader subject

May include photos and captions

Radar image of hurricane approaching west coast of Florida

Classified Ads

Classified ads are short notices that are classified, or put into groups. For example, the "New Today" section groups those items that are appearing for the first time. Look at these ads.

Help Wanted

For Sale

Wanted to Buy

New Today

DOGGY DAY CARE: Wanted dog lover w/time to care for energetic dog 2-3 days per week. 555-1759, lv. msg.

UNICYCLE: Brand new! We can't ride it! $80 OBO. Call 555-2521.

WANTED: Used longboard, 8 ft. or longer. Call Marc 555-8653.

People pay for classified ads by the line, so they use abbreviations.

Abbreviation	Meaning
w/	with
lv. msg.	leave message
obo.	or best offer
ft.	feet

Personal Narrative

When you write a personal narrative, you tell a story about something that happened to you. Because the story is about you, you'll use the words *I*, *me*, and *my* a lot.

Urff

One afternoon, two summers ago, I was walking on the beach. I was looking out at the bay, daydreaming.

Suddenly, something pushed me on my chest, and I fell back a step. A big, hairy dog had just put wet paw prints on my shirt! "Urff!" he barked playfully. Dogs are always romping on the beach. I figured his owner was nearby. I petted the dog. Then I started to walk again.

After a few steps, I noticed the dog was walking beside me. "Go on, now," I said. I tried to gently shoo him away with my hand. I looked around for his owner, but no one seemed to be calling for him.

This happened a couple more times, but he kept following me. He followed me as I left the beach and walked home. He followed me into my house and room, where he slept that night by my bed.

The next day, my mom made me take him to the shelter. I checked on him after a month. No one had claimed him. So I took him home. (Mom said, "OK," after much begging by me.) And Urff has been my best friend ever since.

Play

A play is a story that is acted on stage. Real people, or actors, pretend to be characters in the story.

The actors perform the play *Annie* **on stage**.

The **audience** watches the play in a **theater**.

Lakeside Theater
presents

Annie

a play by
Thomas Meehan

November 17-19

The author of a play is called a **playwright**. The playwright writes the script.

The actor's part in a play is called a **role**.
The girl is performing the role of Annie.

This **scene**, or part of the play,
takes place in the city. The
scenery shows what this place
looks like. The scenery can
change between scenes.

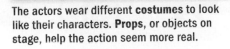

The actors wear different **costumes** to look
like their characters. **Props**, or objects on
stage, help the action seem more real.

Play, continued

You can turn any story into a play. Follow these steps.

1. Start with a story. Make one up or choose one from a book.

THE LEGEND
OF THE
CHINESE ZODIAC

In ancient times, the Jade Emperor wanted to name each year in the twelve-year cycle after an animal. He couldn't decide which animals to honor, however. He invited all the animals on earth to participate in a race. The first twelve to finish the race would each have a year named for them. The rat won the race; the ox was second. The tiger, rabbit, dragon, snake, horse, sheep, monkey, rooster, dog, and boar were the next ten animals to cross the finish line. The Jade Emperor named a year for the animals in the order they finished.

2. Turn the story into a script. The script names the characters and the setting. It describes what the characters say and do.

Write a title and act number.

ACT TWO

The Race

List all the characters.

CHARACTERS: *the Jade Emperor, rat, ox, tiger, rabbit, dragon, snake, horse, sheep, monkey, rooster, dog, boar*

Tell about the setting.

SETTING: Long ago, in front of the Jade Emperor's palace. There is a starting line on the ground. The Jade Emperor is telling all the animals the rules of the race.

JADE EMPEROR *(loudly, to get everyone's attention):* Listen! Listen! We are going to start the race soon. First, I want to explain the course and the rules.

BOAR *(raising his hand):* Will we be allowed to stop for water along the way?

JADE EMPEROR: *Please let me tell you the rules of the whole race before you ask questions. (pointing at the line on the ground) This is the starting line. You must have all of your toes behind this line.*

SNAKE *(raising his tail):* What if you don't have toes?

JADE EMPEROR *(Surprised):* Good point.

Name each character and write the dialogue, or the words the characters say.

Use stage directions to tell how the characters should say lines or move around.

3. Perform the play. Choose people to play the characters. Have them use script to practice. Then put on the play.

Poetry

Rhymed Verse

Rhymed verse follows a set rhyme scheme and often uses a regular rhythm as well.

Stopping By Woods on a Snowy Evening

by Robert Frost

Whose woods these are I think I know.	*a*
His house is in the village, though;	*a*
He will not see me stopping here	*b*
To watch his woods fill up with snow.	*a*
My little horse must think it queer	*b*
To stop without a farmhouse near	*b*
Between the woods and frozen lake	*c*
The darkest evening of the year.	*b*
He gives his harness bells a shake	*c*
To ask if there is some mistake.	*c*
The only other sound's the sweep	*d*
Of easy wind and downy flake.	*c*
The woods are lovely, dark, and deep,	*d*
But I have promises to keep,	*d*
And miles to go before I sleep,	*d*
And miles to go before I sleep.	*d*

This poem has an interesting rhyme pattern, shown by the letters.

Free Verse

Free verse has no fixed rhythm and uses irregular rhyme or no rhyme at all. However, free verse often includes other poetic devices, such as repetition, imagery, or figurative language.

MOTHER

by Maya Angelou

During the years when you knew nothing
And I knew everything, I loved you still.
Condescendingly of course,
From my high perch
Of teenage wisdom.
I grew older and
Was stunned to find
How much knowledge you had gleaned
And so quickly.

Haiku

A haiku is a brief poem that focuses on a single image or emotion. The haiku form originated in Japan and often describes images found in nature. The form traditionally uses three lines with five, seven, and five syllables, respectively.

> by the noonflower
> a rice-pounder cools himself:
> a sight so moving
> —*Bashō*

> the cathedral bell
> is shaking a few snowflakes
> from the morning air
> —*Nicholas Virgilio*

> heat before the storm:
> a fly disturbs the quiet
> of the empty store
> —*Nicholas Virgilio*

> A bitter morning:
> sparrows sitting together
> without any necks.
> —*James Hackett*

Concrete Poem

A concrete poem is written so the words make a picture of what they are describing.

(a poem to be read from the bottom up)

this great oak

into the coming night

its capillary ends

its garbled limbs

against the hazy light

now stretches

to stand winter and the wind

from wells far underground

with strength

girthed itself

upon a trunk

upon a branch

upon a sprig

upon a leaf

spring by spring

a century ago

from under land

this tree unrolled

Simple as a flower

—Dawn L. Watkins

Procedure

A procedure is a list of steps that must be followed to complete a task. When you write a procedure, clearly describe, in order, what needs to be done.

Headings help organize the instructions.

Gives clear, specific, step-by-step instructions

PROCEDURE FOR HOUSE SITTER

<u>When Entering</u>

Open door and close it quickly. Rufus will try to escape if the door is left open!

<u>In the Morning</u>

1. Give Rufus fresh water and dry kibble.
2. Play with Rufus and let him outside for $\frac{1}{2}$ hour.
3. Water plants on kitchen windowsill.
4. Feed fish with flakes next to tank.
5. Bring in the morning's newspaper and leave on kitchen table.

In the Afternoon

1. Bring in the day's mail and leave on kitchen table.
2. Feed Rufus $\frac{1}{2}$ can of dog food.
3. Play with Rufus and walk him for at least 20 minutes.
4. Check the tomato plants and place any ripe tomatoes on the kitchen table.

When Leaving

1. Close windows.
2. Turn off lights and fans.
3. Don't forget to lock the door and deadbolt.

Emergency Phone Numbers

Mr. & Mrs. Rhoades (cell): (212) 555-7834

Dr. Sternberg (vet): (212) 555-4700
Annandale Police Dept.: (212) 555-2299

Story

Writers use their imaginations and make up different types of stories to entertain their readers. They decide where a story will happen, who will be in it, and what will happen.

Parts of a Story

Every story happens in a place at some time. That place and time are called the **setting**.

The people or animals in a story are called the **characters**. In most stories, the characters speak. Their words are called **dialogue**.

Saturday morning in our apartment

woman from the bike store

Alex and his Mom

The things that happen in a story are the events. The order, or **sequence of events**, is called the **plot**.

1. Mom filled out a form for the bike drawing.

2. We went to the bike store.

3. I saw a huge sign that said I won!

Realistic Fiction

Some stories have characters that seem like people you know. They happen in a place that seems real. These stories are called realistic fiction because they tell about something that could happen in real life.

Another Saturday Morning

The **characters** are like people you know.

The events in the **plot** could really happen.

Mom and I were eating breakfast Saturday morning when a woman knocked on the door to our apartment.

"Hello," she said. "I'm from Bikes and Stuff. We're having a drawing for a mountain bike. Would you be interested in signing up?" Mom agreed and filled out a form for me.

"Come by this afternoon to see if you have won," the woman said.

"Anything is possible, but don't count on winning the bike, Alex," Mom said when the woman left.

So I forgot all about the bike and started reading my new book. Before I knew it, Mom came in the room and said it was time to go to the bike store.

When I walked in, the first thing I saw was a huge sign that said: *Mountain bike winner: Alex Sanchez!* I couldn't believe it!

They put my name and photograph in the newspaper in an ad for Bikes and Stuff. That was the day I learned anything is possible on a Saturday morning.

The **setting** is in a time and a place you know.

The **dialogue** sounds real.

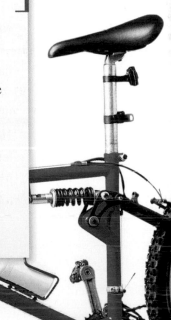

Historical Fiction

Historical Fiction is a story that takes place in the past during a certain time in history. Some of the characters may be real people, and some of the events really happened. Even so, the story is fiction because the writer made it up.

January 13, 1778

The characters act and talk like the people in that time did.

Today when we returned the laundry to the army headquarters, I was astounded to see only General Washington in the parlor, no other officers. I know not where Billy Lee was. The General was sharpening his quill with his penknife. He looked up at us and smiled.

"Thank you, Abigail. Thank you, Elisabeth," he said.

I curtsied, unable to speak. How did he know our names?

He looked at us with kind eyes—they're gray-blue—then he returned to his pen and paper. Mrs. Hewes says Mr. Washington writes at least fifteen letters a day, mostly to Congress. He is pleading for food, clothing, and other supplies for the soldiers, she told us.

It can have **real people** and **made up characters** who lived during that time.

Fantasy

A fantasy is a story that tells about events that couldn't possibly happen in real life. Here is part of a fantasy about some children playing a very unusual board game.

JUMANJI | Chris Van Allsburg   15

At home, the children spread the game out on a card table. It looked very much like the games they already had.

"Here," said Judy, handing her brother the dice, "you go first."

Peter casually dropped the dice from his hand.

"Seven," said Judy.

Peter moved his piece to the seventh square.

"'Lion attacks, move back two spaces,'" read Judy.

"Gosh, how exciting," said Peter, in a very unexcited voice. As he reached for his piece he looked up at his sister. She had a look of absolute horror on her face.

"Peter," she whispered, "turn around very, very slowly."

The boy turned in his chair. He couldn't believe his eyes. Lying on the piano was a lion, staring at Peter and licking his lips. The lion roared so loud it knocked Peter right off his chair. The big cat jumped to the floor. Peter was up on his feet, running through the house with the lion a whisker's length behind. He ran upstairs and dove under a bed. The lion tried to squeeze under, but got his head stuck. Peter scrambled out, ran from the bedroom, and slammed the door behind him. He stood in the hall with Judy, gasping for breath.

"I don't think," said Peter in between gasps of air, "that I want . . . to play . . . this game . . . anymore."

"But we have to," said Judy as she helped Peter back downstairs. "I'm sure that's what the instructions mean. The lion won't go away until one of us wins the game."

The characters can be like real people.

Some of the events could never happen in real life.

Web Site

A Web site can be personal or professional and can be about any subject. Web sites often include images, sound files, video, and links to related pages or sites.

As a Web-site "writer" you have to think "in time."
What happens when you click a link?
How do you get back "home" after listening to a song?

Workplace and Consumer Resources

Instruction Manual

Most products come with directions, often in the form of an **instruction manual**, or booklet. The instruction manual usually describes the product's parts and features and tells how to use the product.

Some products, especially more complicated ones, come with two sets of instructions. A short **quick-start guide** may give you the most essential information, so you can start using the product and its basic features right away. The quick-start guide may be as short as a single page (sometimes a big page!).

The complete instruction manual is sometimes called a **user manual**. A good instruction manual covers everything you might want to know about the product, both right away and later on.

USER MANUAL

LIGHTNING STAR
GAME SYSTEM

③

USER MANUAL

CONTENTS
1: LightningStar 3 Parts and Features
3: Setting Up Your LightningStar 3
4: Loading and Playing Games
7: Using the Controller: Basics
9: Using the Controller: Advanced Play
11: Multiplayer Games
13: Online Play
15: Wireless Play (requires accessories sold separately)
16: Troubleshooting
18: Important Warnings and Safeguards
Back Cover: Customer Support

LIGHTNING STAR
GAME SYSTEM
③

QUICK-START GUIDE

Set-Up

IIn order to start the LightningStar game system, first insert the accompanying cd-rom into your computer. The program will automatically install the necessary software onto your computer. Follow the steps in the Installation Wizard. Your system may need some additional support software to effectively run your LightningStar game system. If this is the case, the system will automatically link you to the site to download the appropriate software for free, as long as you have an active internet connection.

Once you have completed the steps, you will be ready to calibrate, or set up, your LightningStar joystick. Directions on how to calibrate your joystick will follow installation.

Basic Play

LightningStar is a game in which you will explore various solar systems to hunt for life on other planets. Once life is located, you will help the civilizations move forward by helping them develop new tools and methods. For example, in the solar system for Star X587, the planet Zevob has a population that has not yet discovered farming. Your task is to teach the Zevobians about farming, as well as to help the population develop tools to stop the invading Nostrarlans who are from a nearby planet.

Play continues until populations from all of the planets under your supervision have developed useful tools and are no longer at war with others.

Tips

The following tips will help you have the most successful journey through your stars and planets:
- Use the tutorial to walk you through your first planet encounter.
- You can always ask the planet guide to walk you through a difficult task.
- You must solve the problems of the planet you are on before you can travel to another

planet or solar system.
- Multiple planets in a solar system may have life. Be sure to check all of the planets before moving to the next solar system.

Troubleshooting Checklist

LightningStar game system is a quick-installation game system. If you are unable to start or control your game system, check the following:
- Make sure that the joystick is plugged into an active USB port and is turned on.
- Check that the system successfully installed missing software components during the installation process. To ensure this has been done properly, re-install the CD-ROM and go through the installation process once more. If the system sends you an error message for any necessary software, check if your computer has the correct operating system needed to play LightningStar.
- Be sure to calibrate your joystick and set the various controls so that you know what each button does. Improperly calibrated joysticks can have control problems during a game.
- For more troubleshooting help, please visit our Web site or call us at 1-800-555-3939.

Warranty

When you buy a product, you hope it will keep working the way it's supposed to. But what if it doesn't? Most products come with a written **warranty** that states what the manufacturer will do if something goes wrong. It's a good idea to check out the warranty before you buy the product, so you'll know what kind of protection you're getting.

A warranty will usually spell out the following:

• What is (and is not) covered

• How long the warranty period lasts

• What the consumer needs to do to take advantage of the warranty.

USER MANUAL

LIMITED WARRANTY FOR THE LIGHTNINGSTAR GAME SYSTEM

LightningStar warrants to the original purchaser that the LightningStar 3 game system shall be free of defects in material and workmanship for a period of one (1) year from the original date of purchase (the "Warranty Period"). LightningStar will, at its sole discretion, repair or replace a defective system returned during the warranty period in accordance with the instructions below. No other warranty is expressed or implied.

Tells what the warranty covers and how long the warranty period lasts

This warranty shall not apply if the game system has been damaged, misused, or altered after purchase. This warranty does not cover accessories purchased separately.

Tells what is *not* covered

To arrange for service under this warranty, visit the Customer Service section of our website or call the toll-free number listed in the User Manual. You will need to have the product serial number available when you contact us. You will also need a copy of your original purchase receipt when you send the system in for repair. You are responsible for shipping charges to our repair facility. LightningStar is not responsible for units lost or damaged in transit to or from our repair facility.

Tells what to do if you need to use the warranty

Employment Advertisements

When it's time to get your first job, an important source of information for you will be the **Classified** section of your local newspaper. Employers place advertisements for workers they need to hire in this section. By reading an **employment advertisement** carefully, you can find out details about the job, including: hours, tasks, qualifications, and how to apply. Look for each of these pieces of information in the ad below.

Retail Sales

Out of This World gift shop seeks P/T person (eves and weekends) to assist customers as they browse and buy. Our one-of-a kind shop offers a wide range of space-oriented items, and we seek someone who is enthusiastic about our products. Good math skills, friendly personality, and dependability required. Min. wage with attractive sales bonus. Apply in person at City Mall, Saturdays (9:00 a.m.–noon).

Most advertisers use standard abbreviations. *P/T* stands for *part-time*.

Employment Contract

Once you are hired for a job, you might be asked to sign an **employment contract**. This is a legal document, so you will want to read it very carefully before you sign it. The purpose of an employment contract is to ensure that you and your employer agree on the terms of your employment. It usually states when your employment begins, what the expectations are for you on the job, what your starting pay will be, and what special benefits (such as paid vacation) you will receive. A sample is provided below.

EMPLOYMENT AGREEMENT

This Employment Agreement (hereinafter "Agreement") is entered into on December 5, 2014, by and between The Daily Herald (The "Employer") and Starry Jackson (The "Employee")

Employer and Employee each agree with the other as follows:

1. **EMPLOYMENT**   Employer has agreed to employ Employee for the position of Newspaper Delivery Person, and Employee has agreed to accept such employment. Employee's duties shall include: collating and delivering papers and collecting payment from customers.

2. **TERM**   The term of this Agreement shall begin December 6, 2014, and shall continue until terminated in accordance with the terms set forth below.

3. **COMPENSATION**   For services provided, Employer shall employ Employee at a rate of $6.55/hour. The Employee shall be paid weekly. The remuneration is subject to all required withholdings, paid in accordance with Employer's regular payroll policies and procedures.

4. **PROBATION**   The probationary period is 3 months.

5. **VACATION**   Vacation time can be taken at the employee's discretion, with notice to The Daily Herald.

6. **HOURS OF WORK**   The Employee agrees that the working hours are flexible with a minimum of 15 hours per week.

---

7. **CONDUCT**   Employee agrees that during the time of employment with Employer, the Employee shall adhere to all rules, regulations, and policies established by the Employer for the conduct of its employees. Employee agrees to devote his/her full time, attention, and energies to the business of the Employer.

8. **TERMINATION**   The employment of the Employee by the Employer may be terminated by either the Employer or the Employee upon the giving of 14 days prior written notice to the other party. The employment of the Employee by the Employer may be immediately terminated upon the occurrence of any of the following events:

   a. In the event the Employee shall willfully and continuously fail or refuse to comply with the standards, rules, regulations, and policies established by the Employer.

   b. In the event the Employee shall be guilty of fraud, dishonesty, or any other misconduct in the performance of the Employee's duties on behalf of the Employer.

   c. In the event the Employee shall fail to perform any provision of this Agreement to be performed by the Employee.

9. **GOVERNANCE**   This Agreement shall be governed by the Laws of the State of Florida. The parties hereby indicate by their signatures below that they have read and agree with the terms and conditions of this Agreement in its entirety.

Employer: Employee:

_____   _____
Signature   Signature

_____   _____
Name/Title   Printed Name

_____   _____
Date   Date

ONE OF THE HARDEST PARTS of writing is organizing your ideas. You can use graphic organizers and idea organizers to plan and organize what you are going to write. Idea organizers can help you plan how to present your ideas. They help the reader (and the writer—you!) follow your thinking process. You can use graphic organizers to narrow your writing topic or to remember the sequence of your ideas before writing.

Find out more about the different kinds of graphic organizers and idea organizers.

Writing
ORGANIZERS

Logical Order

Chronological Order

Spatial Order

Showing Causes and Effects

Showing Comparisons

Showing Goals and Outcomes

Showing Problems and Solutions

Showing Your Position

Idea Organizers

Writing Organizers

Logical Order

Logical order makes the most sense when you want to group ideas that have something in common, or you want to organize them by importance.

Topic and Main Idea Diagram

A diagram like this can help you plan the focus for each paragraph in an essay.

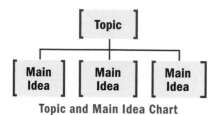

Topic and Main Idea Chart

Main Idea and Detail Diagrams

For each paragraph in the essay, try one of these diagrams to plan the details you'll include.

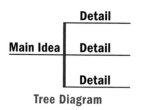

Tree Diagram

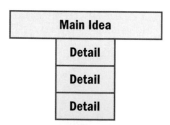

Block Diagram

Category Chart

Try sorting information into groups or categories.

Carlos and Me

Helped me	Caused me problems
helped me pass math class	was rude to my parents
convinced me to try out for the football team	never shows up on time
lent me money to buy concert tickets	went to the concert with someone else

Category

Category Chart

Example

Hypothesis-and-Results Chart

You could use a chart like this to explain the results of a survey.

Question:	Hypothesis:
What percentage of teens at Washington High School sometimes lie to their best friends?	Most teenagers at Washington High lie to their best friends occasionally.
	Data:
	50 teens surveyed 30 have lied about minor things (60%) 5 have lied about something important (10%) 15 always tell their best friends the truth (30%)
Conclusions:	**Observations:**
70% of teens sometimes lie to their best friends.	Most teens will not lie to their best friends about something important.

Hypothesis-and-Results Chart

Outline

You can also use an outline to help you organize your ideas logically. List the main ideas and supporting details using roman numerals, letters, and numbers.

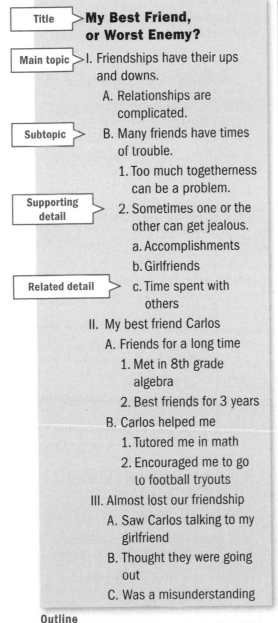

Title → **My Best Friend, or Worst Enemy?**

Main topic → I. Friendships have their ups and downs.

    A. Relationships are complicated.

Subtopic → B. Many friends have times of trouble.

    1. Too much togetherness can be a problem.

Supporting detail → 2. Sometimes one or the other can get jealous.

    a. Accomplishments

    b. Girlfriends

Related detail → c. Time spent with others

II. My best friend Carlos

    A. Friends for a long time

      1. Met in 8th grade algebra

      2. Best friends for 3 years

    B. Carlos helped me

      1. Tutored me in math

      2. Encouraged me to go to football tryouts

III. Almost lost our friendship

    A. Saw Carlos talking to my girlfriend

    B. Thought they were going out

    C. Was a misunderstanding

Outline

Order-of-Importance Diagrams

Sometimes you'll want to organize your ideas by how important they are.

1. You can organize from most important to least important.

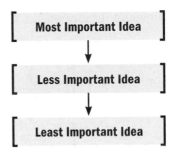

Most Important Idea
↓
Less Important Idea
↓
Least Important Idea

2. Or, you can organize from least important to most important.

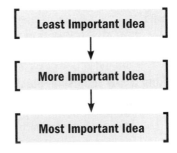

Least Important Idea
↓
More Important Idea
↓
Most Important Idea

Chronological Order

To tell about events in the order in which they happen or to explain the steps in a process, use chronological order.

Sequence Chain

A diagram like this one can help you plan plot events for stories.

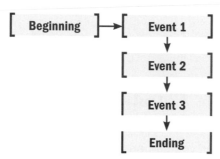

Sequence Chain

Flow Chart

Use a flow chart to explain how to do something or how something works.

Making a 3-D Theatrical Mask

Step 1
A cast of the actor's face is made.

↓

Step 2
The cast is then used to shape the features of the mask.

↓

Step 3
This new character's "face" is then used to make a mold for the final mask.

↓

Step 4
Latex rubber is poured into the mold to create the mask.

↓

Step 5
The mask is then painted and attached to the actor with a special glue.

Flow Chart

Time Line

Use a time line to help you keep track of when important events happened.

Evolution of The Wizard of Oz

1900 — L. Frank Baum publishes The Wonderful Wizard of Oz.

> First event

1925 — The full-length silent film version of the book opens.

1939 — MGM releases the classic film version of The Wizard of Oz.

1956 — The Wizard of Oz is shown on network television for the first time.

> Date

1975 — The Wiz, an African American stage musical based on the story, opens.

1978 — A film version of The Wiz is released.

1995 — Wicked, based on the Oz story, is published by Gregory Maguire.

2003 — The musical Wicked opens on Broadway.

Time Line

Spatial Order

For a description, try using spatial order to tell what you see—from left to right, from near to far, or from top to bottom, for example.

Picture Diagram

Try labeling a picture—or drawing one—to show how you'll organize details for a description.

Circle Diagram

Whether you want to describe an area from the inside to the outside or vice versa, try using a circle diagram to show your plan.

Picture Diagram

beat-up hat

plaster nose

rope belt

hay stuffing

busted shoes

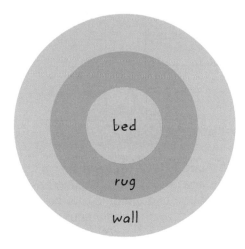

bed

rug

wall

Circle Diagram

Writing Organizers, continued

Showing Causes and Effects

When you write about causes and effects, you explain what happens and why.

Cause-and-Effect Chart

Sometimes a cause leads to a single effect. You might want to show each cause and its effect in a chart.

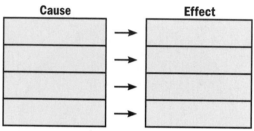

Cause-and-Effect Chart

Cause-and-Effect Diagrams

Maybe what you want to explain has a single cause and multiple effects, or a single effect and multiple causes.

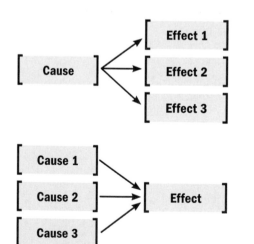

Cause-and-Effect Diagrams

Cause-and-Effect Chain

Sometimes causes and effects form a chain of linked events. One event causes the next event to happen.

Cause-and-Effect Chain

Showing Comparisons

Plan what you'll say about how people, places, or things are alike or different. It'll be easy to see the comparisons if you show your ideas side by side.

T Chart

Use a T Chart to help you compare and contrast specific characteristics of a topic.

What you compare

Buying a Costume	Making a Costume
limits your choices	gives you many choices
requires little work or skill	may require skills, such as sewing or painting
can be done quickly	takes a long time

T Chart

Characteristics

Venn Diagram

A Venn diagram uses overlapping circles to compare and contrast.

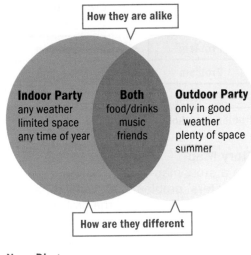

How they are alike

Indoor Party
any weather
limited space
any time of year

Both
food/drinks
music
friends

Outdoor Party
only in good weather
plenty of space
summer

How are they different

Venn Diagram

Showing Goals and Outcomes

Whether you want to share your own personal accomplishments or create a story about a fictional character, try organizing your ideas by goal and outcome.

Goal	Actions	Obstacles	Outcome
I wanted to get the lead role in the school play.	I found out the date and time of the audition. I prepared a monologue. I attended the audition and performed the monologue.	I had a cold on the day of the audition. I kept coughing during my monologue. My best friend tried out for the lead, too.	My friend got the lead role. I got a minor part.

Goal-and-Outcome Chart

What stands in the way?

Showing Problems and Solutions

Both fiction and nonfiction often present problems and solutions.
In your writing, organize the ideas by first telling why something is a
problem and then how the problem is or can be solved.

Problem-and-Solution Chart

A chart like this one works best for
nonfiction in which there are several
problems, each with its own solution.

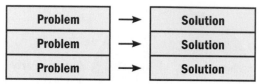

Problem-and-Solution Chart

Story Map

Use a story map to show your
characters' problems, or conflicts, and
how they work to solve the problems.

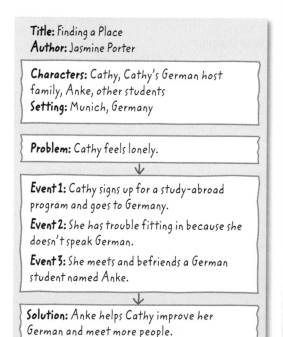

Title: Finding a Place
Author: Jasmine Porter

Characters: Cathy, Cathy's German host
family, Anke, other students
Setting: Munich, Germany

Problem: Cathy feels lonely.

Event 1: Cathy signs up for a study-abroad
program and goes to Germany.
Event 2: She has trouble fitting in because she
doesn't speak German.
Event 3: She meets and befriends a German
student named Anke.

Solution: Anke helps Cathy improve her
German and meet more people.

Story Map

Essay Map

For an essay, complete a map to help
you organize and explain your ideas.

The Problem
Few students are submitting works for
publication in the literary magazine The
Scribbler

Why It Needs to Be Solved
The Scribbler can't survive without any
work to publish.

The Solution
Many students may not know about
The Scribbler, so we need to make the
magazine more visible.

How the Solution Works
The staff will
• add a page about The Scribbler to the
Fowler High School Web site.
• put a notice in the school newspaper.
• ask English teachers to let students submit
work to The Scribbler for extra credit.

Conclusion
If more students know about the literary
magazine, there'll be an increase in the
number of submissions.

Problem-and-Solution Essay Map

Showing Your Position

When you write to persuade, you want to convince people to agree with you. So, to be sure you've included all the important and persuasive details, use a chart or a diagram to plan what you'll say.

Opinion Chart

You can use an opinion chart to organize the reasons and supporting evidence for your opinion.

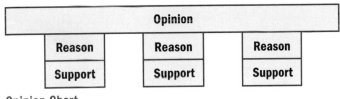

Opinion Chart

Position-and-Support Diagram

Sometimes people will disagree with you. When this happens, you need to plan how to respond to their objections with rebuttals.

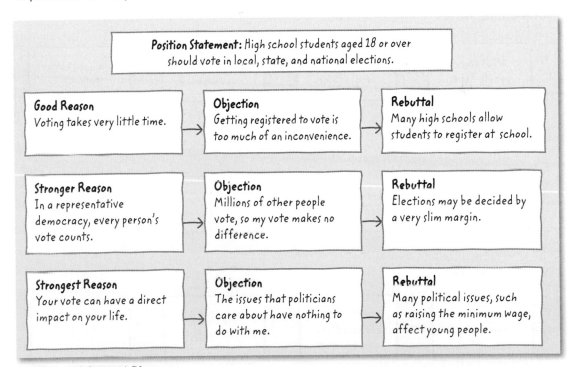

Position-and-Support Diagram

Idea Organizers

Choose an Organizer

Idea organizers can help you plan how to present your ideas. They help the reader (and the writer—you!) follow your thinking process.

The Story of My Thinking

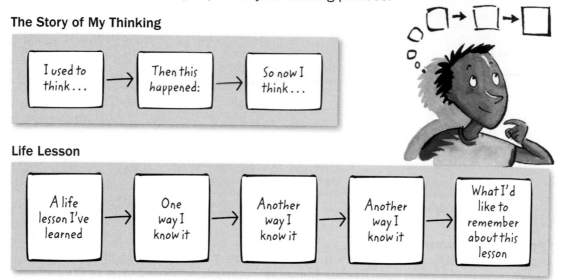

I used to think . . . → Then this happened: → So now I think . . .

Life Lesson

A life lesson I've learned → One way I know it → Another way I know it → Another way I know it → What I'd like to remember about this lesson

Comparing Notes

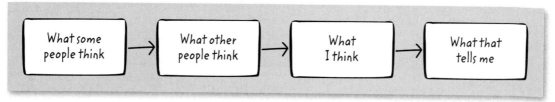

What some people think → What other people think → What I think → What that tells me

Memory Reflections

Where I was → Moment it started → Next moment → Final moment → What I realized

Wrong Assumption

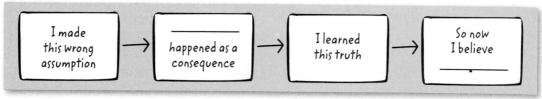

I made this wrong assumption → _____ happened as a consequence → I learned this truth → So now I believe _____

Sensory Associations

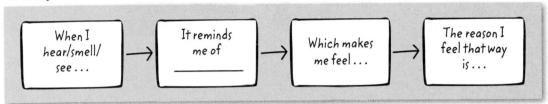

| When I hear/smell/see . . . | → | It reminds me of _____ | → | Which makes me feel . . . | → | The reason I feel that way is . . . |

Something Big

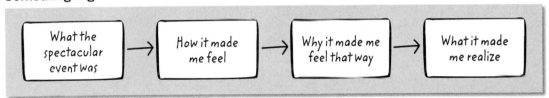

| What the spectacular event was | → | How it made me feel | → | Why it made me feel that way | → | What it made me realize |

Finding Out for Sure

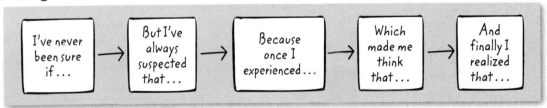

| I've never been sure if . . . | → | But I've always suspected that . . . | → | Because once I experienced . . . | → | Which made me think that . . . | → | And finally I realized that . . . |

Making a Change

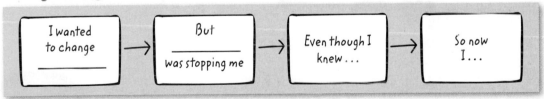

| I wanted to change _____ | → | But _____ was stopping me | → | Even though I knew . . . | → | So now I . . . |

Learning From Mistakes

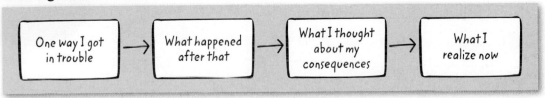

| One way I got in trouble | → | What happened after that | → | What I thought about my consequences | → | What I realize now |

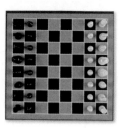

Grammar, Usage, AND Spelling

Sentences

A sentence is a group of words that tells a complete thought.

Subjects and Predicates

A **subject** tells who or what the sentence is about. A **predicate** tells something about the subject. A sentence must have both of these parts to be a **complete sentence**. If one part of a sentence is missing, a **fragment** is the result.

Complete and Simple Subjects and Predicates	Examples
The **complete subject** includes all the words in the subject.	**Many people** visit our national parks. **My favorite parks** are in the West.
The **simple subject** is the most important noun or pronoun in the complete subject.	**Many <u>people</u>** visit our national parks. **My favorite <u>parks</u>** are in the West.
The **complete predicate** includes all the words in the predicate.	Visitors **explore caves in Yellowstone Park**. Some people **climb the unusual rock formations**.
The **simple predicate** is the **verb**. It is the most important word in the predicate.	Visitors **<u>explore</u> caves in Yellowstone Park**. Some people **<u>climb</u> the unusual rock formations**.

Compound Subject and Compound Predicate	Examples
A **compound subject** is two or more simple subjects joined by **and** or **or**.	**<u>Yosemite</u> and <u>Yellowstone</u>** are both in the West. Either **<u>spring</u> or <u>fall</u>** is a good time to visit.
A **compound predicate** has two or more verbs joined by **and** or **or**.	At Yosemite, some people **fish and swim**. My family **hikes** to the river **or stays** in a cabin.

Complete Sentences and Fragments

Sentences and Fragments	Examples
Begin a complete sentence with a capital letter, and end it with a period or other end mark.	<u>These parks</u> / <u>have many tourist attractions</u>. *subject* *predicate*
A **fragment** is a sentence part that is incorrectly used as a complete sentence. For example, the fragment may be missing a subject. Add a subject to correct the problem.	**Incorrect:** Beautiful waterfalls. **Correct:** Many parks have beautiful waterfalls.
Writers sometimes use fragments on purpose to emphasize an idea or for special effect.	I did not camp in bear country. **No way. Too dangerous.**

Subject-Verb Agreement

The subject and verb of a sentence or clause must agree in number.

Subject-Verb Agreement	Examples
Use a **singular subject** with a **singular verb**.	Another popular **park is** the Grand Canyon.
Use a **plural subject** with a **plural verb**.	We **were amazed** by the colors of its cliffs.
If the simple subjects in a **compound subject** are connected by **and**, use a plural verb. If they are connected by **or**, look at the last simple subject. If it is singular, use a **singular verb**. If it is plural, use a **plural verb**.	<u>Rafts</u> and a <u>boat</u> **are** available for a trip down the canyon. These **rafts or** this <u>**boat**</u> **is** the best way to go. This **boat or** these <u>**rafts**</u> **are** the best way to go .
The **subject** and **verb** must agree, even when other words come between them.	The **bikers** in the park **are looking** for animals.

Sentence Structures

Clauses	Examples
A **clause** is a group of words that has both a **subject** and a **predicate**.	<u>California's population</u> / <u>grew during the 1840s.</u> *subject* *predicate*
An **independent clause** can stand alone as a complete sentence.	<u>California's population</u> / <u>increased.</u> *subject* *predicate*
A **dependent clause** cannot stand alone as a complete sentence because it begins with a subordinating conjunction. A dependent clause can be combined with an independent clause to form a complete sentence.	**because** gold / was found there during that time <u>California's population grew</u> <u>because gold was found.</u> *independent clause* *dependent clause*
An **adjective clause** gives more details about the noun or pronoun that it describes.	The news **that gold had been found** spread fast.
An **adverb clause** gives more details about the verb, adjective, or adverb that it describes.	**When someone found gold**, people celebrated.

Sentence Structures, continued

Simple Sentences	Examples
A **simple sentence** is one independent clause with a subject and a predicate. It has no dependent clauses.	Supplies / were scarce. The miners / needed goods and services.

Compound Sentences	Examples
When you join two independent clauses, you make a **compound sentence**. • Use a comma and a **coordinating conjunction** to join independent clauses. • Use a semicolon to join independent clauses that are short and closely related.	People opened stores, **but** supplies were scarce. People went hungry; there was no food.
Joining independent clauses without a conjunction or proper punctuation creates a **run-on sentence**.	**Incorrect:** The miners were hungry supplies were scarce. **Correct:** The miners were hungry, and supplies were scarce.

Complex Sentences	Examples
To make a **complex sentence**, join an independent clause with one or more dependent clauses. If the dependent clause comes first, put a **comma** after it.	Many writers visited camps **where miners worked**. 　　　　independent　　　dependent **While the writers were there**, they wrote stories about the miners.

Compound-Complex Sentences	Examples
You can make a **compound-complex sentence** by joining two or more independent clauses and one or more dependent clauses.	Many miners never found gold, **but** they stayed in California **because they found other jobs there**. 　　　　　　　　dependent

Sentence Structures, continued

Phrases	Examples
A **phrase** is a group of related words that does not have both a subject and a verb. Phrases add details to sentences.	The team won the game **in overtime.** **With only seconds left**, the quarterback scored.
A **prepositional phrase** starts with a preposition and ends with a noun or a pronoun. (See page 461W [Level A], 487W [Level B], or 483W [Level C] for a list of prepositions.) It includes all the words in between. The noun or pronoun is the **object of the preposition.**	I live **near the Chávez Community Center.** preposition object of preposition Tom wants to walk there **with you and me.** preposition objects of preposition
Prepositional phrases can function either as **adjectives** or as **adverbs.** • They function as adjectives when they modify a noun or pronoun. • They function as **adverbs** when they modify a verb, an adjective, or another adverb.	The **guy in the yellow shirt and khaki pants** is my friend Joel. He is **excited about the new Chávez Center.** He wants to **come with us.**
A **participial phrase** begins with a participle. A **participle** is a word made from a verb but used as an adjective (**sizzling** burgers, **burned** hot dogs) Most participles end in **-ing** or **-ed**. A participle phrase includes the participle and its modifiers. Place the phrase next to the noun it describes.	**Correct:** **Standing by the grill**, he soon had the hamburgers cooked to perfection. **Incorrect:** He soon had the hamburgers cooked to perfection standing by the grill.

Parenthetical Phrases and Appositives	Examples
A **parenthetical phrase** adds nonessential information to a sentence. You can leave out a nonessential phrase without changing the meaning of the sentence. Use commas to set off a nonessential phrase.	Most miners did not, **in fact**, find gold. Gold, **every miner's dream**, lay deeply buried.
An **appositive phrase** renames the noun next to it. An appositive phrase usually comes after the noun or pronoun it refers to.	James Marshall, **a mill worker**, started the Gold Rush when he found gold nuggets in 1848.

Sentence Functions

Sentence Types	Examples
A **statement** ends with a period.	The football game was on Friday. The coach made an important announcement.
A **question** ends with a question mark.	Who heard the announcement? What did the coach say?
An **exclamation** shows surprise or strong emotion. It ends with an exclamation mark.	That's fantastic news! I can't believe it!
In an **imperative** sentence, or command, the subject **you** is implied. It is not stated. • An imperative sentence usually begins with a verb and ends with a period. • If an imperative sentence shows strong emotion, it ends with an exclamation mark.	Give the team my congratulations. **Be** on time. Beat the opponent!

Negative Sentences	Examples
A **negative sentence** uses a **negative word** to say "no."	The game in Hawaii was **not** boring!
Negative Words	**Nobody** in our town missed it on TV.
	Our team **never** played better.
no nobody never	**Nothing** is better than watching your team win!
not nothing no one	**None** of us could stop cheering.
none nowhere	**Incorrect:** The cheering **did not** never stop.
Use only one negative word in a sentence. Two negatives in one sentence is called a **double negative**. Two negatives cancel each other out. **I did not see no one** means **I saw someone**.	**Correct:** The cheering **never** stopped The cheering **did not** stop.
	anything The other team could not do ~~nothing~~ right.
	any Their team never scored ~~no~~ points.

Conditional Sentences	Examples
Conditional sentences tell how one action depends on another action. These sentences often use conditional or modal verbs.	**If** our team returns today, **then** we will have a party.
Conditional Verbs	**Unless** it rains, we can have the party outside.
	If you have time, **could** you invite the mayor?
can could might	The mayor **might** come to the party **if** he is available.
will would	

Combining Sentences

Good writers use many different types of sentences. You can combine short, related sentences in different ways.

Combined Sentences	Examples
You can use **appositives**.	Samuel Brannan was a newspaper publisher. He told everyone about the discovery of gold. Samuel Brannan, **a newspaper publisher**, told everyone about the discovery of gold.
You can use **participial phrases**.	The search for gold was dangerous. The miners stood in rushing streams. The search for gold was dangerous for miners **standing in rushing streams**.
You can use **prepositional phrases**.	The trip to California was difficult. People traveled in covered wagons. The trip to California **by covered wagon** was difficult.
You can join clauses. Use **coordination** to join clauses of equal weight, or importance.	Gold was often found next to streams, **and** it was also found deep beneath the earth.
Use **subordination** to join clauses of unequal weight, or importance. Put the main idea in the main clause and the less important detail in the dependent clause.	The miners were called '49ers. *main idea* Many miners arrived in 1849. *less important detail* The miners were called '49ers because they arrived in 1849.

Parts of Speech

All the words in the English language can be put into one of eight groups. These groups are the eight **parts of speech**. You can tell a word's part of speech by looking at how it functions, or the way it is used, in a sentence. Knowing about the functions of words can help you become a better writer.

The Eight Parts of Speech	Examples
A **noun** names a person, place, thing, or idea.	**Erik Weihenmayer** climbed the highest **mountain** in the **world**. The **journey** up **Mount Everest** took **courage**.
A **pronoun** takes the place of a noun.	**He** made the journey even though **it** was dangerous.
An **adjective** describes a noun or a pronoun.	Erik is a **confident** climber. He is **strong**, too.
A **verb** can tell what the subject of a sentence does or has. A **verb** can also link a noun or an adjective in the predicate to the subject.	Erik also **skis** and **rides** a bike. He **has** many hobbies. Erik **is** an athlete. He **is** also blind.
An **adverb** describes a verb, an adjective, or another adverb.	Illness **slowly** took his eyesight, but it **never** affected his spirit. His accomplishments have made him **very** famous. He has been interviewed **quite** often.
A **preposition** shows how two things or ideas are related. It introduces a prepositional phrase.	Erik speaks **to** people **around** the world. **In** his speeches, he talks **about** his life.
A **conjunction** connects words or groups of words.	Courage **and** skill have carried him far. He has one disability, **but** he has many abilities.
An **interjection** expresses strong feeling.	**Wow**! What an amazing person he is! **Hurray**! He reached the mountaintop.

Nouns

A **noun** names a person, animal, place, thing, or idea.
There are different kinds of nouns.

Common and Proper Nouns	Examples
A **common noun** names a general person, place, thing, or idea.	A **teenager** sat by the **ocean** and read a **magazine**.
Capitalize a common noun only when it begins a sentence.	**Magazines** are the perfect thing to read at the beach.
A **proper noun** names a specific person, place, thing, or idea. Always capitalize a proper noun.	**Jessica** sat by the **Pacific Ocean** and read *Teen Talk* magazine.

Regular Plural Nouns	Examples
Plural nouns name more than one person, place, thing, or idea. Add **–s** to most nouns to make them plural.	My favorite **guitar** was made in Spain, but I also like my two American **guitars**.

Other nouns follow different rules to form the plural.

Forming Noun Plurals

When a Noun Ends in:	Form the Plural by:	Examples
ch, **sh**, **s**, **x**, or **z**	adding **-es**	box—box**es** brush—brush**es**
a consonant + **y**	changing the **y** to **i** and adding **-es**	story—stor**ies**
a vowel + **y**	just adding **-s**	boy—boy**s**
a single **f** or **fe**	changing the **f** or **fe** to **v** and adding **-es** **Exceptions**	leaf—lea**ves** knife—kni**ves** belief—belief**s** chief—chief**s** scarf—scarf**s**/scar**ves**
a vowel + **o**	adding **-s**	radio—radio**s** kangaroo—kangaroo**s**
a consonant + **o**	adding **-s** or **-es**. Some words take **-s**, some words take **-es**, some take both **-s** and **-es**.	photo—photo**s** radio—radio**s** potato—potato**es** tomato—tomato**es** tornado—tornado**s**/tornado**es** zero—zero**s**/zero**es**

Irregular Plural Nouns	Examples
Some nouns are **irregular**. These nouns do not follow the rules to form the plural.	At first only one **person** came, but within an hour there were many **people**.

Forming Plurals of Irregular Nouns

For some irregular nouns, change the spelling to form the plural.	one child many **children**	one man several **men**	one mouse a few **mice**
	one foot many **feet**	one ox ten **oxen**	one tooth three **teeth**
	one goose some **geese**	one person two **people**	one woman most **women**
For other irregular nouns, keep the same form for the singular and the plural.	one deer two **deer**	one fish many **fish**	one sheep twelve **sheep**

Possessive Nouns	Examples
Possessive nouns show ownership or relationship of persons, places, or things.	**Ted's** daughter made the guitar. The **guitar's** tone is beautiful.
Follow these rules to make a noun possessive: • Add **'s** to a singular noun or a plural noun that does not end in **s**.	When she plays the piano, it attracts **the children's** attention.
• Add an apostrophe after the final **s** in a plural noun that ends in **s**.	Three **musicians'** instruments were left on the bus.

Noun Phrases	Examples
A **noun phrase** is made up of a noun and its modifiers. Modifiers are words that describe, such as adjectives.	**The flying frog** does not actually fly. It glides on **special skin flaps**. Thailand is a **frog-friendly habitat**.

Articles

An **article** is a word that helps identify a noun.

Articles	Examples
A, **an**, and **the** are **articles**.	It is **an** amazing event when **a** flying frog glides in **the** forest.
A and **an** are **indefinite articles**. Use **a** or **an** before a noun that names a nonspecific thing.	**A flying frog** stretched its webbed feet. **An owl** watched from a nearby tree.
• Use **a** before a word that starts with a consonant sound.	a **f**oot a **p**ool a **n**est a **r**ainbow a **u**nion (*u* is pronounced like *y*, a consonant)
• Use **an** before a word that starts with a vowel sound.	an **e**gg an **a**nimal an **i**dea an **o**cean an **h**our (The *h* is silent.)
The is a **definite article**. Use **the** before a noun that names a specific thing.	Leiopelmids are **the** oldest kind of frog in **the** world. They are survivors of **the** Jurassic period.

Pronouns

A **pronoun** takes the place of a noun or refers to a noun.

Subject Pronouns	Examples
Use a **subject pronoun** as the subject of a sentence. | Singular	Plural
I	we
you	you
he, she, it	they		**Antonio** is looking forward to the dance. **He** is trying to decide what to wear. The **dance** starts at 7:00. **It** ends at 10:00.
The pronoun **it** can be used as a **subject** to refer to a noun. **But:** The pronoun **it** can be the subject without refering to a specific noun.	The **dance** starts at 7:00. **It** ends at 10:00. **It** is important to arrive on time. **It** is fun to see your friends in formal clothes.

Object Pronouns

Use an **object pronoun** after an <u>action verb</u> or after a <u>preposition</u>.

Singular	Plural
me	us
you	you
him, her, it	them

Examples

Tickets are on sale, so <u>buy</u> **them** now.

Antonio invited Caryn. He has flowers <u>for</u> **her**.

Possessive Pronouns

A **possessive pronoun** shows who or what owns something or belongs with something.

A **singular possessive pronoun** shows that one person owns or has something.

A **plural possessive pronoun** shows that more than one person owns or has something.

Singular	Plural
mine	ours
yours	yours
his, hers, its	theirs

Examples

The photographs belong to **John and Marissa**. The photographs are **theirs**.

John has a new camera. The camera is **his**.

I made a video of the event. The video is **mine**.

Have you seen my laptop, Mom?
Yes, that laptop is **yours**.

John, **Marissa**, and **I** posted the photos online. The online photos are **ours**.

Have you seen our photos yet, Zack?
Yes, **yours** are the best!

Demonstrative Pronouns

A **demonstrative pronoun** points out a specific person, place, thing, or idea. Use the correct pronoun to talk about things that are near you or far from you.

	Singular	Plural
Near	this	these
Far	that	those

Examples

This is a good phone. It takes great photos. Look at **these**!

These on my phone are photos of my friends. **This** is my friend, Michael.

Those on the wall are photographs of my grandparents. **That** is a photo of my grandmother when she was young.

Pronouns, continued

Indefinite Pronouns	Examples
Use an **indefinite pronoun** when you are not talking about a specific person, place, or thing.	**Someone** has to lose the game. **Nobody** knows who the winner will be.

Some Indefinite Pronouns

These **indefinite pronouns** are always singular and need a **singular verb**.				
anybody	either	neither	one	**Something is** happening on the playing field.
anyone	everybody	nobody	somebody	
anything	everyone	no one	someone	We hope that **everything goes** well for our team.
each	everything	nothing	nothing	

These **indefinite pronouns** are always plural and need a **plural verb**.				
both	few	many	several	**Many** of us **are** hopeful.

These **indefinite pronouns** can be singular or plural.				
all	any	most	none	some	**Most** of the players **are** tired.
Look at the phrase that follows the indefinite pronoun. If the noun or pronoun in the phrase is plural, use a **plural verb**. If it is singular, use a **singular verb**.				**Most** of the game **is** over.

Relative Pronouns	Examples
A **relative pronoun** introduces **a relative clause**. It connects, or relates, the clause to a word in the sentence.	**Relative Pronouns** who what which whom whoever whatever whose whomever whichever
Use **who**, **whom**, or **whose** for people. The pronouns **whoever** and **whomever**, also refer to people.	The student **who** was injured is Joe. We play **whomever** we are scheduled to play.
Use **which**, **whichever**, **what**, and **whatever** for things.	Joe's wrist, **which** is sprained, will heal.
Use **that** for people or things.	The trainer **that** examined Joe's wrist is sure. The injury **that** Joe received is minor.

Reflexive and Intensive Pronouns	Examples
Reflexive and **intensive pronouns** refer to nouns or other pronouns in a sentence. These pronouns end with **–self** or **–selves**.	**I** will go to the store by **myself**.

Singular	Plural
myself	ourselves
yourself	yourselves
himself, herself, itself	themselves

Use a **reflexive pronoun** when the object **refers back to the subject**.	To surprise her technology teacher, **Kim** taught **herself** how to create a website on the computer.
Use an **intensive pronoun to emphasize a noun or a pronoun** in a sentence.	The technology **teacher himself** learned some interesting techniques from Kim.

Agreement and Reference	Examples
When nouns and pronouns **agree**, they both refer to the same person, place, or thing. The **noun** is the **antecedent**, and the **pronoun** refers to it.	**Rafael and Felicia** visited a local college. **They** toured the campus. *antecedent* *pronoun*
A pronoun must agree (match) in **number** with the noun it refers to. • **Singular pronouns** refer to one. • **Plural pronouns** refer to more than one.	**Rafael** plays violin. **He** enjoyed the music school. **The teenagers** were impressed. **They** liked this college.
Pronouns must agree in **gender** with the nouns they refer to. Use **she**, **her**, and **hers** to refer to females. Use **he**, **him**, and **his** to refer to males.	Felicia told **her** uncle about the college visit. **Her** uncle told **her** that **he** received **his** graduate degree from that school.
When you write, check that your pronouns refer to the correct noun. To correct sentences with unclear or vague pronouns, you can edit the sentence and remove the pronoun, or replace the pronoun with a noun.	Unclear: Bill told Rafael **he** would like the teachers. *Is **he** Uncle Bill or Rafael?* Clear: Bill said that Rafael would like the teachers. Unclear: At the college, **they** give violin lessons. *Who gives the lessons?* Clear: At the college, musicians give violin lessons.

Adjectives

An **adjective** describes, or modifies, a noun or a pronoun. It can tell what kind, which one, how many, or how much.

Adjectives	Examples
Adjectives provide more detailed information about a noun. Usually, an adjective comes before the noun it describes.	Deserts have a **dry** climate.
But an adjective can also come after the noun.	The climate is also **hot**.
Number words are often used as adjectives.	While I was out in the desert I saw **one** roadrunner, **two** Gila monsters, and **six** cacti.
Sometimes the number word tells the **order** that things are in.	The **first** day, I just saw some lizards. The **second** day, I got to see a coyote!

Proper Adjectives	Examples
A proper adjective is formed from a proper noun. It always begins with a capital letter.	Major deserts are found in Africa, Asia, and the Americas. The largest **African** desert is the Sahara.

Possessive Adjectives	Examples
A **possessive adjective** replaces an owner's name. It matches the gender and number of owners.	I have notes about an interesting desert animal. **My** notes are mostly about the Gila monster. A **Gila monster** has a painful bite. **Its** bite is poisonous. **Mia's** report is about a bird called a Roadrunner. **Her** report includes photographs of the bird.

Singular	Plural
my	our
your	your
his, her, its	their

Adjectives That Compare	Examples
Comparative adjectives help show the similarities or differences between two nouns.	Deserts are **more fun** to study **than** forests.
To form the comparative of one-syllable adjectives, add -**er**, and use **than**. Use **more ... than** if the adjective has three or more syllables.	The Sechura Desert in South America is small**er than** the Kalahari Desert in Africa. Is that desert **more interesting than** this one?
Superlative adjectives help show how three or more nouns are alike or different.	Of the Sechura, Kalahari, and Sahara, which is **the largest**?
To form the superlative of one-syllable adjectives, add -**est** and use **the**. Use **most** if the adjective has three or more syllables.	Which of the three deserts is the **smallest**? I think the Sahara is **the most beautiful**.
Irregular adjectives form the comparative and superlative differently. good better best bad worse worst much/many more most little less/fewer least	I had **the best** time ever visiting the desert. But the desert heat is **worse than** city heat. There was **less** traffic **than** before. There were **fewer** buses on the road.
Some two-syllable adjectives form the comparative with either -**er** or **more** and the superlative with either -**est** or **most**. Do not use both more and -er with the same adjective.	Desert animals are usually **more lively** at night than during the day. Desert animals are usually **livelier** at night than during the day. **Incorrect:** Desert animals are usually **more livelier** at night than during the day.

Adjective Phrases and Clauses	Examples
An **adjective phrase** is a group of words that work together to modify a noun or a pronoun. A phrase has no verb.	Plants **in the desert** have developed adaptations.
An **adjective clause** also works to modify a noun or a pronoun. Unlike an adjective phrase, an adjective clause has a subject and a verb.	The saguaro, **whose flowers bloom at night**, soaks up surface water after it rains. Desert plants **that have long roots** tap into water deep in the earth.

Verbs

Every complete sentence has two parts: a subject and a predicate. The subject tells who or what the sentence is about. The predicate tells something about the subject. For example:

The <u>dancers</u> / **performed** on stage.

The **verb** is the key word in the predicate because it tells what the subject does or has. Verbs can also link together words in the subject and the predicate.

Action Verbs	Examples
An **action verb** tells what the subject of a sentence does. Most verbs are action verbs.	Dancers **practice** for many hours. They **stretch** their muscles and **lift** weights.
Some **action verbs** tell about an action that you cannot see.	The dancers **recognize** the rewards that come from their hard work.

Linking Verbs	Examples
A **linking verb** connects, or links, the subject of a sentence to a word in the predicate. Forms of the verb *be* are most commonly used, but other verbs are used as well. **Forms of the Verb *Be*** 	am	are	were
is	was	| **Other Linking Verbs** | appear	seem	become
feel	smell	taste
look				
The word in the predicate can describe the subject.	Their feet **are** calloused.
Or the word in the predicate can rename the subject.	These dancers **are** athletes.

Helping Verbs	Examples
Some verbs are made up of more than one word. They need help to show exactly what is happening.	Ballet **is considered** a dramatic art form. *helping verb* *main verb*
The action word is called the **main verb**. It shows what the subject does, has, or is.	This dance form **has been evolving** over the years. *helping verbs* *main verb*
Any verbs that come before the **main** verb are the **helping verbs**.	Ballet **must have been** very different in the 1500s. *helping verbs* *main verb*

Helping Verbs

Forms of the Verb *Be*	Forms of the Verb *Do*	Forms of the Verb *Have*
am was is were are	do did does	have had has

Other Helping Verbs

To express ability: **can, could**	I **can** dance.
To express possibility: **may, might, could**	I **might** dance tonight.
To express necessity or desire: **must, would**	I **must** dance more often.
To express certainty: **will, shall**	I **will** dance more often.
To express obligation: **should, ought to**	I **should** practice more often. I **ought to** practice more often.

Helping verbs agree with the subject.	Baryshnikov **has performed** around the world. Many people **have praised** this famous dancer.
When used, the adverb *not* always comes between the **helping verb** and the main verb.	If you **have** not **heard** of him, you can watch the film *Dancers* to see him perform.
In questions, the subject comes between the **helping verb** and the **main verb**.	**Have** you **heard** of Mikhail Baryshnikov?

Verb Tense: Past, Present, Future

The **tense** of a verb shows when an action happens.

Present Tense Verbs	Examples
The **present tense** of a verb tells about an action that is happening now.	Greg **checks** his watch to see if it is time to leave. He **starts** work at 5:00 today.

Habitual Present Tense Verbs	Examples
The **habitual present tense** of a verb tells about an action that happens regularly or all the time.	Greg **works** at a pizza shop. He **makes** pizzas and **washes** dishes.

Past Tense Verbs (Regular and Irregular)	Examples
The **past tense** of a verb tells about an action that happened earlier, or in the past.	Yesterday, Greg **worked** until the shop closed. He **made** 50 pizzas.
• The past tense form of **regular verbs** ends with -**ed**.	He **learned** how to make a stuffed-crust pizza. Then Greg **chopped** onions and peppers.
• **Irregular verbs** have **special forms** to show the past tense. See pages 454W-455W [Level A], 480W-481W [Level B], 476W-477W [Level C]. Here are some examples of irregular verbs:	Greg **cut** the pizza. It **was** delicious. We **ate** all of it!

Present Tense	Past Tense
cut	cut
am, is, are	was, were
eat	ate

Future Tense Verbs	Examples
The **future tense** of a verb tells about an action that will happen later, or in the future. To show future tense, use:	Greg **will ride** the bus home after work tonight.
• the helping verb **will** plus a main verb	Greg's mother **will drive** him to work tomorrow. On Friday, he **will get** his first paycheck.
• **am**, **is**, or **are** + **going to** + a main verb	He **is going to take** a pizza home to his family. They **are going to eat** the pizza for dinner.

Verb Tense: Perfect Tenses

All verbs in the **perfect tenses**—**present perfect**, **past perfect**, and **future perfect**—have a helping verb and a form of the main verb that is called the **past participle**.

Present Perfect Tense Verbs	Examples
The **present perfect tense** of a verb uses the helping verb **has** or **have** plus the past participle.	
Use the present perfect tense to tell about something that happened at an unknown time in the past.	I **have looked** things up on the Internet.
You can also use the present perfect tense to tell about something that happened in the past and may still be going on.	The public **has used** the Internet since the 1980s.
For **regular verbs**, the past participle ends in -**ed**.	I like the Internet.
Present Tense like **Past Participle** liked	I **have** always **liked** the Internet.
Irregular verbs have **special forms** for the past participle.	
Present Tense know **Past Participle** known	I know a lot about the Internet. I **have known** about it for a long time.

Past Perfect Tense Verbs	Examples
The **past perfect tense** of a verb tells about an action that was completed before some other action in the past. It uses the helping verb **had**.	My grandmother **had graduated** from high school before computers were even invented!

Future Perfect Tense Verbs	Examples
The **future perfect tense** of a verb tells about an action that will be completed at a specific time in the future. It uses the helping verbs **will have**.	By the end of next year, 100,000 people **will have visited** our website.

Verb Forms

The **form** a verb takes changes depending on when the action happened—in the present, the past, or the future. It also depends on whether the action is in progress.

Progressive Verbs	Examples
The **progressive** verb forms tell about an action that occurs over a period of time.	
The **present progressive** form of a verb tells about an action as it is happening. • It uses the helping verb **am**, **is**, or **are**. The main verb ends in -**ing**.	They **are expecting** a big crowd for the fireworks show this evening. **Are** you **expecting** the rain to end before the show starts?
The **past progressive** form of a verb tells about an action that was happening over a period of time in the past. • It uses the helping verb **was** or **were** and a main verb. The main verb ends in -**ing**.	They **were thinking** of canceling the fireworks. A tornado **was heading** in this direction.
The **future progressive** form of a verb tells about an action that will be happening over a period of time in the future. • It uses the helping verbs **will be** plus a main verb. The main verb ends in -**ing**.	The weather forecasters **will be watching** for tornados. I hope that they **will** not **be canceling** the show.

Transitive and Intransitive Verbs	Examples
Action verbs can be transitive or intransitive. A **transitive verb** needs an **object** to complete its meaning and to receive the action of the verb.	**Not complete:** **Complete:** Many cities **use** Many cities **use** fireworks.
The object can be a **direct object**. A direct object answers the question *Whom?* or *What?*	**Whom:** The noise **surprises** the audience. **What:** The people in the audience **cover** their ears.
An **intransitive verb** does not need an object to complete its meaning.	**Complete:** The people in our neighborhood **clap**. They **shout**. They **laugh**.
An **intransitive verb** may end the sentence, or it may be followed by other words that tell how, where, or when. These words are not objects since they do not receive the action of the verb.	The fireworks **glow** brightly. Then, slowly, they **disappear** in the sky. The show **ends** by midnight.

Active and Passive Voice of Verbs	Examples
Sentences have nouns or pronouns and verbs. You use verbs to tell about actions. You use nouns or pronouns to tell about the subject. The subject does the action. The voice of a verb depends on the subject in a sentence. A verb is in the **active voice** if the subject does, or performs, the action. The subject is the doer. A verb is in the **passive voice** if the subject does not perform the action. The subject is the receiver. A verb in the passive voice always includes a form of the verb be (am, is, are, was, were) and the past participle of the main verb. How does a reader know who does the action? Sometimes the subject is included in a phrase. Sometimes the subject is not mentioned in the sentence.	*doer* *receiver* Many cities **hold** fireworks displays on the Fourth of July. *receiver* *doer* Fireworks displays **are held by** many cities on the Fourth of July. *receiver* Fireworks displays **are held** every Fourth of July.
The first words in a sentence usually get more attention from the reader. Using active or passive voice impacts the focus, or emphasis, of writing. Use the **active voice** when you want more emphasis on the subject. Use **passive voice** when you want less emphasis on the subject. This happens when: • the object, or receiver of the action, is more important than the subject • the subject is not known, not important, or obvious • the writer prefers not to mention who did the action (the subject). For example, the writer might not want to blame a specific person or group.	*doer* The mayor **picked** a safe location. *receiver* A safe location **was picked** by the mayor. The fireworks **were made** in the U.S. An error **was made** in the location choice last year.
When you write for a specific audience or purpose, you choose a tone. Your tone can be formal or informal. Use **active voice** when you write in either a formal tone or an informal tone. When you use passive voice, your writing sounds more objective and impersonal. Use passive voice when you write in a more formal tone.	Formal Tone: The mayor **approved** the location for this year's fireworks display. Informal Tone: The mayor **picked** a really awesome location for this year's fireworks. The location for this year's fireworks display **was approved** by the mayor.

Verb Forms, continued

Two-Word Verbs

A **two-word verb** is a verb followed by a preposition. The meaning of the two-word verb is different from the meaning of the verb by itself.

Some Two-Word Verbs

Verb	Meaning	Example
break	to split into pieces	I didn't **break** the window with the ball.
break down	to stop working	Did the car **break down** again?
break up	to end	The party will **break up** before midnight.
	to come apart	The ice on the lake will **break up** in the spring.
check	to make sure you are right	We can **check** our answers at the back of the book.
check in	to stay in touch with someone	I **check in** with my mom at work.
check up	to see if everything is okay	The nurse **checks up** on the patient every hour.
check off	to mark off a list	Look at your list and **check off** the girls' names.
check out	to look at something carefully	Hey, Marisa, **check out** my new bike!
fill	to place as much as can be held	**Fill** the pail with water.
fill in	to color or shade in a space	Please **fill in** the circle.
fill out	to complete	Marcos **fills out** a form to order a book.
get	to receive	I often **get** letters from my pen pal.
get ahead	to go beyond what is expected	She worked hard to **get ahead** in math class.
get along	to be on good terms with	Do you **get along** with your sister?
get out	to leave	Let's **get out** of the kitchen.
get over	to feel better	I hope you'll **get over** the flu soon.
get through	to finish	I can **get through** this book tonight.
give	to hand something to someone	We **give** presents to the children.
give out	to stop working	If she runs ten miles, her energy will **give out**.
give up	to quit	I'm going to **give up** eating candy.

Verb	Meaning	Example
go	to move from place to place	Did you **go** to the mall on Saturday?
go on	to continue	Why do the boys **go on** playing after the bell rings?
go out	to go someplace special	Let's **go out** to lunch on Saturday.
look	to see or watch	Don't **look** directly at the sun.
look forward	to be excited about something	My brothers **look forward** to summer vacation.
look over	to review	She **looks over** her test before finishing.
look up	to hunt for and find	We **look up** information on the Internet.
pick	to choose	I'd **pick** Lin for class president.
pick on	to bother or tease	My older brothers always **pick on** me.
pick up	to increase	Business **picks up** in the summer.
	to gather or collect	**Pick up** your clothes!
run	to move quickly	Juan will **run** in a marathon.
run into	to unexpectedly see someone	Did you **run into** Chris at the store?
run out	to suddenly have nothing left	The cafeteria always **runs out** of nachos.
stand	to be on your feet	I have to **stand** in line to buy tickets.
stand for	to represent	A heart **stands for** love.
stand out	to be easier to see	You'll **stand out** with that orange cap.
turn	to change direction	We **turn** right at the next corner.
turn up	to appear	Clean your closet and your belt will **turn up**.
	to raise the volume	Please **turn up** the radio.
turn in	to go to bed	On school nights I **turn in** at 9:30.
	to present or submit	You didn't **turn in** the homework yesterday.
turn off	to make something stop	Please **turn off** the radio.

Verb Forms, continued

Irregular verbs do not follow the same rules for changing form as the "regular" verbs do. These verb forms have to be memorized. Here are some irregular verbs.

Irregular Verb	Past Tense	Past Participle	Irregular Verb	Past Tense	Past Participle
be: am, is, are	was, were	been	eat	ate	eaten
beat	beat	beaten	fall	fell	fallen
become	became	become	feed	fed	fed
begin	began	begun	feel	felt	felt
bend	bent	bent	fight	fought	fought
bind	bound	bound	find	found	found
bite	bit	bitten	fly	flew	flown
blow	blew	blown	forget	forgot	forgotten
break	broke	broken	forgive	forgave	forgiven
bring	brought	brought	freeze	froze	frozen
build	built	built	get	got	gotten
burst	burst	burst	give	gave	given
buy	bought	bought	go	went	gone
catch	caught	caught	grow	grew	grown
choose	chose	chosen	have	had	had
come	came	come	hear	heard	heard
cost	cost	cost	hide	hid	hidden
creep	crept	crept	hit	hit	hit
cut	cut	cut	hold	held	held
dig	dug	dug	hurt	hurt	hurt
do	did	done	keep	kept	kept
draw	drew	drawn	know	knew	known
drink	drank	drunk	lead	led	led
drive	drove	driven	leave	left	left

Forms of Irregular Verbs

Irregular Verb	Past Tense	Past Participle	Irregular Verb	Past Tense	Past Participle
let	let	let	sink	sank	sunk
light	lit	lit	sit	sat	sat
lose	lost	lost	sleep	slept	slept
make	made	made	slide	slid	slid
mean	meant	meant	speak	spoke	spoken
meet	met	met	spend	spent	spent
pay	paid	paid	stand	stood	stood
prove	proved	proved, proven	steal	stole	stolen
put	put	put	stick	stuck	stuck
read	read	read	sting	stung	stung
ride	rode	ridden	strike	struck	struck
ring	rang	rung	swear	swore	sworn
rise	rose	risen	swim	swam	swum
run	ran	run	swing	swung	swung
say	said	said	take	took	taken
see	saw	seen	teach	taught	taught
seek	sought	sought	tear	tore	torn
sell	sold	sold	tell	told	told
send	sent	sent	think	thought	thought
set	set	set	throw	threw	thrown
shake	shook	shaken	wake	woke, waked	woken, waked
show	showed	shown	wear	wore	worn
shrink	shrank	shrunk	win	won	won
sing	sang	sung	write	wrote	written

Verbals

A **verbal** is a word made from a verb, but used as a different part of speech.

Gerunds	Examples
A **gerund** is a verb form that ends in **-ing**, and is used as a noun. A gerund can be: • the subject of a sentence. Only use gerunds as the subject when the verb is singular. • a direct object of a verb • an object of a preposition • a predicate nominative, or word in the predicate that renames the subject.	**Cooking** is Jorge's favorite hobby. He enjoys **cooking**. Jorge is very talented at **cooking**. His talent is **cooking**. ⊤ ⊤ subject predicate
A **gerund phrase** is made up of the gerund, its modifiers, and other words that complete its meaning. Use gerunds to vary your sentences. Notice how this writer made improvements by including gerunds.	Jorge makes **creating delicious meals** look easy. following As you learn how to cook, ~~it is a good idea for you~~ ~~to take the time to follow~~ a recipe step-by- is important step. But once you have successfully created the experimenting dish a few times, try ~~to do different things with it~~. Add or change ingredients to make the dish your own.

Infinitives	Examples
An **infinitive** is a verb form that begins with the word **to**.	
• An infinitive can be used as a noun. It can be the **direct object of a verb**.	Jorge likes **to cook**. *noun: direct object*
Sometimes an infinitive can be the **subject** of the sentence. When it is the subject, the verb is singular.	**To cook** is Jorge's passion. *noun: subject*
• An infinitive can also be an **adjective** or an **adverb**.	His beef tamales are a sight **to see**. *adjective* Jorge cooks **to relax**. *adverb*
Remember, a phase is a group of related words. An **infinitive phrase** is made up of the infinitive, its modifiers, and other words that complete its meaning.	Jorge likes **to create his own special dishes**. *infinitive* *infinitive phrase*

Participles	Examples
A **participle** is a verb form that is used as an adjective.	
• For regular verbs, a participle ends in -**ing** or -**ed**.	His **sizzling** fajitas taste delicious. He makes them with **sliced** steak.
• For irregular verbs, a participle takes the past participle form.	Jorge also makes tasty **frozen** desserts.
A **participial phrase** begins with a participle and includes all the words that complete its meaning.	**Starving for a good lunch**, we ask Jorge to cook. *participle* *participial phrase*
Always place a participial phrase next to the noun it describes so the meaning is clear.	**Correct:** He prepared ground beef **mixed with spices**. *Incorrect:* **Mixed with spices**, he prepared ground beef. **Correct: Standing by the grill**, he cooked hamburgers. *Incorrect:* He cooked hamburgers, **standing by the grill**.

Verb Moods

Sometimes writers state facts. Other times, they give commands or express wishes. To show what they intend by the action in sentences, writers use different **verb moods**.

Indicative Mood	Examples
The **indicative mood** is the most common verb mood. Indicate means "to show" or "point out." The indicative mood points out something that exists or is true in real life. Use the indicative mood to • describe events • state a fact or make a statement • express beliefs, thoughts, and ideas that are possible in real life.	 Our class studied the solar system. Jupiter is the largest planet. Thinking about space travel is interesting.

Imperative Mood	Examples
Imperative means "necessary or required," so sentences that use the **imperative mood** • make requests • give commands • give advice. Remember, complete sentences include a subject and a predicate. Sometimes the subject is not directly stated, it is implied. Most of the time, sentences using the imperative mood have an implied subject: *You*.	 Let me see what you've done so far. Sit down. Take a break for a while. (You) Work with your partner.

Interrogative Mood	Examples
To interrogate means "to question." Use the **interrogative mood** to • make requests for action • ask for information.	 Will you show me those photographs now? How many rings does the planet Saturn have?

Conditional Mood	Examples
The **conditional mood** expresses what could or might happen as a result of another event.	**If Ian goes online**, he will find a lot of facts about Saturn.
Sentences in the conditional mood use the words *if, might, could,* or *would* to express possibilities.	**If** he sees what Saturn looks like, he **could** make a model of it.
Sentences using the conditional mood can reflect:	
• facts	A meteoroid will evaporate **if** it collides with Earth's atmosphere.
• activities that are repeated	**If** Ian takes notes, he'll remember what he learned.
• future events or plans	**If** Ian does well on his report, he could get a good grade.

Subjunctive Mood	Examples
The **subjunctive mood** expresses ideas that are not facts, such as wishes or possibilities.	
Sentences using the subjunctive mood tell about things that someone	
• wants to happen	The teacher asks that teams **be** ready by 2 p.m.
• predicts will happen	**If** we aren't ready, the teacher will not have time to finish the presentation.
• imagines happening	**If we were** ready early, she **might** give us more reading time
The subjunctive often	
• uses the words: *If, might, could, would, should*	I **would** do it **if** I had the time. But I don't have the time.
• follows the verbs: *ask, demand, doubt, request, suggest,* or *wish*	Mary **suggests** that we stay late each day this week.
• begins with the phrases: *if I /you/we/they/ were; it is important that; it is necessary that*	**It is important that** he decide as soon as possible.
	If I were to bring a meteor to class, **I would** definitely get an A!
Always use **were**, not **was**, when you use the **if** clause with a form of the verb **be**.	were If I ~~was~~ an alien, I would live on Saturn. ^

Contractions

A **contraction** is a shortened form of a verb plus the word *not*, or of a verb-and-pronoun combination.

Contractions	Examples
Use an **apostrophe** to show which letters have been left out of the contraction.	is n~~o~~t = isn't I w~~oul~~d = I'd can ~~not~~ = can't They ~~a~~re = They're
In contractions made up of a verb and the word **not**, the word **not** is usually shortened to **n't**.	I **can't** stop eating these cookies!

Adverbs

An **adverb** describes a verb, an adjective, or another adverb.

Adverbs	Examples
Adverbs answer one of the following questions: • How? • Where? • When? • How often?	**Carefully** aim the ball. Kick the ball **here**. Try again **later** to make a goal. Cathy **usually** scores.
An adverb can come before or after a **verb**.	Our team **always wins**. The whole team **plays well**.
An adverb can modify the meaning of an **adjective** or another **adverb**.	Gina is **really good** at soccer. She plays **very well**.

Adverbs That Compare	Examples
Some **adverbs** compare actions. Add **-er** to compare the actions of two people. Add **-est** to compare the actions of three or more people.	Gina runs **fast**. Gina runs **faster** than Maria. Gina runs **the fastest** of all the players.
If the adverb ends in **-ly**, use **more** or **less** to compare two actions.	Gina aims **more carefully** than Jen. Jen aims **less carefully** than Gina.
Use **the most** or **the least** to compare three or more actions.	Gina aims **the most carefully** of all the players. Jen aims **the least carefully** of all the players.

Prepositions

A **preposition** comes at the beginning of a prepositional phrase. **Prepositional phrases** add details to sentences.

Uses of Prepositions				Examples
Some prepositions show **location.**				The Chávez Community Center is **by my house.**
behind	between	inside	outside	The pool is **behind the building**
below	by	near	over	
beside	in	on	under	
Some prepositions show **time.**				The Teen Club's party will start **after lunch.**
after	before	during	until	
Some prepositions show **direction.**				Go **through the building** and **around the fountain** to get **to the pool.**
across	down	out of	toward	The snack bar is **down the hall.**
around	into	through	up	
Some prepositions have **multiple uses.**				We might see Joshua **at the party.**
about	among	for	to	Meet me **at my house.**
against	as	from	with	Come **at noon.**
along	at	of	without	

Conjunctions

A **conjunction** connects words or groups of words.

Conjunctions	Examples
A **coordinating conjunction** connects words, phrases, or clauses.	
To show similarity: **and**	Irena **and** Irving are twins.
To show difference: **but**, **yet**	I know Irena, **but** I do not know Irving.
To show choice: **or**	They will celebrate Friday **or** Saturday night.
To show cause/effect: **so**, **for**	I have a cold, **so** I cannot go to the party.
To put negative ideas together: **nor**	My mother will not let me go, **nor** will my father.
Correlative conjunctions are used in pairs. The pair connects phrases or words.	**Some Correlative Conjunctions** both … and not only … but also either … or whether … or
A **subordinating conjunction** introduces a **dependent clause** in a complex sentence. It connects the **dependent clause** to the main clause.	**Some Subordinating Conjunctions** after before till although if until
A **conjunctive adverb** joins two independent clauses. Use a semicolon before the conjunction and a comma after it.	**Some Conjunctive Adverbs** besides however then consequently moreover therefore

Interjections

An **interjection** expresses strong feeling or emotion.

Interjections	Examples
An **interjection** shows emotion. If an interjection stands alone, follow it with an exclamation point.	**Help!** **Oops!** **Oh boy!**
An interjection used in a sentence can be followed by a comma or an exclamation mark. Use a comma after a weak interjection. Use an exclamation mark after a strong interjection.	**Oh**, it's a baby panda! **Hooray**! The baby panda has survived!

Grammar Troubleshooting Guide

In this section, you will find helpful solutions to common problems with sentences and parts of speech.

Sentences: Problems and Solutions

Sentence Fragments

Problem:
An infinitive phrase is punctuated as a complete sentence.

Solution:
Add a complete sentence to the phrase.

Incorrect:
To show students alternative ways to learn.

Correct:
To show students alternative ways to learn, Mr. Harris organized the trip.

Problem:
A clause starting with a relative pronoun is punctuated as a complete sentence.

Solution:
Add a subject and predicate to the sentence.

Incorrect:
Who might be interested in going on the trip.

Correct:
Anyone who might be interested in going on the trip should see Mr. Harris.

Problem:
A prepositional phrase is punctuated as a complete sentence.

Solution:
Add a sentence to the prepostional phrase.

Incorrect:
When traveling overseas.

Correct:
When traveling overseas, always try to speak to people in their native language.

Run On Sentences

Problem:
Two or more independent clauses are run together with no punctuation.

Solution:
Change one of the clauses into a dependent clause. Rewrite the sentence as two sentences.

Incorrect:
I first played guitar at twelve I thought I was great I knew very little then.

Correct:
When I first played guitar at twelve, I thought I was great. However, I knew very little then.

Problem:
Two independent clauses are joined with a conjunction, but without a comma.

Solution:
Use a comma before the conjunction.

Incorrect:
I continued to take lessons and I realized that I had much to learn to become a good guitarist.

Correct:
I continued to take lessons, and I realized that I had much to learn to become a good guitarist.

Parts of Speech: Problems and Solutions

Nouns

Problem:
The sentence has the wrong plural form of an irregular noun.

Incorrect:
Many **deers** live there.

Solution:
Rewrite the sentence using the correct plural form. Check a dictionary.

Correct:
Many **deer** live there.

Problem:
The noun should be possessive, but it is not.

Incorrect:
The beginning should capture the **readers** interest.

Solution:
Add an apostrophe to make the noun possessive.

Correct:
The beginning should capture the **readers'** interest.

Pronouns

Problem:
The pronoun does not agree in number or gender with the noun it refers to.

Incorrect:
Mary called Robert, but **they** did not answer **him**.

Solution:
Match a pronoun's number and gender to the number and gender of the noun it is replacing.

Correct:
Mary called Robert, but **he** did not answer **her**.

Problem:
A pronun does not agree in number with the indefinte pronoun it refers to.

Incorrect:
Everyone brought **their book** to class.

Solution:
Make the pronoun and the word it refers to agree in number, so that both are singular or plural.

Correct:
Everyone brought **his or her book** to class. OR

All the students brought **their books** to class.

Problem:
It's hard to tell which noun in a compound subject is referred to or replaced.

Incorrect:
Ana and Mia own a car, but only **she** drives it.

Solution:
Replace the unclear pronoun with a noun.

Correct:
Ana and Mia own a car, but only **Ana** drives it.

Pronouns, continued

Problem: An object pronoun is used in a compound subject. Remember that subjects do actions and objects receive actions.	**Incorrect:** My brother and **me** rebuild car engines. object pronoun
Solution: Replace the object pronoun with a subject pronoun.	**Correct:** My brother and **I** rebuild car engines. subject pronoun
Problem: A subject pronoun is used in a compound object.	**Incorrect:** Leticia asked my brother and **I** to fix her car. subject pronoun
Solution: Replace the subject pronoun with an object pronoun.	**Correct:** Leticia asked my brother and **me** to fix her car. object pronoun
Problem: A subject pronoun is used as the object of a preposition.	**Incorrect:** Give your timesheet to Colin or **I**. subject pronoun
Solution: Replace the subject pronoun with an object pronoun.	**Correct:** Give your timesheet to Colin or **me**. object pronoun

Adjectives

Problem: The sentence contains a double comparison, using both an -er ending and the word *more*.	**Incorrect:** Joseph is **more older** than he looks.
Solution: Delete the incorrect comparative form.	**Correct:** Joseph is **older** than he looks. OR Joseph is more old than he looks.
Problem: The wrong form of an irregular adjective appears in a sentence that makes a comparison.	**Incorrect:** Cal feels **worser** since he ran out of medicine.
Solution: Replace the wrong form with the correct one. Check a dictionary.	**Correct:** Cal feels **worse** since he ran out of medicine.
Problem: The adjective *good* is used to modify a verb.	**Incorrect:** Julia did **good** on her test.
Solution: Rewrite the sentence using the adverb *well*, or add a noun for the adjective to describe.	**Correct:** Julia did well on her test. OR Julia did a good **job** on her test. noun

Verbs

Problem: In a sentence with two verbs, the tense of the second verb doesn't match the first.	**Incorrect:** Yesterday, Alberto **called** me and **says** he has tickets for the game.
Solution: Keep the verb tense the same unless there is a change in time, such as from past to present.	**Correct:** Yesterday, Alberto **called** me and **said** he has tickets for the game.
Problem: The past tense form of an irregular verb is formed incorrectly.	**Incorrect:** We **bringed** our portable TV to the game.
Solution: Replace the wrong form with the correct one. Check a dictionary.	**Correct:** We **brought** our portable TV to the game.
Problem: The participle form is used when the past-tense form is required.	**Incorrect:** After the game, we **run** over to Marcia's house.
Solution: Replace the wrong form with the correct one. Check a dictionary.	**Correct:** After the game, we **ran** over to Marcia's house.

Adverbs

Problem: An adverb is used to modify a noun or pronoun after the linking verb *feel*.	**Incorrect:** I feel **badly** about the mistake. adverb
Solution: Rewrite the sentence using an adjective.	**Correct:** I feel **bad** about the mistake. adjective
Problem: An adverb is used but does not modify anything in the sentence.	**Incorrect:** **Hopefully**, I didn't make too many mistakes on the test.
Solution: Rewrite the sentence using the adverb as a verb.	**Correct:** **I hope** I didn't make too many mistakes on the test.
Problem: Two negative words are used to express one idea.	**Incorrect:** We **don't** have **no** aspirin.
Solution: Change one negative word to a positive word.	**Correct:** We **don't** have **any** aspirin.

Capitalization

Knowing when to use capital letters is an important part of clear writing.

First Word in a Sentence	Examples
Capitalize the first word in a sentence.	**W**e are studying the Lewis and Clark expedition.

In Direct Quotations	Examples
Capitalize the first word in a **direct quotation**.	Clark said, "**There is great joy in camp.**" "**We are in view of the ocean**," he said. "**It's the Pacific Ocean**," he added.

In Letters	Examples
Capitalize the first word used in the **greeting** or in the **closing** of a letter.	**D**ear Kim, **Y**our friend,

In Titles of Works	Examples
All important words in a **title** begin with a capital letter. Articles (*a*, *an*, *the*) and short prepositions such as *at*, *for*, *of*, and *on* are not capitalized unless they are the first or last word in the title.	**book:** *The Longest Journey* **poem:** "Leaves of Grass" **magazine:** *Flora and Fauna of Arizona* **newspaper:** *The Denver Post* **song:** "The Star-Spangled Banner" **game:** Exploration! **TV series:** "The Gilmore Girls" **movie:** *The Lion King* **play:** Fiddler on the Roof **work of art:** Mona Lisa

Pronoun *I*	Examples
Capitalize the pronoun *I* no matter where it is located in a sentence.	**I** was amazed when **I** learned that Lewis and Clark's expedition was over 8,000 miles.

Capitalization, continued

Proper Nouns and Adjectives	Examples
Common nouns name a general person, place, thing, or idea. Proper nouns name a particular person, place, thing, or idea. All the important words in a **proper noun** start with a capital letter.	**Common Noun: t**eam **Proper Noun: C**orps of **D**estiny
Proper nouns include the following: • names of people and their titles Do not capitalize a title if it is used without a name. • family titles like *Mom* and *Dad* when they are used as names. • names of organizations • names of languages and religions • months, days, special days, and holidays • names of academic courses • historical events and documents	**S**tephanie **E**ddins **C**aptain **M**eriwether **L**ewis The **captain's** co-leader on the expedition was William Clark. "William Clark is one of our ancestors," **Mom** said. I asked my **mom** whose side of the family he was on, hers or my **dad's**. United Nations History Club Wildlife Society Spanish Christianity Islam April Sunday Thanksgiving Algebra I World History Physics Boston Tea Party Bill of Rights
Names of geographic places are proper nouns. Capitalize street, city, and state names in mailing addresses.	**Cities and States**: Dallas, Texas **Regions:** New England **Streets and Roads**: Main Avenue **Bodies of Water**: Pacific Ocean **Countries**: Ecuador **Landforms**: Sahara Desert **Continents**: North America **Public Spaces**: Muir Camp **Buildings, Ships, and Monuments**: *Titanic* **Planets and Heavenly Bodies**: Neptune
A **proper adjective** is formed from a **proper noun**. Capitalize proper adjectives.	Napoleon Bonaparte was from **Europe**. He was a **European** leader in the 1800s.

Abbreviations of Proper Nouns

Abbreviations of geographic places are also capitalized.

Words Used in Addresses

Avenue	Ave.	Drive	Dr.	North	N.	Street	St.
Apartment	Apt.	East	E.	Place	Pl.	Suite	Ste.
Boulevard	Blvd.	Highway	Hwy.	Road	Rd.	West	W.
Court	Ct.	Lane	Ln.	South	S.		

State Names

Alabama	AL	Indiana	IN	Nebraska	NE	South Carolina	SC
Alaska	AK	Iowa	IA	Nevada	NV	South Dakota	SD
Arizona	AZ	Kansas	KS	New Hampshire	NH	Tennessee	TN
Arkansas	AR	Kentucky	KY	New Jersey	NJ	Texas	TX
California	CA	Louisiana	LA	New Mexico	NM	Utah	UT
Colorado	CO	Maine	ME	New York	NY	Vermont	VT
Connecticut	CT	Maryland	MD	North Carolina	NC	Virginia	VA
Delaware	DE	Massachusetts	MA	North Dakota	ND	Washington	WA
Florida	FL	Michigan	MI	Ohio	OH	West Virginia	WV
Georgia	GA	Minnesota	MN	Oklahoma	OK	Wisconsin	WI
Hawaii	HI	Mississippi	MS	Oregon	OR	Wyoming	WY
Idaho	ID	Missouri	MO	Pennsylvania	PA		
Illinois	IL	Montana	MT	Rhode Island	RI		

Abbreviations of Personal Titles

Capitalize abbreviations for a personal title. Follow the same rules for capitalizing a personal title.

Mr. . . . . Mister   **Mrs.** . . . . . . Missus   **Dr.** . . . . Doctor

Jr. . . . . Junior   **Capt.** . . . . . Captain   **Sen.** . . . . . . Senator

Punctuation

Punctuation marks are used to emphasize or clarify meanings.

End Marks	Examples
Use a **period** at the end of a statement or a polite command.	Georgia read the paper to her mom**.**
	Tell me if there are any interesting articles**.**
Or use a period after an indirect question. An indirect question tells about a question you asked.	She asked if there were any articles about the new restaurant on Stone Street near their house**.**
Use a **question mark** at the end of a question.	What kind of food do they serve**?**
Or use a question mark after a question that comes at the end of a statement.	The food is good, isn't it**?**
Use an **exclamation mark** after an interjection.	Wow**!**
Or use an exclamation mark at the end of a sentence to show you feel strongly about something.	The chicken parmesan is delicious**!**

Semicolon	Examples
Use a **semicolon**:	
• to separate two simple sentences used together without a conjunction	A group of Jim's classmates plan to attend the reading**;** he hopes to join them.
• before a conjunctive adverb that joins two simple sentences. Use a comma after the adverb.	Jim wanted to finish reading Josie Ramón's book this evening**;** however, he forgot it at school.
• to separate a group of words in a series if the words in the series already have commas	After school, Jim has to study French, health, and math**;** walk, feed, and brush the dog**;** and eat dinner.

Colon	Examples
Use a **colon**:	
• after the greeting in a business letter	Dear Sir or Madam**:**
• to separate hours and minutes	The restaurant is open until 11**:**30 p.m.
• to start a list	If you decide to hold your banquet here, we can**:** 1. Provide a private room 2. Offer a special menu 3. Supply free coffee and lemonade.

Comma	Examples
Use a comma:	
• before the **coordinating conjunction** in a compound sentence	Soccer is a relatively new sport in the United States, **but** it has been popular in England for a long time.
• to set off words that interrupt a sentence, such as an **appositive phrase** that is not needed to identify the word it describes	Mr. Okada, **the soccer coach,** had the team practice skills like passing, **for example,** for the first hour.
• to separate three or more items in a **series**	Shooting, passing, and dribbling are important skills.
• between coordinate adjectives, or adjectives of equal rank, that tell about the same noun	The midfielder's quick, unpredictable passes made him the team's star player.
• after an **introductory phrase or clause**	**In the last game,** he made several goals.
• before someone's exact words and after them if the sentence continues	Mr. Okada said, "Meet the ball after it bounces," as we practiced our half-volleys.
• before and after a **clause** if the clause is not necessary for understanding the sentence	At the end of practice, **before anyone left,** Mr. Okada handed out revised game schedules.
• before a question at the end of a statement	You talked to Mr. Okada, **didn't you?**
• to set off the name of a person someone is talking to	Mr. Okada said, "That's not how you do it, **Jimmy**."
Use a comma in these places in a letter:	
• between the city and the state	Milpas, AK
• between the date and the year	July 3, 2008
• after the greeting of a personal letter	Dear Mr. Okada,
• after the closing of a letter	Sincerely,

Punctuation, continued

Apostrophe	Examples
Use an **apostrophe** to punctuate a **possessive noun**.	
If there is one owner, add **'s** to the owner's name, even if the owner's name ends in **s**.	Mrs. Ramos**'s** sons live in New Mexico.
If there is more than one owner, add **'** if the plural noun ends in **s**. Add **'s** if it does not end in **s**.	Her sons**'** birthdays are both in January. My children**'s** birthdays are in March.
Use an **apostrophe** to replace the letters left out of a contraction.	could n~~o~~t = couldn**'t** he ~~woul~~d = he**'d**

Hyphen	Examples
Use a **hyphen** to:	
• connect words in a number and in a fraction	**One-third** of the people surveyed used at least **thirty-two** gallons of water every day.
• join some words to make a compound word	A **15-year-old** boy and his **great-grandmother** have started an awareness campaign.
• connect a letter to a word	They designed a **T-shirt** for their campaign.
• divide words at the end of a line. Always divide the word between two syllables.	Please join us today in our awareness **cam-paign**. It's for the good of the planet.

Dash	Examples
Use a **dash** to show a break in an idea or the tone in a sentence.	Water—a valuable resource—is often taken for granted.
Or use a dash to emphasize a word, a series of words, a phrase, or a clause.	It is easy to conserve water—wash full loads of laundry, use water-saving devices, fix leaky faucets.

Ellipsis	Examples
Use an **ellipsis** to show that you have left out words.	A recent survey documented ... water usage.
Or use an ellipsis to show an idea that trails off.	I don't know ... so much waste ...

Quotation Marks	Examples
Use **quotation marks** to show:	
• a speaker's exact words	"Listen to this!" Jim said.
• the exact words quoted from a book or other printed material	The announcement in the paper was: "The writer Josie Ramón will be at Milpas Library on Friday."
• the title of a song, poem, short story, magazine article, or newspaper article	Her famous poem "Speaking" appeared in the magazine article "How to Talk to Your Teen."
• the title of a chapter from a book	She'll be reading "Getting Along," a chapter from her new book.
• words used in a special way	We will be "all ears" at the reading.

Italics and Underlining	Examples
When you are typing or using a computer, use **italics** for the names of:	
• magazines and newspapers	I like to read *Time* magazine and the *Daily News*.
• books	They help me understand our history book, *The U.S. Story*.
• plays	Did you see the play *Abraham Lincoln in Illinois*?
• movies	It was made into the movie *Young Abe*.
• musicals	The musical *Oklahoma!* is about Southwest pioneers.
• music albums	*Greatest Hits from Musicals* is my favorite album.
• TV series	Do you like the singers on the TV show *American Idol*?
If you are using handwriting, underline.	

Parentheses	Examples
Use **parentheses** around extra information in a sentence.	The new story (in the evening paper) is very interesting.

Using Words Correctly

This section will help you to choose between words that are often confused or misused.

a lot • allot

A lot means "many" and is always written as two words, never as one word. *Allot* means "to assign" or "to give out."

> I have **a lot** of friends who like to eat.

> We **allot** one hour for lunch.

a while • awhile

The two-word form *a while* is often preceded by the prepositions *after*, *for*, or *in*. The one-word form *awhile* is used without a preposition.

> Let's stop here for **a while**.

> Let's stop here **awhile**.

accept • except

Accept is a verb that means "to receive." *Except* can be a verb meaning "to leave out" or a preposition meaning "excluding."

> I **accept** everything you say, **except** your point about music.

advice • advise

Advice is a noun that means "ideas about how to solve a problem." *Advise* is a verb and means "to give advice."

> I will give you **advice** about your problem today, but do not ask me to **advise** you again tomorrow.

affect • effect

Affect is a verb. It means "to cause a change in" or "to influence." *Effect* as a verb means "to bring about." As a noun, *effect* means "result."

> Sunshine will **affect** my plants positively.

> The governor is working to **effect** change.

> The rain had no **effect** on our spirits.

ain't

Ain't is not used in formal English. Use the correct form of the verb *be* with the word *not*: *is not, isn't; are not,* or *aren't*.

> We **are not going** to sing in front of you.

> I **am not going** to practice today.

all ready • already

Use the two-word form, *all ready*, to mean "completely finished." Use the one-word form, *already*, to mean "previously."

> We waited an hour for dinner to be **all ready**.

> It is a good thing I have **already** eaten today.

alright • all right

The expression *all right* means "OK" and should be written as two words. The one-word form, *alright*, is not used in formal writing.

> I hope it is **all right** that I am early.

all together • altogether

The two-word form, *all together*, means "in a group." The one-word form, *altogether*, means "completely."

> It is **altogether** wrong that we will not be **all together** this holiday.

among • between

Use *among* when comparing more than two people or things. Use *between* when comparing a person or thing with one other person, thing, or group.

> How can we share one piece of pizza **among** the four of us?

> We will split the money **between** Sal and Jess.

amount of • number of

Amount of is used with nouns that cannot be counted. *Number of* is used with nouns that can be counted.

> The **amount of** pollution in the air is increasing.

> A record **number of** people attended the game.

assure • ensure • insure

Assure means "to make certain." *Ensure* means "to guarantee." *Insure* means "to cover financially."

> I **assure** you that he is OK.

> I will personally **ensure** his safety.

> If the car is **insured**, the insurance company will pay to fix the damage.

being as • being that

Neither of these is used in formal English. Use *because* or *since* instead.

> I went home early **because** I was sick.

beside • besides

Beside means "next to." *Besides* means "plus" or "in addition to."

> Located **beside** the cafeteria is a vending machine.

> **Besides** being the fastest runner, she is also the nicest team member.

bring • take

Use *bring* to speak of transporting something to where you are now. Use *take* to speak of transporting something to a place where you're not now.

> **Bring** the snacks here to my house, and then we'll **take** them to the party at Ann's.

bust • busted

Neither of these is used in formal English. Use *broke* or *broken* instead.

> I **broke** the vase by accident.

> The **broken** vase cannot be fixed.

can't • hardly • scarcely

Do not use *can't* with *hardly* or *scarcely*. That would be a double negative. Use only *can't*, or use *can* plus a negative word.

> I **can't** get my work done in time.

> I **can scarcely** get my work done in time.

capital • capitol

A *capital* is a place where a government is located. A *capitol* is the actual building the government meets in.

> The **capital** of the U.S. is Washington, D.C.

> The senate met at the **capitol** to vote.

cite • site • sight

To *cite* means "to quote a source." A *site* is "a place." *Sight* can mean "the ability to see" or it can mean "something that can be seen."

> Be sure to **cite** all your sources.

> My brother works on a construction **site**.

> Dan went to the eye doctor to have his **sight** checked.

> The sunset last night was a beautiful **sight**.

complement • compliment

Complement means "something that completes" or "to complete." *Compliment* means "something nice someone says about another person" or "to praise."

> The colors you picked really **complement** each other.

> I would like to **compliment** you on your new shoes.

could have • should have • would have • might have

Be sure to use "have" not "of" with words like *could*, *should*, *would*, and *might*.

> I **would have** gone, but I didn't feel well last night.

council • counsel

A *council* is a group organized to study and plan something. To *counsel* is to give advice to someone.

> The city **council** met to discuss traffic issues.

> Mom, please **counsel** me on how to handle this situation.

different from • different than

Different from is preferred in formal English and is used with nouns and noun clauses and phrases. *Different than*, when used, is used with adverbial clauses.

> My interest in music is **different from** my friends.

> Movies today are **different than** they used to be in the 1950s.

farther • further

Farther refers to a physical distance. *Further* refers to time or amount.

> If you go down the road a little **farther**, you will see the sign.

> We will discuss this **further** at lunch.

fewer • less

Fewer refers to things that can be counted individually. *Less* refers to things that cannot be counted individually.

> The farm had **fewer** animals than the zoo, so it was **less** fun to visit.

good • well

The adjective *good* means "pleasing," "kind," or "healthy." The adverb *well* means "ably."

> She is a **good** person.

> I am glad to see that you are **well** again after that illness.

> You have performed **well**.

immigrate to • emigrate from

Immigrate to means "to move to a country." *Emigrate from* means "to leave a country."

> I **immigrated to** America in 2001 from Panama.

> I **emigrated from** El Salvador because of the war.

it's • its

It's is a contraction of *it is*. *Its* is a possessive word meaning "belonging to it."

> **It's** going to be a hot day.

> The dog drank all of **its** water already.

kind of • sort of

These words mean "a type of." In formal English, do not use them to mean "partly." Use *somewhat* or *rather* instead.

> The peanut is actually a **kind of** bean.

> I feel **rather** silly in this outfit.

lay • lie

Lay means "to put in a place." It is used to describe what people do with objects. *Lie* means "to recline." People can *lie* down, but they *lay* down objects. Do not confuse this use of *lie* with the verb that means "to tell an untruth."

> I will **lay** the book on this desk for you.

> I'm tired and am going to **lie** on the couch.

> If you **lie** in court, you will be punished.

learn • teach

To *learn* is "to receive information." To *teach* is "to give information."

> If we want to **learn**, we have to listen.

> She will **teach** us how to drive.

leave • let

Leave means "to go away." *Let* means "to allow."

> **Leave** the keys on the kitchen table.

> I will **let** you borrow my pen.

like • as

Like can be used either as a preposition or as a verb meaning "to care about something." *As* is a conjunction and should be used to introduce a subordinate clause.

> She sometimes acts **like** a princess. But I still **like** her.

> She acts **as** if she owns the school.

loose • lose

Loose can be used as an adverb or adjective meaning "free" or "not securely attached." The verb *lose* means "to misplace" or "to be defeated."

> I let the dog **loose** and he is missing.

> Did you **lose** your homework?

> Did they **lose** the game by many points?

passed • past

Passed is a verb that means "to have moved ahead of." *Past* is a noun that means "the time before the present."

> I **passed** my English test.

> Poor grades are in the **past** now.

precede • proceed

Precede means "to come before." *Proceed* means "to go forward."

> Prewriting **precedes** drafting in the writing process.

> Turn left; then **proceed** down the next street.

principal • principle

A *principal* is "a person of authority." Principal can also mean "main." A *principle* is "a general truth or belief."

> The **principal** of our school makes an announcement every morning.

> The **principal** ingredient in baking is flour.

> The essay was based on the **principles** of effective persuasion.

raise • rise

The verb *raise* always takes an object. The verb *rise* does not take an object.

> **Raise** the curtain for the play.

> The curtain **rises**.

> I **rise** from bed every morning at six.

real • really

Real means "actual." It is an adjective used to describe nouns. *Really* means "actually" or "truly." It is an adverb used to describe verbs, adjectives, or other adverbs.

> The diamond was **real**.

> The diamond was **really** beautiful.

set • sit

The verb *set* usually means "to put something down." The verb *sit* means "to go into a seated position."

> I **set** the box on the ground.

> Please **sit** while we talk.

than • then

Than is used to compare things. *Then* means "next" and is used to tell when something took place.

> She likes fiction more **than** nonfiction.

> First, we will go to the bookstore; **then** we will go home.

they're • their • there

They're is the contraction of *they are*. *Their* is the possessive form of the pronoun *they*. *There* is used to indicate location.

> **They're** all on vacation this week.

> I want to use **their** office.

> The library is right over **there**.

> **There** are several books I want to read.

this • these • that • those

This indicates something specific that is near you. *These* is the plural form of *this*. *That* indicates something specific that is farther from you. *Those* is the plural form of *that*.

> **This** book in my hand belongs to me.
> **These** pens are also mine.

> **That** book over there is his. **Those** notes are his, too.

where

It is not necessary to use *at* or *to* with *where*.

> **Where** are you going?

> **Where** is Ernesto?

who • whom

Who is a subject. *Whom* is an object. If you can replace *who* or *whom* with *he*, *she*, *they*, or *it*, use *who*. If you can replace the word with *him*, *her*, or *them*, use *whom*.

> **Who** is going to finish first?

> My grandmother is a woman to **whom** I owe many thanks.

who's • whose

Who's is a contraction of *who is*. *Whose* is the possessive form of *who*.

> **Who's** coming to our dinner party?

> **Whose** car is parked in the garage?

you're • your

You're is a contraction of *you are*. *Your* is a possessive pronoun meaning "belonging to you."

> **You're** going to be late if you don't hurry.

> Is **your** backpack too heavy?

Spelling Handbook

Spelling. It's one of those subjects that seem to make a lot of people anxious. You now—like going to the dentist or taking a pop quiz. It's time to take control of spelling and turn worries into word work!

The truth is that spelling can be fun, especially when you see yourself getting better and better at it. It's also true that once you learn the spelling basics, you will know how to spell six out of seven words. That's right! Most words follow spelling patterns. Most words obey spelling rules. Tricky words are definitely in the minority.

Don't just read this guide. Apply it! Think like a speller. Here are some ideas:

- Start your own lists of related words.

- Make other lists of unusual words.

- Become a pattern finder. As you figure out a pattern, write the rule down in your own words.

- Create your own dictionary for words that are tricky for you.

- Make up your own ways to remember a tough word.

Write it all down, and watch your personal spelling guide grow right along with your spelling skills!

Don't forget every speller's best friend—the dictionary! ▶

Learning New Words

Follow six steps when you are learning how to spell a new word.

STEP 1: **Look** at the word carefully.

STEP 2: **Say** the word aloud. Look at the word as you say it, and listen to yourself saying it.

STEP 3: **Picture** the whole word in your mind.

STEP 4: **Spell** the word aloud, letter by letter.

STEP 5: **Write** the word. Use your memory.

STEP 6: **Check** the word. You can use a dictionary, a computer spell checker, or a word list.

If you find errors in **STEP 6**, circle them. Write the word correctly. Then repeat the steps again for the word.

Use all Your Senses

Good spellers remember how words look and how they sound. When you are learning how to spell a new word, you should also get the rest of your senses involved. Try these ideas to use all of your senses together:

Ideas for Learning New Words

See it.	Really study the word. Look at every letter.
Hear it.	As you study the word, say it aloud. Say each sound and notice how it matches the letters.
Work it.	As you say each sound, tap your finger or foot. As you look at each letter, write it in the air.
Feel it.	Write the word slowly. Shape the letters carefully. Imagine writing the word in sand to really feel it!

Making Words Your Own

Every person has trouble spelling some words. The secret is to help yourself remember these troublesome words. You can make up your own memory tools that fit your way of thinking. Here are some examples.

Rhymes

Here's a famous rhyme to use when deciding whether to use *ie* (brief) or *ei* (receive).

> "*i* before *e*
> except after *c*
> or when sounded *a*
> as in *neighbor* and *weigh* . . .
> and *weird* is just weird!"

Acronyms

Think of a word that begins with each letter. The words in the correct order should be easy for you to remember.

EXAMPLES	**because** big elephants can always understand small elephants **rhythm** rhythm helps your two hips move **ocean** only cats' eyes are narrow

Explanations

Think of a clever way to remember *why* letters appear or not in a word.

EXAMPLES	**argument** "I lost an *e* in an argument." **dessert** "It has two *s*'s for sweet stuff!" **necessary** "It is *necessary* for a shirt to have one collar (one *c*) and two sleeves (two *s*'s)."

Stories

Make up a story that will help you remember how to spell a word.

EXAMPLES

cemetery
I got scared walking through the cemetery and yelled, "e-e-e!" as I ran away. (The word *cemetery* has three *e*'s.)

separate
A lady was married to a man named Sep. One day she saw a rat. She yelled, "Sep! A rat! E!"

The best memory tools are the ones you make up. Here are examples from students' personal spelling guides.

from Grace's Memory Tricks

When I get a bargain, I feel like I gain money.

from Alphonso's Explanations

The desert is too dry to grow more than one s.

from Anna's Amazing Acronyms

said: Sailor Al is daring.

from Julian's Spelling Stories

My aunt always says that I have "cute scarlet cheeks." (Scarlet is another word for red.) When I am embarrassed, my two scarlet cheeks turn really red. The word embarrassed takes two r's and two s's, to match my two red or scarlet cheeks.

Reflect

- Which memory tool looks most fun?

- Which memory tool would probably work best for me because of how I am able to remember things?

Finding and Fixing Errors

Spelling and the Writing Process

You focus on spelling during the editing and proofreading stage of writing. But what should you do while drafting? When you are drafting, let your ideas flow. Keep writing even if you are unsure of how to spell a word. When you want to write a word and are unsure of the spelling, follow these steps:

1. Recall spelling rules you know. Think about related words and how they are spelled.

2. Write the word down.

3. Circle the word so you remember to check the spelling.

Check Your Spelling

Read your paper carefully, word by word. Study each spelling. Think about the rules you know. Remember, six out of every seven words follow common spelling rules.

How do you know if a word is spelled wrong? Trust what you know. If you are not sure, circle it. Many of the words you circle and check may be spelled correctly! There are common errors that many writers make. Look out for these problems:

- Missing letters
- Missing syllables
- Flipped letters
- Words that sound alike
- Sounds that can be spelled many different ways

My Spelling List

lovable
lovely
happiness
funny
dirty

Whether you work alone or with a partner, keep track of the words that you misspell. Create a personal spelling list. Review the words on a regular schedule and you will see your spelling improve.

Bryon used these spelling tips to find the errors in his personal narrative.

Byron's First Draft

I really enjoyed our family reunion this summer. More than 20 of us got together at Clear Lake for the Fourth of July. There were some surprises. My Uncle Al hadn't seen me for two years, and he was amazed by my (hieght.) There were three new (babys) born since last year's reunion, including twin girls! Other things at the reunion were expected, includeing great food, lots of laughs, fun games, and warm feelings.

Byron thinks:

" This word follows the *i* before *e* rule, but it just doesn't look right."

" I need to think about how to make a word that ends in y plural."

You should always check your own spelling. It's also helpful to have a friend or classmate check your work. Remember we all have different words that challenge us. Ask your friend to circle words to check. Talk about the words. Work together to use a dictionary to find the correct spellings.

Byron's Edited Draft

I really enjoyed our (famly) reunion this summer. More than 20 of us got together at Clear Lake for the Fourth of July. There were some surprises. My Uncle Al hadn't seen me for two years, and he was amazed by my height. There were three new babies born since last year's reunion, including twin girls! Other things at the reunion were expected, (includeing) great food, lots of laughs, fun games, and warm feelings.

" I remember to really say the middle syllable to myself so I don't leave it out: *fam·i·ly.*"

" Remember to drop the e before adding an ending that starts with a vowel."

Making Sound-Spelling Connections

English words are made up of combinations of more than 40 different sounds. You can expect each sound to be spelled by certain letters. (Yes, there are exceptions!) Let's start with vowel sounds.

LONG VOWELS	
Spellings	**Example Words**
i ie igh i_e _y	**i**tem p**ie** n**igh**t f**i**n**e** cr**y**
o oa ow o_e	**o**pen s**oa**p gr**ow** v**o**t**e**
u ew ue ui u_e oo	**u**nit f**ew** bl**ue** fr**ui**t p**u**r**e** t**oo**th

OTHER VOWELS	
Spellings	**Example Words**
au aw	**au**thor sh**aw**l
al all	**al**so b**all**
ow ou	c**ow** sc**ou**t
oy oi	t**oy** b**oi**l
oo u	f**oo**t b**u**sh
ar	y**ar**d
er ir ur	ov**er** b**ir**d c**ur**l
or	h**or**n
a e i o u	**a**bout **e**ffect rabb**i**t sec**o**nd circ**u**s

Now let's look at consonant sounds.

CONSONANT SOUNDS	
Spellings	**Example Words**
ch _tch	chin patch
d	did
f ph	first graph
g	gum
h	hen
j g _dge	jump giant fudge
k c ck	king camp luck
x	six
qu	quack
l	left
m mb	make lamb

CONSONANT SOUNDS	
Spellings	**Example Words**
n kn	namc know
p	pond
r wr	red wrist
s c	safe pencil
sh	shell
t	time
th	thank
th	this
v	van
w	wash
wh	when
y	yell
z s	zebra news

Breaking Words Down

One great way to learn how to spell a word is to break it into parts. You can break words into **syllables**. Learn how to spell each syllable. Then put them together.

Syllable Rules (Look in the middle of the word. Look for the patterns named below. Say the word aloud.)	Examples
The VCV Rule: **A consonant between two vowels** If the first vowel is long, the break usually comes before the consonant. If the first vowel is short, the break usually comes after the consonant.	before:　be·fore vacant:　va·cant music:　mu·sic cabin:　cab·in wagon:　wag·on linen:　lin·en
The VCCV Rule: **Two consonants between vowels** The break comes between the consonants, unless the consonants work together to make one sound (as in *sh* and *th*).	blanket:　blan·ket perhaps:　per·haps picture:　pic·ture fashion:　fash·ion weather:　weath·er
The VCCCV Rule: **Three consonants between vowels** The break comes between the two consonants that work together to make a sound and the third consonant.	pumpkin:　pump·kin exchange:　ex·change instead:　in·stead although:　al·though
Compound Words: Always divide a compound word between the two smaller words forming it.	afternoon:　after·noon driveway:　drive·way skateboard:　skate·board

Look for these patterns in longer words, too. For example:

possible: pos•si•ble

controversy: con•tro•ver•sy

responsibility: re•spon•si•bil•i•ty

Making Words Plural

Once you learn how to spell a word, you also need to learn how to get it right in its different forms. For example, when you make nouns plural, you might need to make some spelling changes.

Plural Rules	Examples
Make most nouns plural by adding –s to the end.	author ⟶ authors crowd ⟶ crowds principal ⟶ principals niece ⟶ nieces
If the word ends in s, sh, ch, x, or z, add –es.	business ⟶ businesses brush ⟶ brushes speech ⟶ speeches fox ⟶ foxes waltz ⟶ waltzes
If the word ends in a consonant followed by y, change the y to i and add –es.	category ⟶ categories puppy ⟶ puppies library ⟶ libraries fly ⟶ flies
If the word ends in a vowel followed by y, just add –s.	birthday ⟶ birthdays toy ⟶ toys turkey ⟶ turkeys key ⟶ keys
If the word ends in a consonant followed by o, add –es.	hero ⟶ heroes potato ⟶ potatoes
If the word ends in a vowel followed by o, just add –s.	video ⟶ videos radio ⟶ radios
Words that end in f or fe are tricky. Sometimes you change the f to v and add –es. Sometimes you just add –s.	knife ⟶ knives half ⟶ halves roof ⟶ roofs belief ⟶ beliefs

Making Words Plural, continued

Some words have irregular plural forms. They do not follow the normal rules for creating plurals.

Singular	Plural	Singular	Plural
auto	autos	man	men
axis	axes	medium	media
basis	bases	mouse	mice
child	children	oasis	oases
crisis	crises	ox	oxen
criterion	criteria	parenthesis	parentheses
datum	data	piano	pianos
Eskimo	Eskimos	radius	radii
focus	foci	solo	solos
foot	feet	stimulus	stimuli
goose	geese	tooth	teeth
index	indices	woman	women

Some words are used for both the singular and the plural forms: deer, fish, moose, series, sheep, traffic, trout, wheat.

Knowing Your Roots

Many English words came from other languages. In many modern English words, you can see Greek and Latin roots. In some cases, you can find the same root in several words. So, if you learn how to spell these common roots, you will be on your way to knowing how to spell many words!

Root	Origin	Meaning	Examples
act	Latin	do	action, enactment
alter	Latin	other	alternate, alternative
anim	Latin	life	animated, inanimate
ann	Latin	year	annual, anniversary
aqua	Latin	water	aquarium, aquatic
ast	Greek	star	astronaut, astronomy
aud	Latin	hear	auditorium, audible
bio	Greek	life	biography, biology
cred	Latin	believe	credit, incredible
cycl	Greek	circle	bicycle, recycle
dic	Latin	speak	dictate, verdict
form	Latin	shape	uniform, transform
geo	Greek	earth	geologist, geography
gram	Greek	written	grammar, telegram
loc	Latin	place	location, local
meter	Greek	measure	thermometer, diameter
nat	Latin	born	native, national
phon	Greek	sound	phonics, telephone
poli	Greek	city	politics, cosmopolitan
port	Latin	carry	portable, import

Root	Origin	Meaning	Examples
rect	Latin	straight	rectangle, erect
rupt	Latin	break	erupt, interrupt
san	Latin	health	sane, sanitary
sci	Greek	know	science, conscious
sign	Latin	mark	signal, signature
spec	Latin	see	spectacles, inspect
struct	Latin	build	instruct, destruction
terr	Latin	land	terrace, territory
tract	Latin	pull	tractor, subtract
trib	Latin	give	contribution, attribute
vac	Latin	empty	vacant, evacuate
var	Latin	different	variety, variable

Adding Inflected Endings

Other word forms are made when certain endings, called **inflected endings**, are added. These endings include –*ed, -ing, –er,* and –*est*. Sometimes the spelling of a word changes when these endings are added.

Inflected Endings Rules	Examples
If the word ends with one vowel and two consonants, just add the ending.	weigh → weighed, weighing grand → grander, grandest
If the word ends with two vowels and one consonant, just add the ending.	repair → repaired, repairing great → greater, greatest
If the word ends in silent e, drop the e before adding the ending.	acquire → acquired, acquiring safe → safer, safest

Inflected Endings Rules, continued	Examples, continued
If the word ends in one vowel and one consonant (except *x*), double the consonant before adding the ending	trim → trimmed, trimming wet → wetter, wettest
If the word ends in *y*, change the *y* to *I* before adding –ed, –er, or –est. However, keep the *y* if you are adding –ing.	study → studied easy → easier, easiest study → studying
If the word ends in *c*, add a *k* before the ending.	panic → panicked, panicking

Adding Suffixes and Prefixes

Other **suffixes** (the letters after the root word) can also change the spelling of a word.

Suffix Rules	Examples
If the word ends in silent *e*, drop the *e* before adding a suffix that starts with a vowel. However, if the suffix starts with a consonant, just add it to the word.	lie + -ar → liar white + -en → whiten life + -less → lifeless confine + ment → confinement
If the word ends in a consonant and *y*, change the *y* to *i* before adding the suffix.	pretty + -ly → prettily silly + -ness → silliness
If the word ends in a vowel and *y*, just add the suffix.	enjoy + -ment → enjoyment play + -ful → playful
If the word ends in *le*, drop the final *le* before adding the suffix –ly.	able + -ly → ably comfortable + -ly → comfortably
If the word ends in *l*, just add –ly to the end.	usual + -ly → usually annual + -ly → annually

When it comes to **prefixes** (the letters before the root word), you are lucky. You do not have to memorize any spelling rules to add prefixes! The spelling of a word does not change when you add a prefix.

Prefix Examples
disagree, impossible, reheat, unable

Knowing the Long and Short of It

Compound Words

- A **compound word** is made up of two smaller words. The compound word has a new meaning.

Examples
sailboat
high school
well-known

- Most of the time, you just put the two short words together without changing their spellings. These are called **closed compounds**.

Examples
baseball
homework
raincoat

- Sometimes compound words are **open compounds**. They are spelled with a space between the two words.

Examples
potato chips
vacation home
health food

- **Hyphenated compounds** use a hyphen to join the two words.

Examples
ice-cold
brand-new
long-term

- When a compound word is used as an adjective or adverb, it is usually hyphenated, except when part of the compound is an adverb ending in –*ly*.

Examples
The track meet was an all-day event.

Exception
The badly injured woman was taken away in an ambulance.

Contractions

When two words are joined into one with a loss of one or more letters, the word is called a **contraction**. The missing letter is replaced by an apostrophe.

- Many contractions are formed with a pronoun and the verb forms *am, are, is, have,* or *will.*

  EXAMPLE

I + am	→	I'm
we + are	→	we're
he + is	→	he's
they + have	→	they've
she + will	→	she'll

- Many other contractions are formed with a verb and the word *not*. To make this kind of contraction, an apostrophe replaces the *o* in *not*.

  EXAMPLES

  | could + not | → | couldn't |
  | does + not | → | doesn't |

  EXCEPTIONS

  | can + not | → | can't (just one n) |
  | will + not | → | won't (a different word) |

Making Spelling Generalizations

You can memorize certain rules about spelling patterns within words. These rules are nearly always true, so they are known as **generalizations**.

Generalizations	Examples	Exceptions
ie or *ei* for the long e sound: Write *i* before *e* except right after *c*.	chief, relief, shield, receive	weird, seize, either, leisure, neither
words ending with a syllable pronounced "shent": This ending is spelled *cient*.	efficient sufficient ancient	
the letter *q*: Always follow the letter *q* with *u*.	quantity, quiet, request, inquiry, antique	Iraq, Iraqi, Qatar
the schwa sound followed by /l/ at the end of a word: These two sounds combined at the end of the word will be spelled –*le*, –*el*, or –*al*.	staple, jewel, dental	
c: the /k/ or /s/ sound When *c* is followed by *e*, *i*, or *y*, it makes the sound /s/. When *c* is followed by *a*, *o*, or *u*, it makes the sound /k/.	celery, city, fancy camera, copy, cushion	
words ending with a short vowel followed by /k/: The /k/ sound is spelled ck.	pack, check, sick, lock, buck	
words ending with a short vowel followed by /j/: The /j/ sound is spelled *dge*.	badge, ledge, ridge, dodge, fudge	
words ending with /v/: Final /v/ is spelled *ve*.	brave, dive, cove	names like Tel Aviv and Isaac Asimov
words with endings pronounced /shon/: This final syllable is spelled *cion*, *sion*, or *tion*. If the base word has a *t*, the spelling is –*tion*. If the base word has a *d* or an *s*, the spelling is –*sion*.	suspicion, tension creation delete, deletion decide, decision confuse, confusion	attend, attention

Learning to Spell Tricky Words

Some words are tricky because they just don't follow the rules or sound-spelling connections. Other words are confusing because they sound alike but are spelled differently and have different meanings. These words are called **homophones**. Still other words are easily confused because they sound similar.

Lists of homophones and easily confused words are started here. On the next page, see more lists of common words that don't follow the rules. Add your own words to these lists as you come across them. Remember to make the words your own by coming up with good ways to connect their meanings to their spellings.

Homophones and Meanings	Examples
all together (in a group) altogether (completely)	It is **altogether** wrong that we will not be **all together** this holiday.
capital (a place where a government is located) capitol (the actual building the government meets in)	We saw the senate vote in their chambers at the **capitol** during our tour of the **capital**.
cite (to quote a source) site (a place) sight (the ability to see or something that can be seen)	Be sure to **cite** your sources. My brother works on a construction **site**. The sunset last night was a beautiful **sight**.
council (a group organized to study and plan something) counsel (to give advice to someone)	The city **council** asked a lawyer to come and **counsel** them about civil rights.
it's (a contraction of *it is*) its (a possessive word meaning "belonging to it")	**It's** true that the dog drank all of **its** water already.
passed (to have moved ahead of) past (the time before the present)	In the **past** my brother drove too fast and often **passed** cars when he shouldn't.
principal (a person of authority or main) principle (a general truth or belief)	Our school **principal** makes announcements every morning. The **principal** ingredient in baking is flour. The essay was based on the **principles** of effective persuasion.
they're (contraction of *they are*) their (possessive form of the pronoun *they*) there (used to indicate location)	**They're** all on vacation this week. I want to use **their** office. The library is right over **there**.

Homophones and Meanings	Examples
who's (contraction of *who is*) whose (possessive from of *who*)	**Who's** coming to our dinner party? **Whose** car is parked in the garage?
you're (contraction of *you are*) your (possessive pronoun meaning "belong to you")	**You're** going to be late if you don't hurry. Is **your** backpack too heavy? **from Grace's Memory Tricks** My principal is my PAL. A ruLE can be called a principLE.

Easily Confused Words and Meanings	Examples
accept (to receive) except (to leave out or excluding)	I **accept** everything you say **except** your point about music.
advice (ideas about how to solve a problem) advise (to give advice)	I will give you **advice** about your problem today, but do not ask me to **advise** you again tomorrow.
affect (to cause a change in or to influence) effect (to bring about or the result)	Sunshine will **affect** my plants in a positive way. The rain will have a good **effect** on my plants, too.
assure (to make certain) ensure (to guarantee) insure (to cover financially)	I **assure** you that he is OK. I will personally **ensure** his safety. If the car is **insured**, the insurance company will pay to fix the damage.
beside (next to) besides (in addition to)	A parking lot is right **beside** the store. **Besides** being the fastest runner, she is also the nicest team member.
farther (refers to a physical distance) further (refers to time or amount)	If you go down the road a little **farther**, you will see the sign. We will discuss this **further** at lunch.
loose (free or not securely attached) lose (to misplace or to be defeated)	The dog got **loose** and now he is missing. First I **lose** my homework, and then we **lose** the game!
precede (to come before) proceed (to go forward)	Prewriting **precedes** drafting in the writing process. Please **proceed** carefully on the icy sidewalk.
than (used to compare things) then (next)	She likes to read fiction more **than** nonfiction. First, we will go to the bookstore; **then** we will go home.

Learning to Spell Tricky Words continued

Some of the most common words in the English language do not follow spelling rules. Check out these examples from the 25 most frequently used words:

are   have   of   on   to   they   you   was

You see these words so often that you tend to learn them by sight. You memorize what they look like. For this reason, these common words are sometimes called *sight* words.

A list is started here of other tricky words that just don't follow the usual rules and patterns. These words come from the 1,000 most common words in the English language and from lists of words that students your age often misspell. You will probably have more words that are tricky for you to spell for one reason or another. Add those words to this list.

A	C	F	K	O
above	century	father	knowledge	ocean
accurate	certain	favorite		often
ache	chocolate	February	**L**	once
again	city	foreign	language	one
aisle	clothes	four	laughed	only
although	color	friend	listen	opposite
among	come	from		other
ancient	conquer		**M**	
answer	conscience	**G**	many	**P**
anxious	control	give	marriage	people
any	cough	gone	material	persuade
	country	great	meant	picture
B		group	measure	piece
balloon	**D**	guard	minute	put
bargain	design	guess	money	
beautiful	determine		mother	**Q**
become	discipline	**H**	mountain	quarterly
been	does	heard	move	quarter
both	done	height		
bought			**N**	**R**
brilliant	**E**	**I**	necessary	receipt
brought	earth	iron	none	restaurant
building	early	island	notice	rhythm
bury	engine			route
busy	enough	**J**		
buy	evening	jealousy		
	experience			

S	T	V	XYZ
said	though	vacuum	yacht
says	thought	valley	young
several	through	various	youth
shoes	toward	very	
should	trouble	villian	
sign			
soldier	**U**	**W**	
some	usually	want	
southern		watch	
special		water	
sugar		Wednesday	
sure		were	
surface		what	
		where	
		whose	
		woman	
		work	
		would	

My Word List

mansion

gorgeous

daughter

fruit

chalk

Index of Skills and Strategies

W

At-a-Glance Index

Acknowledgments

Bill Smith Studios: Design and artwork of "Space" from *The World Almanac for Kids 2003.* Copyright © Bill Smith Studios. Used by permission.

Encyclopædia Britannica: Reprinted with permission from Encyclopædia Britannica, © 2008 by Encyclopædia Britannica, Inc.

John Eng: Quote from Dr. John Eng was originally published in "Taking on a monster" by Terri Somers from the *San Diego Union-Tribune,* April 29, 2005. By permission.

Grove/Atlantic, Inc.: *This Boy's Life* © 1989 by Tobias Wolff. Used by permission of Grove/Atlantic, Inc.

James W. Hackett: "A bitter morning" by James W. Hackett from hacketthaiku.com. Reprinted by permission.

Henry Holt and Company: "Stopping by Woods on a Snowy Evening" by Robert Frost from *The Poetry of Robert Frost,* edited by Edward Connery Lathem. Copyright 1923, 1969 by Henry Holt and Company. Copyright 1951 by Robert Frost. Reprinted by permission of Henry Holt and Company, LLC.

Highlights for Children: "Oak" by Dawn Watkins. Copyright © 1997 by Highlights for Children, Inc., Columbus, Ohio. Reprinted by permission.

Houghton Mifflin Harcourt Publishing Company: Excerpt from *Jumanji* by Chris Van Allsburg. Copyright © 1981 by Chris Van Allsburg. Reprinted by permission of Houghton Mifflin Harcourt Publishing Company. All rights reserved.

Marshall Cavendish Corporation: Reprinted from *Juvenile Diabetes* by Johannah Haney with permission of Marshall Cavendish.

McGraw-Hill: "southward" through "Spanish" from the *Macmillan Dictionary for Children.* Copyright © 1997 by Simon & Schuster and was originally published in the McGraw-Hill School Dictionary.

National Geographic Society: Cover of the *Family Reference Atlas of the World, Second Edition.* Copyright © 2007 National Geographic Society. All rights reserved.

Cover of *National Geographic Historical Atlas of the United States.* Copyright © 2004 National Geographic Society. All rights reserved.

Cover of the *National Geographic Road Atlas, Adventure Edition.* Published by National Geographic Maps in association with MapQuest, Inc. Copyright © 2007 by MapQuest, Inc. and Adventure section copyright © 2007 National Geographic Society. Cover photo by Steve Casimiro. All rights reserved.

Oxford University Press: "good" from *Oxford American Writer's Thesaurus.* Copyright © 2004 by Oxford University Press. Used by permission of Oxford University Press, Inc.

Random House, Inc.: Excerpt from *Mother* by Maya Angelou, copyright © 2006 by Maya Angelou. Used by permission of Random House, Inc.

Excerpt from *The Watson's Go to Birmingham* – 1963 by Christopher Paul Curtis. Copyright © 1995 by Christopher Paul Curtis.

"Funny in Farsi" excerpt was originally titled "Hot Dogs and Wild Geese," from *Funny in Farsi* by Firoozeh Dumas, copyright © 2003 by Firoozeh Dumas. Used by permission of Villard Books, a division of Random House, Inc.

Scholastic Library Publishing, Inc.: "Mars" by Elaine Landau. All rights reserved. Reprinted by permission of Franklin Watts an imprint of Scholastic Library Publishing, Inc. Background image on title page is from NASA.

Scholastic, Inc.: Adapted from *Dear America: The Winter of Red Snow: The Revolutionary War Diary of Abigail Jane Stewart* by Kristiana Gregory. Copyright © 1996 by Kristiana Gregory. Reprinted by permission of Scholastic Inc.

SUNY Press: Reprinted by permission from *Basho's Haiku: Selected Poems of Matsuo Basho* by Matsuo Basho, translated by David Landis Barnhill, the State University of New York Press © 2004, State University of New York. All rights reserved.

Teen Ink Magazine: "Book Review of When I Was Puerto Rican by Esmeralda Santiago" by Jennifer K. Reprinted with permission of Teen Ink Magazine and teenink.com

Anthony Virgilio: "heat before the storm" and "the cathedral bell" by Nicholas Virgilio from *Selected Haiku* (Second Edition) by Nicholas Virgilio co-published by Burnt Lake Press and Black Moss Press, copyright © 1988 Nicholas A. Virgilio. Reprinted by permission by Anthony Virgilio.

World Almanac Education Group: "Space" from the *World Almanac for Kids 2003.* Copyright © 2002 World Almanac Education Group. All rights reserved. Used by permission.

The YGS Group: "Molding Troubled Kids into Future Chefs" by Kathy Blake. Used with permission of Nation's Restaurant News © 2008 All Rights Reserved. "Tropical Storm Florence Forms in Atlantic" by The Associated Press, September 5, 2006. Used with permission of The Associated Press © 2008 All Rights Reserved.

Photography

Cover, Back Cover ©Patrick Endres/ Visuals Unlimted/Corbis. **2W** ©Ian Shaw/ Alamy. **4W** ©Robert Morris/Alamy. **7W** ©National Geographic Television and Film. **8W–9W** ©Tim Davis/Corbis. **11W** ©Larry Foster/National Geographic. **13W** (r) ©Stephen Frink/Getty Images. **13W** (l) ©Andy Rouse/Corbis. **15W** ©Brandon Cole Marine Photography/Alamy. **18W** ©David Young-Wolff/Alamy. **18W** (b) ©Ocean/ Corbis. **20W** ©Jack Hollingsworth/ Corbis. **21W** (l) ©Comstock/Jupiter images. **21W** (r) ©George Doyle & Ciaran Griffin/Stockbyte/Getty Images. **22W** ©Tom & Dee Ann McCarthy/ Bridge/ Corbis. **23W** (tr) ©Paul Harizan/Getty Images. **23W** ©Lee Page/Stone/Getty Images. **23W** (tl) ©Ariel Skelley/Comet/ Corbis. **23W** (bl) ©Eureka Premium/ Corbis. **24W** (tr) ©Roger Viollet/Getty Images. **24W** (t) ©Bettmann/Corbis. **24W** (b) ©Stuart McCall/Getty Images. **24W** (tl) ©Pictorial Press Ltd/Alamy. **24W** ©Steven Puetzer/ Nonstock/ Getty Images. **24W** ©Jose Luis Pelaez

Acknowledgments, continued

PhotoEdit. **371W** ©Jay Adeff.
372W ©Corbis/Jupiterimage.
376W (t) ©Frank Cezus/Getty Images.
376W ©Paul Spinelli/MLB Photos
vis Getty Images. **390W** (tr) ©William
Whitehurst/Bridge/Corbis.
390W ©PhotoDisc. **390W** ©siamimages/
Big Stock Photo. **390W** ©PhotoDisc.
390W ©PhotoDisc. **390W** ©PhotoDisc.
390W ©PhotoDisc. **390W** ©PhotoDisc.
391W ©PhotoDisc. **392W** ©Anthony
Nex/Newscom. **392W** ©Image courtesy
of Advertising Archives. **393W** ©Damien
Lovegrove/ Science Photo Library.
394W ©Aicha ystrom. **395W** (tr) ©The
Granger Collection NYC. **395W** (c) ©The
Granger Collection. **396W** ©University
of New Mexico Press. **397W** ©Russell
Monk/Masterfile. **398W** ©Todd Gipstein/
Corbis. **399W** ©Odilon Dimier/PhotoAlto
sas/Alamy. **400W** (b) ©Studio Eye/
Corbis. **400W** (t) ©Patrick LaCroix/
Alamy. **401W** ©Corbis/Jupiterimages.
402W ©Jupiter Images/Creatas/
Alamy. **403W** ©Moodboard/Corbis.
404W ©Digital Vision/Alamy.
405W (t) ©Fernando Bengoechea/
Haven/Beateworks/Corbis.
405W© Leah Warkentin/Design Pics/
Corbis. **407W** ©Donovan Reese/Getty
Images. **408W** (l) ©SKirchner/
photocuisine/Corbis. **408W** ©Jeff
Greenberg/PhotoEdit. **409W** ©Andrew
Paterson/Alamy. **410W–413W** ©Big
Stock Photos. **412W** ©Reuters/Larry
Downing. **414W** ©Tom Bean/Corbis.
415W (b) ©Ocean/Corbis. **415W** ©From
"When I Was Puerto Rican" by
Esmerelda Santiago. Used by Permission
of Vintage Books a division of random
House Inc. **416W** ©Marty Snyderman/
Spirit/Corbis. **417W** ©Franz Marc Frei/
Encyclopedia/Corbis. **418W** ©Corel
Photo Jeff Greenberg/Alamy. **419W** ©Jeff
Greenberg/Alamy. **420W** Photos
Courtesy of the Fredricksburg Theater
Co Mary Washington College Department
of theater and dance Fredricksburg VA.
421W ©Tetra Images/Getty Images.
421W Photos Courtesy of the
Fredricksburg Theater Co Mary
Washington College Department of
theater and dance Fredricksburg VA.
422W, 423W ©Leong Kin Fei/
istockphotoscom. **424W**© Bruce Dale/
National Geographic/Getty Images.
426W ©Christie's Image Corbis.
428-429W ©Linda/zefa/Corbis.

430W ©Jessica Secheret.
431W ©Lawrence Manning/Spirit/
Corbis. **437W** ©Big Stock Photos.
439W ©David Young-Wolff/Photo
Edit. **441W** ©Stockbyte/Alamy.
442W (cl) ©Antar Dayal/Illustration
Works/Motif/Corbis. **442W** (tr)
©Anthony Nex/FoodPix/Getty Images.
442W, 512W ©Andrew_Howe/
istockphoto.com. **442W** ©Stockbyte.
442W ©PhotoDisc. **442W** ©PhotoDisc.
442W ©PhotoDisc. **442W** ©PhotoDisc.
446W ©20th Century Fox/The Kobal
Collection/Picture Desk. **454W** ©C
Squared Studios/Photodisc/Getty
Images. **454W** (bc) ©Duncan Smith/
Flame/Corbis. **454W** ©Alex Grimm/
Reuters/Corbis. **454W** ©Steve Cole/
Photodisc/Getty Images.
454W ©Big Stock Photos. **454W** ©Big
Stock Photos. **454W** ©David Toase/Getty
Images. **454W** ©David Toase/Getty
Images. **454W** ©Metaphotos.
455W ©PhotoDisc. **455W** ©PhotoDisc.
487W ©Nation Wong/Zefa/Corbis.
v ©Martin O'Neill: Mental Health
>Memory. **vi** ©Martin O'Neill: E Design>
Internet Research. **viii** ©Martin O'Neill:
Nabakov > Speak Memory. **xvi** ©Martin
O'Neill: Mental Health> Memory.
xv (l) ©Andrew_Howe/istockphoto.com.
xv (c, r) ©Photodisc.

Illustration

**55W, 63W, 159W, 166W, 167W, 187W,
197W, 199W** ©Steve Bjorkman.

Common Core State Standards

CHAPTER 1: The Building Blocks of Writing

Project 1: Paragraph Structure: Ways to Organize

Pages	Lesson	Code	Standards Text
2W–13W	Sentences and Paragraphs: Model Study and Writing Strategy: Organize Your Paragraphs		Write informative/explanatory texts to examine a topic and convey ideas, concepts, and information through the selection, organization, and analysis of relevant content.
		W.7.2.a	Introduce a topic clearly, previewing what is to follow; organize ideas, concepts, and information, using strategies such as definition, classification, comparison/contrast, and cause/effect; include formatting (e.g., headings), graphics (e.g., charts, tables), and multimedia when useful to aiding comprehension.
14W–15W	Paragraph: Plan and Write	W.7.2	Write informative/explanatory texts to examine a topic and convey ideas, concepts, and information through the selection, organization, and analysis of relevant content.
		W.7.2.a	Introduce a topic clearly, previewing what is to follow; organize ideas, concepts, and information, using strategies such as definition, classification, comparison/contrast, and cause/effect; include formatting (e.g., headings), graphics (e.g., charts, tables), and multimedia when useful to aiding comprehension.
		W.7.2.b	Develop the topic with relevant facts, definitions, concrete details, quotations, or other information and examples.
		W.7.4	Produce clear and coherent writing in which the development, organization, and style are appropriate to task, purpose, and audience.
		W.7.5	With some guidance and support from peers and adults, develop and strengthen writing as needed by planning, revising, editing, rewriting, or trying a new approach, focusing on how well purpose and audience have been addressed.
		W.7.10	Write routinely over extended time frames (time for research, reflection, and revision) and shorter time frames (a single sitting or a day or two) for a range of discipline-specific tasks, purposes, and audiences.

Common Core State Standards, continued

Project 2: Use the Writing Process, continued

Pages	Lesson	Code	Standards Text
		W.7.5	With some guidance and support from peers and adults, develop and strengthen writing as needed by planning, revising, editing, rewriting, or trying a new approach, focusing on how well purpose and audience have been addressed.
		W.7.10	Write routinely over extended time frames (time for research, reflection, and revision) and shorter time frames (a single sitting or a day or two) for a range of discipline-specific tasks, purposes, and audiences.
40W–41W	**Writing Strategy: Write Effective Sentences**		Write arguments to support claims with clear reasons and relevant evidence.
		W.7.1.c	Use words, phrases, and clauses to create cohesion and clarify the relationships among claim(s), reasons, and evidence.
		W.7.5	With some guidance and support from peers and adults, develop and strengthen writing as needed by planning, revising, editing, rewriting, or trying a new approach, focusing on how well purpose and audience have been addressed.
			Demonstrate command of the conventions of standard English grammar and usage when writing or speaking.
		L.7.1.b	Choose among simple, compound, complex, and compound-complex sentences to signal differing relationships among ideas.
			Use knowledge of language and its conventions when writing, speaking, reading, or listening.
		L.7.3.a	Choose language that expresses ideas precisely and concisely, recognizing and eliminating wordiness and redundancy.
42W–47W	**Problem-and-Solution Paragraphs: Revise**		Write arguments to support claims with clear reasons and relevant evidence.
		W.7.1.a	Introduce claim(s), acknowledge alternate or opposing claims, and organize the reasons and evidence logically.
		W.7.1.b	Support claim(s) with logical reasoning and relevant evidence, using accurate, credible sources and demonstrating an understanding of the topic or text.
		W.7.1.e	Provide a concluding statement or section that follows from and supports the argument presented.

Common Core State Standards, continued

Project 2: Use the Writing Process, continued

Pages	Lesson	Code	Standards Text
		W.7.4	Produce clear and coherent writing in which the development, organization, and style are appropriate to task, purpose, and audience.
		W.7.5	With some guidance and support from peers and adults, develop and strengthen writing as needed by planning, revising, editing, rewriting, or trying a new approach, focusing on how well purpose and audience have been addressed.
48W–56W	**Problem-and-Solution Paragraphs: Edit and Proofread**	W.7.5	With some guidance and support from peers and adults, develop and strengthen writing as needed by planning, revising, editing, rewriting, or trying a new approach, focusing on how well purpose and audience have been addressed.
		W.7.6	Use technology, including the Internet, to produce and publish writing and link to and cite sources as well as to interact and collaborate with others, including linking to and citing sources.
		W.7.10	Write routinely over extended time frames (time for research, reflection, and revision) and shorter time frames (a single sitting or a day or two) for a range of discipline-specific tasks, purposes, and audiences.
		L.7.1	Demonstrate command of the conventions of standard English grammar and usage when writing or speaking.
		L.7.2	Demonstrate command of the conventions of standard English capitalization, punctuation, and spelling when writing.
		L.7.2.b	Spell correctly.
		L.7.3	Use knowledge of language and its conventions when writing, speaking, reading, or listening.
		L.7.4.c	Determine or clarify the meaning of unknown and multiple-meaning words and phrases based on grade 7 reading and content, choosing flexibly from a range of strategies. Consult general and specialized reference materials (e.g., dictionaries, glossaries, thesauruses), both print and digital, to find the pronunciation of a word or determine or clarify its precise meaning or its part of speech.
57W	**Grammar Workout: Check for Complete Sentences**	L.7.1	Demonstrate command of the conventions of standard English grammar and usage when writing or speaking.
		L.7.3	Use knowledge of language and its conventions when writing, speaking, reading, or listening.

Project 2: Use the Writing Process, continued

Pages	Lesson	Code	Standards Text
58W	**Spelling Workout:** **Check Plural Nouns**	L.7.1	Demonstrate command of the conventions of standard English grammar and usage when writing or speaking.
		L.7.2	Demonstrate command of the conventions of standard English capitalization, punctuation, and spelling when writing.
		L.7.2.b	Spell correctly.
59W	**Mechanics Workout:** **Check Sentence Punctuation**	L.7.2	Demonstrate command of the conventions of standard English capitalization, punctuation, and spelling when writing.
60W–63W	**Problem-and-Solution** **Paragraphs:** **Publish, Share, and Reflect**	W.7.5	With some guidance and support from peers and adults, develop and strengthen writing as needed by planning, revising, editing, rewriting, or trying a new approach, focusing on how well purpose and audience have been addressed.
		W.7.6	Use technology, including the Internet, to produce and publish writing and link to and cite sources as well as to interact and collaborate with others, including linking to and citing sources.
64W–65W	**Presentation Manual:** **Use Multimedia**	SL.7.1	Engage effectively in a range of collaborative discussions (one-on-one, in groups, and teacher led) with diverse partners on grade 7 topics, texts, and issues, building on others' ideas and expressing their own clearly.
		SL.7.1.a	Come to discussions prepared, having read or researched material under study; explicitly draw on that preparation by referring to evidence on the topic, text, or issue to probe and reflect on ideas under discussion.
		SL.7.1.c	Pose questions that elicit elaboration and respond to others' questions and comments with relevant observations and ideas that bring the discussion back on topic as needed.
		SL.7.2	Analyze the main ideas and supporting details presented in diverse media and formats (e.g., visually, quantitatively, orally) and explain how the ideas clarify a topic, text, or issue under study.
		SL.7.4	Present claims and findings, emphasizing salient points in a focused, coherent manner with pertinent descriptions, facts, details, and examples; use appropriate eye contact, adequate volume, and clear pronunciation.
		SL.7.5	Include multimedia components and visual displays in presentations to clarify claims and findings and emphasize salient points.

Common Core State Standards, continued

Pages	Lesson	Code	Standards Text
68W–71W	**Personal Narrative: Model Study and Prewrite**	W.7.5	With some guidance and support from peers and adults, develop and strengthen writing as needed by planning, revising, editing, rewriting, or trying a new approach, focusing on how well purpose and audience have been addressed.
72W–73W	**Personal Narrative: Draft**	W.7.3	Write narratives to develop real or imagined experiences or events using effective technique, relevant descriptive details, and well-structured event sequences.
		W.7.3.a	Engage and orient the reader by establishing a context and point of view and introducing a narrator and/or characters; organize an event sequence that unfolds naturally and logically.
		W.7.3.c	Use a variety of transition words, phrases, and clauses to convey sequence and signal shifts from one time frame or setting to another.
		W.7.3.d	Use precise words and phrases, relevant descriptive details, and sensory language to capture the action and convey experiences and events.
		W.7.3.e	Provide a conclusion that follows from and reflects on the narrated experiences or events.
		W.7.5	With some guidance and support from peers and adults, develop and strengthen writing as needed by planning, revising, editing, rewriting, or trying a new approach, focusing on how well purpose and audience have been addressed.
		W.7.10	Write routinely over extended time frames (time for research, reflection, and revision) and shorter time frames (a single sitting or a day or two) for a range of discipline-specific tasks, purposes, and audiences.
74W–75W	**Personal Narrative: Revise**		Write narratives to develop real or imagined experiences or events using effective technique, relevant descriptive details, and well-structured event sequences.
		W.7.3.b	Use narrative techniques, such as dialogue, pacing, and description, to develop experiences, events, and/or characters.
		W.7.3.d	Use precise words and phrases, relevant descriptive details, and sensory language to capture the action and convey experiences and events.

Project 3: Write as an Eyewitness, continued

Pages	Lesson	Code	Standards Text
		W.7.4	Produce clear and coherent writing in which the development, organization, and style are appropriate to task, purpose, and audience.
		W.7.5	With some guidance and support from peers and adults, develop and strengthen writing as needed by planning, revising, editing, rewriting, or trying a new approach, focusing on how well purpose and audience have been addressed.
		L.7.3.a	Use knowledge of language and its conventions when writing, speaking, reading, or listening. Choose language that expresses ideas precisely and concisely, recognizing and eliminating wordiness and redundancy.
76W	Personal Narrative: Edit and Proofread	W.7.5	With some guidance and support from peers and adults, develop and strengthen writing as needed by planning, revising, editing, rewriting, or trying a new approach, focusing on how well purpose and audience have been addressed.
		L.7.1	Demonstrate command of the conventions of standard English grammar and usage when writing or speaking.
		L.7.2	Demonstrate command of the conventions of standard English capitalization, punctuation, and spelling when writing.
		L.7.2.b	Spell correctly.
		L.7.3	Use knowledge of language and its conventions when writing, speaking, reading, or listening.
77W	Grammar Workout: Check Pronouns	L.7.1	Demonstrate command of the conventions of standard English grammar and usage when writing or speaking.
		L.7.3	Use knowledge of language and its conventions when writing, speaking, reading, or listening.
78W	Spelling Workout: Check Plural of Nouns Ending in y	L.7.2	Demonstrate command of the conventions of standard English capitalization, punctuation, and spelling when writing.
		L.7.2.b	Spell correctly.
79W	Mechanics Workout: Check Capitalization of Proper Nouns	L.7.2	Demonstrate command of the conventions of standard English capitalization, punctuation, and spelling when writing.

Common Core State Standards, continued

Project 4: Write as a Storyteller

Pages	Lesson	Code	Standards Text
80W–89W	**Short Story: Model Study and Writing Trait: Organization**	W.7.4	Produce clear and coherent writing in which the development, organization, and style are appropriate to task, purpose, and audience.
		W.7.5	With some guidance and support from peers and adults, develop and strengthen writing as needed by planning, revising, editing, rewriting, or trying a new approach, focusing on how well purpose and audience have been addressed.
		W.7.10	Write routinely over extended time frames (time for research, reflection, and revision) and shorter time frames (a single sitting or a day or two) for a range of discipline-specific tasks, purposes, and audiences.
90W–91W	**Writing Strategy: How to Make Your Ideas Flow**		Write narratives to develop real or imagined experiences or events using effective technique, relevant descriptive details, and well-structured event sequences.
		W.7.3.c	Use a variety of transition words, phrases, and clauses to convey sequence and signal shifts from one time frame or setting to another.
		W.7.5	With some guidance and support from peers and adults, develop and strengthen writing as needed by planning, revising, editing, rewriting, or trying a new approach, focusing on how well purpose and audience have been addressed.
92W–93W	**Writing Strategy: How to Connect Your Paragraphs**		Write narratives to develop real or imagined experiences or events using effective technique, relevant descriptive details, and well-structured event sequences.
		W.7.3.c	Use a variety of transition words, phrases, and clauses to convey sequence and signal shifts from one time frame or setting to another.
		W.7.5	With some guidance and support from peers and adults, develop and strengthen writing as needed by planning, revising, editing, rewriting, or trying a new approach, focusing on how well purpose and audience have been addressed.
94W–97W	**Short Story: Prewrite**		Write narratives to develop real or imagined experiences or events using effective technique, relevant descriptive details, and well-structured event sequences.
		W.7.3.d	Use precise words and phrases, relevant descriptive details, and sensory language to capture the action and convey experiences and events.

Project 4: Write as a Storyteller, continued

Pages	Lesson	Code	Standards Text
		W.7.5	With some guidance and support from peers and adults, develop and strengthen writing as needed by planning, revising, editing, rewriting, or trying a new approach, focusing on how well purpose and audience have been addressed.
98W–99W	Short Story: Draft	W.7.3	Write narratives to develop real or imagined experiences or events using effective technique, relevant descriptive details, and well-structured event sequences.
		W.7.3.a	Engage and orient the reader by establishing a context and point of view and introducing a narrator and/or characters; organize an event sequence that unfolds naturally and logically.
		W.7.3.b	Use narrative techniques, such as dialogue, pacing, and description, to develop experiences, events, and/or characters.
		W.7.3.c	Use a variety of transition words, phrases, and clauses to convey sequence and signal shifts from one time frame or setting to another.
		W.7.3.d	Use precise words and phrases, relevant descriptive details, and sensory language to capture the action and convey experiences and events.
		W.7.3.e	Provide a conclusion that follows from and reflects on the narrated experiences or events.
		W.7.5	With some guidance and support from peers and adults, develop and strengthen writing as needed by planning, revising, editing, rewriting, or trying a new approach, focusing on how well purpose and audience have been addressed.
		W.7.10	Write routinely over extended time frames (time for research, reflection, and revision) and shorter time frames (a single sitting or a day or two) for a range of discipline-specific tasks, purposes, and audiences.
100W–101W	Short Story: Revise		Write narratives to develop real or imagined experiences or events using effective technique, relevant descriptive details, and well-structured event sequences.
		W.7.3.a	Engage and orient the reader by establishing a context and point of view and introducing a narrator and/or characters; organize an event sequence that unfolds naturally and logically.

Common Core State Standards, continued

Project 4: Write as a Storyteller, continued

Pages	Lesson	Code	Standards Text
		W.7.3.c	Use a variety of transition words, phrases, and clauses to convey sequence and signal shifts from one time frame or setting to another.
		W.7.3.e	Provide a conclusion that follows from and reflects on the narrated experiences or events.
		W.7.4	Produce clear and coherent writing in which the development, organization, and style are appropriate to task, purpose, and audience.
		W.7.5	With some guidance and support from peers and adults, develop and strengthen writing as needed by planning, revising, editing, rewriting, or trying a new approach, focusing on how well purpose and audience have been addressed.
102W	**Short Story: Edit and Proofread**	W.7.5	With some guidance and support from peers and adults, develop and strengthen writing as needed by planning, revising, editing, rewriting, or trying a new approach, focusing on how well purpose and audience have been addressed.
		L.7.1	Demonstrate command of the conventions of standard English grammar and usage when writing or speaking.
		L.7.2	Demonstrate command of the conventions of standard English capitalization, punctuation, and spelling when writing.
		L.7.2.b	Spell correctly.
		L.7.3	Use knowledge of language and its conventions when writing, speaking, reading, or listening.
103W	**Grammar Workout: Check Subject-Verb Agreement**	L.7.1	Demonstrate command of the conventions of standard English grammar and usage when writing or speaking.
		L.7.3	Use knowledge of language and its conventions when writing, speaking, reading, or listening.
104W	**Spelling Workout: Check Words with Tricky Consonant Sounds**	L.7.2	Demonstrate command of the conventions of standard English capitalization, punctuation, and spelling when writing.
		L.7.2.b	Spell correctly.
105W	**Mechanics Workout: Check Style with Dialogue**	L.7.2	Demonstrate command of the conventions of standard English capitalization, punctuation, and spelling when writing.

Project 4: Write as a Storyteller, continued

Pages	Lesson	Code	Standards Text
106W	**Short Story: Publish, Share, and Reflect**	W.7.5	With some guidance and support from peers and adults, develop and strengthen writing as needed by planning, revising, editing, rewriting, or trying a new approach, focusing on how well purpose and audience have been addressed.
		W.7.6	Use technology, including the Internet, to produce and publish writing and link to and cite sources as well as to interact and collaborate with others, including linking to and citing sources.
107W	**Presentation Manual: How to Read a Story Aloud**	SL.7.1	Engage effectively in a range of collaborative discussions (one-on-one, in groups, and teacher led) with diverse partners on grade 7 topics, texts, and issues, building on others' ideas and expressing their own clearly.
		SL.7.1.c	Pose questions that elicit elaboration and respond to others' questions and comments with relevant observations and ideas that bring the discussion back on topic as needed.

Project 5 Write Realistic Fiction

Pages	Lesson	Code	Standards Text
108W–111W	**Realistic Short Story: Model Study and Prewrite**	W.7.5	With some guidance and support from peers and adults, develop and strengthen writing as needed by planning, revising, editing, rewriting, or trying a new approach, focusing on how well purpose and audience have been addressed.
112W–113W	**Realistic Short Story: Draft**	W.7.3	Write narratives to develop real or imagined experiences or events using effective technique, relevant descriptive details, and well-structured event sequences.
		W.7.3.a	Engage and orient the reader by establishing a context and point of view and introducing a narrator and/or characters; organize an event sequence that unfolds naturally and logically.
		W.7.3.b	Use narrative techniques, such as dialogue, pacing, and description, to develop experiences, events, and/or characters.
		W.7.3.e	Provide a conclusion that follows from and reflects on the narrated experiences or events.
		W.7.5	With some guidance and support from peers and adults, develop and strengthen writing as needed by planning, revising, editing, rewriting, or trying a new approach, focusing on how well purpose and audience have been addressed.
		W.7.10	Write routinely over extended time frames (time for research, reflection, and revision) and shorter time frames (a single sitting or a day or two) for a range of discipline-specific tasks, purposes, and audiences.

Common Core State Standards, continued

Project 5: Write Realistic Fiction, continued

Pages	Lesson	Code	Standards Text
114W–115W	Realistic Short Story: Revise		Write narratives to develop real or imagined experiences or events using effective technique, relevant descriptive details, and well-structured event sequences.
		W.7.3.a	Engage and orient the reader by establishing a context and point of view and introducing a narrator and/or characters; organize an event sequence that unfolds naturally and logically.
		W.7.3.d	Use precise words and phrases, relevant descriptive details, and sensory language to capture the action and convey experiences and events.
		W.7.4	Produce clear and coherent writing in which the development, organization, and style are appropriate to task, purpose, and audience.
		W.7.5	With some guidance and support from peers and adults, develop and strengthen writing as needed by planning, revising, editing, rewriting, or trying a new approach, focusing on how well purpose and audience have been addressed.
			Use knowledge of language and its conventions when writing, speaking, reading, or listening.
		L.7.3.a	Choose language that expresses ideas precisely and concisely, recognizing and eliminating wordiness and redundancy.
116W	Realistic Short Story: Edit and Proofread	W.7.5	With some guidance and support from peers and adults, develop and strengthen writing as needed by planning, revising, editing, rewriting, or trying a new approach, focusing on how well purpose and audience have been addressed.
		L.7.1	Demonstrate command of the conventions of standard English grammar and usage when writing or speaking.
		L.7.2	Demonstrate command of the conventions of standard English capitalization, punctuation, and spelling when writing.
		L.7.2.b	Spell correctly.
		L.7.3	Use knowledge of language and its conventions when writing, speaking, reading, or listening.
117W	Grammar Workout: Check Adjectives	L.7.1	Demonstrate command of the conventions of standard English grammar and usage when writing or speaking.
		L.7.3	Use knowledge of language and its conventions when writing, speaking, reading, or listening.

Project 5: Write Realistic Fiction, continued

Pages	Lesson	Code	Standards Text
118W	**Spelling Workout: Check Compound Words**	L.7.2	Demonstrate command of the conventions of standard English capitalization, punctuation, and spelling when writing.
		L.7.2.b	Spell correctly.
119W	**Mechanics Workout: Check Commas Between Adjectives**		Demonstrate command of the conventions of standard English capitalization, punctuation, and spelling when writing.
		L.7.2.a	Use a comma to separate coordinate adjectives (e.g., It was a fascinating, enjoyable movie but not He wore an old[,] green shirt).
		L.7.3	Use knowledge of language and its conventions when writing, speaking, reading, or listening.

Project 6 Write as a Reporter

Pages	Lesson	Code	Standards Text
120W–129W	**Cause-and-Effect Essay: Model Study and Writing Trait: Focus and Unity**		Write informative/explanatory texts to examine a topic and convey ideas, concepts, and information through the selection, organization, and analysis of relevant content.
		W.7.2.a	Introduce a topic clearly, previewing what is to follow; organize ideas, concepts, and information, using strategies such as definition, classification, comparison/contrast, and cause/effect; include formatting (e.g., headings), graphics (e.g., charts, tables), and multimedia when useful to aiding comprehension.
		W.7.2.b	Develop the topic with relevant facts, definitions, concrete details, quotations, or other information and examples.
		W.7.2.f	Provide a concluding statement or section that follows from and supports the information or explanation presented.
		W.7.4	Produce clear and coherent writing in which the development, organization, and style are appropriate to task, purpose, and audience.
		W.7.5	With some guidance and support from peers and adults, develop and strengthen writing as needed by planning, revising, editing, rewriting, or trying a new approach, focusing on how well purpose and audience have been addressed.
		W.7.10	Write routinely over extended time frames (time for research, reflection, and revision) and shorter time frames (a single sitting or a day or two) for a range of discipline-specific tasks, purposes, and audiences.

Common Core State Standards, continued

Project 6: Write as a Reporter

SE Pages	Lesson	Code	Standards Text
130W–133W	Writing Strategy: State a Central Idea		Write informative/explanatory texts to examine a topic and convey ideas, concepts, and information through the selection, organization, and analysis of relevant content.
		W.7.2.a	Introduce a topic clearly, previewing what is to follow; organize ideas, concepts, and information, using strategies such as definition, classification, comparison/contrast, and cause/effect; include formatting (e.g., headings), graphics (e.g., charts, tables), and multimedia when useful to aiding comprehension.
134W–135W	Writing Strategy: Stay Focused on the Central Idea	W.7.5	With some guidance and support from peers and adults, develop and strengthen writing as needed by planning, revising, editing, rewriting, or trying a new approach, focusing on how well purpose and audience have been addressed.
136W–137W	Cause-and-Effect Essay: Prewrite	W.7.5	With some guidance and support from peers and adults, develop and strengthen writing as needed by planning, revising, editing, rewriting, or trying a new approach, focusing on how well purpose and audience have been addressed.
138W–139W	Cause-and-Effect Essay: Draft	W.7.2	Write informative/explanatory texts to examine a topic and convey ideas, concepts, and information through the selection, organization, and analysis of relevant content.
		W.7.2.a	Introduce a topic clearly, previewing what is to follow; organize ideas, concepts, and information, using strategies such as definition, classification, comparison/contrast, and cause/effect; include formatting (e.g., headings), graphics (e.g., charts, tables), and multimedia when useful to aiding comprehension.
		W.7.2.b	Develop the topic with relevant facts, definitions, concrete details, quotations, or other information and examples.
		W.7.3.c	Use a variety of transition words, phrases, and clauses to convey sequence and signal shifts from one time frame or setting to another.
		W.7.2.d	Use precise language and domain-specific vocabulary to inform about or explain the topic.
		W.7.2.e	Establish and maintain a formal style.
		W.7.2.f	Provide a concluding statement or section that follows from and supports the information or explanation presented.

Project 6: Write as a Reporter, continued

Pages	Lesson	Code	Standards Text
		W.7.5	With some guidance and support from peers and adults, develop and strengthen writing as needed by planning, revising, editing, rewriting, or trying a new approach, focusing on how well purpose and audience have been addressed.
		W.7.10	Write routinely over extended time frames (time for research, reflection, and revision) and shorter time frames (a single sitting or a day or two) for a range of discipline-specific tasks, purposes, and audiences.
140W–143W	Cause-and-Effect Essay: Revise		Write informative/explanatory texts to examine a topic and convey ideas, concepts, and information through the selection, organization, and analysis of relevant content.
		W.7.2.a	Introduce a topic clearly, previewing what is to follow; organize ideas, concepts, and information, using strategies such as definition, classification, comparison/contrast, and cause/effect; include formatting (e.g., headings), graphics (e.g., charts, tables), and multimedia when useful to aiding comprehension.
		W.7.2.b	Develop the topic with relevant facts, definitions, concrete details, quotations, or other information and examples.
		W.7.2.c	Use appropriate transitions to create cohesion and clarify the relationships among ideas and concepts.
		W.7.4	Produce clear and coherent writing in which the development, organization, and style are appropriate to task, purpose, and audience.
		W.7.5	With some guidance and support from peers and adults, develop and strengthen writing as needed by planning, revising, editing, rewriting, or trying a new approach, focusing on how well purpose and audience have been addressed.
144W	Cause-and-Effect Essay: Edit and Proofread	W.7.5	With some guidance and support from peers and adults, develop and strengthen writing as needed by planning, revising, editing, rewriting, or trying a new approach, focusing on how well purpose and audience have been addressed.
		L.7.1	Demonstrate command of the conventions of standard English grammar and usage when writing or speaking.
		L.7.2	Demonstrate command of the conventions of standard English capitalization, punctuation, and spelling when writing.
		L.7.2.b	Spell correctly.
		L.7.3	Use knowledge of language and its conventions when writing, speaking, reading, or listening.

Common Core State Standards, continued

Project 6: Write as a Reporter, continued

Pages	Lesson	Code	Standards Text
145W	**Grammar Workout: Check Adverbs**	L.7.1	Demonstrate command of the conventions of standard English grammar and usage when writing or speaking.
		L.7.3	Use knowledge of language and its conventions when writing, speaking, reading, or listening.
146W	**Spelling Workout: Check Adverbs Ending in -ly**	L.7.2	Demonstrate command of the conventions of standard English capitalization, punctuation, and spelling when writing.
		L.7.2.b	Spell correctly.
147W	**Mechanics Workout: Check Capitalization of Proper Nouns**	L.7.2	Demonstrate command of the conventions of standard English capitalization, punctuation, and spelling when writing.
		L.7.3	Use knowledge of language and its conventions when writing, speaking, reading, or listening.
148W	**Cause-and-Effect Essay: Publish, Share, and Reflect**	W.7.5	With some guidance and support from peers and adults, develop and strengthen writing as needed by planning, revising, editing, rewriting, or trying a new approach, focusing on how well purpose and audience have been addressed.
		W.7.6	Use technology, including the Internet, to produce and publish writing and link to and cite sources as well as to interact and collaborate with others, including linking to and citing sources.
149W	**Presentation Manual: How to Stay Focused**		Engage effectively in a range of collaborative discussions (one-on-one, in groups, and teacher led) with diverse partners on grade 7 topics, texts, and issues, building on others' ideas and expressing their own clearly.
		SL.7.1.c	Pose questions that elicit elaboration and respond to others' questions and comments with relevant observations and ideas that bring the discussion back on topic as needed.
		SL.7.4	Present claims and findings, emphasizing salient points in a focused, coherent manner with pertinent descriptions, facts, details, and examples; use appropriate eye contact, adequate volume, and clear pronunciation.

Project 7: Write as a Researcher

Pages	Lesson	Code	Standards Text
150W–159W	**Research Report: Model Study and Research Strategy: Develop a Game Plan**	W.7.4	Produce clear and coherent writing in which the development, organization, and style are appropriate to task, purpose, and audience.
		W.7.5	With some guidance and support from peers and adults, develop and strengthen writing as needed by planning, revising, editing, rewriting, or trying a new approach, focusing on how well purpose and audience have been addressed.
		W.7.7	Conduct short research projects to answer a question, drawing on several sources and generating additional related, focused questions for further research and investigation.
160W–167W	**Research Strategy: Locate Information Sources**	W.7.5	With some guidance and support from peers and adults, develop and strengthen writing as needed by planning, revising, editing, rewriting, or trying a new approach, focusing on how well purpose and audience have been addressed.
		W.7.6	Use technology, including the Internet, to produce and publish writing and link to and cite sources as well as to interact and collaborate with others, including linking to and citing sources.
		W.7.7	Conduct short research projects to answer a question, drawing on several sources and generating additional related, focused questions for further research and investigation.
		W.7.8	Gather relevant information from multiple print and digital sources, using search terms effectively; assess the credibility and accuracy of each source; and quote or paraphrase the data and conclusions of others while avoiding plagiarism and following a standard format for citation.
168W–171W	**Research Strategy: Get Information from the Web**	W.7.6	Use technology, including the Internet, to produce and publish writing and link to and cite sources as well as to interact and collaborate with others, including linking to and citing sources.
		W.7.7	Conduct short research projects to answer a question, drawing on several sources and generating additional related, focused questions for further research and investigation.
		W.7.8	Gather relevant information from multiple print and digital sources, using search terms effectively; assess the credibility and accuracy of each source; and quote or paraphrase the data and conclusions of others while avoiding plagiarism and following a standard format for citation.

Common Core State Standards, continued

Project 7: Write as a Researcher, continued

Pages	Lesson	Code	Standards Text
172W–175W	**Research Strategy: Sort through the Information**	W.7.8	Gather relevant information from multiple print and digital sources, using search terms effectively; assess the credibility and accuracy of each source; and quote or paraphrase the data and conclusions of others while avoiding plagiarism and following a standard format for citation.
176W–179W	**Research Strategy: Take Good Notes**	W.7.8	Gather relevant information from multiple print and digital sources, using search terms effectively; assess the credibility and accuracy of each source; and quote or paraphrase the data and conclusions of others while avoiding plagiarism and following a standard format for citation.
		W.7.9	Draw evidence from literary or informational texts to support analysis, reflection, and research.
		W.7.9.b	Apply grade 7 Reading standards to literary nonfiction (e.g. "Trace and evaluate the argument and specific claims in a text, assessing whether the reasoning is sound and the evidence is relevant and sufficient to support the claims").
180W–183W	**Research Strategy: Avoid Plagiarism**	W.7.8	Gather relevant information from multiple print and digital sources, using search terms effectively; assess the credibility and accuracy of each source; and quote or paraphrase the data and conclusions of others while avoiding plagiarism and following a standard format for citation.
		L.7.2	Demonstrate command of the conventions of standard English capitalization, punctuation, and spelling when writing.
184W–189W	**Research Strategy: Organize Your Notes**	W.7.5	With some guidance and support from peers and adults, develop and strengthen writing as needed by planning, revising, editing, rewriting, or trying a new approach, focusing on how well purpose and audience have been addressed.
		W.7.9	Draw evidence from literary or informational texts to support analysis, reflection, and research.
		W.7.9.b	Apply grade 7 Reading standards to literary nonfiction (e.g. "Trace and evaluate the argument and specific claims in a text, assessing whether the reasoning is sound and the evidence is relevant and sufficient to support the claims").

Project 7: Write as a Researcher, continued

Pages	Lesson	Code	Standards Text
190W–191W	**Research Strategy: Develop an Outline**	W.7.2	Write informative/explanatory texts to examine a topic and convey ideas, concepts, and information through the selection, organization, and analysis of relevant content.
		W.7.2.a	Introduce a topic clearly, previewing what is to follow; organize ideas, concepts, and information, using strategies such as definition, classification, comparison/contrast, and cause/effect; include formatting (e.g., headings), graphics (e.g., charts, tables), and multimedia when useful to aiding comprehension.
		W.7.4	Produce clear and coherent writing in which the development, organization, and style are appropriate to task, purpose, and audience.
		W.7.5	With some guidance and support from peers and adults, develop and strengthen writing as needed by planning, revising, editing, rewriting, or trying a new approach, focusing on how well purpose and audience have been addressed.
		W.7.7	Conduct short research projects to answer a question, drawing on several sources and generating additional related, focused questions for further research and investigation.
192W–195W	**Research Report: Draft**	W.7.2	Write informative/explanatory texts to examine a topic and convey ideas, concepts, and information through the selection, organization, and analysis of relevant content.
		W.7.2.a	Introduce a topic clearly, previewing what is to follow; organize ideas, concepts, and information, using strategies such as definition, classification, comparison/contrast, and cause/effect; include formatting (e.g., headings), graphics (e.g., charts, tables), and multimedia when useful to aiding comprehension.
		W.7.2.b	Develop the topic with relevant facts, definitions, concrete details, quotations, or other information and examples.
		W.7.2.d	Use precise language and domain-specific vocabulary to inform about or explain the topic.
		W.7.2.e	Establish and maintain a formal style.
		W.7.2.f	Provide a concluding statement or section that follows from and supports the information or explanation presented.
		W.7.4	Produce clear and coherent writing in which the development, organization, and style are appropriate to task, purpose, and audience.

Common Core State Standards, continued

Project 7: Write as a Researcher, continued

Pages	Lesson	Code	Standards Text
		W.7.5	With some guidance and support from peers and adults, develop and strengthen writing as needed by planning, revising, editing, rewriting, or trying a new approach, focusing on how well purpose and audience have been addressed.
		W.7.7	Conduct short research projects to answer a question, drawing on several sources and generating additional related, focused questions for further research and investigation.
		W.7.10	Write routinely over extended time frames (time for research, reflection, and revision) and shorter time frames (a single sitting or a day or two) for a range of discipline-specific tasks, purposes, and audiences.
196W–199W	**Research Report: How to Cite Sources**	W.7.8	Gather relevant information from multiple print and digital sources, using search terms effectively; assess the credibility and accuracy of each source; and quote or paraphrase the data and conclusions of others while avoiding plagiarism and following a standard format for citation.
200W–201W	**Research Report: Revise**		Write informative/explanatory texts to examine a topic and convey ideas, concepts, and information through the selection, organization, and analysis of relevant content.
		W.7.2.a	Introduce a topic clearly, previewing what is to follow; organize ideas, concepts, and information, using strategies such as definition, classification, comparison/contrast, and cause/effect; include formatting (e.g., headings), graphics (e.g., charts, tables), and multimedia when useful to aiding comprehension.
		W.7.2.b	Develop the topic with relevant facts, definitions, concrete details, quotations, or other information and examples.
		W.7.4	Produce clear and coherent writing in which the development, organization, and style are appropriate to task, purpose, and audience.
		W.7.5	With some guidance and support from peers and adults, develop and strengthen writing as needed by planning, revising, editing, rewriting, or trying a new approach, focusing on how well purpose and audience have been addressed.

Project 7: Write as a Researcher, continued

Pages	Lesson	Code	Standards Text
202W	**Research Report: Edit and Proofread**	W.7.5	With some guidance and support from peers and adults, develop and strengthen writing as needed by planning, revising, editing, rewriting, or trying a new approach, focusing on how well purpose and audience have been addressed.
		L.7.1	Demonstrate command of the conventions of standard English grammar and usage when writing or speaking.
		L.7.2	Demonstrate command of the conventions of standard English capitalization, punctuation, and spelling when writing.
		L.7.2.b	Spell correctly.
		L.7.3	Use knowledge of language and its conventions when writing, speaking, reading, or listening.
203W	**Grammar Workout: Check Possessive Adjectives**	L.7.1	Demonstrate command of the conventions of standard English grammar and usage when writing or speaking
		L.7.3	Use knowledge of language and its conventions when writing, speaking, reading, or listening.
204W	**Spelling Workout: Check the Spelling of Long Words**	L.7.2	Demonstrate command of the conventions of standard English capitalization, punctuation, and spelling when writing.
		L.7.2.b	Spell correctly.
205W	**Mechanics Workout: Check Apostrophes in Possessive Nouns**	L.7.2	Demonstrate command of the conventions of standard English capitalization, punctuation, and spelling when writing.
		L.7.3	Use knowledge of language and its conventions when writing, speaking, reading, or listening.
206W	**Research Report: Publish, Share, and Reflect**	W.7.5	With some guidance and support from peers and adults, develop and strengthen writing as needed by planning, revising, editing, rewriting, or trying a new approach, focusing on how well purpose and audience have been addressed.
		W.7.6	Use technology, including the Internet, to produce and publish writing and link to and cite sources as well as to interact and collaborate with others, including linking to and citing sources.

Common Core State Standards, continued

Project 7: Write as a Researcher, continued

Pages	Lesson	Code	Standards Text
207W	**Presentation Manual: Use Multimedia**	W.7.6	Use technology, including the Internet, to produce and publish writing and link to and cite sources as well as to interact and collaborate with others, including linking to and citing sources.
		SL.7.1	Engage effectively in a range of collaborative discussions (one-on-one, in groups, and teacher led) with diverse partners on grade 7 topics, texts, and issues, building on others' ideas and expressing their own clearly.
		SL.7.1.a	Come to discussions prepared, having read or researched material under study; explicitly draw on that preparation by referring to evidence on the topic, text, or issue to probe and reflect on ideas under discussion.
		SL.7.1.c	Pose questions that elicit elaboration and respond to others' questions and comments with relevant observations and ideas that bring the discussion back on topic as needed.
		SL.7.2	Analyze the main ideas and supporting details presented in diverse media and formats (e.g., visually, quantitatively, orally) and explain how the ideas clarify a topic, text, or issue under study.
		SL.7.5	Include multimedia components and visual displays in presentations to clarify claims and findings and emphasize salient points.

Project 8: Write a Story Scene

Pages	Lesson	Code	Standards Text
228W–231W	**Story Scene: Model Study and Prewrite**		Write narratives to develop real or imagined experiences or events using effective technique, relevant descriptive details, and well-structured event sequences.
		W.7.3.d	Use precise words and phrases, relevant descriptive details, and sensory language to capture the action and convey experiences and events.
		W.7.5	With some guidance and support from peers and adults, develop and strengthen writing as needed by planning, revising, editing, rewriting, or trying a new approach, focusing on how well purpose and audience have been addressed.

Project 8: Write a Story Scene, continued

Pages	Lesson	Code	Standards Text
232W–233W	**Story Scene: Draft**	W.7.3	Write narratives to develop real or imagined experiences or events using effective technique, relevant descriptive details, and well-structured event sequences.
		W.7.3.a	Engage and orient the reader by establishing a context and point of view and introducing a narrator and/or characters; organize an event sequence that unfolds naturally and logically.
		W.7.3.b	Use narrative techniques, such as dialogue, pacing, and description, to develop experiences, events, and/or characters.
		W.7.3.d	Use precise words and phrases, relevant descriptive details, and sensory language to capture the action and convey experiences and events.
		W.7.5	With some guidance and support from peers and adults, develop and strengthen writing as needed by planning, revising, editing, rewriting, or trying a new approach, focusing on how well purpose and audience have been addressed.
		W.7.10	Write routinely over extended time frames (time for research, reflection, and revision) and shorter time frames (a single sitting or a day or two) for a range of discipline-specific tasks, purposes, and audiences.
234W–235W	**Story Scene: Revise**	W.7.3	Write narratives to develop real or imagined experiences or events using effective technique, relevant descriptive details, and well-structured event sequences.
		W.7.3.a	Engage and orient the reader by establishing a context and point of view and introducing a narrator and/or characters; organize an event sequence that unfolds naturally and logically.
		W.7.3.b	Use narrative techniques, such as dialogue, pacing, and description, to develop experiences, events, and/or characters.
		W.7.3.d	Use precise words and phrases, relevant descriptive details, and sensory language to capture the action and convey experiences and events.
		W.7.4	Produce clear and coherent writing in which the development, organization, and style are appropriate to task, purpose, and audience.
		W.7.5	With some guidance and support from peers and adults, develop and strengthen writing as needed by planning, revising, editing, rewriting, or trying a new approach, focusing on how well purpose and audience have been addressed.

Common Core State Standards, continued

Project 8: Write a Story Scene, continued

Pages	Lesson	Code	Standards Text
236W	**Story Scene: Edit and Proofread**	W.7.5	With some guidance and support from peers and adults, develop and strengthen writing as needed by planning, revising, editing, rewriting, or trying a new approach, focusing on how well purpose and audience have been addressed.
		L.7.1	Demonstrate command of the conventions of standard English grammar and usage when writing or speaking.
		L.7.2	Demonstrate command of the conventions of standard English capitalization, punctuation, and spelling when writing.
		L.7.2.b	Spell correctly.
		L.7.3	Use knowledge of language and its conventions when writing, speaking, reading, or listening.
237W	**Grammar Workout: Check Frequently Misused Words**	L.7.1	Demonstrate command of the conventions of standard English grammar and usage when writing or speaking.
		L.7.3	Use knowledge of language and its conventions when writing, speaking, reading, or listening.
238W	**Spelling Workout: Check Words with Suffixes**	L.7.2	Demonstrate command of the conventions of standard English capitalization, punctuation, and spelling when writing.
		L.7.2.b	Spell correctly.
239W	**Mechanics Workout: Check Serial Commas**	L.7.2	Demonstrate command of the conventions of standard English capitalization, punctuation, and spelling when writing.

Project 9 Write as a Reader

Pages	Lesson	Code	Standards Text
240W–249W	**Literary Response: Model Study and Writing Trait: Development of Ideas**		Write arguments to support claims with clear reasons and relevant evidence.
		W.7.1.a	Introduce claim(s), acknowledge alternate or opposing claims, and organize the reasons and evidence logically.
		W.7.1.b	Support claim(s) with logical reasoning and relevant evidence, using accurate, credible sources and demonstrating an understanding of the topic or text.
		W.7.1.e	Provide a concluding statement or section that follows from and supports the argument presented.
		W.7.4	Produce clear and coherent writing in which the development, organization, and style are appropriate to task, purpose, and audience.

Project 9: Write as a Reader, continued

Pages	Lesson	Code	Standards Text
		W.7.5	With some guidance and support from peers and adults, develop and strengthen writing as needed by planning, revising, editing, rewriting, or trying a new approach, focusing on how well purpose and audience have been addressed.
		W.7.10	Write routinely over extended time frames (time for research, reflection, and revision) and shorter time frames (a single sitting or a day or two) for a range of discipline-specific tasks, purposes, and audiences.
250W–253W	**Writing Strategy: Good Beginnings and Endings**		Write arguments to support claims with clear reasons and relevant evidence.
		W.7.1.a	Introduce claim(s), acknowledge alternate or opposing claims, and organize the reasons and evidence logically.
		W.7.1.e	Provide a concluding statement or section that follows from and supports the argument presented.
254W–257W	**Writing Strategy: Explain and Support Your Ideas**		Write arguments to support claims with clear reasons and relevant evidence.
		W.7.1.a	Introduce claim(s), acknowledge alternate or opposing claims, and organize the reasons and evidence logically.
		W.7.1.b	Support claim(s) with logical reasoning and relevant evidence, using accurate, credible sources and demonstrating an understanding of the topic or text.
		W.7.1.e	Provide a concluding statement or section that follows from and supports the argument presented.
		W.7.5	With some guidance and support from peers and adults, develop and strengthen writing as needed by planning, revising, editing, rewriting, or trying a new approach, focusing on how well purpose and audience have been addressed.
		W.7.9	Draw evidence from literary or informational texts to support analysis, reflection, and research.
		W.7.9.a	Apply grade 7 Reading standards to literature (e.g., "Compare and contrast a fictional portrayal of a time, place, or character and a historical account of the same period as a means of understanding how authors of fiction use or alter history").

Common Core State Standards, continued

Project 9: Write as a Reader, continued

Pages	Lesson	Code	Standards Text
258W–259W	**Literary Response: Prewrite**	W.7.4	Produce clear and coherent writing in which the development, organization, and style are appropriate to task, purpose, and audience.
		W.7.5	With some guidance and support from peers and adults, develop and strengthen writing as needed by planning, revising, editing, rewriting, or trying a new approach, focusing on how well purpose and audience have been addressed.
		W.7.9	Draw evidence from literary or informational texts to support analysis, reflection, and research.
		W.7.9.a	Apply grade 7 Reading standards to literature (e.g., "Compare and contrast a fictional portrayal of a time, place, or character and a historical account of the same period as a means of understanding how authors of fiction use or alter history").
260W–261W	**Literary Response: Draft**	W.7.1	Write arguments to support claims with clear reasons and relevant evidence.
		W.7.1.a	Introduce claim(s), acknowledge alternate or opposing claims, and organize the reasons and evidence logically.
		W.7.1.b	Support claim(s) with logical reasoning and relevant evidence, using accurate, credible sources and demonstrating an understanding of the topic or text.
		W.7.1.e	Provide a concluding statement or section that follows from and supports the argument presented.
		W.7.5	With some guidance and support from peers and adults, develop and strengthen writing as needed by planning, revising, editing, rewriting, or trying a new approach, focusing on how well purpose and audience have been addressed.
		W.7.9	Draw evidence from literary or informational texts to support analysis, reflection, and research.
		W.7.9.a	Apply grade 7 Reading standards to literature (e.g., "Compare and contrast a fictional portrayal of a time, place, or character and a historical account of the same period as a means of understanding how authors of fiction use or alter history").
		W.7.10	Write routinely over extended time frames (time for research, reflection, and revision) and shorter time frames (a single sitting or a day or two) for a range of discipline-specific tasks, purposes, and audiences.

Project 9: Write as a Reader, continued

Pages	Lesson	Code	Standards Text
262W–263W	Literary Response: Revise		Write arguments to support claims with clear reasons and relevant evidence.
		W.7.1.a	Introduce claim(s), acknowledge alternate or opposing claims, and organize the reasons and evidence logically.
		W.7.1.b	Support claim(s) with logical reasoning and relevant evidence, using accurate, credible sources and demonstrating an understanding of the topic or text.
		W.7.1.c	Use words, phrases, and clauses to create cohesion and clarify the relationships among claim(s), reasons, and evidence.
		W.7.1.e	Provide a concluding statement or section that follows from and supports the argument presented.
		W.7.4	Produce clear and coherent writing in which the development, organization, and style are appropriate to task, purpose, and audience.
		W.7.5	With some guidance and support from peers and adults, develop and strengthen writing as needed by planning, revising, editing, rewriting, or trying a new approach, focusing on how well purpose and audience have been addressed.
		W.7.9	Draw evidence from literary or informational texts to support analysis, reflection, and research.
		W.7.9.a	Apply grade 7 Reading standards to literature (e.g., "Compare and contrast a fictional portrayal of a time, place, or character and a historical account of the same period as a means of understanding how authors of fiction use or alter history").
264W	Literary Response: Edit and Proofread	W.7.5	With some guidance and support from peers and adults, develop and strengthen writing as needed by planning, revising, editing, rewriting, or trying a new approach, focusing on how well purpose and audience have been addressed.
		L.7.1	Demonstrate command of the conventions of standard English grammar and usage when writing or speaking.
		L.7.2	Demonstrate command of the conventions of standard English capitalization, punctuation, and spelling when writing.
		L.7.2.b	Spell correctly.
		L.7.3	Use knowledge of language and its conventions when writing, speaking, reading, or listening.

Common Core State Standards, continued

Project 9: Write as a Reader, continued

Pages	Lesson	Code	Standards Text
265W	**Grammar Workout: Check Past Tense Verbs**	L.7.1	Demonstrate command of the conventions of standard English grammar and usage when writing or speaking.
		L.7.3	Use knowledge of language and its conventions when writing, speaking, reading, or listening.
266W	**Spelling Workout: Check Verbs with Endings**	L.7.2	Demonstrate command of the conventions of standard English capitalization, punctuation, and spelling when writing.
		L.7.2.b	Spell correctly.
267W	**Mechanics Workout: Check Titles of Literary Works**	L.7.2	Demonstrate command of the conventions of standard English capitalization, punctuation, and spelling when writing.
268W	**Literary Response: Publish, Share, and Reflect**	W.7.5	With some guidance and support from peers and adults, develop and strengthen writing as needed by planning, revising, editing, rewriting, or trying a new approach, focusing on how well purpose and audience have been addressed.
		W.7.6	Use technology, including the Internet, to produce and publish writing and link to and cite sources as well as to interact and collaborate with others, including linking to and citing sources.
269W	**Presentation Manual: How to Conduct a Book-Club Meeting**		Engage effectively in a range of collaborative discussions (one-on-one, in groups, and teacher led) with diverse partners on grade 7 topics, texts, and issues, building on others' ideas and expressing their own clearly.
		SL.7.1.a	Come to discussions prepared, having read or researched material under study; explicitly draw on that preparation by referring to evidence on the topic, text, or issue to probe and reflect on ideas under discussion.
		SL.7.1.b	Follow rules for collegial discussions, track progress toward specific goals and deadlines, and define individual roles as needed.
		SL.7.1.c	Pose questions that elicit elaboration and respond to others' questions and comments with relevant observations and ideas that bring the discussion back on topic as needed.
		SL.7.4	Present claims and findings, emphasizing salient points in a focused, coherent manner with pertinent descriptions, facts, details, and examples; use appropriate eye contact, adequate volume, and clear pronunciation.

Project 10: Write to Summarize

Pages	Lesson	Code	Standards Text
270W–273W	**Summary Paragraph: Model Study and Prewrite**	W.7.5	With some guidance and support from peers and adults, develop and strengthen writing as needed by planning, revising, editing, rewriting, or trying a new approach, focusing on how well purpose and audience have been addressed.
		W.7.9	Draw evidence from literary or informational texts to support analysis, reflection, and research.
		W.7.9.b	Apply grade 7 Reading standards to literary nonfiction (e.g. "Trace and evaluate the argument and specific claims in a text, assessing whether the reasoning is sound and the evidence is relevant and sufficient to support the claims").
274W–275W	**Summary Paragraph: Draft**	W.7.2	Write informative/explanatory texts to examine a topic and convey ideas, concepts, and information through the selection, organization, and analysis of relevant content.
		W.7.2.a	Introduce a topic clearly, previewing what is to follow; organize ideas, concepts, and information, using strategies such as definition, classification, comparison/contrast, and cause/effect; include formatting (e.g., headings), graphics (e.g., charts, tables), and multimedia when useful to aiding comprehension.
		W.7.2.b	Develop the topic with relevant facts, definitions, concrete details, quotations, or other information and examples.
		W.7.5	With some guidance and support from peers and adults, develop and strengthen writing as needed by planning, revising, editing, rewriting, or trying a new approach, focusing on how well purpose and audience have been addressed.
		W.7.9	Draw evidence from literary or informational texts to support analysis, reflection, and research.
		W.7.9.b	Apply grade 7 Reading standards to literary nonfiction (e.g. "Trace and evaluate the argument and specific claims in a text, assessing whether the reasoning is sound and the evidence is relevant and sufficient to support the claims").
		W.7.10	Write routinely over extended time frames (time for research, reflection, and revision) and shorter time frames (a single sitting or a day or two) for a range of discipline-specific tasks, purposes, and audiences.

Common Core State Standards, continued

Project 10: Write to Summarize, continued

Pages	Lesson	Code	Standards Text
276W–277W	**Summary Paragraph: Revise**		Write informative/explanatory texts to examine a topic and convey ideas, concepts, and information through the selection, organization, and analysis of relevant content.
		W.7.2.a	Introduce a topic clearly, previewing what is to follow; organize ideas, concepts, and information, using strategies such as definition, classification, comparison/contrast, and cause/effect; include formatting (e.g., headings), graphics (e.g., charts, tables), and multimedia when useful to aiding comprehension.
		W.7.2.b	Develop the topic with relevant facts, definitions, concrete details, quotations, or other information and examples.
		W.7.4	Produce clear and coherent writing in which the development, organization, and style are appropriate to task, purpose, and audience.
		W.7.5	With some guidance and support from peers and adults, develop and strengthen writing as needed by planning, revising, editing, rewriting, or trying a new approach, focusing on how well purpose and audience have been addressed.
278W	**Summary Paragraph: Edit and Proofread**	W.7.5	With some guidance and support from peers and adults, develop and strengthen writing as needed by planning, revising, editing, rewriting, or trying a new approach, focusing on how well purpose and audience have been addressed.
		L.7.1	Demonstrate command of the conventions of standard English grammar and usage when writing or speaking.
		L.7.2	Demonstrate command of the conventions of standard English capitalization, punctuation, and spelling when writing.
		L.7.2.b	Spell correctly.
		L.7.3	Use knowledge of language and its conventions when writing, speaking, reading, or listening.
279W	**Grammar Workout: Check Object Pronouns**	L.7.1	Demonstrate command of the conventions of standard English grammar and usage when writing or speaking.
		L.7.3	Use knowledge of language and its conventions when writing, speaking, reading, or listening.
280W	**Spelling Workout: Check Words Ending in -y**	L.7.2	Demonstrate command of the conventions of standard English capitalization, punctuation, and spelling when writing.
		L.7.2.b	Spell correctly.
281W	**Mechanics Workout: Check Apostrophes with Contractions**	L.7.2	Demonstrate command of the conventions of standard English capitalization, punctuation, and spelling when writing.

Project 11: Write a Letter to the Editor

Pages	Lesson	Code	Standards Text
282W–287W	**Letter to the Editor: Model Study and Prewrite**	W.7.5	With some guidance and support from peers and adults, develop and strengthen writing as needed by planning, revising, editing, rewriting, or trying a new approach, focusing on how well purpose and audience have been addressed.
288W–289W	**Letter to the Editor: Draft**	W.7.1	Write arguments to support claims with clear reasons and relevant evidence.
		W.7.1.a	Introduce claim(s), acknowledge alternate or opposing claims, and organize the reasons and evidence logically.
		W.7.1.b	Support claim(s) with logical reasoning and relevant evidence, using accurate, credible sources and demonstrating an understanding of the topic or text.
		W.7.1.d	Establish and maintain a formal style.
		W.7.1.e	Provide a concluding statement or section that follows from and supports the argument presented.
		W.7.5	With some guidance and support from peers and adults, develop and strengthen writing as needed by planning, revising, editing, rewriting, or trying a new approach, focusing on how well purpose and audience have been addressed.
		W.7.10	Write routinely over extended time frames (time for research, reflection, and revision) and shorter time frames (a single sitting or a day or two) for a range of discipline-specific tasks, purposes, and audiences.
290W–291W	**Letter to the Editor: Revise**		Write arguments to support claims with clear reasons and relevant evidence.
		W.7.1.a	Introduce claim(s), acknowledge alternate or opposing claims, and organize the reasons and evidence logically.
		W.7.1.b	Support claim(s) with logical reasoning and relevant evidence, using accurate, credible sources and demonstrating an understanding of the topic or text.
		W.7.1.d	Establish and maintain a formal style.
		W.7.4	Produce clear and coherent writing in which the development, organization, and style are appropriate to task, purpose, and audience.
		W.7.5	With some guidance and support from peers and adults, develop and strengthen writing as needed by planning, revising, editing, rewriting, or trying a new approach, focusing on how well purpose and audience have been addressed.

Common Core State Standards, continued

Project 11: Write a Letter to the Editor, continued

Pages	Lesson	Code	Standards Text
292W	**Letter to the Editor: Edit and Proofread**	W.7.5	With some guidance and support from peers and adults, develop and strengthen writing as needed by planning, revising, editing, rewriting, or trying a new approach, focusing on how well purpose and audience have been addressed.
		L.7.1	Demonstrate command of the conventions of standard English grammar and usage when writing or speaking.
		L.7.1.c	Place phrases and clauses within a sentence, recognizing and correcting misplaced and dangling modifiers.
		L.7.2	Demonstrate command of the conventions of standard English capitalization, punctuation, and spelling when writing.
		L.7.2.b	Spell correctly.
		L.7.3	Use knowledge of language and its conventions when writing, speaking, reading, or listening.
293W	**Grammar Workout: Check for Prepositional Phrases**		Demonstrate command of the conventions of standard English grammar and usage when writing or speaking.
		L.7.1.c	Place phrases and clauses within a sentence, recognizing and correcting misplaced and dangling modifiers.
		L.7.3	Use knowledge of language and its conventions when writing, speaking, reading, or listening.
294W	**Spelling Workout: Check Sound-Alike Words**	L.7.2	Demonstrate command of the conventions of standard English capitalization, punctuation, and spelling when writing.
		L.7.2.b	Spell correctly.
295W	**Mechanics Workout: Check Use of Commas and Dashes**	L.7.2	Demonstrate command of the conventions of standard English capitalization, punctuation, and spelling when writing.

Project 12: Write as a Consumer

Pages	Lesson	Code	Standards Text
296W–299W	**Business Letter: Model Study and Prewrite**	W.7.5	With some guidance and support from peers and adults, develop and strengthen writing as needed by planning, revising, editing, rewriting, or trying a new approach, focusing on how well purpose and audience have been addressed.
		W.7.8	Gather relevant information from multiple print and digital sources, using search terms effectively; assess the credibility and accuracy of each source; and quote or paraphrase the data and conclusions of others while avoiding plagiarism and following a standard format for citation.

Project 12: Write as a Consumer, continued

Pages	Lesson	Code	Standards Text
300W–301W	**Business Letter: Draft**	W.7.1	Write arguments to support claims with clear reasons and relevant evidence.
		W.7.1.a	Introduce claim(s), acknowledge alternate or opposing claims, and organize the reasons and evidence logically.
		W.7.1.b	Support claim(s) with logical reasoning and relevant evidence, using accurate, credible sources and demonstrating an understanding of the topic or text.
		W.7.1.d	Establish and maintain a formal style.
		W.7.1.e	Provide a concluding statement or section that follows from and supports the argument presented.
		W.7.5	With some guidance and support from peers and adults, develop and strengthen writing as needed by planning, revising, editing, rewriting, or trying a new approach, focusing on how well purpose and audience have been addressed.
		W.7.10	Write routinely over extended time frames (time for research, reflection, and revision) and shorter time frames (a single sitting or a day or two) for a range of discipline-specific tasks, purposes, and audiences.
302W–303W	**Business Letter: Revise**		Write arguments to support claims with clear reasons and relevant evidence.
		W.7.1.a	Introduce claim(s), acknowledge alternate or opposing claims, and organize the reasons and evidence logically.
		W.7.1.b	Support claim(s) with logical reasoning and relevant evidence, using accurate, credible sources and demonstrating an understanding of the topic or text.
		W.7.1.c	Use words, phrases, and clauses to create cohesion and clarify the relationships among claim(s), reasons, and evidence.
		W.7.1.d	Establish and maintain a formal style.
		W.7.1.e	Provide a concluding statement or section that follows from and supports the argument presented.
		W.7.4	Produce clear and coherent writing in which the development, organization, and style are appropriate to task, purpose, and audience.
		W.7.5	With some guidance and support from peers and adults, develop and strengthen writing as needed by planning, revising, editing, rewriting, or trying a new approach, focusing on how well purpose and audience have been addressed.

Common Core State Standards, continued

Project 12: Write as a Consumer, continued

Pages	Lesson	Code	Standards Text
304W	Business Letter: Edit and Proofread	W.7.5	With some guidance and support from peers and adults, develop and strengthen writing as needed by planning, revising, editing, rewriting, or trying a new approach, focusing on how well purpose and audience have been addressed.
		L.7.1	Demonstrate command of the conventions of standard English grammar and usage when writing or speaking.
		L.7.2	Demonstrate command of the conventions of standard English capitalization, punctuation, and spelling when writing.
		L.7.2.b	Spell correctly.
		L.7.3	Use knowledge of language and its conventions when writing, speaking, reading, or listening.
305W	Grammar Workout: Check Subject and Object Pronouns	L.7.1	Demonstrate command of the conventions of standard English grammar and usage when writing or speaking.
		L.7.3	Use knowledge of language and its conventions when writing, speaking, reading, or listening.
306W	Spelling Workout: Check Words with Greek or Latin Roots	L.7.2	Demonstrate command of the conventions of standard English capitalization, punctuation, and spelling when writing.
		L.7.2.b	Spell correctly.
307W	Mechanics Workout: Check Colons and Semicolons	L.7.2	Demonstrate command of the conventions of standard English capitalization, punctuation, and spelling when writing.

Project 13: Write to Tell What Happened

Pages	Lesson	Code	Standards Text
308W–311W	Paragraphs in Chronological Order: Model Study and Prewrite	W.7.4	Produce clear and coherent writing in which the development, organization, and style are appropriate to task, purpose, and audience.
		W.7.5	With some guidance and support from peers and adults, develop and strengthen writing as needed by planning, revising, editing, rewriting, or trying a new approach, focusing on how well purpose and audience have been addressed.

Project 13: Write to Tell What Happened, continued

Pages	Lesson	Code	Standards Text
312W–313W	**Paragraphs in Chronological Order: Draft**	W.7.2	Write informative/explanatory texts to examine a topic and convey ideas, concepts, and information through the selection, organization, and analysis of relevant content.
		W.7.2.a	Introduce a topic clearly, previewing what is to follow; organize ideas, concepts, and information, using strategies such as definition, classification, comparison/contrast, and cause/effect; include formatting (e.g., headings), graphics (e.g., charts, tables), and multimedia when useful to aiding comprehension.
		W.7.2.b	Develop the topic with relevant facts, definitions, concrete details, quotations, or other information and examples.
		W.7.2.c	Use appropriate transitions to create cohesion and clarify the relationships among ideas and concepts.
		W.7.5	With some guidance and support from peers and adults, develop and strengthen writing as needed by planning, revising, editing, rewriting, or trying a new approach, focusing on how well purpose and audience have been addressed.
		W.7.10	Write routinely over extended time frames (time for research, reflection, and revision) and shorter time frames (a single sitting or a day or two) for a range of discipline-specific tasks, purposes, and audiences.
314W–315W	**Paragraphs in Chronological Order: Revise**	W.7.2	Write informative/explanatory texts to examine a topic and convey ideas, concepts, and information through the selection, organization, and analysis of relevant content.
		W.7.2.a	Introduce a topic clearly, previewing what is to follow; organize ideas, concepts, and information, using strategies such as definition, classification, comparison/contrast, and cause/effect; include formatting (e.g., headings), graphics (e.g., charts, tables), and multimedia when useful to aiding comprehension.
		W.7.2.b	Develop the topic with relevant facts, definitions, concrete details, quotations, or other information and examples.
		W.7.2.c	Use appropriate transitions to create cohesion and clarify the relationships among ideas and concepts.
		W.7.2.f	Provide a concluding statement or section that follows from and supports the information or explanation presented.

Common Core State Standards, continued

Project 13: Write to Tell What Happened, continued

Pages	Lesson	Code	Standards Text
		W.7.4	Produce clear and coherent writing in which the development, organization, and style are appropriate to task, purpose, and audience.
		W.7.5	With some guidance and support from peers and adults, develop and strengthen writing as needed by planning, revising, editing, rewriting, or trying a new approach, focusing on how well purpose and audience have been addressed.
316W	Paragraphs in Chronological Order: Edit and Proofread	W.7.5	With some guidance and support from peers and adults, develop and strengthen writing as needed by planning, revising, editing, rewriting, or trying a new approach, focusing on how well purpose and audience have been addressed.
		L.7.1	Demonstrate command of the conventions of standard English grammar and usage when writing or speaking.
		L.7.2	Demonstrate command of the conventions of standard English capitalization, punctuation, and spelling when writing.
		L.7.2.b	Spell correctly.
		L.7.3	Use knowledge of language and its conventions when writing, speaking, reading, or listening.
317W	Grammar Workout: Check Verb Tenses	L.7.1	Demonstrate command of the conventions of standard English grammar and usage when writing or speaking.
		L.7.3	Use knowledge of language and its conventions when writing, speaking, reading, or listening.
318W	Spelling Workout: Check Words You Have to Know or Look Up	L.7.2	Demonstrate command of the conventions of standard English capitalization, punctuation, and spelling when writing.
		L.7.2.b	Spell correctly.
		L.7.3	Use knowledge of language and its conventions when writing, speaking, reading, or listening.
319W	Mechanics Workout: Check for Commas before Conjunctions	L.7.2	Demonstrate command of the conventions of standard English capitalization, punctuation, and spelling when writing.
		L.7.3	Use knowledge of language and its conventions when writing, speaking, reading, or listening.

Project 14: Write About Someone's Life

Pages	Lesson	Code	Standards Text
320W–329W	**Biography: Model Study and Writing Trait: Voice and Style**	W.7.4	Produce clear and coherent writing in which the development, organization, and style are appropriate to task, purpose, and audience.
		W.7.5	With some guidance and support from peers and adults, develop and strengthen writing as needed by planning, revising, editing, rewriting, or trying a new approach, focusing on how well purpose and audience have been addressed.
		W.7.10	Write routinely over extended time frames (time for research, reflection, and revision) and shorter time frames (a single sitting or a day or two) for a range of discipline-specific tasks, purposes, and audiences.
330W–333W	**Writing Strategy: Choose the Right Voice**	W.7.10	Write routinely over extended time frames (time for research, reflection, and revision) and shorter time frames (a single sitting or a day or two) for a range of discipline-specific tasks, purposes, and audiences.
334W–337W	**Writing Strategy: Use Figurative Language**		Write narratives to develop real or imagined experiences or events using effective technique, relevant descriptive details, and well-structured event sequences.
		W.7.3.d	Use precise words and phrases, relevant descriptive details, and sensory language to capture the action and convey experiences and events.
		L.7.5	Demonstrate understanding of figurative language, word relationships, and nuances in word meanings.
338W–339W	**Biography: Prewrite**	W.7.4	Produce clear and coherent writing in which the development, organization, and style are appropriate to task, purpose, and audience.
		W.7.5	With some guidance and support from peers and adults, develop and strengthen writing as needed by planning, revising, editing, rewriting, or trying a new approach, focusing on how well purpose and audience have been addressed.
340W–341W	**Biography: Draft**	W.7.2	Write informative/explanatory texts to examine a topic and convey ideas, concepts, and information through the selection, organization, and analysis of relevant content.
		W.7.2.a	Introduce a topic clearly, previewing what is to follow; organize ideas, concepts, and information, using strategies such as definition, classification, comparison/contrast, and cause/effect; include formatting (e.g., headings), graphics (e.g., charts, tables), and multimedia when useful to aiding comprehension.

Common Core State Standards, continued

Project 14: Write About Someone's Life, continued

Pages	Lesson	Code	Standards Text
		W.7.2.b	Develop the topic with relevant facts, definitions, concrete details, quotations, or other information and examples.
		W.7.2.c	Use appropriate transitions to create cohesion and clarify the relationships among ideas and concepts.
		W.7.2.d	Use precise language and domain-specific vocabulary to inform about or explain the topic.
		W.7.5	With some guidance and support from peers and adults, develop and strengthen writing as needed by planning, revising, editing, rewriting, or trying a new approach, focusing on how well purpose and audience have been addressed.
		W.7.10	Write routinely over extended time frames (time for research, reflection, and revision) and shorter time frames (a single sitting or a day or two) for a range of discipline-specific tasks, purposes, and audiences.
342W–343W	Biography: Revise	W.7.2	Write informative/explanatory texts to examine a topic and convey ideas, concepts, and information through the selection, organization, and analysis of relevant content.
		W.7.2.a	Introduce a topic clearly, previewing what is to follow; organize ideas, concepts, and information, using strategies such as definition, classification, comparison/contrast, and cause/effect; include formatting (e.g., headings), graphics (e.g., charts, tables), and multimedia when useful to aiding comprehension.
		W.7.2.b	Develop the topic with relevant facts, definitions, concrete details, quotations, or other information and examples.
		W.7.2.c	Use appropriate transitions to create cohesion and clarify the relationships among ideas and concepts.
		W.7.2.d	Use precise language and domain-specific vocabulary to inform about or explain the topic.
		W.7.4	Produce clear and coherent writing in which the development, organization, and style are appropriate to task, purpose, and audience.
		W.7.5	With some guidance and support from peers and adults, develop and strengthen writing as needed by planning, revising, editing, rewriting, or trying a new approach, focusing on how well purpose and audience have been addressed.

Project 14: Write About Someone's Life, continued

Pages	Lesson	Code	Standards Text
344W	**Biography: Edit and Proofread**	W.7.5	With some guidance and support from peers and adults, develop and strengthen writing as needed by planning, revising, editing, rewriting, or trying a new approach, focusing on how well purpose and audience have been addressed.
		L.7.1	Demonstrate command of the conventions of standard English grammar and usage when writing or speaking.
		L.7.2	Demonstrate command of the conventions of standard English capitalization, punctuation, and spelling when writing.
		L.7.2.b	Spell correctly.
		L.7.3	Use knowledge of language and its conventions when writing, speaking, reading, or listening.
345W	**Grammar Workout: Check Consistency in Verb Tenses**	L.7.1	Demonstrate command of the conventions of standard English grammar and usage when writing or speaking.
		L.7.3	Use knowledge of language and its conventions when writing, speaking, reading, or listening.
346W	**Spelling Workout: Check Words with Silent Consonants**	L.7.2	Demonstrate command of the conventions of standard English capitalization, punctuation, and spelling when writing.
		L.7.2.b	Spell correctly.
		L.7.3	Use knowledge of language and its conventions when writing, speaking, reading, or listening.
347W	**Mechanics Workout: Check Semicolons**	L.7.2	Demonstrate command of the conventions of standard English capitalization, punctuation, and spelling when writing.
		L.7.3	Use knowledge of language and its conventions when writing, speaking, reading, or listening.
348W	**Biography: Publish, Share, and Reflect**	W.7.5	With some guidance and support from peers and adults, develop and strengthen writing as needed by planning, revising, editing, rewriting, or trying a new approach, focusing on how well purpose and audience have been addressed.
		W.7.6	Use technology, including the Internet, to produce and publish writing and link to and cite sources as well as to interact and collaborate with others, including linking to and citing sources.

Common Core State Standards, continued

Project 14: Write About Someone's Life, continued

Pages	Lesson	Code	Standards Text
349W	Presentation Manual: Emphasize Your Points		Engage effectively in a range of collaborative discussions (one-on-one, in groups, and teacher led) with diverse partners on grade 7 topics, texts, and issues, building on others' ideas and expressing their own clearly.
		SL.7.1.c	Pose questions that elicit elaboration and respond to others' questions and comments with relevant observations and ideas that bring the discussion back on topic as needed.
		SL.7.1.d	Acknowledge new information expressed by others and, when warranted, modify their own views.
		SL.7.4	Present claims and findings, emphasizing salient points in a focused, coherent manner with pertinent descriptions, facts, details, and examples; use appropriate eye contact, adequate volume, and clear pronunciation.

Project 15: Write as an Advocate

Pages	Lesson	Code	Standards Text
350W–355W	Public Service Announcement: Model Study and Writing Strategy: Write Effective Sentences		Write arguments to support claims with clear reasons and relevant evidence.
		W.7.1.c	Use words, phrases, and clauses to create cohesion and clarify the relationships among claim(s), reasons, and evidence.
		W.7.4	Produce clear and coherent writing in which the development, organization, and style are appropriate to task, purpose, and audience.
356W–357W	Public Service Announcement: Prewrite		Write arguments to support claims with clear reasons and relevant evidence.
		W.7.1.a	Introduce claim(s), acknowledge alternate or opposing claims, and organize the reasons and evidence logically.
		W.7.1.b	Support claim(s) with logical reasoning and relevant evidence, using accurate, credible sources and demonstrating an understanding of the topic or text.
		W.7.4	Produce clear and coherent writing in which the development, organization, and style are appropriate to task, purpose, and audience.
		W.7.5	With some guidance and support from peers and adults, develop and strengthen writing as needed by planning, revising, editing, rewriting, or trying a new approach, focusing on how well purpose and audience have been addressed.

Project 15: Write as an Advocate, continued

Pages	Lesson	Code	Standards Text
358W–359W	**Public Service Announcement: Draft**	W.7.1	Write arguments to support claims with clear reasons and relevant evidence.
		W.7.1.a	Introduce claim(s), acknowledge alternate or opposing claims, and organize the reasons and evidence logically.
		W.7.1.b	Support claim(s) with logical reasoning and relevant evidence, using accurate, credible sources and demonstrating an understanding of the topic or text.
		W.7.1.c	Use words, phrases, and clauses to create cohesion and clarify the relationships among claim(s), reasons, and evidence.
		W.7.1.d	Establish and maintain a formal style.
		W.7.1.e	Provide a concluding statement or section that follows from and supports the argument presented.
		W.7.5	With some guidance and support from peers and adults, develop and strengthen writing as needed by planning, revising, editing, rewriting, or trying a new approach, focusing on how well purpose and audience have been addressed.
360W–361W	**Public Service Announcement: Revise**	W.7.1	Write arguments to support claims with clear reasons and relevant evidence.
		W.7.1.a	Introduce claim(s), acknowledge alternate or opposing claims, and organize the reasons and evidence logically.
		W.7.1.b	Support claim(s) with logical reasoning and relevant evidence, using accurate, credible sources and demonstrating an understanding of the topic or text.
		W.7.1.c	Use words, phrases, and clauses to create cohesion and clarify the relationships among claim(s), reasons, and evidence.
		W.7.1.e	Provide a concluding statement or section that follows from and supports the argument presented.
		W.7.4	Produce clear and coherent writing in which the development, organization, and style are appropriate to task, purpose, and audience.
		W.7.5	With some guidance and support from peers and adults, develop and strengthen writing as needed by planning, revising, editing, rewriting, or trying a new approach, focusing on how well purpose and audience have been addressed.

Common Core State Standards, continued

Project 15: Write as an Advocate, continued

Pages	Lesson	Code	Standards Text
362W	**Public Service Announcement: Edit and Proofread**	W.7.5	With some guidance and support from peers and adults, develop and strengthen writing as needed by planning, revising, editing, rewriting, or trying a new approach, focusing on how well purpose and audience have been addressed.
		L.7.1	Demonstrate command of the conventions of standard English grammar and usage when writing or speaking. Demonstrate command of the conventions of standard English capitalization, punctuation, and spelling when writing.
		L.7.2.a	Use a comma to separate coordinate adjectives (e.g., It was a fascinating, enjoyable movie but not He wore an old[,] green shirt).
		L.7.2.b	Spell correctly.
		L.7.3	Use knowledge of language and its conventions when writing, speaking, reading, or listening.
363W	**Grammar Workout: Check Present Perfect Tense**	L.7.1	Demonstrate command of the conventions of standard English grammar and usage when writing or speaking.
		L.7.3	Use knowledge of language and its conventions when writing, speaking, reading, or listening.
364W	**Spelling Workout: Spelling Words Ending with -y**	L.7.2	Demonstrate command of the conventions of standard English capitalization, punctuation, and spelling when writing.
		L.7.2.b	Spell correctly.
365W	**Mechanics Workout: Check Commas Between Adjectives**		Demonstrate command of the conventions of standard English capitalization, punctuation, and spelling when writing.
		L.7.2.a	Use a comma to separate coordinate adjectives (e.g., It was a fascinating, enjoyable movie but not He wore an old[,] green shirt).
		L.7.3	Use knowledge of language and its conventions when writing, speaking, reading, or listening.

Project 16: Write as a Citizen

Pages	Lesson	Code	Standards Text
366W–371W	Persuasive Essay: Model Study and Writing Strategy: Appeal to Logic	W.7.1.b	Write arguments to support claims with clear reasons and relevant evidence. Support claim(s) with logical reasoning and relevant evidence, using accurate, credible sources and demonstrating an understanding of the topic or text.
		W.7.4	Produce clear and coherent writing in which the development, organization, and style are appropriate to task, purpose, and audience.
372W–373W	Writing Strategy: Appeal to Emotion	W.7.1.b	Write arguments to support claims with clear reasons and relevant evidence. Support claim(s) with logical reasoning and relevant evidence, using accurate, credible sources and demonstrating an understanding of the topic or text.
		W.7.4	Produce clear and coherent writing in which the development, organization, and style are appropriate to task, purpose, and audience.
374W–375W	Writing Strategy: Support Your Arguments	W.7.1.b	Write arguments to support claims with clear reasons and relevant evidence. Support claim(s) with logical reasoning and relevant evidence, using accurate, credible sources and demonstrating an understanding of the topic or text.
		W.7.4	Produce clear and coherent writing in which the development, organization, and style are appropriate to task, purpose, and audience.
376W–377W	Writing Strategy: Use Charts, Tables, and Pictures	W.7.1.b	Write arguments to support claims with clear reasons and relevant evidence. Support claim(s) with logical reasoning and relevant evidence, using accurate, credible sources and demonstrating an understanding of the topic or text.
378W–379W	Persuasive Essay: Prewrite	W.7.4	Produce clear and coherent writing in which the development, organization, and style are appropriate to task, purpose, and audience.
		W.7.5	With some guidance and support from peers and adults, develop and strengthen writing as needed by planning, revising, editing, rewriting, or trying a new approach, focusing on how well purpose and audience have been addressed.

Common Core State Standards, continued

Pages	Lesson	Code	Standards Text
380W–381W	Persuasive Essay: Draft	W.7.1	Write arguments to support claims with clear reasons and relevant evidence.
		W.7.1.a	Introduce claim(s), acknowledge alternate or opposing claims, and organize the reasons and evidence logically.
		W.7.1.b	Support claim(s) with logical reasoning and relevant evidence, using accurate, credible sources and demonstrating an understanding of the topic or text.
		W.7.1.c	Use words, phrases, and clauses to create cohesion and clarify the relationships among claim(s), reasons, and evidence.
		W.7.1.e	Provide a concluding statement or section that follows from and supports the argument presented.
		W.7.10	Write routinely over extended time frames (time for research, reflection, and revision) and shorter time frames (a single sitting or a day or two) for a range of discipline-specific tasks, purposes, and audiences.
382W–383W	Persuasive Essay: Revise	W.7.1	Write arguments to support claims with clear reasons and relevant evidence.
		W.7.1.a	Introduce claim(s), acknowledge alternate or opposing claims, and organize the reasons and evidence logically.
		W.7.1.b	Support claim(s) with logical reasoning and relevant evidence, using accurate, credible sources and demonstrating an understanding of the topic or text.
		W.7.1.c	Use words, phrases, and clauses to create cohesion and clarify the relationships among claim(s), reasons, and evidence.
		W.7.1.e	Provide a concluding statement or section that follows from and supports the argument presented.
		W.7.5	With some guidance and support from peers and adults, develop and strengthen writing as needed by planning, revising, editing, rewriting, or trying a new approach, focusing on how well purpose and audience have been addressed.

Project 16: Write as a Citizen, continued

Pages	Lesson	Code	Standards Text
384W	**Persuasive Essay: Edit and Proofread**	W.7.5	With some guidance and support from peers and adults, develop and strengthen writing as needed by planning, revising, editing, rewriting, or trying a new approach, focusing on how well purpose and audience have been addressed.
		L.7.1.c	Demonstrate command of the conventions of standard English grammar and usage when writing or speaking. Place phrases and clauses within a sentence, recognizing and correcting misplaced and dangling modifiers.
		L.7.2	Demonstrate command of the conventions of standard English capitalization, punctuation, and spelling when writing.
		L.7.2.b	Spell correctly.
		L.7.3	Use knowledge of language and its conventions when writing, speaking, reading, or listening.
385W	**Grammar Workout: Check Participial Phrases**	L.7.1.c	Demonstrate command of the conventions of standard English grammar and usage when writing or speaking. Place phrases and clauses within a sentence, recognizing and correcting misplaced and dangling modifiers.
		L.7.3	Use knowledge of language and its conventions when writing, speaking, reading, or listening.
386W	**Spelling Workout: Check Words with *q, ie,* and *ei***	L.7.2	Demonstrate command of the conventions of standard English capitalization, punctuation, and spelling when writing.
		L.7.2.b	Spell correctly.
		L.7.3	Use knowledge of language and its conventions when writing, speaking, reading, or listening.
387W	**Mechanics Workout: Participial Phrases and Appositives**	L.7.2	Demonstrate command of the conventions of standard English capitalization, punctuation, and spelling when writing.
		L.7.3	Use knowledge of language and its conventions when writing, speaking, reading, or listening.
388W	**Persuasive Essay: Publish, Share, and Reflect**	W.7.5	With some guidance and support from peers and adults, develop and strengthen writing as needed by planning, revising, editing, rewriting, or trying a new approach, focusing on how well purpose and audience have been addressed.
		W.7.6	Use technology, including the Internet, to produce and publish writing and link to and cite sources as well as to interact and collaborate with others, including linking to and citing sources.

Common Core State Standards, continued

Project 16: Write as a Citizen, continued

Pages	Lesson	Code	Standards Text
389W	**Presentation Manual: How to Give a Persuasive Speech**		Engage effectively in a range of collaborative discussions (one-on-one, in groups, and teacher led) with diverse partners on grade 7 topics, texts, and issues, building on others' ideas and expressing their own clearly.
		SL.7.1.c	Pose questions that elicit elaboration and respond to others' questions and comments with relevant observations and ideas that bring the discussion back on topic as needed.
		SL.7.1.d	Acknowledge new information expressed by others and, when warranted, modify their own views.
		SL.7.4	Present claims and findings, emphasizing salient points in a focused, coherent manner with pertinent descriptions, facts, details, and examples; use appropriate eye contact, adequate volume, and clear pronunciation.